Assuming the I

D0338890

Pittsburgh Series in
Composition, Literacy, and Culture

David Bartholomae and
Jean Ferguson Carr,
Editors

ASSUMING THE POSITIONS

Cultural Pedagogy and the Politics
of Commonplace Writing

Susan Miller

. . .

. . .

University of
Pittsburgh
Press

How I envied those dusty bone-jockeys, cradling their pick-axes close to their sweat-stained safari jackets, and standing triumphantly over the remains of some poor wretch who had been buried alive.

PETER MCLAREN, *Schooling as Ritual Performance*

Published by the University of Pittsburgh Press, Pittsburgh, Pa., 15260
Copyright © 1998, University of Pittsburgh Press
All rights reserved
Manufactured in the United States of America
Printed on acid-free paper

10 9 8 7 6 5 4 3 2 1

LIBRARY OF CONGRESS CATALOGING-IN-PUBLICATION DATA
Miller, Susan, 1942–
    Assuming the positions : cultural pedagogy and the politics of commonplace writing / Susan Miller.
        p.   cm. — (Pittsburgh series in composition, literacy, and culture)
    Includes bibliographical references and index.
    ISBN 0-8229-3991-6 (alk. paper). — ISBN 0-8229-5637-3 (pbk. : alk. paper)
    1. English language—Rhetoric—Study and teaching—United States.
2. English language—Rhetoric—Study and teaching—Theory, etc. 3. Authorship—Political aspects—United States. 4. Authorship—Social aspects—United States. 5. Language and culture—United States. 6. Books and reading—United States. 7. Authorship—Sex differences. 8. Commonplace-books—History. 9. Critical pedagogy. I. Title. II. Series.
PE1405.U6M54   1997   97-4792
808'.042'07073—dc21   CIP

    A CIP catalog record for this book is available from the British Library.

For Jack, Barbara, and Natter Miller

Contents

Acknowledgments

Many people and groups have provided encouragement and expertise that give me confidence about my purposes for undertaking this project. I am particularly indebted to Frances Pollard and her staff in the library of the Virginia Historical Society in Richmond, for more than the usual resourcefulness of reference librarians. She now denies that when I wandered in and said, "I'm interested in writing," she answered, "We have a lot of that here—could you be more specific?" But this book verifies her willingness to discuss issues outside conventional uses of archives, which both helped to determine categories of analysis and supported my application for the Mellon Fellowship that made many later visits to the collection possible. As a Fellow of the Society in 1990 and 1995, I was fortunately befriended by historian Thomas Buckley, who generously shared his hard-won discoveries of early nineteenth-century divorce petitions and other documents that demonstrate the inaccuracy of conventional visions of republican and antebellum sexual relationships. His project, like the work of historian Suzanne Lebstock, allowed me to overcome my reluctance to differ openly with traditional histories of a monolithic South and to question supposedly firm gender boundaries around education and literate practices. In addition, Cynthia Kierner, John Kneebone (director of the Dictionary of Virginia Biography at the Virginia State Library and Archives), and Joan Scott have been expert readers of parts of this study and supportive conversants about its data and theoretical inferences. During many trips to Richmond, Bill Smith, Dona Hickey, and James

Kinney, valued colleagues in composition studies, took a substantial interest in the processes and content revealed by these texts, supporting my hope that rhetoric and composition studies might welcome more attention to indigenous composing. I have also had unfailing encouragement from Linda Brodkey, Jean Ferguson Carr, Sharon Crowley, Todd Gernes, Ann Ruggles Gere, Shirley Brice Heath, Gary Olson, Catherine Hobbes Peaden, Kathleen Welsh, and John Trimbur, who showed me the thesis under this project. I thank each of them for parallel work, for needed information and correction, and for setting standards I attempted to meet.

The educational focus of this study benefited enormously from long conversations with Karl Kaestle, whose knowledge of literacy education in America is unparalled, and with Michael Apple, whose radical take on teaching reminds me to ask, in his words, "Who benefits?" and "Who loses?" after any first thought about the cultural purposes of these texts. Both very generously guided me toward both standard and revisionist histories of American education. Mary Carruthers's complex understanding of memory as the small space of difference between *oral* and *literate* inspires many of my goals. In addition, Jane Gallop and Kathleen Woodward, in continuing friendship, have helped me argue for the significance of theorizing connections among feminist theory, pedagogy, and social constructions of identity.

This study has had the support of the National Endowment for the Humanities, which provided a Summer Stipend in 1989 that allowed me to begin research in the collection of nineteenth-century women's periodicals at Ohio State University. The University of Utah Tanner Humanities Center awarded me a 1992–1993 fellowship that provided time to draft it. During that year of writing, visitors to the Center and historians at the University of Utah were kind resources. Director Lowell Durham and his staff made writing an unusually comfortable and interactive undertaking. Visiting Fellow Jane Hunter, whose study of nineteenth-century New England adolescent girls' diaries often brought us together, willingly shared new materials that pointed out many anomalies in both traditional and new histories and theories of gender and family practices. Historians Larry Gerlach, James Lehning, and Dean May also took a great deal of time to question and review this work, applying their expertise in Virginia history, French history, and the history of education and the family in the West. I also thank students and colleagues in Utah's University Writing Program and Department of English, who have been amazingly willing to share ideas and responses to this work-in-progress. Katherine Fitzgerald, Nicole Hoffman, Dean Rehberger, Ron Severson, and Jackie Skibine in the Writing Program, and colleagues in English, Srinivas Aravamudan, Brooke Hopkins and Wilfred Samuels Jr. have been particularly helpful. Finally, I am deeply grateful to the University of Utah for the Distinguished Research Award that made completing this manuscript possible, and to Shaleane Gee, University of Chicago, and George Myerson, King's College, London, for detailed responses to its final form.

Note on Primary Sources

Discovering what people write is an empirical task. Here, it involved transcribing unevenly preserved holograph manuscripts, which are presented in their original graphic forms. I have preserved their omissions, repetitions, local spellings, at times lengthy strikeovers, and other signs of composing processes. I have made this choice to provide texts that may be cited accurately by others and, more important, to remind readers that current graphic "standards" result from relatively recent printing conventions, not from moral probity, and especially not from gender, entitled class status, or prestigious education. I am deeply indebted to the University of Utah College of Humanities Career Development Fund and to the University's Research Committee for support that made this difficult form of transcription feasible, as I am to Terry Hansen, Greg Rode, Sharon Schlagel, and Marcus Sherman for help with transcribing and verifying the accuracy of transcriptions. My colleague Michael Rudick donated crucial expertise in paleography.

Unless otherwise obtained, the manuscript sources are cited in notes by their Virginia Historical Society catalogue numbers. Both analyses of these manuscripts in my text and the list of references indicate authorship, if known; the type or title of the document; and date(s) of composition, if known. This information will, I hope, both advertise the rich resources revealed by archival research and allow others to retrieve, reexamine, and correct the original holograph and other works on which I have inevitably placed errors. I thank Frances Pollard and the staff at the Virginia Historical Society for helping to verify references in last-minute searches.

I also want to thank the Society for permission to reproduce the texts donated to and purchased by it, and for permission to reproduce some of these in this book's illustrations. I am indebted to Nathaniel Morrison, Welbourne Plantation, Middleburg, Virginia, for the precisely typed copy of his ancestor Rebecca Dulany's diary that is analyzed in chapter 4.

Introduction

This book is an experiment, both in its persuasive intent to address David Hall's bewilderment about "high" and "low" modes of writing, and in the composition I have needed to explain the circulation of familiar cultural tropes. I began with a question that values production over reception: what and how did Americans write when they had access to literacy but not the national mass schooling that made it a "problem" for perplexity like Hall's? The answers I present here persuade me that many humanistic fields would benefit enormously from acknowledging the cultural work of a largely invisible but copious group of texts: commonplace writings whose analysis rearranges many points of reference in textual studies. Ordinary, seemingly unimportant writing—diaries, letters, essays, social advice, affidavits, travel notes, recipes, remedies, and other seemingly ephemeral jotting—tells a great deal about the issues that motivate Hall to confess puzzlement about textual hierarchies. This material residue circulates discourses whose simultaneous preservation and inevitable alteration in occasional settings goes a long way toward explaining our professional theories, educational practices, and the still vexed politics of cultural reproduction.

Briefly, this study shuffles these theories, practices, and politics to highlight how ordinary acts of writing simultaneously appropriate and mutate an expanding range of human identities that become available in specific cultures over time. My focus on how discourse determines what specific groups of people can and cannot *be* suggests that much of the writing we choose not to see is a surface on which cultural norms and shifting desires meet. Plain texts (which is not to say "bad writing") embody the always provisional human identities that are unevenly available in discourse, subject positions that experimental moments of utterance constitute. Ordinary texts unite experience, official discursive practices, and fleeting statements on graphic surfaces that make specific cultural signatures legible.

The claim that various subject positions are unevenly available for writers in specific cultures, and that these subject positions are realized in acts of writing, may itself appear quite ordinary if I do not stress that writing in any setting is a powerfully productive cultural process. Ordinary writing inevitably tints any moment with verbal traces of the learned traditions that make writing possible. Even the most offhand notes register unstable cultural traditions in moment-to-moment alliances between experience and textuality. These always forged signatures can be recognized—they "communicate," as Derrida says.[1] But, as he does not remark, their separate signings take specific discursive actions on behalf of particular ways of life.

This is not only to say that language constitutes us and thereby constitutes culture. That proposition is now common even among the least poststructuralist perspectives in cultural studies, as in theorized history, literary studies, and rhetoric and composition—fields among which my experiment negotiates. But if language is not a transparent pipeline for an always emerging core truth, scholars who work in and across these fields might more pointedly consider how human identity is always layered within accumulated prior texts and therefore always politically constructed by disparate but never entirely ephemeral acts of writing. Discovering what people have written in any setting intrigues us because it seems to bring dead or muted voices into our presence. But such discoveries do not tell what was on a people's "mind." They instead reveal the intersections of social vectors, forces that produce discursive actions that have simultaneously material, aesthetic, and ideological consequences.

This further claim expands the arguments of studies that analyze reading and writing as sites of subject formation, like Steven Justice's *Writing and Rebellion: England in 1321,*[2] Janice Radway's *Reading the Romance,*[3] Regenia Gagnier's *Subjectivities: A History of Self Representation in Britain, 1832–1920*[4] and David Vincent's *Bread, Knowledge and Freedom: A Study of Nineteenth-Century Working Class Autobiography.*[5] It adds to this work and other studies that reconfigure the history of formal rhetoric and written composition as gendered, class-biased, and ethnocentric, by asserting that we do not simply fall into status positions that "hail" us, nor set them aside in conscious resistance to calls from ideology. Positions in discourse are always provisional, even when they are assumed through language that is rooted in tradition and directly copied in a new circumstance. Consequently, ordinary texts force us to consider the irony always dogging a quotation. Especially when it writes a cultural signature, a quotation measures and then remeasures the inescapable but impossible "moral progress" implied by George Eliot's joke on humanism and history in *Middlemarch:* "In those days the world in general was more ignorant of good and evil by forty years than it is at present."

Eliot hereby reminds us that human agents do not have opinions about their selfhood, or ways of expressing them, that are not already available in the commonplace opinion, or *doxa,* that regulates them. When scholars argue on the contrary that identity exists "outside language," they easily make relative evaluations of texts that are covertly based on fixed opinions about their human sources. The fields of history, literary theory, and rhetoric and composition, that is, can tacitly accept the uneven distribution of social status as ranked positions that may acquire equal claims on the attention of interpretive studies, but no chance of being changed. They can professionally ignore the fact that individuals do not have equal access to the subject positions, or to the power or passivity they entail, in specific cultural settings.

This human inequity becomes visible, however, when we recognize that discursive and material circumstances are identical. It is restricted possibilities for articulating desire that deserve new attention, not the relative quality of ranked texts that appear to contain it, unevenly but somehow "essentially." Discovering meanings in hierarchically ranked texts is in this view a poor substitute for what might be a new humanism that would examine the conditional inequality of substance, and of discursive provisions for it, among specific groups. Ironically again, only by breaking out of a canon, and the habit of categorizing that sustains interest in its formation, can we fulfill the values that make it worth bothering with in the first place.

Consequently, I have assumed that ordinary acts of writing can reveal limits on the central method in humanistic studies: interpretation. The historically persistent will to write requires a different kind of attention, a focus on how students of culture actually produce it. Attention to the powers of writing can stay within textuality, yet avoid liberal interpretive inclusiveness, the strategy that frames the most recent arrivals at the doors of gatekeepers in anthropological descriptions of their easily dismissed "folkways." The impact of circulating cultural pedagogies, spontaneous and traditional, is hidden in limited studies of cultures that are wrongly labeled "popular" or "oral," as it is in descriptions of the exchange value of reading that are imposed on marginal groups to testify to their always dour "literacy." Unpacking the drive to inscribe requires that textual studies instead desist from assigning absolute quality to a text on the basis of its official yet ambiguous meanings. We might, that is, explore ordinary writing as ongoing constitutive teachings, a continuous process of cultural pedagogy. Society's "workings" become visible in the purposes, imagined audiences, content, and outcomes of the texts that specific cultures make possible, even those already canonized. From this rhetorical, not semiotic, perspective, it is acts of writing, not interpreted texts, that warrant analysis by humanists interested in revealing the texture of a culture.

Of course, it is much easier to reproduce and analyze what people read, or should read, than to retrieve and make available what they write, just as it is more comfortable to appreciate or critique what people hear and see than to argue for the circulating power of what they say and make. Most, even among culturalists who are willing to acknowledge the energies of a "populace," specify those energies in a tight narrative in which people choose or reject art, civic responsibilities, the news media, and even encounters with nature, all of which are usually portrayed as entirely available but willfully misjudged. Students of culture rarely examine the productivity of the commonplace and its textual regulation of identity. They most often portray the responses that a professionally unpopular populace make to the language of others, or faintly praise the craft of (misnamed) oral traditions, in anxious justifications of discourses outside formal categories. Even Richard Hoggart's *The Uses of Literacy*, often cited for its ground-breaking recognition of the identity between mass culture and textuality, projects onto the masses a self-demeaning desire to write. In his analysis,

> Interest in serious publications is more common than is generally thought. There is often a continuous line from elementary promptings to learn "kynamatic [?] speech and writing" to some forms of membership in the "minor intelligentsia," from an obsessive and often rather bizarre interest in some panacea for the world's ills (by means of a system) to a condition of formidably dense "opinionation."[6]

From Hoggart to de Certeau, commonplaces are mistaken for a population's hackneyed (if noble) acts of submission or resistance to the better natures of their observers. Nonetheless, the active power of ordinary writing offers textual studies more than biography or glimpses of authorship, and a great deal more than bringing into line a new corpus from foreordained Others. Historical events, a cultural history of discourse, and changing constructions of the human subject all occur in diverse graphic practices that have remained largely in the realm evoked by Tillie Olsen's collecting title, "String Too Short to Be Saved."

I call this case experimental not to upstage the productive, socially active tenor of the criticism, theory, and cultural studies whose oppositions to textual hegemony have already expanded humanistic studies. Especially in the examinations of literate practices cited above and in Linda Brodkey's *Writing Permitted in Designated Areas Only*,[7] the power of discourse (and of the cultural pedagogies that regulate its production) to shape culture is well documented. That power is similarly acknowledged in studies of rhetoric such as Sharon Crowley's *The Methodical Memory*,[8] Cheryl Glenn's *Rhetoric Retold*,[9] Susan Jarratt's *Re-Reading the Sophists*,[10] and in work by Ann Gere, Thomas Miller, Takis Poulakis, C. Jan Swearingen, Kathleen Welsh, and many others. But examining a corpus of transcribed ordinary writing without ranking it or denying its informing traditions is a largely untried project, as is exposing how the act of writing itself constitutes shifting interventions in human possibilities.

These were my goals in transcribing and analyzing the commonplace book collection of the Virginia Historical Society, a framed remnant I chose for reasons that support these claims about ordinary writing in specific ways. First, this collection thoroughly challenges the typical division between elevated and demeaned texts, a division that usually relies on marking categories of writers. Certainly, upper-class Virginians in the eighteenth and nineteenth centuries did not write the politically marginal, feminized, ethnic, lower-class, racial, or folk texts that now warrant systematic attention, yet only infrequent salutes to their cultural agencies. The examples of ordinary writing contained in this collection exemplify an elite practice carried out by women and men with access to many entitlements, including elaborately schooled literacy. Nonetheless, to see this kind of writing as only elitist jottings, as is conventional in works of history and criticism, too easily hides the mobility of all inscribed identities, the simultaneous presumption and submissiveness of "assuming positions" that is suggested by this book's title.

Despite the high social status of most of their writers, and arguably because of it, the language of these texts is embedded in regulations, duties, and deprivations that imitate many sorts of personal molestation. The three focal points of this study—the cultural persistence of hegemonic common opinion despite philosophy's attempts to erase it, formal and home lessons in discourse, and evolving gender positions that mark members of each sex as simultaneously themselves and Other—appear in both dominant and defeated aspects. These texts especially manifest the cultural force of extracurricular educational practices, which they themselves fashion and to which they subject their writers. As anxious slaveowners, and as eventually defeated victims of the southern identity that they had coveted from the time of Jefferson's *Notes on Virginia* on, these writers are not unconflicted supporters of exclusionary identity politics. Their desire to assure both a republican and a literary identity renders them simultaneously admired and rejected models, for if they express the commonplaces of one state's patrician class they never entirely translate them into later received wisdoms of American bourgeois hegemony. Their characteristic visions of race hierarchy remain offensive objects of interest in a now unarguably subordinated history. Consequently, the writing of members of these now disregarded but persistently visible First Families both does and does not carry what Barthes calls "the disease of thinking in essences,"[11] a later full-blown affliction. But these texts do trace the headwaters of that misfortune in their circulation of conventional utterances that form and reform commonplace desires. This writing invites us to imagine a radically textualized writing subject, the writer who acts in the context of discursive limits and opportunities that include, but are not limited to, fictionalizing its own core as a unified and coherent identity.

This group of commonplace books also results from an exemplary prior circumstance around ordinary acts of writing, a colonial while colonized historical situation that fostered (but was very different from) the later political project of social ranking inside a privileged middle distance. This collection was written during a postrevolutionary era that ended with the emergence of a nationalized American state that centralized educational institutions, stratified writers, categorized their cultural habits, and demeaned ordinary writing. But these writers were not yet writing against the institutionalized norms of a later "public." They took writing to be a function of acquisitive self-development, a process that constituted and confirmed their class status, according to Enlightenment doctrines of universal individualism.

Particularly in letters of fathers to sons (see chapter 6), these writers restate rules of conduct and other rhetorical traditions that develop the ancient discourse pedagogies revived by Renaissance humanism. But they move those traditions into family and individual sites for composing, not merely for storing, artifacts of vernacular literacy. Unlike the humanist gatherings of earlier commonplace volumes, which were largely repositories for copied exempla and moral sayings, these texts comprise a pivotal "textual memory" that we can unpack without falling prey to nostalgia for an irretrievable cultural past. They are a graphic site of participatory policy making through cultural continuities and social inventions, not a medium that merely transmits either schooled perceptions or those experienced outside textuality. Thus these volumes of ordinary discourse show how vernacular writing has long been a primary way for people to become situated. They demonstrate how culture is made by repetitions that vary ordinary language.

In sum, this rhetorically unpredictable group of texts exposes the source of David Hall's bewilderment—the temptation to classify all writing as high or low, major or minor. These texts enact the identity between discursive and material circumstances and advertise the power of writing we are apt to overlook, power that is written here as a Lockean awareness of the equivalence between propriety and property. They occupy what Catherine Clement calls an imaginary "zone for what we exclude," a zone that "in a manifest position of exclusion, [keeps] the system together, latently, by virtue of [its] very exclusion."[12] They reveal the hidden cooperation of privilege and disenfranchisement in discursive networks.

These writers portray this cooperation in diverse ways, constructing a southern history that differs remarkably from the now dominant version. During what might be described as a movement from elite to mass democracy in America, they leave aristocratic literary self-possession for a marginal and predominantly generic identity. Yet they take with them entitlements to discourse that gradually relocate their society's opinions in another protected space, an emerging hermeneutics of experience. Their acts of writing persistently transform fragmented events and dominant discourses into a socialized propriety that becomes the accepted paradox of private cultural property.

Nonetheless, this property is not yet "personal" in the privatized, capitalist sense, nor entirely contained by the Virginia Historical Society, where these texts now rest both metaphorically and in fact. As Locke explains in "Of Property" and in his often imitated commonplace book, these graphic "labours" are evidence of a private work whose worth is verified only by its resonance with common social values.[13] Mary Beth Norton argues in *Founding Mothers and Fathers* that *public* and *private,* terms that appear to separate shared from individual work, might be set aside in this setting in favor of *authority* and *consent,* terms that also characterize the combined elements of any act of writing.[14] As Norton says, colonial Maryland and Virginia were a "practical laboratory for the dichotomous theory of authority years before Locke systematically formulated his ideas" because the earliest settlement of these colonies by men without families prevented the opposition of family and state.[15] In that specific seventeenth-century circumstance, *public* and *private* were contested terms. It was accepted that *public* could mean either something well known or pertaining to official authority, but the word might also describe informal relations among neighbors. The meaning of the term *private,* moreover, was still unsettled, "ambiguous and obscure, open to many interpretations." *Private* generally meant not public, as in secret, exclusive, or unofficial. But its meaning in the colonies was not fixed, and none of the possibilities for its connotations at this time was gendered or psychologized. "The colonists, while acknowledging the theoretical opposition *public/private,* found it extremely difficult to draw a line between the two."[16]

This blurring meant that when Locke later rejected the Filmerian concept of absolute authority over both family and state and posited an alternative, contractual consent, his concern for the investment of *private* labor in property and propriety was easily realized in American texts. Writing that might be discarded as minor because it appears to exemplify the modern category of *private* did important work in constructing such a culture. In this particular system, being minor or major was not a matter of losing or gaining a fixed relation to current understandings of *private* or *public.* This socially and discursively experimental setting warranted writing that was indeed undertaken in private, but never as an act exempt from unavoidable confrontations with the demands of socially warranted self-perception.

These texts thereby suggest what it meant to write before elevation and deflation of literate practices became the sustaining activity of a cultural pedagogy now based on ranked texts. This writing recursively imagines and re-imagines how it feels to be ordinary in relation to entitled textuality. It was never part of a canon, yet was always implicated in dominant discourse, so it realigns our ideas about what does and does not count as culturally formative acts of writing. Like the unsettled colonial meanings of *private,* whose ambiguity warranted these moments of inscription, these texts show how writers inevitably enact the sacrificial tension between immediate events and literary precedents.

These claims require that my own writing conveys discomfort with currently traditional methods of literary and historical interpretation, and thus that it attempts simultaneously to display the texts we do not see and to argue that we know them all too well. It brings together insights and practices from multiple disciplines, to retrieve ordinary writing while theorizing about its cultural results. In that interdisciplinary space, this study draws on what scholars have learned about writing processes to assess their cultural significance. It weaves transcribed holograph manuscripts, relevant historical data, theoretical perspectives, and rhetorical analysis to make a new material on which the identical productivity of material and discursive culture is visible.

This method may seem to give only superficial attention to each of these sources. For instance, I do not dwell on historical and biographical data about these writers and their circumstances, information that might encourage the telling of a comforting, seamless narrative about the status of a given text. Such stories make texts into containers for cultures that we think we already know, not the traces of multiply constitutive discourses that they always are. In approaching these texts as examples of discursive practices, not regional history, I present them with as few editorial omissions as feasible. Intriguing sound bites inevitably encourage a reader to imagine that a text was unified around a brief message or a scholar's interpretation of it. Short quotations also hide the multiple discourses at work in even the most transient act of inscription, so as often as possible I quote at length. I also avoid, where possible, the few published versions of these texts in favor of the holograph manuscripts held by the Virginia Historical Society, thus by-passing previous interpretations of their content and instead looking for evidence of the composing processes at work as they were written. Examining these sources in their original form also allowed me to re-experience the material situation of those who wrote these donations to family and cultural resources.

These choices should not foretell a fragmented description of miscellaneous artifacts. This analysis is organized to show how American postrevolutionary acts of writing accumulated and deployed available subject positions in fluid relations to three sites of authority within the well-known exigencies of this time, especially the Civil War. Both parts of this study examine traditional Western forms of circulating common opinion, formal instruction in writing and its results, and home-based extracurricular pedagogies. Isolating these sites suggests fresh inferences about how acts of writing draw an unstable boundary of gender, transmit male patriarchal identity, and create a liminal space for attempted authorship. In these texts, gender boundaries are always linked to class—a connection that, I argue, suggests that prebourgeois gendered identity was articulated to acquire and defend class standing. These texts also portray patriarchy as a universal male identity whose inheritance or acquisition, surprisingly, was equated with obeying codified rules for writing. Finally, homemade local authorship, a mode of writing that is now ignored because *high* and *low* levels leave no room for its analysis, is a shifting context for graphic identity. In this context, earlier contests over the meaning of privacy slowly become a hegemonic agreement to privilege a modern, psychologized internal creativity and its collateral coded emotions. That progress, from consequential homemade texts that are neither private nor public in any fixed sense, to self-conscious "literary" writing, offers an intriguing exposition of how a fixed subject position for an "author" partially derives from sporadic productions of locally influential texts.

Part 1 (chapters 1–3) focuses on how the regulation of culture operates through the commonplace, a term for both a specific practice prescribed across the history of rhetorical education and for a diffuse literate tradition that has accumulated many religious, political, and other regulatory implications. The persistence of the uses of commonplaces and their generic realizations in this collection are outlined in chapter 1. Writing and preserving homemade texts is a highly sanctioned, enduring family practice that links the individual to diverse discourse communities. But in the specific economy of republican citizenship, commonplace books were also material sites that produced cultural property. Chapter 1 stresses this reformed purpose for the often noted humanistic gathering of cultural wisdoms, a purpose that later commonplace books only partially enact.

Chapters 2 and 3 treat writing as an artifact of education, but this education is not divided between high and low, sanctioned and inadequate versions, as is common in traditional histories of schooling. Until recently, it has been assumed that the formation of public schools and colleges, and the nationalizing purposes of composition and formal rhetoric they achieved, was only a sign of democratic moral and intellectual progress. Instead, I will examine the family's responsibility for "improving" children as the model for institutionalized formal instruction of later "masses," as suggested in the pivotal student texts contained in these archives. These chapters demonstrate the legitimacy of local educational practices in which "family values" are never codes or metaphors, but contexts in which both formal and informal acquisition of educational capital becomes a family "valuable." This family property is exhibited in both published and informal texts about the new importance of writing, in student essays on the value of composition, and in detailed memoirs that describe the home education of a Virginia governor and of a daughter of a keeper of a rigorous girls' school. These home lessons are a mode of acquisition and exchange that simultaneously creates both material and discursive belonging. But this writing was a way to collect the elements of decidedly republican, not "private," propriety. These texts mingle relationships between inherited discourses, which commonplace books both embody and contain, and new rhetorical conduct lessons that constitute their subjects as virtuoso social actors, not as masters of regimes of truth.

These commonplace educational discourses also invite a revision of the now traditional image of gender identity, especially (but not exclusively) for women. They emphatically critique accepted interpretive perspectives in cultural, feminist, and social histories, which regularly portray women as marginal, "uneducated," and culturally demeaned across class boundaries. Part II (chapters 4–6) addresses the inadequacy of the usual categories of gender, patriarchy, and authorship—categories both learned and resisted in this ordinary writing.

Chapter 4 presents advice documents that connect the category of gender to character, to show the economic and class advantages to be achieved by fixing one's identity in a gender category. Formal gender advice and the ordinary off-color stories demeaning women that reiterate its implications attempt simultaneously to create and to impose the exclusionary force of so-called universal standards of evaluation for both sexes. As a particular sort of individual and family property, and propriety, gender obviously entails a multiplicity of learned behaviors, or "characters." But chapter 5, which attaches gender to the genres represented in these commonplace books, argues that we might reconsider gender theories that emphasize the stability of these always provisional characters. Gender, that is, is here only a borrowed identity, taken on in moments of crisis or in self-educational practices (including reading and writing fiction) that are our only sources for social constructions and analyses of men and women. Neither formalized genres nor their content in this group of texts confirms the expectations of outworn blueprints for gender analyses. Both chapters 4 and 5 suggest that gender is often analyzed and reinforced as a category to avoid explaining how the class prerogatives of elite females were models for later bourgeois domestic propriety.

Chapter 6 additionally details the transmission of patriarchy as an identity conveyed literally "on the pulse," in instructive letters from fathers to sons. Examples of this genre make it clear that *property* and *economy* should be read not only as vivid metaphors for entitled male identity. Both terms, that is, are intimately bound up in stringently enforced family education in gender, class, and bodily differences. Each of those topics is frequently embedded in surprising and otherwise unaccountable connections between achieving manhood and mastering correct writing. These letters invite us to set aside Marxist reproduction theories, to instead analyze how generations reappear in an active discursive capitalism. A belief in gender entitlements for males, like class and racial prejudice, is often identical to relative evaluations of texts. Fathers rank both reading and writing explicitly to preserve property by paying diligent attention to the letters of patriarchal law. Universal identity is endowed, that is, to males who write correctly. And it is lost by youngsters who do not attend to correct spelling and vocabulary.

This family correspondence also plants the historical seeds of institutionalized composition teaching and its tenacious commitment to equating linguistic norms with the spiritual good of its students. In only sparse comments, early writing teachers avoided a harsh or sarcastic tone. But marginal remarks by many English teachers today often echo these fathers' vitupertive judgments against their errant sons. Now multiplied communications technologies transmit such supposedly universal standards from one patriarchal keeper of the language to another, as we see in the paternalism of writers like William Safire and E. D. Hirsch.

As a coda for this two-part recursive analysis of self-education, gender, and patriarchy, the final chapter shows how both real and imagined advantages accrue to those who assume temporarily fixed positions in discourse and thereby articulate themselves as "authors" in shifting registers of individualism. The emerging commonplace convention of psychologizing the subject to create "an intriguing *cultural category*"[17] translates the gestures of earlier, abstract social Characters into internal responses to modern private experience.

Three documents represent exemplary moments in this changing nineteenth-century patriarchal and textual politics. An abused wife, a son who witnesses his father's death, and a daughter who equates the South with her father's personality all realign male gender identities to normalize shifted power relations in consequential ways. Each of these texts differently reconfigures universalized mankind. A rare successful divorce petition to the Virginia General Assembly, a highly stylized theatrical account of death, and a memoir of the Civil War that portrays its effects on "My Father's Household" all practice what I term *local authorship,* writing that manipulates commonplace identities in specific exigencies. Each of these examples relies on familiar rhetorical conventions to defamiliarize patriarchy, at last re-endowing it with a silent psychology. These texts struggle with traditional sites of authority, consenting to them in greater and lesser measure, showing how single writers might take new subject positions as temporarily singular authors.

This persuasive and formal experiment takes ordinary writing to be a most serious subject, a complex cultural process that scholars in textual studies could address to recuperate many categories that have lost much of their buoyancy, even in apparently radical attempts to rearrange official evaluations of texts and to expose the politics of conventional common sense about the human subject. But the ordinary writing in folder after folder of this collection requires little of the drudgery we have been so well schooled to expect in reading it. Making these holograph texts available and suggesting theorized ways to explain their results has rewarded me, as I hope it does others, with participation in the discursive energies that I try to make visible. Moments of quaint sententiousness are certainly overcome by the surprising insecurity, self-aware humor and pride, sly seduction, courage, rage, and grief that make a catalogued collection of commonplace volumes a living construction of American discursive culture.

These texts cheerfully demonstrate that to demean the writing we do not see and to justify its dismissal by assigning to its writers unified, coherent, and boring identities is to succumb to the notion of readers' superiority to writers and the politics of safely organized fables of interpretation. But as anthropologist Richard Price says in introducing his study of the Saramaka, we are not here reading "'the history of the bare-assed' [discursive] native."[18] Tracking everyday writing, like following people we have not previously noticed, is accepting an invitation to watch how cultures are made, remade, and finally ensconced in "memory," the miscellaneous space for writing that teaches us to ourselves.

PART I · A Textual Tradition

Ordinary Writing as Cultural Pedagogy

A World Lettered by Codes

Commonplace Powers

From a perspective that considers various kinds of literacy, "reality" would not be understood as a world without writing, but rather a world written or lettered by different codes—not by the institutions produced by the transmission of classical literature but by the political and economic situations whose "lettering" of society constitutes a different kind of regulation. What, then, prevents these other brands of literacy from becoming the objects of "literary" study?

NANCY ARMSTRONG and LEONARD TENNENHOUSE, eds., *The Violence of Representation*

Subjectivity originally is no relation of the real, but of a syntax which engenders in the real the signifying mark.

JACQUES LACAN, *Ecrits*

Three Common Topics

The Purloined Commonplace

First, we search for power in ordinary writing. It escapes us. Yet this embodiment of common opinion outside systematic thought is a structure of desire, even in its ancient articulations as the domain of a philosophically trivialized formal rhetoric. Projected onto the syntax of the human unconscious, the cultural force of plain texts seems imaginary. But even as they peek out of that kind of analysis, ordinary desires remain obvious and demanding, taking shapes that, Lacan says, are structured like a language. In either commonplace form—as the ancients' ordinary but precisely unreasonable desires, which formal rhetoric outlines as its organizing lessons in "common topics," or as the unvoiced syntax of a contemporary unconscious—desire appears only in specific, historical cultural logics. Desires are visible, finally, only as specific circulating discursive practices and power relations they write.

Yet these practices and relationships are simultaneously visible and invisible, in more than one way. *Doxa,* the doctrinaire content of common sense, appears only in specific instances, perhaps in model passages that exemplify rhetoric's instructive catalogue of inventive topoi, the prescriptions for speaking well within patriarchal norms associated with Aristotle and other Western cultural trainers. The regulatory limits of a culture's *doxa* circulate, consequently, precisely not *as* doctrinaire common opinion, not as a wish list. The items in that catalogue remain invisible, to prevent the feared (yet culturally constructive) process of thinking outside the limits, the transgression against philosophy's *thought* and *truth* that formal rhetoric flirts with only to restrain. Transgressions by common opinion can be detected only as the Other of high culture—as supposedly uninformed preferences, as pitifully imitative "originality," and as the strict principles that constitute subjects taken up outside formal education.

In those displaced forms, desires unorganized by official reason are precisely a syntax, but the syntax of a cultural system. The invisible power of this syntax over what is and is not said is reproduced in its photogenic negatives, which we recognize as pliable human subjectivities. *Doxa* is thus only lost letters, as invisible as Poe's purloined letter and as plain to the eye once we know where to look for it. It is rediscovered now in its obvious places by the professions that can see only internal locales of desire, the language of the psychology installed by twentieth-century descriptive magic. Before that descriptive trick, regulated desires remained a hidden and prescriptive cultural rhetoric. But this is not, we see, as it must be.

Lacan's definition of subjectivity, as "a relation . . . of a syntax which engenders in the real the signifying mark," hereby places human subjectivity at a distance from that mark itself, not where we are looking. Human language is not an independent Real. The power of desire is not simply transmitted in direct statements of systematic wishes that stay outside the content we recognize as conventional sense. The discourse that is *doxa* is circulated, says Lacan, in the human identities it creates. But how? Althusser answers that we are "hailed" into subject positions, the identities in common discourses, which are already written by a supposedly self-reproducing "outside," a "society" described by Marx. But neither Lacan's active inner unconscious nor the constructed recipient of cultural "calls" to identity explains how circulating desires survive.

Of course, this denied access to the circulation of *doxa* is an artifact of material circumstances. Productive yet restrained uses of ordinary language are absorbed and mystified by the Western transcendent universal/individual, who appeared just when history itself became a written text, a by-product of Foucault's archive. *Doxa* is easily dismissed, it is said, because it was not written. We console ourselves with the idea that it was lost with those who doomed us to repeat it. When the individual's transcendent and com-modified authorship finally makes a modern category for *doxa,* it sends it packing, clearly labeled as "memory." As this comforting lost gossip, *doxa* becomes systematic but always opaque cultural glue, coded as "oral," the Fix-odent we never discuss in polite company unless to isolate and patronize our Others.

In that sticky situation, the power of déclassé commonplaces seems safely transient. Just when ordinary texts become recognized cultural artifacts, their witness to the circulation of *doxa* is denied as insignificant. Their tes-timony is moved outside history and literature, disciplines that lack a cat-egory for extracanonical and extracurricular textual action. The historical correspondence we might have received, and have already absorbed, never arrives, despite its visibility in the most obvious places. So to learn *how* en-during Western cultural arrangements are matters of active (if only semioffi-cial) rhetorical education, we must peruse places that recently constructed psychologies teach us to call *personal.* Renaming this personal as the domes-ticated discourse to which letters (like Poe's) always return, we can perhaps see the power of ordinary writing. But, we remember, the cultural erasure of *doxa* is a project of our most honored traditions.

Home Improvements

Western education, from a beginning acknowledged as our "heritage" until now, undertakes this cultural erasure of its commonplace and formative syn-tax in a diversionary way, deploying privilege to correct the power of the or-dinary. A line drawn in Aristotle's *Rhetoric,* as in Socrates' joyful humiliation of anyone willing to talk to him, discredits the supposedly fluid and uncer-tain realm of opinion in favor of the exercise of reason. Western traditions first cast this opposition as a difference between systems of rhetoric and of dialectic, with dialectic winning the West in its devotion to seeking general truth. Nonetheless, opinion and the acquisitive emotions that appear to war-rant it are more than processes absorbed by authorship and Enlightenment constructions of the transcendent individual. That is, Aristotle's attention to feelings in Book II of the *Rhetoric* is not the final analysis of the "inner" lives of old, young, and moderate men, even in his canny prescriptions of what each may "say." But in his attempt to organize the verbal structures that con-stitute favorite tendencies among varieties of entitled men, we discover com-mon opinion as a discourse—one that is carefully taught.

To say that common opinion is carefully taught may directly contradict many cherished tenets, primarily the convenient distinction drawn between theory and practice. That separation exempts both formal rhetoric and active ordinary utterances from the power to shape culture by making them schema without content, another Lacanian "syntax." As a practice paired with a theory, rhetoric may remain only a system that describes discourse, leaving its traditional opposite, Western philosophy, safely outside desire. Its practice and theory, in this view, both train "thought," though they do not activate its results.

Rhetoric nonetheless is a discipline that instructs and punishes in equal measure. Admittedly, it describes discursive processes in the name of instruction. It teaches a calculus for tracing movements but not, it is assumed, their substance. But rhetoric is also, if covertly, much like dialectic, limiting what it is possible to think, as the Socratic dialogues openly insist. Both subdivisions of cultural training inculcate rhetorical forms that are comprehended only in examples of "successful" sayings, practices that voice theoretically acceptable desires. As George Kennedy admits in his introduction to Aristotle's *Rhetoric,* "Both dialectic and rhetoric build their arguments on commonly held opinions *(endoxa)* and deal only with the probable (not with scientific certainty)."[1] This hint allows us to reason further: Systematic rhetorical pedagogy, no matter how diffuse and initiative it may seem in post-Cartesian rationalist curricula that appear to erase it, still manages centuries of cultural anxiety. Formal literate education has always asked, and answered, the question: What will happen if *doxa*—Kennedy's *"endoxa"* and "the probable"— are not controlled, both organized and debased in ways that sustain privileged social and philosophical structures that manage a populace?

The rhetorics of Aristotle and others, we see, circumscribe otherwise erratic opinion; they do not merely recapitulate it. Rhetoric is both a tamed descriptive noun and a deceptively abstract verbal form of the quaint content of "conduct." Like the *doxa* it claims only to systematize, rhetoric is a visibly invisible, entirely successful means to circulate, reproduce, and maintain a limited range of categories. In this syntax, common opinion can be thought. The treatise *about* opinion, that is, prescribes it—as a theory always does.

Roland Barthes, with studied bewilderment, discerns this slippage between practice and theory in *The Semiotic Challenge:*

> There is a kind of stubborn agreement between Aristotle (from whom rhetoric proceeded) and our mass culture, as if *Aristotelianism . . . survived* in a corrupt, diffused, inarticulate state in the cultural *practice* of Western societies. . . . A kind of *Aristotelian vulgate still defines a type of trans-historical Occident,* a civilization (our own) which is that of the *endoxa.*[2]

Rhetoric, as Barthes suggests in his references to "a kind of" agreement and to philosophy, is a surreptitious process. It limits, and means to limit, the political opportunities through speech that are in fact its content. Its "survival," a menace to Barthes and to others schooled in suspicion about potentially uncontrolled ordinary discourse, might be recast. Staying alive, for rhetoric, is a persistent renewal of and variation on cultural contexts.

So we can access the power of circulating desire, despite its invisibility. Superficially dull and haphazardly preserved "commonplaces," embodied in the ordinary writing of particular groups of writers at specific times, represent the practice that is identical to theory. These utterances simultaneously organize, arrange, and root culturally transmitted common opinion as the active discursive substance of a culture that appears to be only an object of interpretation. When commonplaces are treated as manifestations of theory, as Barthes accurately suspects them to be, they become decidedly uncommon self-constructions and political actions. Commonplace texts remember where we learned the categories of "inside" and "outside," designations that made the word *canon* relevant far beyond its theological context. Such homemade texts are not equivalent to items in an archeological log of officially designated trash or ephemera, for they perform, on the contrary, perhaps the most active and formative literate practice, the composition of private scripts that are purposefully excluded from official hermeneutic sense.

At last, ordinary writing offers more than the unkempt memorial lore often attributed to silent yet urbane natives. It shows us to ourselves, precisely as products of the texts we produce. It transmits both formal and informal versions of later culturally active categories that it can now gloss—education, gender, authorship, and especially the rationalist fiction of an enduring individual/universal human subject. All of these interests, that is, were made possible *as* categories by antecedent systems circulated in ordinary discourse networks.

Of course, such circulation is visible only in specific and common places. The early Virginia patriarchs who authorized the collection of commonplace volumes that this book transcribes and analyzes are part of a productively ambivalent elitist history. They defamiliarize and thereby empower the implications of the "ordinary." As a product of American "history" in upper-class Virginia from colonial times to the late nineteenth century, these commonplace books embody discourses against which forces promoting national unity and character would work to create an "America" that replaced the "United States" after the Civil War. Robert Beverley's 1705 *History of Virginia* describes the class from which they came as "well-inclined gentlemen," members of a society praised in histories of colonial education for attempting to establish a free public school that enrolled Indians in 1621.[3]

This colonial human subtext, biological and figurative ancestors of the discourses of nationalized America, managed a complex textual tradition that is often mistaken for peripheral, derivative, rural orality by later attempts to purify literary culture. Yet this community sent its first scholar to Oxford in 1635 and endowed a school without tuition or fees in the same year.[4]

The commonplace books kept by these early settlers, like those of later families eager to join Virginia's self-constructed, "aristocratically" traced public memory, provide a core sample of textual practices preserved in specific ways at a specific time in publicly held "history." This ordinary writing demonstrates how common purposes for inscription are entwined in all American fantasies. Its idiom articulates slogans, constructs a catalogue of "roles" attached to rifts in human identity, and forecasts later hierarchical stratifications among them. But this writing also embodies productive social practices that reappear as traces in the formal genres now taught as public and educationally sanctioned purposes for writing.

In all these contexts, the always local access of these texts to the ongoing cultural productivity of ordinary writing reveals commonplaces to be diverse sites of home improvement. The autodidacticism of this writing is now partially described as "self-fashioning" and by similar terms that give only nodding recognition to indigenous cultural productivity. That is, such terms ignore the unity of rhetoric, pedagogy, *doxa,* and culture, the totality that Barthes articulates in his worried rejection of Aristotelian common opinion.

Under Separate Heads: A Literary History

Historians of rhetorical education explain that commonplace books and their equivalents provided schoolboys in ancient Greece and other literate communities in that tradition with a portable memory that enriched and guided their exercises in composing. For instance, in the *Topica,* Aristotle alluded to this relation between an individual human subject and notable discursive practice. He directs students to keep these compilations, to "select also from the written handbooks of arguments, and . . . draw up sketch-lists of them upon each several kind of subject, putting them down under separate headings. . . . In the margin, too, one should indicate also the opinions of individual thinkers."[5] Quintilian, always attentive to practical composing, believed that absorbing the language of others by preparing and memorizing specific passages would increase a student's flow of words. But his "fluent" student orator participates not in a generative, but in a re-collected production of language. As opposed to easy expression, the fluent *memory* uses commonplaces for public speech as *loci*, the places where common ideas useful in argumentation visually "appear," hung on well-stocked, familiar mental images.[6]

Such ancient directions to keep commonplace books have not disappeared from Western educational practice, but they receive only occasional attention as concrete intertextual agencies in the modern literary or rhetorical studies they helped to legitimate. Even after Harold Bloom's proclamation of a generational "anxiety of influence," students may read Milton without connecting his early school exercises (prolusions) to assigned commonplace topics like arguing "whether day or night is more excellent." A modern editor of Ben Jonson, surely unable to imagine an "author" writing from what moderns call plagiarism, overlooked the commonplace implications of Jonson's complete title: *Timber,—or, Discoveries upon Men and Matter as They Have Flowed Out of His Daily Readings* (1616).[7] But as indicated by Milton's "literary" achievement after becoming blind, it is only when a later property right is invested in the printed word that physical manifestations of memory like Jonson's can be treated as original or as the sole authority for a discursive origin.

Mary Carruthers demonstrates in *The Book of Memory* how, contrary to modern wishes for transhistorical "originality," medieval society deployed commonplaces (or personal florilegia) for the purpose of building character. Early compilations, more accurately preserved in human memory than in (often miscopied) texts, stimulated participation in a collective identity and the forms by which it was regulated. Of Cassiodorus's definition of the educational value of such compilations to the human mind, Carruthers writes, "The commonplaces are understood here to be habits of thought, habits of character as well. . . . One *cannot think at all*, at least about the world of process and matter . . . except in commonplaces, which are, as it were, concentrated 'rich' schemata of the memory, to be used for making judgments and forming opinions and ideas."[8] Collecting commonplaces was *the* way to mold one's character, a formation that depended not on private experience, but "the experiences of others."[9]

Guided ethical participation in others' experience, a humanist motive, defined later modes of literary education. In her study of Renaissance commonplaces, Joan Marie Lechner describes how educators such as Melancthon, Vives, and Brinsley (*A Consolation for Our Grammar Schools*, 1622) and Hoole (*New Discovery of the Old Art of Teaching School*, 1660) promoted the keeping of commonplace books as a basis for the inventive and stylistic *copia* presented in Erasmus's *De Copia* (1550), the locus classicus of such texts.[10] In these and other Renaissance treatises on conduct, commonplace books were specific aids to the artificial, "secondary" memory. They supplemented school lessons "as a subsidiary or auxiliary to the primary memory and [to] assist in recalling to mind what may be forgotten."[11] But, as Lechner points out, use of these books in the European Renaissance involved the possession of ideas "not alone by the students and instructors, but by anyone who nurtured a desire to be, or to be thought, learned."[12] They became populist repositories, material aids to memory in which a single but infinitely divisible image could stand for an entire textual structure shared by many keepers of such books, inside and outside the elite educational tradition.

This form of populist textual character building was a vital element in Renaissance humanistic education, an emblem of the humanists' promotion of more democratic attitudes. Commonplace collecting, Mary Thomas Crane argues in *Framing Authority*, was "a version of authorship that was collective instead of individualist, published instead of private, inscriptive instead of voice-centered, and aphoristic or epigrammatic instead of lyric or narrative, but which shaped and informed the lyric tradition even as it countered it."[13] Max W. Thomas also emphasizes the simultaneously material and immaterial implications of such texts in his essay on their authorship.[14] Renaissance manuscript poetry collections, Thomas argues, are imagined as repositories that cull and reproduce "already written material as an integral part of the process of composition, which cobbles together new texts from words others have used."[15]

Understanding the authorship of these books, as Roger Chartier explains in *The Order of Books*,[16] requires historicizing the "author-function" that Foucault divorced from unified, transcendent productive consciousness in "What Is an Author?"[17] In this "already written" process of composing, commonplace books were first copies of others' works, then objects to be read: "Produced by lay people unfamiliar with the traditional institutions of manuscript production and for whom the act of copying was a necessary preliminary to reading, [they] characteristically show no sign of the author-function. The unity of such a book comes from the fact that its producer is also its addressee."[18]

In the model Renaissance that Lechner imagines, all of these results of keeping commonplaces became available from powerful booksellers, whose distribution of blank indexes established the format that frequently appears in the Virginia collection (to be discussed later). They offered alphabetized, numbered, and topically labeled pages for noting memorable passages from civic, religious, academic, and ultimately more general sources. For instance, William Fulwood's *The Enimie of Idleness: Teaching the manner and style how to endite, compose, and write all sorts of Epistles and Letters as well by answer . . .* (1568), like medieval epistolary guides, prescribed writing letters as mini orations. Success as a social and business correspondent depended not only on a writer's knowledge of traditional Ciceronian principles of argumentation, but equally on a private stock of allusions and standard phrases such as those kept in a collection of commonplaces. What Lechner calls "assembling an abundance of literary wealth" informed both institutional and personal claims on a writer's literate identity.[19]

Walter Ong also notes in his study of Ramus that in this pedagogic "wealth" of ideas, memories and allusions appear to derive from dual images used by medieval-Renaissance schoolmasters and logicians to define and explain nature.[20] On the one hand, that is, the *loci,* or places, were systematic compartments, boxes used both to contain and to generate materials in speech making and other forms of composition. In this sense, commonplace collections were systematic preservations. But from another perspective (as titles like Ben Jonson's *Timber* and Francis Bacon's *A Forest of Forests* indicate) the contents of commonplace books store "felled timber," a "superfluous quantity" of profuse "concepts and/or things."[21]

Ong refers this second sense of "material" to "literary composition and . . . the mystery of communication between person and person."[22] He says, "One is not surprised to find that the concepts used to represent operations in the topical logics metamorphose and proliferate in countless forms and directions. But always in vain: 'sorting,' 'cutting out,' 'arranging,' 'seats,' 'treasure chests,' 'woods,' and the rest [are] hopelessly inadequate as representations."[23] He sees these inevitably inadequate containers collapsing, or exploding, under the pressure of a modern psycho-logic. New technologies for capturing materials, that is, involve a cognitive deficiency that evidently did not plague Cassidorus, Acquinas, or Jerome, who lived in worlds whose materials were supposedly narrowed by the absence of print. But failures of keeping that Ong describes psychologically are better cast as a human inability to keep absolutely separate the categories that became applicable to all available reality, the limit addressed by Bacon and post-Cartesian intellectualism. As Chartier comments on the attempts of Doni and La Croix du Maine to compile grandiose universal "libraries without walls" in sixteenth-century France, "The irreducible gap between ideally exhaustive inventories and necessarily incomplete collections was experienced with intense frustration."[24]

Nonetheless, the rationalist, antirhetorical projects of philosophy that begin early modern history promised that the disabled storage technologies of a new, scientized "reality" might be repaired, largely with the help of writing. The supposed remedy for the proliferation of memorable knowledge was new faith in the increasing circulation of duplicable print itself, a fantasy of absolute control over the materials exploding from rationalist self-awareness. But focusing on concerns about storing discourse—like the emphasis in Crane and Thomas on a supposed populist motive for Renaissance and later humanist education—diverts us from the primary issue of how these books came to be a medium of self-regulatory autodidacticism. The keeping of commonplace books became a Puritan "progress," and later a way to record the syntax of Lacanian unconsciousness. But both of these uses are very different from the Renaissance aristocratic vision of writing as occurring within the hierarchial social structure to which genres are attached, for instance, in Sidney's *Apology for Poetry.* Ann Moss calls this shift a "decline" in her study of French printed commonplace books. She attributes fears of plagiarism and desires for originality to a newly independent, masterful, and personalized construction of authorship. But as she says, "The commonplace-book was so firmly entrenched in the European mentality (and in the school system) that even writers who saw little or no profit in its quotations and places, did retain it as a working tool."[25]

Addison's *Spectator* (nos. 411, 412) invests still later versions of private writing with "property of the Imagination," a middle-class version of propriety that was finally warranted by Locke's philosophical break with absolute authority. As David Simpson says, "At precisely the point of emergence of a readership with very little property or none at all, Addison plays up the property of the imagination, which gives us . . . 'a kind of Property' in everything we see."[26] In early Virginia society, the use of written language to create literate "holdings" certainly fulfilled the desires of a displaced gentry to achieve formative control and self-possession, especially in a rural country that sought to minimize its cultural distance from Addison's London until well after the Revolution.

But the Virginia gentry had their reasons for adding to the humanist-Renaissance self-educational purpose for keeping commonplace books. Their motives, like those of New England Puritans, help to explain the general proliferation of personal journals, and later "day timers." Far from merely connecting their keepers to a recognizable religious or social "self-fashioning" or pure Rousseauistic "expression," their use taught, and restrained, the tenets of dominant desires in specific historic circumstances. The genteel labor of early Virginia makers of such family properties made their writing a representation of "self"-invested proprietary workings of property held in common, not of romantic inspiration. As Overton's *Arrows Against All Tyrants* (1646) puts it, "I may be but an Individall, enjoy my selfe, and my selfe propriety, *and may write my selfe no more than my selfe,* or presume any further, if I doe, I am an encroacher & invader upon another mans Right, to which I have no Right."[27]

David Simpson notes that finding in historical texts a concern with postmodern identity issues—"history backwards"—justifies only an "author's perception of the needs of the present."[28] Yet to understand the cultural work of the commonplace book in colonial and early republican culture, it is useful to notice that seventeenth-century and later civic contexts for keeping such books enact the postmodern view of writing as imaginary assurance of always unrealized cultural norms and personal presence. As Marshall Alcorn suggests about the rhetorical, social work of literary production: "Writing offers an imaginary representation of self-consciousness as a commodity for recognition and appropriation. The text . . . provides a space, a habitation . . . , inviting an other to take up presence. It offers, in a subtle form, a verbal body to shore up the insecurity of a self's presence."[29] Alcorn's psychoanalytic perspective verifies the social history of emergent class consciousness that Simpson sketches. It restates the reasons for textual practices that "work" the physical spaces of a new country into written "habitations" where a family can "take up presence." These books, that is, worry about children, education, property, and especially losses from all these domains in the Civil War, to juxtapose a very "real" imaginary security in discourse against rising and falling material fortunes.

Ordinary discourse and its growing power to give its keepers a self-preserving social identity also became a political site during revolutionary formations of the European national state during the eighteenth century. The discursive identity politics I allude to was enacted in state-sponsored emphases on ethical self-regulation. An arresting example of such regulation, described in Furet and Ozouf's monumental study of literacy in France, is a Jacobin report to the French Council of the Five Hundred. The draconian Jacobins proposed to reform bad habits of royalist thought by inspecting the "private morals" of citizens, "their family life, by instituting a 'family book.'"[30] This little-noted proposal projected the civic imagination onto an earlier way of joining the formation of ethical character with an authoritarian agenda. The proposal did not go so far as to imagine what are now recognized primarily as domestic storage sites that serve private, otherwise unaccountable "minds." Yet it foreshadowed how nineteenth-century state education, unlike contemporary religious self-surveillance in the name of literate (and thus godlike) "intelligence," would rely on forming "masses" to become available for political conformity.

The Jacobin proposal suggests not only that commonplace keeping needs historic analysis to mark the rupture in the philosophy of human identity occasioned by Locke, Hume, and others. Equally important, this French proposal identifies the commonplace as the purloined letters of obvious but unremarked political controls on shared cultural memory.

Furet and Ozouf explain the textual politics of the Jacobin project, the

spirit of which was postponed until Euro-American mass education substituted supervised reading of national canons for regulated writing in which
students could self-inscribe their own conformity:

> [Family books] were to contain civil records (birth, marriage, etc.) as well as deeds
> relating to the interests of the family, so as to furnish each family with precise in-
> formation about itself. But it would relate this private history in moral terms, so
> that the record of it might serve as an example and a matter for celebration.
> Lastly, it would at all times serve the Republic, since this instrument of what Le-
> clerc termed "domestic surveillance" also helped to ensure public morality. As an
> infallible substitute for individual recollection, as the principal repository of vir-
> tue, elevated into a ritual, *the written word was given the task of reconstituting re-*
> *publican society from its basic units upwards;* the family had become the focus of
> the beneficial commemoration which the written word made possible.[31]

This particular attempt at grass-roots colonization, socializing the records
of the populace, was not realized. But subsequent state schooling in France,
as in England, its colonies, and post–Civil War America articulated a similar
desire to make universal literacy a means of surveillance increasingly denied
to the Church. This late eighteenth-century vision of literate self-policing reminds us that Renaissance manuscript copies of poetry, the later inscribed
Lockean "consciousness" that linked propriety to property among these Virginia writers, and centralized vernacular curricula in public schools were all
reinventions of Aristotle's perceptive organization of general knowledge presented in the *Rhetoric.* What most people think, *doxa,* is the power of notable
language held in common, a power recast in specific historical instances that
have accumulated visions of linguistic cultural education.

In 1838, Sarah Hale urged readers of *Godey's Ladies Magazine* to keep commonplace books to *respond* to their reading, so that they would have a record
of *their* judgments on its morality, style, and applicability to their own lives.[32]
Hale's directive highlights a persistent social electricity running through the
ordinary, which proliferates in cultural currents that commonplaces both
shape and accommodate. Acts of writing themselves, particularly those
"kept" by individuals, serve as cultural mediators in various ways. Even as
bland repositories for approved "important" ideas and well-turned phrases,
these autodidactic compilations are never culturally neutral. They are the
designated places of dominant discourse. They chronicle variously imagined
relations among available linguistic technologies, constructing both variously
active and passive "selves" and shifting discursive desires. Despite Barthes's
studied bewilderment about the persistence of *doxa,* they openly announce
its force as the site of self-naming.

To modify Althusser's terms, these are the places where individuals hail themselves into specific identities, where people move among available ideologies. Any version of such books materializes the complex relation between *culture* and *civilization* that Raymond Williams describes.[33] Their individual keepers are obviously under various daily institutional and social pressures to mark and activate self-regulatory political statements. They spontaneously, yet with great regularity, have connected their lives to a process usually figured abstractly: the reproduction of simultaneously internal and official self-definitions. These books substantiate the immaterial, Idealist "substance" that once signified only a philosophic and theological "soul."

Having Advantages and Taking Them:
Textual Property and Propriety

Despite the self-awareness it appears to promote, ordinary writing is often recognized as no more than Mikhail Bakhtin's "unpublished speech . . . freed from the shackles of sense." But everyday texts are never, in fact, "outside the usual logical conditions" that they instead actually shape.[34] Obviously, the written word can be described figuratively as only ancillary to voices of memory. As a contested space repeatedly demarcating class and educational boundaries, vernacular writing easily becomes a channel for watchful governance of the populace, the hope of the Jacobin proposal. This hope was realized in common institutional uses of record keeping, in the period when most of these collections were kept, as in Hale's invitation to self-monitoring readers. But the surveillance implied in the earlier ancient, Renaissance, and Puritan pedagogic uses of the genre—to design a socialized and mobile self—was complicated by print and publication, which enhanced the status of self-incriptions with another sort of material: property. That seventeenth-century concept underlies the modern energy of the semi-authored commonplace, as I have suggested, uniting character, or propriety, with material words.

The volumes in the Virginia Historical Society are classified under the specific archival designation, "commonplace books," which the society's archivists often speak of as an unaccountable surplus, anomalous contributions to many large donations of more readily negotiable family papers. These volumes often appear to have been contributed accidentally within large family gifts or deposits, but they have also received scrupulous professional attention befitting the prominence of their authors, members of Virginia's First (and many other) Families. They thus occupy territory somewhere between entropy and formalized expectation, a space where only accidents are expected to occur. They could easily be dismissed as "excess."

Nonetheless, their scrupulous preservation draws attention to the complex relation between purposeful making and chance durability. They embody the contradictory implications of preserving seemingly disposable "content" within carefully conserved textual objects. They offer new access to the "political and economic situations whose 'lettering' of society constitutes a regulation" in the multiply coded "reality" that Armstrong and Tennenhouse imagine.[35] Their obviously marginal place among more prominent holdings, their typically informal graphic forms, and their overflowing, miscellaneous content suggest an almost pure sample of the mobile and conflicted ordinary supports undergirding the elite position of their compilers. They draw attention to invisible cultural "resources" that make any writing possible.

These commonplace books thus exhibit both material privileges and discursive entitlements that have specifically been "left." They are endowed signs of prosperity, both in family genealogies and in enduring public display. They certify the discursive entitlements that supported family, civic, and cultural ecology in literate eighteenth- and nineteenth-century America. Time for writing, various forms of literary expertise, and a keen sense of significant identity all enable the long traditions governing the keeping of such textual records. Both aristocratic leanings and these surplus resources transformed material acquisitions and motley daily events into simultaneously informal and highly codified textual forms.

But as their discrete catalogue designation also emphasizes, commonplace books are generally *left out* of the usual categories of correspondence, treatises, and literary remains that are treasured in public collections and mined by historians for Foucauldian "statements." They are *left over* from among the more familiar artifacts and chattel we view as material culture. Thus their "collecting" itself shows how material and textual culture were joined in well-crafted, tangible representations of a cultural "elite" who are often imagined to have imported, but not to have built, a local discursive tradition.

These carefully preserved texts hereby portray both value and indifference in the local settings they define. As cultural focal points, they nonetheless have no particular stake in the economies of later cultural professions. These upper-class writers, when they were self-conscious "writers" at all, imagined self-defining composition as one discursive action among other social actions that constituted their culture as an emerging civic *bricolage*. Both young social initiates and older citizens deployed written language to link their society both to the authorized past and to later inheritors of the significant tension between that past and a new order.

Exceptions are, of course, obvious. The literary commonplace book of Thomas Jefferson and the many volumes kept by William Byrd receive professional attention befitting the status of their renowned "authors," the result of a selective tradition of historical interpretation.[36] Yet those special examples, as instances of the commonplace, serve mainly to highlight how modern constructions of literary authority reproduce past inequities. Jefferson and Byrd wrote no more, and no better, than many whose names do not call attention to their ordinary literate practices.

We should notice, of course, that literary and cultural histories do suggest the ruptures and renewals visible in this otherwise seemingly unremarkable literate practice. The commonplace acts of writing in this collection are discrete transformations of a lost generic origin perhaps best represented by the numbered list of Ten Commandments. They specifically show how fragmented events and transmitted dominant discourses constituted a socialized but still preinstitutional *propriety*. This particular form of human property is not yet personal in a privatized, capitalist sense. It is not precisely Bourdieu's cultural capital, possessed or not by individuals identified in later class demarcations.[37] Still later philosophic categories warrant that now common class paradigm for analyzing the formation of "masses" and their stratification. Neither is this cultural property entirely isolated in its public museum setting. As shown in Locke's "Of Property" and his much imitated commonplace book, these examples of graphic "labours" are evidence of an ambiguously private work, in Mary Beth Norton's sense (see introduction). The worth of these private investments, that is, is verified only by their resonance with common social values. Consequently, they are pivotal spaces between the acquisition and the transmission of personal worth. The republican collector's "sense of self" hereby acquires a relation that both includes and goes beyond its ethical "character," a relation to real and figurative *earnings*, assets acquired by simultaneously individual and culturally warranted discursive labors.

C. B. Macpherson argues in *The Political Theory of Possessive Individualism* that seventeenth- and eighteenth-century social philosophies authorized the appropriation of cultural doctrines, and the textually verifiable social identities traditionally connected to them, through inscribed family properties.[38] These entitlements to identity reside primarily in Locke's reasoning about ownership and use, mirrored in his commonplace method itself, an emblem for his philosophy's self-surprised investigation of its own reliance on conventional discursive practice. In Locke's analysis of property rights, the absolute right to possession of one's own labor overrides the moral claims of a larger society. Using an image for commonplace materials later circulated in Keats's metaphor for the compression of poetic meanings— "load every rift with Ore"—Locke explicitly promotes the individual's claim on otherwise "common" property that one has "worked": "The *labour* that was mine, removing [natural resources and] the Ore I have digg'd in any place where I have a right to it out of that common state they were in, hath *fixed* my *Property* in them."[39] David Silverman and Brian Torode explain this appropriation of "resources" by labor in this way: "Labour, which expresses the social (and the transcendence of given forms of the social), is used by Locke to represent the private; . . . the grounds of my speech are now private property."[40]

Locke works this shift from social to private, however, at a time when the range of definitions for *private* was still unsettled, well before a general acceptance of isolated authorship and the investiture of socially held language with internal "meaning." Locke's labor of writing was instead *production,* even in the form of copying to produce a personally owned manuscript that appropriates an event—such as, for instance, the copy of Cornwallis's surrender document in the Historical Society collection—or formative advice about character. Such labor, writes Locke, "fixes my property" in me, but as an acquisition of a *cultural structure,* not of an "original" or "inner" identity. As he also emphasizes in the *Essay on Human Understanding* (3, XI), where he identifies commerce with communication, language use requires precautions. We must take "care to apply . . . words as near as may be to such ideas as common use has annexed them to. For words, especially of languages already framed, *being no man's private possession, but the common measure of commerce and communication,* it is not for any one at pleasure to change the stamp they are current in, nor alter the ideas they are affixed to."[41] Speech, like other capital, should not go to waste. But it will unless it has public (common) value.

Consequently, the copying and imitation that licensed commonplace acquisitions under republican rationalism also invested them with a transformative dynamism, the social energy that warranted their commodification. But this energy equally permitted the social practice of self-inscribing acquisition that is exemplified in the volumes analyzed here. Writing to "fix my property" in dominant, well-circulated discourses was a way of keeping alive the ethical character of the models traditionally copied and imitated as sources for fluent composition. Yet this frame around scribal labor not only warranted the extensive social practice of keeping household "books" and journals. It also explains the modern mystique surrounding acts of writing by individuals, an aura often imagined to be the result of a cultural shift from oral to written modes of cognition. Such making, circulating "my property" in Locke's sense, opens a space for imagining an independent writer's work, not inscribed collectively held language, as a source of social identity. The slightly odd concepts of *writer* and published *author,* characters nervously alluded to in these texts only after the 1830s, became sanctioned yet startling autonomous identities only after ownership of written language, as "the Ore I have digged," had transformed that language into a domain of aesthetic and conscious originality. The Lockean perspective, that is, looked back to a Shakespeare who would have been made anxious by this supposed autonomy and forward to the thousands of "creative writers" stimulated by it.

This progress from private labor to common but not yet authorial identity is the space traversed by the early American writing presented here. Socialized moral claims on discursive property were not entrenched, either legally or psychologically, in the early republic. Even through the Civil War, recursive interactions between *doxa* and episteme, rhetorical practice and regimes of truth, only tentatively constructed what Richard Schwartz calls the "notion of a self-defining, self-validating author, who serves as *the final source* of the text's internal coherence and its aesthetic, cultural, and moral value."[42] Macpherson points out that for Locke, "ownership of property [does not] involve social obligations" nor does it take place in a socialist "community" that starts with the "traditional assumption that the earth and its fruits had originally been given to mankind for their common use."[43] But the material and discursive capitalism at work is distinct from a (yet unrealized, still irrelevant) social isolation that later housed the supposedly univocal source of singular discourse.

In the preindustrial capitalism of colonial and antebellum Virginia, class differentials and making an effort beyond those of one's neighbors justified appropriations of land, produce, and cultural identity. But these positions were not yet imagined as states of psychological autonomy. Discursive properties so acquired were still warranted for *use,* for the increase of a culturally embedded individual and its family's wealth. This self-possession was not the action that "expressed" an entirely privatized self as an author, but a differently "individual" right to own "the Ore I have digged" as both language and the desirable identities attached to it. A "social contract" figured identity, not the powerfully constructed fiction of potentially isolated discursive independence that produced radically private bourgeois subjectivity.

This pivotal difference is evident in Locke's advice in *A New Method of Making Common-Place Books.*[44] This widely influential work shifts the definition of the genre to a modernist historical stake in assuring its keepers' social identity in a mode of self-composition that can plausibly be situated outside religious, civic, and academic spheres. Locke's method, which is specifically executed and theorized in the examples described below, suggests that keeping commonplace books became a material ontology. These books, that is, assured their keepers that *an* "identity of person-as-consciousness" endured substantially, in a physical location. They comforted the necessarily unmarked insecurity of the Enlightenment's universalized, supposedly coherent individual in a written record that *literally* embodied the unstable moment-to-moment awareness of its compiler. A commonplace book installed on sequential pages a fleeting, and therefore troubling and unverifiable, accountability for disparate actions of the mind, simultaneously acknowledging and undoing that dispersal.[45]

The endurance of this method of using organized, self-aggrandizing discursive access to bifurcated, simultaneously whole and mobile identity is most evident today in the competitive models that characterize documentation in professional research. There, footnotes both display an inevitably disorganized selectivity and support the fiction of coherent omniscience that, under Locke's *New Method,* transformed commonplace compilations. The alliances and conflicts visible in notes and in lists of cited works trace Locke's instructions to peruse, recreate, and invest in a universal narrative "history," taking from it an identity realized as a textual consciousness.[46]

An Embodied Textual Tradition

Obviously, no single collection can prove that keeping commonplace books was a widespread practice with the cultural implications I claim for it. Accidents and exigencies affect preservation itself, determining which texts survive. Donations to particular collections depend on geographic proximity, coincidental personal affinities, and concerns for social status, all unpredictable and untraceable. In Virginia, the Historical Society and the State Library and Archives in Richmond, the University in Charlottesville, the Williamsburg Trust, and various local historical libraries all purchase such collections and acquire them as gifts or deposits from differently motivated donors. The Historical Society, founded in 1831, was the earliest and remains the most prominent public repository for donated family records, but its carefully catalogued commonplace books only partially exemplify this local textual history.

We know, however, that most contributions in this site exhibit a particular kind of sociotextual elitism. Their donors are presenting the archive with examples of lettered behavior by both male and female ancestors over many generations, a display that depicts the donors as significant participants in memories that become, by virtue of their preservation, a public history. These texts insist on an overwhelming sense of conservation and continuity among families from the state that is significantly called the "cradle of the republic." They are the product of material circumstances and social connections that mark them as privately held family possessions; only later were they delivered, read, and paintakingly archived as leftovers, a superfluity of writing. But these donations justify our interest in this collection as an exemplary redundancy.

These commonplace texts reveal the relations between local cultures and generalized textuality. They certainly announce a blended, local "historical" demeanor, but they also reveal a specific historic process—the self-display of cultural virtue that becomes organized institutional standards. Their informality and readers' schooled negative reactions to it help show how presuppositions about quality are now the *doxa* of nationalized education and professional literary and literacy studies.

But this informal while generically traditional collection is most valuable as a way to juxtapose multiple social and discursive sites of production. It is tempting to begin with simple questions: "Who wrote?" "When?" and "For what purposes?" But identifying biographical authorship, dates of writing, and purposes only obliquely describes these collected examples of a much more elastic textual tradition.

Dates, Generic Scope, and Authorship of This Collection

Commonplace books often include the copied quotations that first defined their purpose, as well as notes, self- and school-sponsored essays, journals, correspondence, speeches, legal documents, school exercises, and many other familiar forms that now occupy literary, historical, and cultural analysis. But in these post-Cartesian manifestations, they are not only repositories for rhetoric's common topics. Their content in this later tradition also circulates the *process* of keeping, so just as often they contain receipts, crude drawings, practice signatures, artifacts like pressed flowers and theater tickets, and directions for domestic and cultural activities, the "ephemera" of cultural anthropology. In this case, these 349 separately catalogued compilations take the form of bound volumes of once blank pages, folders of loose sheets, printed almanacs, calendar-diaries, account books, and pocket books, in which their owners attempted only sporadically to author often partially completed texts.[47] Yet these informal or preliminary inscriptions were undertaken by widely read and educated people whose crudest jottings show ways of characterizing a concurrent elite and marginal "literacy."

The commonplace books in this collection were begun between 1650 and 1880, although continuous collections of family papers also contain examples begun before these dates and continued in the twentieth century. Four books were begun in the 1650s, whereas the last twenty-four were begun in the 1880s. As we might expect, if only because of the vagaries of preservation,

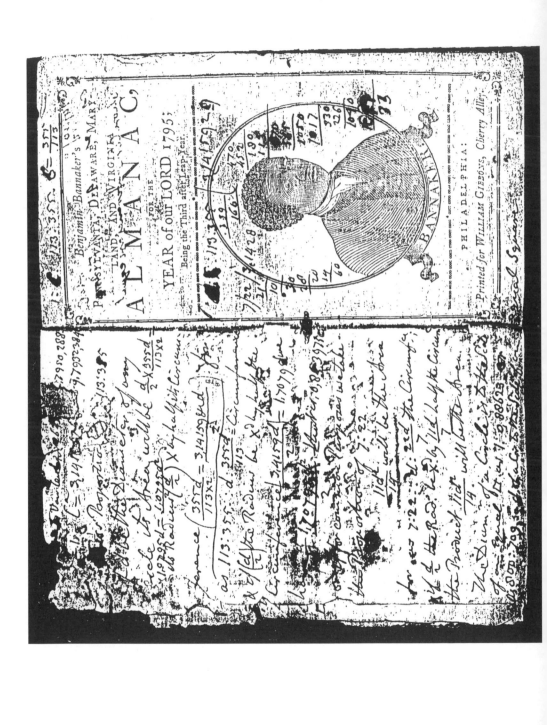

each fifty-year period from 1650 to 1850 provides an increased number of examples. In 1650–1700, six commonplace books were begun, four by men, one by a woman, and one by an unidentified author. There are fifteen examples from 1700–1750, eight by men (including Thomas Jefferson), four by women, and three unidentified.[48] Fifty-two date from 1750–1800, thirty-eight by men, ten by women, and four by unidentified compilers.

Most examples in this collection were undertaken in the nineteenth century, as families were becoming convinced of the plausible significance of their members' writing. The collection includes 267 examples begun from 1800 to 1880. Of the 114 begun between 1800 and 1840, 64 were kept by men, 43 by women, and 7 by unidentified authors. There are 153 examples from the period 1850–1880, of which 109 were kept by men, 38 by women, and 6 by unidentified authors.

Women kept a significant proportion of these books: the percentage kept by women are as follows: 20 percent for 1650–1699; 19 percent for 1700–1749; 29 percent for 1750–1799; 37 percent for 1800–1849; 25 percent for 1850–1880s. These figures verify that upper-class families educated children of both sexes. In the total collection, 29 percent (101) were kept by women, 71 percent (248) by men.

But such figures about gender, like dates of origin, apply to a mode of authorship that is quite different from the proprietary, yet not consistently individual, acts of writing that produced these books. Twelve commonplace books, for instance, are catalogued as having multiple authors. In four cases, two or more women shared the same book; in three cases, two or more men did; and five books were kept by both men and women. In other instances, two, three, and sometimes four siblings, parents and their children, cousins, or relatives by marriage joined in an evolving authorship. In one instance, the letters of a grandfather to a father were faithfully copied for generations to follow, so that the "author" of Charles Mortimer's letters to his son in Philadelphia (1784–1789) is both Mortimer and his granddaughter, Mary

· 1 ·

(Facing page) Title page and notes on inside cover of commonplace book of John Page (1744–1808), kept in Benjamin Bannaker's *Pennsylvania, Delaware, Maryland, and Virginia Almanac* (Philadelphia, 1794). The volume includes notes about the boundaries of Rosewell Plantation, lists of slaves, birth records, and algebra and geometry problems. Mss55P1432, 1, Virginia Historical Society. Reprinted by permission of Margaret Bemiss.

Anne Fauntleroy Mortimer Randolph (see chapter 6). Mary Randolph's 1850 commonplace book, a typical, multiply kept family "working book," contains copies of these letters, with occasional explanations in the hand (we assume) of their recipient, who may have reread her later preserved copies. Copies of a text written by an ancestor, perhaps itself copied from another source, are not uncommon. A fragmentary letter that was recopied to assure its survival is labeled only "copied from paper in Welly [Wellington] chest." This text, advice to a "New Wife," appears in a commonplace book containing both original and recopied holograph versions.[49] Often a commonplace book is catalogued only by the name of a family (e.g., "Blanton family papers"), indicating that although kept by an unidentified writer it was included in an ongoing household collection of holograph texts.

Consequently, this collection is not the product of particular individuals who wrote at specific times for one of the regularly identified purposes for composing. William Byrd's 1722–1733 commonplace book ranges from "love letters to Charmante to a random assortment of ribald anecdotes, epigrams, verse, and puns . . . even 'Some Rules for preserving health,'" which, as Richard Beale Davis says, were kept for transformation "into more enduring prose."[50] But Byrd never systematically worked these later transformations. His and others' specifically commonplace mode of "authorship" remains a puzzle if one measures it by later authorial tropes that identify a unified, single-voiced source of writing. It is tempting to remainder these books as their cataloguers have done, attributing their importance to the contexts in which they may be interpreted as "historical information," or "minor writings," like many catalogue entries under the names of William Byrd and Thomas Jefferson.

The widely differing physical characteristics of the media used by these writers reinforce this conclusion. Many examples are leather-bound, originally blank books of 100–250 pages, measuring 6 × 10 or 4 × 6 inches. Sixty-nine still contain many blank pages. Some books kept over two or more generations were turned upside down and written from back to front for fresh purposes, or by other writers. Most (240) are handwritten, many in an easily read school script. But many are almost indecipherable, and still others contain newspaper clippings or typescripts of earlier texts, with indications of their significance for the family or its donor.

The content of these books also varies so enormously that in some cases it is difficult to imagine how they fulfilled any of the educationally prescribed reasons for their keeping; they claim no organized attempt at self-education or desires to perform civic, religious, and cultural duties. The range of genres and topics addressed suggests the entire historical spectrum of motives for writing, from transcribing aids to memory in graphic record keeping, to reflecting on experience and organizing a modern version of a "self." The collection includes the following generic categories, in order of frequency: ninety-six lines of verse copied, and often composed by the writer or friends; ninety-six accounts and records of work performed; thirty-six lists of addresses, places visited, visitors, books read, household goods, and other material; twenty-seven genealogical records; twenty-seven letters; twenty-five school exercises; nineteen slave records; eighteen receipts for purchases; seventeen school compositions; seventeen prescriptions for home remedies and useful compounds like lye or soap; seventeen day-by-day diaries kept while traveling or at home; fifteen copies of documents such as affidavits, wills, and deeds; and six speeches delivered by family members. In addition, these volumes were repositories for actual and facsimile autographs, bookplates, literary quotations, epitaphs, obituary notices, and coats of arms.

The topics addressed within these genres include the local and civic interests and necessities of family life across almost every category of public and private activity, although these writers rarely discuss intimate physical matters. (Even the journal kept by Martha Ballard, a New England midwife, does not include detailed obstetric or gynecological details.)[51] Various books include commentaries, numerous judicial and legal notes, records of judgments made by lawyers, historical and travel information about specific countries, and descriptive anecdotes of the lives of relatives and important people. For instance, as befits the propertied status of the families preserving them, the collection includes accounts of the Virginia Conventions of 1776 and 1829, records of supplies for Virginia's struggling forces during the Revolution and the Civil War, and a copy of the articles of surrender signed by Cornwallis in 1781. Nine books include religious memorabilia—records of sermons delivered and attended, notes on religion, devotional passages, and Bible verses. Others preserve domestic records—recipes, lists of slave births and clothing, horses and farm implements, instructions for planting fruit trees, notes on marriage and children, and boundary lines and land transfers—along with descriptions of ships, lighthouses, navigational aids, and mining and mineral resources. Six writers include minutes or membership lists from the college, social, and recreational clubs to which they belonged. Many inserted report cards, bills, and evaluations from their attendance at school.

There are intriguing anomalies, examples of formulaic genres used to organize idiosyncratic perceptions. Timothy Chandler, for instance, had a taste for "events." From 1821 to 1823, he recorded every murder, calamity of weather, instance of public insanity, and gruesome accident he encountered.

William Howard faithfully copied the legal procedures entailed in a declaration of insanity, thereby simultaneously telling and not telling the story of his father's affliction. A book by an unidentified compiler contains a letter by John Yeats Beall written shortly before he was executed for spying during the Civil War. Anne Page Friend listed each escort in whose company she attended receptions and lectures at Hampden-Sydney College in the late 1880s; and Ida Lownes's commonplace book includes a list of gentlemen callers at her home in Petersburg—280 in all—as well as the names of 48 female schoolmates. But these and similarly peculiar records rely on conventional modes—the list, the "last letter," or carefully dated diary entry—for their credibility in a particular family's inscribed memory. These writers tacitly explain these diverse records as a "property" of graphic genres, using conventional formats, not their singular content, as permission to display it.

Examples that are clearly relevant to literary composition occasionally mark the writer as a self-identified author. George Brydon and Johan Bocock included lists of their activities as "authors"; William Palmer and George Bagby listed their writings. Hugh Blair Grigsby's numerous volumes include poetry and drawings by himself and his cousins, as well as numerous letters from Yale classmates saying goodbye after his brief sojourn as a student (see chapter 4). But allusions to specifically literary activity most often emphasize reading or compilations of broadly "literary" information. Maria DeRieux, for example, listed more than 1,100 books read between 1806 and 1823, an achievement noted in her obituary. Mary Dupuy's commonplace book outlines Kane's *Elements of Criticism*, and Mary Jane Wimbish recorded her school notes on logic, metaphysics, and philosophy. Clearly, the collection is not the product of self-conscious attempts at private *or* public authorship, nor at literary analysis. Only Jane Taylor Lomax Worthington (1821–1846) appears to have used the two commonplace books she began at age sixteen as sites for drafting short stories. In *Women of the South Distinguished in Literature* (1861), written after many of the stories had been published, Mary Forrest says Worthington is "not yet an author."[52]

Composing Commonplaces: Writing Processes

These mundane, often incomplete texts are sometimes difficult to read, literally and in a professional sense. They are often sloppily written, holographically unpredictable, illegible because of erasures, on torn or fragmentary paper, even when obviously kept as "fair copies." They are organized in heavy folders that suggest a drawer in which one tosses documents too trivial or personal to be filed, a kitchen junk drawer, or an overstuffed glove compartment. But their physical condition, and occasionally their content, help us to reconstruct the composing processes that formed them, processes that in turn often reveal their writers' immediate social purposes. Blair Bolling, for instance, self-consciously earmarks "a final poem if ever my compositions be published" in his extensive but family-oriented history of various members' encounters with "bon mots and anecdotes."[53] More frequently, however, in volumes kept by younger writers, authorial prerogatives and ownership reside only in emphatic demands for privacy. James Minor Holladay repeated such a notification at the front of his book: "The property of JMH" (signed twice), and on the next page, "The undisputed property of JMH" (again signed twice).[54] But as often, pages are torn out or parts of them are neatly excised, indicating that keepers or donors do not trust future generations to protect their privacy.

The content of these books is often copied material, "passages" that one expects in a medium first conceived as a copybook. They contain copies of entire poems and other compositions that apparently warranted preservation as the social property of the copyist. But copying, a nineteenth-century profession, was a necessary scribal function long before that time, in a premechanized society. Its endurance as a way to earn money helps to explain why both school curricula and parents paid so much attention to handwriting as a vocational and social skill. For instance, Elizabeth Virginia Lindsay Lomax (1796–1867), author of *Leaves from an Old Washington Diary, 1854–1863,* was a copyist. Widowed after the Seminole Wars of 1835–1838, she supported six children by working in Washington City. A note on her records from January 16, 1857, reads: "[I am] agreeably surprised by a note from the State Department sending me more copying to do immediately."[55] The copy work in these volumes was also deeply embedded in inherited textual and family traditions. Frances Lee Jones annotates her father's copying as a ritual moment of preservation: "Written by lamented and tenderly beloved Father Walter Jones, on a blank leaf of an old copy of Youngs night thoughts, one Sunday as we were reading in the dining room, he picked up the book lying with several others on a chaise by my side, and as was often usual with him, when he particularly admired a sentiment transcribed it on a blank leaf of the volume."[56]

Hugh Blair Grigsby, arguably the most prolific writer in Virginia of his time, memorialized not only the texts that fill his many commonplace volumes, but his motives at particular moments for recopying them:

(Sept 19, 1845)

The above bagatelle [three stanzas of a poem entitled "Kerchief"] was written in 1822 in consequence of my friend Miss McElhanay having had her face covered with a handkerchief while suffering from a sharp [?] of the toothache. She has since married Judge Fry.

Lines written in the Album of Miss S. B. of Union, Monroe, Va., Jan 5, 1833: Edgehill, Sept 19, 1843: The above lines were written at Mount Prospect in the Album of Miss Susan Beinne [H?], at the request of some of the young ladies then on a visit to Mrs. Calder, as they wished to see what I could say in the book of a lady I knew nothing about. Afterwards knew Miss Beinne. She is now married. Gen Chapman of Monroe, now in Congress, married her elder sister. Peace be with them; for I enjoyed many pleasant hours in their neighbourhood.

Amused myself this morning by copying into this book several little pieces written during my visit to Monroe in 1822; and more especially have I done so, as my wife has repeatedly begged me to do it.[57]

Grigsby's many comments also show how writing processes were a medium of social exchange in this society. They offer a glimpse of graphically supported relationships with many female friends, in circumstances that are rarely recalled more explicitly than in the following example:

Written in the Album of Mary Miller Ershene of the Salt Sulphur Springs in January, 1833: stanzas "Edgehill, Sept 29, 1845. The above lines were written in 1833 when I was pretty considerably smitten with Mary Erskine—who was then about seventeen, and as exquisitely formed as if she were the product of the chisel of Cleomenes, and not common flesh and blood of the back woods. Her complexion was as the rose. She danced with exceeding grace, and waltzed splendidly. No wonder that I, who had before that time been too busy to think of the girls, became fascinated by his charming [girl] creature. But the affair never proceeded to extremities. I soon left the county of Monroe, and for years I saw not Mary Erskine, until in '36 or '37, I received a message from her father at French's Hotel in Norfolk informing me of his presence in that town. I hastened to meet him, and, as I was ascending the stairs, who should I see but Mary, now fully developed in age and beauty, coquetting with a couple of midshipmen. I chatted with her that evening, and saw her depart for Charleston. My old feelings came over me, but nothing farther. I enclosed her an invitation to a 22nd February-ball, and wrote some nice things in the envelope. Thereby hangs a tale. I have never seen her since. God bless her![58]

These keepers of the commonplace also played with the graphic elements of language. Numerous books contain tables for "finding a lady's age," or for calculating dates, in imitation of time, tide, and weather charts found in almanacs. These writers also composed acrostics, arranging a name in a vertical column so that each letter begins a line of verse.

In sum, describing this collection itself complicates obvious questions: "Who wrote?" "When?" and "For what purposes?" These texts frequently defy classification as either generic, entirely conventional family records or as the introspective narrative accounts we are later schooled to hope for in a collection easily characterized as merely domestic, private writing.

Exemplary Templates for Experience:
"To Preserve a Clue"

Three examples exactly reproduce the discursive space of the commonplace textual work that these early Virginia inheritors transformed. These model volumes help theorize this literate practice as a habit that centered their writers in superimposed property and cultural propriety as they "labored" in selected discourse.

In the earliest example, dating from 1722 to 1729, an unidentified compiler made indexed notes of sermons "preached at London, Puttenham and Whitchurch, England, by a member of the clergy of the Church of England." These notes, recorded neatly in vaguely alphabetical order in a 7 × 9 1/2 inch book, are an index of sermon topics that the compiler delivered or that he heard and read. The list of topics, marked "incomplete" by its cataloguer, is divided by large headings with detailed outlines of possible divisions of these topics. The headings include the following:

> Of the Severity of God's Laws gains [against] EVIL-DOERS: of His
>   Patience or Forbearance to put his Laws in execution against them, &
>   of ye ill use Sinners make thereof.
> [In minuscule print] Eccles [Ecclesiastes]:
> of Evil Speaking
> The Excellency of ye Xtian Religion.
> The Nature, Cause, Degrees, Eficacy of Kinds of FAITH
> The true Notion of FAITH & its Necessity to Salvation.
> How to Keep a Truly Religious FAST
> Men not to GLORY in their Wisdom
> Of Numbering our DAYS
> The Necessity, Nature, Time, & Advantages of EDUCATION.
> The Misery of MAN'S natural State
> Messiah
> Miricales
> . . . A Conscience void of Offence toward men and God
> The Nature & Benefit of CONSIDERATION[59]

These topics, such as "Evil Speaking" and "Consideration," were transformed into many school essays on "Gossip" and "Small Talk." "The Necessity, Nature, Time, & Advantages of Education" was also treated under each of its subdivisions in many school essays. This book shows, that is, that recirculated biblical hermeneutics contributed to topics assigned for early vernacular school compositions (see chapter 2). This holograph index, possibly compiled as a source for future sermons by its keeper, is much like two others, published works that show both the persistence of commonplaces and the results of their printed transformations.

John Henry Ducachet Wingfield (1833–1898) kept his sermon notes in the prepared blank spaces in *A Theological Common-Place Book*. This volume contains both already headed and blank pages, on which Wingfield noted references to topics like "Episcopacy," "Last Judgment," "Religion," and "Councils." The notes are also marked by page numbers inserted in the index that comprises most of the book's print, placed at its end. The book's publisher prefaces it by claiming its superiority over both homemade compilations and printed sources where one might "read the passages we deem important, in a printed volume."[60] It offers, he says, a system superior to common practice:

> Its chief use is to consist in its becoming a *general index* to the passages to which a Theologian may wish to preserve a clue. It is intended not for a reservoir of mere extracts, but . . . of references. Instead of making a reference, on the blank leaves of a book, where it may be forgotten, or on loose scraps of paper, which may be misplaced or lost; with this volume at hand, one can place it, here it will be safely preserved and always tangible. . . . This volume . . . will help greatly to economize [time].

This explanation stresses "the value of time" for the student. The book's user should gradually "systematize his acquirements" and, "by turning over the pages of this Index, and pausing here and there upon the titles which cover them," will learn "the comprehensiveness of Theology." The long printed index is indeed comprehensive; according to the preface, "it might easily have been longer." It includes entries that remind us of the implications of theology in a world of "materials" whose categories were constructed when theology, together with law and medicine, were the only official goals of advanced education. A brief sample of included topics now detached from theology includes the following: "Absurd," "Alphabet," "Bribe," "Century," "Classic," "Paraphrase," "Periodicals," "Persuasion," "Poetry" ("study of" and "use of"), "Press," "Tenses," "Text," "Theory," "Trope," and "Variety."[61]

A third example, Rev. John Todd's *Index Rerum: or Index of Subjects; Intended as a Manual to Aid the Student and the Professional Man, in Preparing Himself for Usefulness* (1835), generalizes this theological tradition to all knowledge.[62] Its spirit displaces the "tangible" benefits of Wingfield's book onto a more vivid equation drawn between secular knowledge and the economy of memory. Todd's book appears to be, as he says, a transparently simple bound filing system. The "Directions for Using this Index" describe its uses as follows:

> [It is] ruled with blue ink, with a wide margin on the left hand of each page . . . to contain the word selected as a guide to the subject noted down. Ten pages are allotted for each letter of the alphabet, printed on the corners of the pages. In the centers of the pages are printed the vowels a, e, i, o, u, with two pages allotted for each vowel. When you read any thing which you may hereafter need, place the principal word in the margin, under the first letter in that word, and the first vowel in it. . . . Suppose I wish to note something relating to America. I turn to A. and the vowel e. because A. is the first letter, and e. is the first vowel. (6)

In this complicated way, Todd's *Index Rerum* localizes and individualizes the commonplace book tradition that is briefly reviewed in its introduction. Todd asserts that his project grew out of "the author's own wants" and that conversations "with gentlemen of different professions" have revealed "an earnest wish that *it may become the property of every student*" (1, emphasis added). Echoing the compiler of Wingfield's blank book, Todd comments on what is clearly *the* competitive "printed volume," noting that "the Commonplace Book of Locke is the only one that has come into much notice; and if that has, it is not owning to any intrinsic merit which it possesses, but to its bearing his own great name, and professing to be the result of his experience. But neither that nor any other [will be used or] be of any essential advantage to the student, and the man of literary habits" (1). Nonetheless, Todd continues, keeping one's own collections requires too much time, labor, and patience. "Every thing that is saved must be copied out in full, and then noted also in the Index. . . . Books are so common, and so constantly multiplying, that few have the courage to . . . make extracts, and to copy what is really valuable. I have seen multitudes of such books commenced, but have seen but very few which were not abandoned at an early hour" (1–2).

Todd also exhibits the historical instruction in formal rhetoric that promoted the tradition emphasized by Walter Ong, with whom he vividly describes memory as a material process that occupies physical space:

> Every one is aware that we frequently want [need] the thoughts, or the materials of thought . . . in books . . . we have read, but which, though now sought after in every corner of the memory, are not to be found. Their faint impressions are seen . . . but too distant and too undefined. . . . Nor can we recollect the books in which we met them. . . . Few are aware . . . how much of all our valuable reading is lost. (2)

Todd follows Plato in assuming that mature men are the best rhetorical performers. But he casts this tradition in educational doctrines that postponed
rhetorical instruction to a man's thirties, in an extended conceit that equates
memory with thrifty banking—in the interest, we can assume, of encouraging readers to spend the price of his book:

> Let a young man when he begins life, be in the habit of making an Index to all
> that he reads which is truly valuable, (and he ought to read nothing else,) and at
> the age of thirty-five or forty, he has something of his own, and which no price
> could purchase. Many would think hundreds of dollars well spent, could they
> purchase what they have thrown away; and what each one might most easily save
> for himself; and to aid in saving which, this Book is prepared. (4)

Lest we miss his economic tenor, Todd quotes another scholar, William
Wirt, who significantly equates material "saving" with the collection of
knowledge:

> Old-fashioned economists will tell you never to pass an old nail, or an old horse-
> shoe, or buckle, or even a pin, without taking it up; . . . you may not want it now,
> [but] you will find a use for it some time or other. I say the same . . . with regard
> to knowledge. . . . There is not a fact . . . nor even a fugitive anecdote that you
> read in a newspaper, or hear in conversation, that will not come in play, some
> time or other. (4)

Todd stresses that "this is certainly a *valuable* thought, and a *valuable* opinion
of a great man." He could appropriate it for this introduction, he says, because he has kept an index like the one he is promoting. Even those whose
"youth is past" will benefit: "Knowledge, like the seed of the fruit-tree which
you put into the ground today, will yield its fruits soon; and . . . memory, as
life advances, becomes more treacherous, and needs something to assist it" (5).

Finally, this introduction notes Todd's peculiar "authorial" status as the
purveyor of blank pages, reminding us of the mobility these texts require us
to impose on their writing:

> The idea of publishing blank sheets is not very cheering to the fame of author-
> ship; but mortified pride may have this consoling reflection, that many who fill
> out their sheets, had better have left them blank; and that each one can fill out
> this book more to his own satisfaction and benefit, than the most gifted mind
> could do for him. (6)

This self-defensive apology, itself replete with commonplaces, highlights the
dual status of these texts as windows on the supposed dichotomy between
"lived" and "textual" worlds. The sometimes questionable, better-if-left-
blank, "fame of authorship" that Todd cannot claim is dispersed here to

"each one" of his purchasers. They will accumulate discursive wealth, while saving time. Yet each one so propertied, as Todd is, will be simultaneously relaying and spending the authorially famous resources of others.

Todd had one success at least among the commonplace book keepers in this collection, Hugh White Sheffer, who kept his commonplace collection in another copy of the *Index Rerum*.[63] On its pages, under the appropriate alphabetical categories, Sheffer summarized and cited quotations, as the prefatory material recommends. His page "C o," for instance, lists quotations that use the following words: "Crown (English), Consanguinity, Common Law, Courts, Common-places: (recommended to lawyer Note to Black, V. 1. ? 22), Counties, Comedy, Conscience, Commerce." Page "G o " includes citations on "Government" and from "Goldsmith," while page "W e " notes "Wales." Yet the book also indicates its use in more than only collective ways. On the blank pages at the end, Sheffer summarizes the content of two novels: "Marriage," ("by the author of Inheritance") and "Newton Foster. A novel by Capt. Manyalt." Sheffer somewhat ambiguously notes under his signature, "purchased June 18, 1836, N. B. all this is in it will not of course be of what I have read since the above date; but if I collect any thing and can refer to it I shall here note it down." Again, textual memory escapes the boundaries it needs to remain stable, suggesting excess and a tension between what can and cannot be saved.

Sheffer's demur recalls the larger implications of ordinary authorship, for his scrupulous qualification of the match between his actual experience and this record indicates how the diverse members of this collection might be encountered productively. They are, that is, simultaneously subtexts—"material" that becomes other writing, other thinking, and other speaking—and texts themselves, organized copies and paraphrases of written "sources." As subtexts, their items in "place" signify memorable language, although not always language from published or literary discourse. Their passages capture common linguistic structures that are *ordinary* both in the sense of being held in common and often reiterated. As subtextual "items," they fix limits on what a dominant Western text may *do* with a subject. They establish the precisely common topics of rhetorical invention—comparison, contrast, classification, degree, narratives of processes, et cetera. They sustain the introjected, domineering, and necessary source of authority and anchor of intelligibility across Western texts.

But as "text itself," commonplace collections like these and the many more free-handed items in this collection affirm the situational appropriateness of formulaic discursive doings. On the authority of subtexts, they write both individual histories and cultural memories as fluid and mobile sites of recognition and recognizance. They transform to printed volumes of blank yet already coded pages many collections of "items" that forecast individualism in their decidedly personal ownership of intertextuality. Like any collation of memorable language, they are always poised for projection into arrangements that will assert a keeper's *personal* participation, to become another story, a constructed reality of "original" contributions from self-sponsored acquisitions. Again, the uncertain perception of Ben Jonson's collection in *Timber*—was it "original" or a copied "list"?—restates this ambivalent relation between textuality and ownership. The "oversight" of Jonson's modern editor, that is, is also canny perspicacity about the fulcrum on which any commonplace discourse is poised. By gathering textual, material "wealth" into a private collection, Jonson took the property of others to become himself actually rich in invention, as his dramas and poetry demonstrate. Consequently, his and other well-stocked collections of language are not museums where artifacts made by others are respectfully viewed with an access granted by codified "tradition." They are also originary sources of disposable wealth, entitlements to authorial spending.

In all of these senses, commonplace books portray a scene of writing made intelligible by the many uses of the word *material*. These books are now actual property. Like family china, silver, and land, they have been transferred into the hands of survivors. But they are equally a surplus, private property that ironically purchases a revised public history of writing. They allow us to reimagine the certified discourse of more prominent textual categories, for they are both precedents to those ways of thinking and speaking and the results of still other precedents.

Focusing on the materiality of these texts allows us, that is, to disintegrate binary oppositions between public and private language in favor of attending to the cultural functions of textual production. As simultaneously important and inconsequential material goods, these ambivalent, mobile texts reevaluate categorical as well as selective, "tasteful," evaluations of texts. These leftover items in family inheritances are "papers" that have little market value, yet are substantial American cultural capital. Thus they are both a substance and an "excess," what Georges Bataille differently describes as an "excess energy (wealth) [that] can be used for the growth of a system."[64] These books have absorbed the memories of the "system" that now embeds textuality in professional study, that insists on the constructed "importance" of any object of interpretation. Especially as sites of educational, gendered, and authorial identities, they once increased the literate property of their producers. But now, outside their circumscribed places of origin, in a later sociotextual context that calls origins and inheritance into question, they uncover the cultural energies of writers for whom the act of making a text was a productive luxury, a claim on and a witness to mental, emotional, and social prosperity. In the changing circumstances of early America and the successive upheavals that these books portray, they also remind us of Bataille's caveat that "if [a] system can no longer grow, or if the excess cannot be completely absorbed in its growth, it must necessarily be lost without profit; it must be spent, willingly or not, gloriously or catastrophically."[65] Consequently, while they are themselves discursive and material "excess," the analysis of these texts also enacts a particular Derridian "supplement." They picture the active, mobile creation by writing of the social, enlarging its accepted history by recalling the making of texts as an act that often overshadows the "content" they record. Their liminal relations to intertextuality explain a great deal about institutionalized social, educational, and gendered discourses that came later, in very different configurations of the "common."

· 2 ·

The Schooled Commonplace
Writing Along New Lines

Somewhere every culture has an imaginary zone for what it excludes, and it is that zone we must try to remember *today.* The same goes for women as for madmen: in a *manifest* position of exclusion, they keep the system together, *latently,* by virtue of their very exclusion.

CATHERINE CLEMENT, *The Lives and Legends of Jacques Lacan*

Most standard histories of education obscure the cultural agendas of writing instruction, just as they exclude the extent and nature of supposedly irregular settings for schooling. But as Catherine Clement suggests, it is time to notice how education in indigenous texts becomes a site that maintains "the system." At the least, focusing on examples of instruction in writing reveals material and social exchanges on which both recognized and seemingly random cultural identities depend. As chapter 1 suggests, the specific contents of the volumes in this collection, and the composing processes that produced them, circulate a magnificent self-pedagogy that is unimagined in histories of education that compare and contrast their topics to the supposed norms of state public education. These records, however, display vestiges of socially and politically active identities that a later, more passive common opinion of schooling would obliterate, largely by declaring writing to be always problematic.

To understand the historical cultural work of these texts, we must set aside typical divisions between high and low literate culture and the evaluative categories that characterize current ideas of normal American bourgeois education. Insofar as many of these books preserve children's first writing exercises and encode educational *doxa* for their descendants, they suggest that many forms of discourse were both identified and confidently owned as locally powerful actions through language. This self-educational writing predates the rigid separation of authors from a student mass, a division that portrays high literacy as a privileged but largely unattainable goal from the late nineteenth century on. It thereby also uncovers differences *within* the most prevalent explanations of why writing is taught.

This chapter looks at how a selected group of Virginia families memorialized formal, but not always institutional, lessons in composition. It first examines the blend of public and private schooling in the republic as a civic system. It then turns to emerging doctrines about writing to uncover the context for early indigenous education, a context visible in examples of lessons that exhibit emerging social purposes for writing. Texts both about writing lessons and within them show the inaccuracy of denigrating the varieties of schooling available in this setting. They expose the social energy of purposes for writing instruction before common schooling and university classes made it a way to nationalize students in state-sponsored imitations of families. Most striking is the extrainstitutional confidence revealed in these early examples of student texts and student polemics about writing. The assurance of these youngsters about their ability to write and their social superiority to the educational institutions their class established for them challenges the idea that literacy education of a century or two ago was narrowly limited. This writing about writing helps lift a veil obscuring the uneven but significant results of early teaching.

Statements in these commonplace books asserting the need for advanced lessons in writing present those lessons as providing needed access to local, privately realized versions of universal, enduring public fame, a traditional objective of formal rhetorical training. Well before the wide distribution of advanced writing lessons such as "Harvard Composition" after 1870, writing was a school subject that aimed to produce autonomous texts, not practice for oratory. Student compositions themselves recirculate the value of fame, but as an agent in local circumstances, not a universal reputation. They show a new emphasis on local purposes for learning to write as a means of social and material advancement. Lessons in writing, that is, embody the Lockean labor of discursive acquisitiveness. But these lessons do not demonstrate later, institutional judgments made by the state acting as *the* school, nor do student compositions reveal the individual "consciousness" whose construction accomplished the regulatory function of that evaluative structure. Consequently, these texts about learning to write for specific reasons are on a historical cusp. Emerging systems of education would find ways to center *English* and imagine the mass of students as discursively disenfranchised, as a people whose language is inadequate for public influence. The very self-possession of these texts reveals the difference made by later, much more sharply divided constructions of the *student* and the *teacher* of discursive practices.

A Local Education

A prevalent assumption in most branches of textual studies is that learning to write, like learning interpretative reading, depends on organized formal instruction. This assumption is basic to the sort of elementary school instruction that produces statistics measuring popular literacy and to the pointedly "higher" learning imagined necessary to produce culturally intelligible texts. The politics of an educational apparatus that distinguishes between high and low mass literacy is described by Lawrence Levine in *Highbrow/Lowbrow*,[1] by Ian Hunter in *Culture and Government*,[2] and by many analysts of the emerging nineteenth-century bourgeois empires. Mass schooling in literacy became, and largely remains, what Hunter calls "a special *social technology*," a Foucauldian force gathered from the cooperation among unevenly positioned governments, disparate colonial administrations, and various pressures on prior forms of schooling.[3] The European West established this force nationally as an instrument of middle-class entitlement.

The precise nature of that entitlement to be an observed collective identity is exemplified in the linkage between people and institutions observed by Robert Owen, the British educational reformer. In 1813 Owen explicitly connected the subjection of "character" to "governing powers": "The governing powers of all countries should establish rational plans for the *education and general formation of the characters of their subjects*—These plans must be devised to train children from their earliest infancy in good habits . . . which will of course prevent them from acquiring those of falsehood and deception."[4] As Hunter says, this "new kind of educational apparatus [was] capable of combining a concern for 'self-expression'"—what Owen called "character"—with new techniques of discipline and observation operative at the level of the population."[5] It took the form of centralized studies in "English":

> The aesthetic as a practice of the self permitted the teacher to occupy the position of ethical regard built into the architecture of the classroom and into the teacher-student couple. The full flowering of these developments occurs of course in the discipline of "English" or popular literary education. In the teaching of English the techniques for relating to the self as the subject of aesthetic experience are integrated with the techniques of supervision and emulation forming the relation of teacher to student. The new school provided the space in which the virtuoso techniques of self-problematization and self-modification would be administered as pedagogical techniques . . . through which the children of the popular classes would come to problematize and modify the conduct of their own lives.[6]

This combination of organized "concern" and a "new technique" that makes aesthetic textual analysis equal to "self-problematization and self-modification" was a chief constituent of the formative chauvinism of English studies in nineteenth-century Britain, its colonies, and industrial America. This blend of care and method still characterizes European education, as Jacques Rancière says of French philosophy. Rancière critiques sociology and social histories that problematize pedagogy for the ignorant "worker." Contemporary bourgeois observers and intellectuals, like their earlier counterparts, "know, and thus 'speak for,' or explicate, the privileged other of political modernity."[7]

But these nationalist common wisdoms were the artifacts of a politics that established a specifically European mass education. They differ from the expedients that underlay its diverse American precedents in towns, parishes, and colonies. Those who read and wrote after the states' Revolution, yet before the Civil War, made schooling a national rather than local project, had a different stake in vernacular literacy. Their discourse on writing joined traditional letters with the personal goals and local traditions well before nineteenth-century institutions, corporations, and wide book distribution could unify middle-class cultures. Consequently, these texts comment on the emerging nationalist categories that would bifurcate public from private discourse, the boundaries that Ian Hunter highlights to explain a shift in discursive regulation. Hunter names this prior system "erstwhile caste practices of aesthetic self-culture, or criticism." Using his parlance, the caste practices that produced these texts were only later reorganized as a discipline, an "apparatus aimed at the cultural transformation of whole populations."[8] To read this instructional difference accurately, we need a better understanding of local, preinstitutional schooling, especially of how it treated the slippery phenomenon of *writing*, before a public definition of education was launched, contested, and only partially accepted.

Propertied Virginians were always a decidedly literate community. They valued both reading and the activities that resulted in making texts, if not always education and guided practice in vernacular composition. They were also literate in the earliest and continuing sense of "acquainted with letters." They heard, recognized, recited, and discussed texts regarded as marks of culture and status, even when they were not fluent readers.[9] As female, lower-class, or African-American members of local communities, they might be thoroughly familiar with legal and political texts and current news that they had not themselves read and could not imagine writing. But as the colonial group transmitting responsibility for a new American commonwealth, they were highly self-conscious about their educational status, as about the links between access to learning and the sociopolitical survival of the new republic.

These Virginians, like their peers in other colonies, only partially deserved their reputation for denying a "good" education—usually equated with classical study—to all but a few privileged males, or for favoring the illiteracy of females and African Americans. In the early years of the republic, Virginians did pursue policies that caused Jefferson's frustration with the lackadaisical pace attending the creation of the University of Virginia. (The university opened in 1825, tainted, in Jefferson's view, by religious leanings.) But propertied voters, before their negative reputation became a national trope after the Civil War, thought of themselves as particularly scrupulous about the education of their children and, until the tight-fisted nineteenth century, about the education of the less fortunate, especially Native Americans and paupers.

Upper-class colonists regularly dispatched children of both sexes to England for training through the mid-eighteenth century, after which time, thrift, republican pride, and fear that young people would sink into dissipation curtailed interest in education abroad. In 1685 Ursula Byrd voyaged without her parents at the age of four; advertisements in Virginia newspapers encouraged such voyages as late as 1769.[10] The Lee, Byrd, and Custis families all sent sons to England, in keeping with Governor Berkeley's perception of the "course of study" in the colony: "[It is] the same course that is taken in England out of town, every man according to his ability instructing his children."[11] When in 1671 Berkeley "thanked God that there were no free schools in Virginia," he meant precisely that, adding that such schools undid proper class distinctions, presumably by providing access to social advancement across class boundaries. By the word *free*, however, the governor meant Latin grammar schools that provided instruction in classical languages. He was not criticizing the legislature's mandated, tuition-free schools for apprentices, orphans, and indentured children of both sexes that had been established in various early Virginia settlements.[12] Increasingly, such intra-"national" colonial traditions developed into various indigenous sites for education: plantation schoolrooms overseen by tutors; town and country boarding schools (academies, seminaries, preparatory schools) that were advertised as safe refuges from the urban temptations of London or Williamsburg; locally supported "free schools" or "oldfield schools" undertaken by the formerly indentured; and a legal system of apprenticeship to families who were legally required to provide basic education.[13]

Like Massachusetts, Virginia in 1642 passed a law requiring county officials to "take up" children whose parents were "disabled to maintaine and educate them."[14] This maintenance, which applied to privileged children as to those apprenticed in trades to masters, often took the form of hiring a tutor, the obvious way to move the expensive mountain of an English education to the more accessible hills near widely separated river villages and plantation homes.[15] John Ascough recorded in the Middlesex County *Deed Book, 1679–1694* that his stepson was to be apprenticed to Christopher Robinson for eight years, stipulating that Robinson should "instruct said apprentice in all business as concerns his said office of the court."[16] In 1705, the master of an orphaned apprentice was required to teach him to read and write "the necessary basis for religious instruction."[17]

Propertied families were, in these ways, legally and morally responsible for the education of their own children and children of the colony's (and later the commonwealth's) poor. The state did not establish the universal free education that Jefferson proposed in 1779. But in 1811, twenty-five years before Massachusetts passed Horace Mann's high school law, Virginia instituted an alternative, the remarkably titled Literary Fund. What had been voluntary (if unpredictable) endowments in wills and donations for free, pauper, and orphan schools were transformed by the Assembly's fund law into collections from "all escheats, fines, confiscations, penalties and forfeitures,"[18] and later also from a lottery. This money was administered by state and local school commissioners until 1870. After 1818, county courts appointed school commissioners to "direct the education of indigent children."[19] By 1819, the Middlesex County commissioners could report that of the sixty-one poor white children who "ought to be educated," forty-five were "actually sent to school" in seven separate schools whose aggregate expenditures were $356. The commissioners noted, "There is indeed among the number one or two geniuses of the first rate and more unusually bad— Owing to the great distance some had to go to school, the actual worth of the labor of others by their parent has prevented as regular attendance at school by some as we could have wished."[20]

As in Massachusetts, where the 1837 high school law was first enforced in 1869, statewide (and therefore state) public schools were not provided in Virginia until 1870, after the Civil War. But extensive nonpublic education was well established in Virginia, as elsewhere in America, from the eighteenth century on, in academies, seminaries, and their offshoots, manual labor schools and military schools. Dale G. Robinson identifies two categories: "local, modest, transient and often short lived" schools that extended private home tutoring to a more public constituency, and "those of wide patronage" with "creditable equipment, and . . . substantially endowed."[21] The first transient sort, as Robinson notes, left few records that are found only in casual notes and accounts, but they probably numbered in the hundreds.

Middlesex County records begun in 1879 describe at least seven private schools in the county, established on the important model of how families should provide for their children. These included a school conducted by Mrs. S. S. Mountain for "the negroes in her community." "On Sunday afternoons negroes of all ages met in a vacant building near her home where Dr. Mason Evans, Mr. R. D. Hilliard, Mrs. Mountain and Mrs. Healy, then a very small girl, taught the negroes reading, spelling, singing and religion. . . . Later, Mrs. Mountain taught the negroes in the little field school at Royal Oakes."[22]

The second category, the better-documented academies that are strategically overlooked in later histories of education, were attended by many who kept these commonplace books. Academies were both male and female institutions, although they offered widely dissimilar curricula to women. Suzanne Lebstock emphasizes that the eighteenth-century illiteracy rate of 50 percent among free women reinforced the poverty often imposed on women by patriarchy.[23] Many, like Martha Washington in her advice to a widowed niece, recognized the importance of women's sometimes legal right to a separate estate, but women were nonetheless denied full control of their destiny by inadequate education. Supported by appeals to provide educated mothers for "free men" who could sustain a new republic, cognizant women began to establish academies not only for themselves, but for the daughters of the poor. Such schools were opened in Fredericksburg in 1803, Norfolk in 1804, Richmond in 1805, Petersburg in 1811, and Alexandria in 1812.

There were, of course, differences between the various curricula for females and the traditional male curriculum, which included classical study. Few schools for women included foreign languages other than socially useful French. But education itself was not imagined as a male prerogative, for practical reasons. In 1819, Maria Campbell of Abingdon wrote, "Education is considered equally [a daughter's] due."[24] Aware that education was as important to women as to men in maintaining class status and thus enhancing their marriageability, a father wrote, "A girl will be more respected with an education than with wealth."[25] In 1822, men debated the question—and thereby made it possible to respond in the negative—"Is the mind of man naturally superior to that of women?"[26]

In 1880, John R. Purdie wrote a "History of Education in Isle of Wight County from Colonial Times," a local memoir that validates these anecdotes and the views of many others that temper popular assumptions about the historical inadequacy of female education. But Purdie perceived a decline after revolutionary times. He notes the limitations addressed by a girls' school opened between 1825 and 1830 by "a Mrs. Julia Hayden, a highly educated lady of Connecticut" at the invitation "of the late Honorable A. Atkinson":

> When Mrs. Hayden's school was established, the education of females in this county comprised generally Reading, Writing and Arithmetic to the Rule of three and a little Grammar. Many were not taught to read the Bible or write their names. A few men of wealth and good social position deemed it a duty to have their daughters instructed in the branches that are now considered essential accomplishments. . . . Good female schools in country and small towns were rare.[27]

Purdie also complains about the abundant female academies established after the Civil War, where all the students do is read novelettes and dress up. Times have declined, he says. "I ask with trembling suspense," he writes, "can we expect them to become the mothers of such men as filled the Confederate ranks in our late civil revolt?"[28] He thereby recirculates early republican commonplaces that privilege motherhood, "almost . . . a fourth branch of Government" in the early republic, writes Linda Kerber in *Women of the Republic*.[29] But Purdie deploys this trope to address a local and—considering the destructive effects of the war—more pressing political worry.

This continuing logic of revolutionary motherhood, based on appeals like many documented by Lebstock, also reminds Purdie of his own better education. His distinction between his home and "book" learning underscores how treacherous it is to attempt to interpret descriptions of early, pre–common school curricula by more recent codes of pedagogical value. He writes:

> When I entered school I could answer every question in Ruddeman's Rudiments of Latin Grammar, acquired entirely from oral instruction *having never seen the book until syntax was reached*. I will also declare in my whole school life, I never recited a lesson in English Grammar; *the principles of grammar I possess, if any, were derived from the Latin, Greek and French and from association with those who spoke the English correctly*.[30]

Clearly, Purdie learned advanced skills at home, without being formally taught writing or reading, at a pace and to a standard entirely independent of the curricular levels in the later social technology described by Ian Hunter.

The educational responsibilities that constituted adult interactions with the young were, given this anecdotal but common evidence, carried out in competing forms that, over time, collided with and shaped each other. The mixture of private and public, elite and inclusive, and male and female, educational opportunities for various classes was not a homogenous system devised to unify diverse groups or equalize gender relations. Until the late nineteenth century, education in Virginia and elsewhere did not aspire to equality-as-unification in an ideologically "public" form. Nor did these earlier sites operate systematically in a uniform sequence of lessons and levels.

Nonetheless, educational practices in separated social and school classes informed habits in other settings. Edmund Morgan's sentimentalized social history, *Virginians at Home,* notes that apprenticeship was not an exclusively trade-oriented nor a lower-class custom.[31] In New England and in other colonies, it was not unusual to send orphans and other children to live in the homes of other families for vocational education, discipline, and rearing. Wealthy English families also sent their children to live with sometimes un-related families as servants or as moral charges—for no discernible economic or specialized educational reasons.

Clearly, the "family" constructed by such diverse customs was not neces-sarily a biological unit, nor a privatized social nucleus. Its economics and ide-ology did not necessarily include "natural" filial attachment or a divison be-tween separate gender spheres, nor validate its relation to its children against the monitorial social practices of now normal educational systems. But to the degree that its economic situation allowed, this family, while not entirely in the public realm, was responsible for its children's education.

This structure of neither entirely privatized nor state responsibility for ed-ucation helps explain what is often seen as opposition to common schools by powerful Virginians, an attitude readily understood as support for traditional family prerogatives in the face of nineteenth-century economic shifts. Karl F. Kaestle, in his study of common schools from 1780 to 1860, stresses that op-ponents of emerging common school agendas acted on principle.[32] Antago-nists connected their situation to the same imaginary realms of localism—a distinct colonial and familial identity and religious independence—that emerged in their class's support for a new meaning of "writing." As Kaestle says, "The very devotion to liberty that schooling was designed to protect also made local citizens skeptical of new forms of taxation . . . and of new in-stitutional regulation; . . . it was not clear to the members of . . . legislatures that the republic would collapse without new systems of common schooling, or that *the existing mode of local and parental initiative was insufficient.*"[33]

In this context of parental initiative, Thomas Jefferson defended to Nathaniel Burwell his plan for public schooling without expressing the spe-cific form of gender prejudice that would later influence ideas about educa-tion. He wrote, "A plan of female education has never been a subject of *sys-tematic* contemplation with me. It has occupied my attention so far only as to the education of *my own* daughter occasionally required."[34] Jefferson need not be interpreted as desiring to exclude daughters from *any* education, a view embraced by many of his peers. He makes a precise distinction in his plea for *public* responsibility for schooling, promoting public, state-spon-sored education for boys, while assuming that fathers would educate their

daughters. He was only partially joking in a letter to François de Barbe Marbois, December 5, 1783, as he outlined his motives for a reading plan for his
daughter Martha:

> The plan of reading which I have formed for her is considerably different from
> what I think would be most proper for her sex in any other country than Amer
> ica. I am obliged in it to extend my views beyond herself, and consider her as
> possibly at the head of a little family of her own. The chance that in marriage she
> will draw a blockhead I calculate at about fourteen to one.[35]

Harold Hellenbrand summarizes this distinction in Jefferson's thought between the prospects for boys and for girls:

> Jefferson's laws concerning inheritance and education evolved out of his under
> standing of a good parent's and a good mentor's primary obligation: to provide
> all his wards "with a true and solid happiness" so that they could merit and sus
> tain reasonable independence.[36]

Kaestle's revisionist history of prenational schooling also questions much
traditionally accepted data about the advantages of public schooling. He
notes that tutors, select boarding schools, and an "array of independent pay
schools and academies" served children across class lines and produced both
men and women who were extensively acquainted with many categories of
literacy.[37] In 1825, for instance, the Greenbriar County, Virginia, commissioners reported that "by the aid of a few indigent children to make a sufficient number," schools had been established across the county. In 1848, the
eight poor children attending "Mr. Hardy's school" in District 5 were described by visiting commissioner Richard Jeffries: "[They are] employed in
spelling, reading, writing, cyphering, and . . . [in one case] the study of English grammar. Several are intellectual in appearance, and all I think were
learning tolerably fast. Mr. Hardy had 38 scholars, and . . . must I think have
had his hands rather full."[38] In addition, laws against teaching African Americans to read were not enacted in Virginia until 1831, almost two centuries after the arrival of the first slaves, and then were unevenly enforced or flouted.
Robert E. Lee's daughter, Agnes Lee (1841–1873), often mentions home
lessons for slaves in her journal, a book kept to improve her "style & handwriting."[39] Like other families represented in this collection, the Lees did not
assume that a centralized regulatory system should control literacy. They
took the liberty of providing it to children in home schooling and in other
forms of quasi-private schooling, as they did for their own continuing self-
education. After the war, Agnes wrote to her sister Mildred about the Reading Club of Lexington, Virginia, joking that attending its meetings was an
excuse for meeting young men.[40]

But attempting to match the equally verifiable facts of class-limited educational opportunities, sexism, and racism in early Virginia and elsewhere only encourages us to support one side of the binary that divides high from low writers and texts, the components of good and marginal education. As Lynne Templeton Brickley shows in her survey of secondary education for women in the United States, 1790–1830, the necessity of presenting a triumphant political "story of democratic public high schools" requires both traditional and revisionist historians to ignore the blended private-public realm that constituted education for children of both sexes in diverse family-sponsored settings.[41] The extent of this educational system is largely ignored in the interest of focusing on its successors, a focus that encourages scholars to report only low literacy rates and evidence of the exclusion from these settings of lower-class, slave, Native-American, and female populations.

Similarly, many feminist historians and advocates of literacy studies mistakenly reflect the same views exhibited by late nineteenth-century critics of any educational process that was not public or national. Like Emma Willard, Catharine Beecher, and Mary Lyon, who wanted to establish their own new mode of schooling in bourgeois values by denigrating the academies, current promoters of gender equality inadvertently dismiss as inferior any instructional project that denies the patriarchy that is privileged in supposedly standard curricula—thereby validating the centralized, masculinist ideals underlying systematic, "universal" education. As Brickley says, "Criticisms . . . of the earlier female educational institutions . . . represent a major theoretical problem for historians of women's education. Their criticisms reveal a *hunger for the formal institutions and tangible credentials that the colleges of the period were offering men.*"[42] Gerda Lerner notes in her comprehensive history of women that "when education began to be institutionalized, the exclusion of girls from higher education was an actual deprivation." That is, regulation of education reduced females' access to formerly available home and local schooling, systems of education that came to imply lower status.[43] Judgments that favor progressivism and "reform" movements in nationalizing late nineteenth-century educational agendas distort the writing and obscure the discursive positions of writers whose texts do not conform to what now pass for politically neutral educational conventions. These writers articulated antecedent, differently informed, not publicly schooled statements about educational culture. They circulated *doxa* that privileged education before it became a state-sponsored totality.

Bernard Bailyn's description of early academies sets an acutely historicized agenda for understanding this difference. He describes how literacy and the subject positions available within its widely various practices were circulated in relatively anarchic forms of schooling. What we now may think of as "original" student writing preserved in these commonplace books represents the "erstwhile caste practices" of education—what Bailyn describes as "a powerful movement in which large numbers of people, organizing locally, built for themselves, without prescriptive traditions, plans or principles of education, institutions to serve vague, unformed cultural needs."[44] The exact nature of this familial and local community power appears in multiple commonplace modes of discursive ownership.

New Directions for "Writing"

We now have careful historical and theoretical critiques of a supposed de facto cultural empowerment through unified *literacy*. That always value-laden term has been dismantled by Harvey Graff in *The Literacy Myth*, Brian Street in *Literacy in Theory and Practice*, Cole and Scribner in *Culture and Thought*, and by studies of local literate practices like Niko Besnier's *Literacy, Emotion, and Authority*.[45] But older progressive histories of education, seemingly developmental lists of curricula in school advertisements, and evaluatively interpreted statistics about signing documents nonetheless continue to inaccurately present early writing lessons as though they occurred, or should have occurred, in a monitorial cultural system. These sources portray successful, or failed, access to "authorship" determined by a professionalized vision of democratic civilization. Nonetheless, well before the hegemony of organized institutional discourses that imagine literacy as access to a privileged conformity, many texts about writing document its earlier local role in education of a different sort.

One such text, a casually kept self-instructional note entitled "Directions for Writing," helps us begin to defamiliarize *writing* and thereby to accept that writing took significant new directions in the society of these keepers of commonplaces.[46] Sometime between 1839 and 1843, at about age twenty-seven, Dr. Sextus Barbour of Orange County wrote himself the following reminder. (It fills the page to its edges, as many of these manuscripts do, evidently to save paper.)

DIRECTIONS FOR WRITING

In notes in the third person, the address, and date, are to be placed, on the right side just below the last line. Both letters, and notes, are to be addressed, to the persons for whom they are intended, on the left side, of the lower part of the paper. The place of abode of the person to whom sent, to be first. This is the case when they are in the third person. The letter, or note should never be carried so, near the bottom, as not to have room for the usual conclusion, and signature or to crunch it. Postscripts should if possible be avoided, and, on no account should civilities be postponed to this part. All letters should be enveloped but such as are sent by the post. Nothing should be written when [?] the inside of [reverse side of paper] the envelope; nor must any address, be put on the enclosed letter. A half sheet to be used for the envelope.

If we imagine Barbour at any age carefully noting these details, available in many manuals on graphic etiquette, his preservation of these directions says a great deal about the *writing* announced in his careful title. The word remains intransitive and opaque despite the very specificity of its definition, on a sheet that includes other practical information he thought worth preserving—planting information and a recipe for making plaster of Paris, both useful to Barbour as a professional and planter. This note on writing is, however, a clearly codified, situationally specific, social action. It prescribes skill in a quite complicated procedure. We learn, for instance, that "civilities" in "notes in the third person" should not be postponed for postscripts—which should be avoided, probably because a writer cannot be sure of having enough space for afterthoughts on the single sheet of paper that was expensive enough to have delivered.

Barbour's note suggests, that is, an absolute identity between graphic form and the purpose of writing, a specific material connection seldom attributed to discourse production today. His abstract summarizes how to place addresses and signatures to produce the document itself, including the half-sheet envelope necessary to convey it. In these copied directions, the form and delivery of documents is at stake, not traditional manuals' concerns with appropriate sentiments, fitting occasions for writing them, or an abstract normative correctness. The writing of notes, which involves knowing how to discriminate between those delivered by the relatively new postal service and by private arrangements, was for Barbour an unfamiliar matter of crucial, precisely meant "documentation" and precautions against its mishandling.

Academic curricula for the daughters and sons of upper-class Virginians, as elsewhere, included traditional collegiate subjects—mathematics, astronomy, geography, natural history, the history of nations, and very practical chemistry. But many academies also offered courses described in advertisements and student report cards as "orthography, reading, writing, grammar, composition, *[and]* belles lettres."[47] This scrupulous discrimination among the various subjects associated with literacy reveals equally unfamiliar forms of writing instruction, which ironically are hidden by modern uses of this same language. But earlier connotations of these terms show that writing lessons realized and promoted habits, like Barbour's, of creating and preserving property.

These itemized lists, that is, name discrete, separately taught and separately evaluated lessons; composition was assumed to follow instruction in other skills, like the spelling always associated with reading and forming letters well to make legible copies. Current understandings of the words *writing* and *composition* are only vaguely tied to any of the listed items, which collectively indicate a subtly different place for texts and their making in local educational practices. In that setting, language around the subject that we now label *composition* was irrelevant to ideological biases that tacitly promise that lessons in literacy are always teleological, aiming toward "independent" reading of sanctioned texts and "original" writing that will never (in their subtextual assumptions) occur.

For example, quantified accounts of literacy in early America identify those who could or could not write according to class, gender, and race at particular times. But measurements made of acts combined as "writing," as Harvey Graff demonstrates, fail to discriminate among many discrete and still vividly separated graphic acts. Writing, that is, might be *signing,* the supposedly essential knowledge of how to write one's own name that, despite his Harvard education, one early Virginian gave over in favor of making his mark on a public document.[48] But writing might also apply to specific knowledge of various text acts: how to draw up wills, deeds, and affidavits, and how to follow set forms of correspondence for important social, legal, and business purposes. Writing might also mean, differently, good handwriting or the spelling that was taught early as an aid to pronunciation.[49] Finally, writing might be a rarely taught and apparently only formulaically intended vernacular *composition,* a way to combine practice in some of these uses while improving one's ability to construct effective oratorical sentences in stylistic exercises like those undertaken by Agnes Lee in her journal.

We now make similar semantic distinctions, but we rarely invest each with a discrete sense of purpose, a compartmentalized audience, a specialized reading experience, or the separate results that were assumed to follow such multiple pedagogies. Given this diversity, *cultural literacy* in eighteenth- and nineteenth-century America would signify only vaguely as a class attribute. It certainly would not imply objects of universal knowledge, even among the upper class. More important, the word *literacy* is itself useless in analyses of early American inscription and reading. The implications of the term, like corollary connotations of *illiterate,* are only rarely clarified even now. Early American literates could do less, and illiterates more, with cultural texts than we now easily imagine.

Nonetheless, histories of literacy education regularly elide topics they claim to distinguish. For instance, it is common in histories of education to note that writing was a subject taught after the basics of reading, spelling, and handwriting, the "orthography" that Mrs. Barbour of Petersburg (perhaps Sextus Barbour's source of directions for writing) announced as one part of her early nineteenth-century curriculum in "letters."[50] But it is rarely noted that in the lists of courses advertised by specific schools, a very different "writing" was often linked to instruction in arithmetic or mathematics. Mid-eighteenth-century records tell of masters advertising "writing and arithmetick" schools, one of which is described by making yet another scrupulous distinction between modes of writing: "Writing and arithmetic will be taught to such as desire it, and letter writing in form."[51] The 1789 legislation authorizing schools throughout the city of Boston made provisions for teaching discrete forms of written language as writing and as reading. This law also highlights the common pairing of writing and arithmetic:

> There shall be one writing school at the south part of the town, one at the center, and one at the north part, that in these schools the children of both sexes shall be taught writing and also arithmetic in the various branches of it usually taught in the town schools, including vulgar and decimal fractions.
>
> That there be one reading school in the south part of town [and in the center and north] that . . . the children of both sexes be taught to *spell, accent, and read both prose and verse* and also be instructed in English grammar and composition.[52]

The journal *Education* in 1881 explained this pairing in terms of a related precept in composition instruction: "Teachers should aim to induce in their pupils habits of mind that are as distinct, rigid, and certain *in regard to writing as are those which relate to mathematics.*"[53]

The division of activities associated with reading from separate forms of writing, and writing's further links to arithmetic, appear in many guises. Quaker Dolly Madison was said to have had "writing [that] was well taught, but her spelling was always erratic."[54] "Literate" girls learned reading, handwriting, spelling, and grammar. But in many places, including German settlements in Pennsylvania, "writing was probably not at first taught girls, such an acquirement being considered necessary only for boys."[55] In any form, writing was usually considered a subject to be taught later and was often linked to the study of arithmetic. It was frequently placed in the middle of a curricular list that ended with elocution, rhetoric, composition (for oratorical speeches and essays), and the "natural philosophy" or faculty psychology that still informs the mentalistic "modes" of some composition textbooks. This mentalism, a seed of modernist faith in models, is enclosed in a historical triad of composing, mathematics, and the rhetorical psychology of "faculties." A nineteenth-century educator clarified this necessary rigidity of "thought," both mathematical and discursive:

> A second object of study is to give you the power to hold the mind down to a subject or to a point, as long as it is necessary. In doing a long sum in arithmetic, in demonstrating a difficult problem in Euclid, or in evolving a complicated question in algebra, you must hold the mind down to the point, and hold it there till you understand it and can explain it to others. When you write a letter, or a composition, you want the power to hold the mind or the thought till you know what to say [and] and how to say it. How many people lose almost the whole of a lecture, or a sermon, or a public speech, because they cannot hold their minds fast till it is through![56]

In this joining, faculty psychology objectified the "mind," making it capable of physical, even coerced, exercise. Before the language of "points" and "holding the mind down" became acceptable dead educational metaphors, the "point" of either composition or mathematics was mental strengthening of the memory for oral presentations. Geometry, composition, and "thought" merge as equal contributors to an important, essentialized human "power."

But this nineteenth-century statement also justifies an even longer tradition in which writing was a discrete area of study, one unnecessary for girls because of its functional link to the arithmetic needed for business management or a trade. As evinced by many exercises kept in these commonplace books and separate, elaborate volumes, the study of mathematics relied on written language. Geometry, especially, required painstaking presentations of proofs that included both drawings and precise quotations of theorems and their corollaries. Peter Stubblefield (1777–1839), born in Spotsylvania County, Virginia, left a large bound "Arithmetic Book," a work of expert drawings and calligraphy, with explicit and correctly inscribed word problems as examples (what he calls keys) to the "frequently used symbols."[57] Schools advertising "writing and arithmetic" were precisely named; one learned and practiced each skill in the practical context of the other.

Many such statements invite us to reconsider what was meant by lessons in writing. Writing lessons were not logistically joined, advanced ways to combine elements of a supposedly complete curriculum in language, nor a developmental capstone on a teleological sequence that began with the alphabet and ended with either a classical or a psychologized "faculty" rhetoric. *Composing,* in the sense of originating texts, played only a slight, if complex, part among other social and vocational needs that were addressed by learning to write.

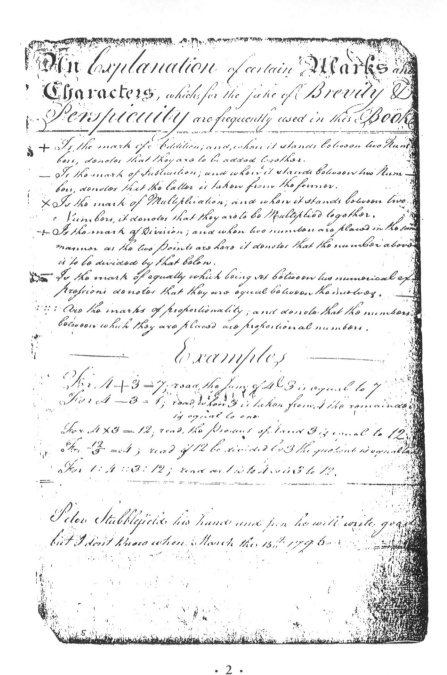

An Explanation of certain Marks and Characters, which for the sake of Brevity & Perspicuity are frequently used in this Book

+ Is the mark of Addition; and when it stands between two Numbers, denotes that they are to be added together.

− Is the mark of Subtraction; and when it stands between two Numbers, denotes that the latter is taken from the former.

× Is the mark of Multiplication; and when it stands between two Numbers, it denotes that they are to be Multiplied together.

÷ Is the mark of Division; and when two numbers are placed in the same manner as the two points are here it denotes that the number above is to be divided by that below.

= Is the mark of equality which being set between two numerical expressions denotes that they are equal between themselves.

∷ Are the marks of proportionality; and denote that the numbers between which they are placed are proportional numbers.

Examples

For 4 + 3 = 7; read, the sum of 4 & 3 is equal to 7

For 4 − 3 = 1; read, when 3 is taken from 4 the remainder is equal to one

For 4 × 3 = 12; read, the product of 4 and 3 is equal to 12.

For 12⁄3 = 4; read if 12 be divided by 3 the quotient is equal to 4

For 1 : 4 ∷ 3 : 12; read as 1 is to 4 so is 3 to 12.

Peter Stubblefield his hand and pen he will write good but I don't know when: March the 15th 1796

· 2 ·

A page from 1796 arithmetic book kept by Peter Stubblefield (1777–1839), headed "An Explanation of certain marks and Characters, which for the sake of Brevity & Perspecuity are frequently used in this Book." At the foot of the page is a note added later: "Peter Stubblefield his hand and pen he will write good but I don't know when. March the 15th, 1796." Mss51735. Reprinted by permission of the Virginia Historical Society.

On the Value of Writing: At Home, in Seclusion,
to "Cooperate with Circumstances"

The unfamiliarity today of the functional concept of writing exhibited by Sextus Barbour and others shows how important it is to reexamine the shift to inscription that supports modern assumptions about graphocentric discourse. George E. Dabney's address "On the Value of Writing," delivered before the University of Virginia Society of Alumni in June 1849, exemplifies and closely analyzes this shift.[58] The text of this speech by an elected alumnus is worth considering in detail, for it pits traditional lessons—in inscribing a well-educated student's thought in preparation for public speech—against an emerging conception of writing as a site of personal presence. *Presence* itself, we see, is a new social process that is engaged in increasingly consequential acts of shaping vernacular written discourse. In his address, Dabney compares and contrasts oral and written discourse in ways we recognize from ethnocentric twentieth-century literacy studies such as Walter Ong's *Orality and Literacy* and David Olson's *From Utterance to Text.*[59] But Dabney's speech differently highlights two pleasures of writing that it joins in a novel way—creating texts and recalling texts through their material purchase on cultural memory. Dabney actively relocates the enduring *fama* that motivated oratorical virtuosity, placing reputation in a specifically graphic reiteration and dissemination of an individual's language. His speech argues for a newly socialized mode of utterance that can be accomplished only by writing, defined specifically here as individual inscriptions.

Dabney's speech was both delivered and published. It calls on powerful men to reform traditions of manly ambition at their hidden heart, sites of education. It emphasizes local values—immediate sites of learning and readerships of friends and acquaintances. It privileges topics whose exploration will encourage an inner, not external, change that is the proper goal of isolated individual authorship. The speech thereby also encourages a specific cultural change. It rearranges traditional definitions of "private" and "public" relations to posterity, in ways manifested as "local authorship" in functional civic and memorial documents. (See chapter 7.) Finally, by calling for new pedagogical practices, it supports an emerging retheorization of "heroic" linguistic forces.

Dabney's speech recalls the precepts of Edward Channing, Harvard's Boylston Professor of Rhetoric, whose lectures between 1819 and 1851 argued that modern orators should reject the spoken polemics of old fashioned heroism, to favor "more quiet ways of forming and expressing public sentiment."[60] Dabney says that university graduates are men who appreciate and foster "domestic" discourses, thereby defining a new gender position made available precisely by *writing,* but in isolated, potentially limited, spheres. Consequently, his speech is a particularly revealing attempt to defamiliarize and then refigure writing as an ongoing social process, not a physically manifest *virtu.*

Dabney's introduction emphasizes his place among a contributory citizenry. He announces himself as one of the "older alumni of this now flourishing University" (then only twenty years old).[61] He agreed to speak "as a western citizen" of the state, eager to show loyalty, to dispel selfishness and bigotry, and to celebrate his election for the occasion. He might have chosen other topics, but writing, his subject, is an emerging triad of law, education, and composition, "intimately connected with every department of human knowledge" (7). Writing is not what it was; it is "that art, which highly valuable at its first invention, has constantly increased in value with the progress of the other arts, with the advance of the sciences, and with the extent of human intercourse" (7). He will consider the advantages of cultivating this renovated definition of writing for students' "intellectual training," "happiness," "reputation," and finally "usefulness" (7). Under each head, Dabney makes points that are now familiar in discourse theory but are surprising in mid-nineteenth-century agendas around written language.

For instance, the speech's first subtopic, the intellect, is treated as writing-as-process. Since "all education is intended rather to train the mind for subsequent effort and acquisition, than to store it with an ample fund of practical information," education in writing should be emphasized as a way to improve "the accuracy of our thoughts" (7). Dabney specifically distinguishes textualized from mental and spoken ideas, which are necessarily inferior, because "floating through our own minds, or orally communicated to others, they may often seem clear and well-arranged, when, if written, they could not bear the ordeal of examination" (7). He praises making outlines of subjects, in the Scottish and European tradition of extensive note taking to reproduce academic lectures,[62] explaining that the "neglect of writing" causes a disorganized store of knowledge: "Who, that knows the carelessness of thought, orthography, and expression, apparent in the compositions of many of our so-called men of education, can fail to deplore that deficiency?" (8). But he also distinguishes the purpose of writing systematically to store others' ideas from another use—writing as a way of learning that promotes "cultivating, in the best manner, the taste and the imagination" (8). Some, he says, can perform "mental" writing by virtue of a prodigious memory, but most need paper itself.

Thus Dabney, although recalling Quintilian in Book X of the *Institutes*, is differently prepared by similar reasoning to advocate teaching university-level composition. He does so in a series of statements that emphatically privilege the regular process of making texts over the genius of their content:

> Carefully prepared original composition should constitute an essential part of education, from elementary schools up to universities. Early and continued habit is necessary to make it, as it ought to be, easy and agreeable. [In] many illustrious examples . . . literary talent and industry have risen superior to the want of this training. . . . Not a few of those who have thus mounted to literary distinction, apparently by the mere buoyancy of genius, trace their ardour in its pursuit, if to no other school, to that best and earliest, the domestic hearth. (8)

This praise for an unexpected source of manly education, the "best and earliest" domestic hearth where Dabney finds the ember for reigniting lessons in writing, connects writing to "private" life. This link is a theme in the three other divisions of his topic, which contrast grandiose oratorical eloquence with the potential actions of new discursive heroes. Happiness, the next subtopic, oscillates between traditions associated with public address and private, isolated, composition. It is enhanced by "correspondence with our friends, from a comparison of those jeux d'esprit, those fugitive lines, or occasional essays, which amuse or interest our own circle, although never meant for the public eye" (9). Yet composition is also one of the principal "avenues to the temple of fame," a way to "hand down our names to coming generations"; it fulfills ambition, which Dabney distinguishes from traditional manifestations of self-pride: "Action, speaking, and writing are the three great highways to distinction" (9). He agrees with Cicero's preference for oration, giving credit to rhetors who unified action and oratory to move nations—William Tell, Patrick Henry, General Gordon, Martin Luther. But speech is often "evanescent." Writing has been the medium of the most practical geniuses, despite its dangerous possibility of encouraging impractical thinking in its requisite isolation; Aristotle, Aeschylus, and Aristophanes all wrote. "Every man who has any political ambition . . . sets up for an orator, and spouts away, too often 'in one weak, washy, everlasting flood'" (12). Yet even those whose "orations have been embalmed in finished composition" could not preserve "the aroma, the enchantment of . . . delivery" (13).

Yet, Dabney adds, "One of the most important points on which . . . to fix your attention, is the immense increase in the rapidity and extent of circulation, which printing has given to all written compositions" (13). Private composition can compete with impassioned public oratory for the rewards of

reputation, his third heading under happiness. Ancient oratorical rep-
utations grew but slowly, but moderns like Daniel Webster and Warren
Hastings quickly attained vast audiences. Consequently, writing is not a
mere "auxiliary" of oratory, but the prime instrument of "Washington,
Franklin and the founder of this University": "The statements of the press
falling, with the silent constancy of dew, on the public mind, furnish its ali-
ment, and usually give it its direction" (15). Religious, literary, and political
periodicals reach a copious readership—"public and private men, . . . young
and old, male and female, learned and unlearned, grave and gay, pious and
irreligious, *and are not the less potent because they address themselves only to the
eye*" (15–16, emphasis added). Dabney laments the "tide of cheap publications . . . poured over the land." But to promote the teaching and learning of
his selected subject, he encourages the audience to write: "It is worthy the
ambition of every educated man, to contribute even a few drops to this puri-
fying and salutary stream" (16).

Dabney hereby subtly reverses the traditional loci of fame, moving "action" into isolation, and redefining "significance" as this isolated influence,
action through the pen. He acknowledges that ephemeral publications are
not the best way to elevate writing, and he introduces the theme of the "absent" American literature common in nineteenth-century discussions of
letters by invoking the shared native history of his audience. Without the in-
terruption of "revolution and the critical period that followed it," the country's elder statesmen would have created the national literature that is now
possible in the prosperity, active professions, and a spreading "taste for reading" of his own time (16). American authors can reach vast spaces and enor-
mous audiences, despite the "masses of foreign emigrants, the engrossment
of gain, and . . . indolence and lethargy" that "have left multitudes without
education." Dabney predicts that America will nonetheless produce "a more
extended and enlightened reading public, than Europe, with all its scholars,
libraries and universities" (16). American literature, in his time an unrealized
"poetry of hope," will draw on the country's scenery, its history of revolution,
the spirit of its frontiers, and its grand new discoveries, to leave its "promising boyhood" and "wake to ecstasy" (17). In significant opposition to Whitman's nationalistic call for American authorship in *Democratic Vistas* (1871),[63]
Dabney suggests that literary writing will celebrate social differences, not the
(as yet unimagined) unity of a national American middle class. After all, he
identifies himself as a westerner in his state, highlighting his regional difference within the educational history he shares with his audience.

The fourth subtopic, the usefulness of writing and writers, is ranked
above intellectual training, personal and public happiness, and the new ver-

sion of fame promised by the medium. Writing is useful to "our associates, our country, and to mankind," increasingly broad categories of service. Significantly, Dabney emphasizes that "the pen in the service of friends" can replace "the bloody duel" (17–18). In his society, skillful writing by experienced intermediaries did prevent violence after most challenges in affairs of honor. In a prescribed, highly codified interchange, friends of the antagonists managed a graceful discourse around exactly what had or had not been said. Steven M. Stowe analyzes such combat as a culturally purposeful conflict that maintained acceptable social stratification among men—status defined precisely by reputation.[64] In addition, Dabney notes that skillful writing in memoirs and obituaries often "set down the memory of the worthy dead unsullied to posterity" (18).

Next, in the prescribed place for oratorical digression, Dabney returns to the superiority of writing to speaking. This earlier general comparison now specifically connects personal to cultural advantages produced by individual writing *processes*, which become social virtues. When undertaken "for posterity," composition allows the individual writer's thoughts to mature and to be measured in perfected language. "Calm deliberation" is encouraged by writing, since thoroughly considered discourse can influence others after the moment of its production. The "empires of the mind" controlled by an intriguing precanonical canon of "Voltaire, Goethe, Rousseau, Burke, Hannah More, Scott and Byron . . . are no less real, powerful and extensive" for having neither "fasces nor regalia" (19).

To this point, Dabney has remained well within the conventional praise for writing that one might find in a "finished" curricular and extracurricular education in classical and vernacular letters. But this proposal for curricular change requires an outcome very different from education for speeches, debate, and civic participation. Dabney proposes instead that vernacular exercises in composition should be required in academic courses and produced spontaneously in extracurricular activity:

> These considerations prove writing, especially since the printing press has given it wings, an invention of incalculable importance. . . . All men of education [should] cultivate this means of immortalizing themselves, amusing, instructing, refining and elevating their kind. [I]n every institution of the first class, composition in our own language, may well monopolize the talents and time of the most gifted professor; and . . . students should regard it, not as a dry and irksome task, but as an accomplishment which demands all their powers, and deserves all their enthusiasm. (20)

Well before vernacular composition was institutionalized either in advanced or lower-division university courses or as a link between common schools and the study of "English," Dabney announces both—composition courses and a central "English" built around them—as the best possible outcome of privileging vernacular writing. The bizarre idea that "all men of education" should cultivate immortality in this way is but one indication of the weird yet "common" angle of vision that unites literacy and the literary in self-conscious ordinary writing. Sure that they never quite get it right, writers focus only on that: getting it, and themselves, right.

This proposal vividly exposes the preferences of the broad community imagined in this speech, a young republic in 1849 comprised of distinct states, commonwealths, and unexplored territories. Education, specifically education in vernacular writing, will secure a startling list of local advantages. "We need," Dabney says, "every influence among us, to correct our tastes, to fix our habits, and change us from the roving, unsettled nation we now are, into a home-loving and home-improving population" (19). America is unfortunately "tinged by the transient character" of speeches "prepared to catch the popular breeze," a speech-making Dabney compares to temporary "buildings and improvements" (19). Shoddy construction of language and of material culture both result from "the migratory spirit" that causes Americans to "expect soon to leave the home of our childhood for some imaginary El Dorado" (19). Despite the virtues of pioneering, "fixedness of principle will usually be found connected with fixedness of residence," which an explicitly modern process of writing can promote. Writing keeps us at home, in seclusion, to "cooperate with circumstances" (19).

In that local place, we need not become "great" writers to benefit "mankind": "He who puts forth the simplest school-book" or "a tract which brings one soul from vice to virtue" may do more good "in this land" and in "those heathen regions now opening to Christian civilization." Dabney concludes by praising the "young men assembled" for "commencing a periodical, which is to be the exponent of their views, and the stimulant of their powers in composition," both a product of and a process for encouraging writing. This and other local "literary distinction" compete with "the giddy heights" of ambition traditionally ascribed to statesmanship or heroic action. Even after the university "crumbles to dust," the writing of its students will remain (20).

Dabney's imagined heathen probably did not read English language tracts, but his point is equally hyperbolic: increased attention to writing will stabilize new practices made possible by print, and in turn stabilize the people who constitute a republican America. From the first mention of the educational "domestic hearth" to a consideration of domestic home improvements in a fixed residence where immobilized writers absorb "fixed principles," this address insistently turns intellect, happiness, and fame away from grandiose public conquest and toward isolated, time-consuming, and physically constraining written composition. In the paradox that later became the logic of centralized courses in self-corrective composition, writing about specialized topics for a limited readership in private, not "authored," modes will serve the entire country. Education in vernacular composition will accomplish inner changes and local benefits within a broad range of political action that fixes the American definition of *private,* so imprecise in the seventeenth century, in the bifurcated allegiances of newly opposed identities.[65]

Of course, the plausibility of Dabney's claims is not at issue. They interest us insofar as they redefine writing, precisely *as* composing and executing vernacular texts. In this move, Dabney announces connotations of *composition* that are familiar today. Composition fosters the development of personal qualities like organization, thoughtfulness, reconsideration, and the ability to define oneself as a local, not a universal hero. Domesticity is not for Dabney a gendered "domestic sphere," the logic of which emerged in his lifetime, but an arena of local and special responsibilities that crosses gender categories, as his allusions to both men and women and to Hannah More indicate. Writing includes care for friends, for marginal groups, and especially for the social education of the self and others. The speech seems to instate a now common bourgeois desire for local domestication in stable, privatized, physical and social spaces. But it instead works out a precisely *discursive* version of emerging cultural categories, established by an unfamiliar force in formal higher education, organized vernacular composition.

Both Dabney's speech and Barbour's deceptively conventional "Directions for Writing" map unfamiliar territory. They highlight a new space for the purposeful inscription of vernacular language as autonomous social texts. Making notes by following a precise format, like codifying a new vision in an isolating, locally directed, at once socially and mentally improving inscription, were unfamiliar codifications of vernacular writing. This move creates identities that merge formerly separate versions of public and private, high and low spheres. Writing becomes an indigenous project undertaken to assert family and community, not to diminish them before state interests. It is domesticated to home and local concerns that compete with formerly universal and elite images of fame. It acquires connotations, that is, beyond ancient and modern representations of speech in graphic signs, the definition still traced in educational claims for its universal, quasi-religious effects. These texts suggest a discrete and influential movement toward emerging articulations of private, psychologized selves and newly classified audiences—friends, duelists, schoolchildren, even the heathen.

In the social context for writing that George Dabney's address enlarges, the student texts discussed in the next section represent a framed *possessive* activity, one not yet absorbed by later social projects. These statements about writing address an emerging cultural formation that is immediately problematized. It requires both advocacy and detailed explanations of matters that now appear obvious, to justify a new educational project. This new version of *writing* documents a subtle shift in cultural categories, overlaying classical traditions of discourse education on new differences between a private and a public domain.

Writing About Writing: Self-Possessed Schooling

Just as Barbour's "Directions" and Dabney's reconception of writing only sketch emerging cultural forces, school essays by upper-class Virginia youth preclude easy assumptions about the cultural work they undertake. Against a modern notion of the universality of both education and writing, this scribal energy needs careful attention, with help from revisionist historians like Brickley, Kaestle, and Bailyn. These secondary and primary texts do not, of course, paint detailed portraits of the schooling that produced this assigned "original" writing by young elite Virginians. But it is clear that these texts do not exemplify the same reproductive effects of schooling that cultural theory grapples with in the imagined totality but actual fragmentation that confronts it.

Our task is to read otherwise, aware of different historical conditions surrounding school writing from this era. Obviously, school and personal essays in the Virginia Historical Society collection were written before nationalism was fully conceptualized or entrenched. But they were also written within institutions that simultaneously blurred, redefined, and mobilized differences between the home and the public realm. To discern this distinction, of course, we must not read these student texts with the attitude that student writing has no significance beyond practice. Histories of composition generally assume that such practice furthered the mastery of formal oratorical rhetoric, that it was aimed only at producing textual objects for stringent correction, or, after 1890, that it embodied pedagogical reforms in personal writing about topics that addressed "what the students know."[66] But no matter how imitative, institutionalized, or self-expressive, any brand of "original" student writing exemplifies a fluidly "public" textuality, not one trapped in organized schooling. Practicing writing as process, these students wrote before categories in literary or composition studies privileged an aesthetic culture and its universalized, "inner" self or valued the reflexive writing that sustains regulated mass subjectivity.

But these texts do not arouse nostalgia for the "public" or "political" discourse that is assumed to have preceded them educationally, the supposed result of elite rhetorical training. The imagined public they address is well within Dabney's local horizon. They find their social purposes instead in ordinary places where emerging and established discursive positions mix amiably, with little competition. They participate in a social, not a classically heroic mode of writing, as Dabney suggests they should. Student texts in these commonplace books reveal a precisely "cultural" history of acts of writing. These writers shift their discursive positions and adopt multiple stances toward graphic identities. These texts contain both writerly positions and statements *about* writing that were only later arranged in a literacy hierarchy. They highlight their writers' very different takes on themselves *as* writers and critique later assumptions about the social purposes of schooling for writing.

Compositions and School Curricula

Of course, prose compositions of more than one kind were preserved. Essays appear in seventeen of this collection's commonplace books, kept by fourteen writers, of whom seven are male, six are female, and one is unidentified. Many are not school writers. Two of fourteen essay writers kept more than one volume: John Langbourne Williams (1831–1915) kept volumes in 1879, 1880, and 1888 that include abstracts of philosophical and religious writings.[67] Virginia Eliza Price (1833?–1908) kept two volumes, for 1849–1850 and 1850–1851, which contain essays about the history of Greece and Italy and lines of verse that accompany her school compositions.[68] Two eighteenth-century examples of prose practice are also preserved: Robert Bolling's (1738–1775) "A Collection of Diverting Anecdotes, Bonmots and other Trifling Pieces . . . 1764," copied in 1869 by a Robert Alonzo Brock from a copy of the original (belonging to Thomas Bolling of Bolling Island, Goochland County);[69] and John Robinson's commonplace book, kept from 1735 to 1747, which includes religious writings, accounts of tobacco shipments, and a separate compilation entitled "Religious Writings of John Robinson."[70]

The other original or copied prose compositions in the collection were written between 1826 (by Mary Jefferson Randolph, 1803–1876) and approximately 1882 (by Alfred Byrne Horner, 1861–1934). These include an unfinished novel, short stories, literary abstracts, and essays—in one case, essays in Spanish (by John Fauntleroy Mortimer, ?–1867; see chapter 6). Most are productions of youth, written either when at school or for home entertainments like the poems, essays, and short stories by Jane Tayloe Lomax Worthington (1821–1847). This assortment of authors, dates, and generic categories, if casual evidence, suggests that gender determined neither the likelihood of including original writing in a family collection nor the genres in which one wrote.

The schooling of other writers and their children shows a similar variety of information and artifacts. Twenty-five commonplace books contain school records of various sorts by twenty-one writers. Of these, the earliest are notes on Greek history, poetry, and shorthand by Waller Holladay (1776–1860) in his 1799 commonplace book; the latest are notes on ancient history, botany, and arithmetic in a volume kept by John Couper (1856–1917) from 1869 to 1871. Such primary data about school curricula verifies the findings in other sources (such as Robinson's *Academies of Virginia, 1776–1861*). But actual student notebooks, exercises, and attendance and grade reports highlight how a carefully protected curriculum was transformed into family property; it was not always created when the schooling took place, nor always by the students themselves. The nine distinct subject heads about which students kept notes include chemistry (two examples), arithmetic (four examples that include algebra and geometry problems and miscellaneous exercises), history (three examples that include ancient and Greek history), law (two examples, one from the University of Göttingen), French (two examples of grammar lessons), and one example each of lessons in German, Arabic, and Hindi, music, and philosophy. Three members of the Holladay family, including Waller Holladay, also saved sample penmanship exercises, found in three commonplace books kept by Virginia Holladay (1829–1888) in her 1843–1844 and 1844–1845 volumes, and by James Minor Holladay (1823–1891) in his 1832 volume. Waller Holladay also preserved examples of his shorthand.

In addition, six commonplace books contain attendance and grade reports. Eliza Ann Spragins Clark (1821–1897) saved her 1838 grade reports from Salem Female Academy in Winston-Salem, N.C.; Amanda Jane Cooley Roberts (1820–1854) saved a record of attendance at Mrs. Roberts's school in Carroll County in her 1846–1848 commonplace book. John Denis Keiley (?–1891) included attendance and grade reports from his education at Petersburg Gymnasium, 1862–1866. These were preserved in three of his four commonplace books: 1844–1866, 1858–1860, and 1866–1870.

In preserving such records, of course, students and their families were no different from their modern counterparts who still celebrate their children's accomplishments by keeping such tokens. But they were saved not primarily as records of performance, signs of meeting criteria set by an established institution, *the* school. More complicated relationships between the family and both actual and metaphoric versions of "school" are evident here in the way these writers position themselves and their traditional topics, especially when they write about the social functions of writing itself.

Cultivating a Taste for Composition

On April 6, 1853, at the Alexandria Female Seminary, Jane Thompson wrote a school essay, "On the Advantage of Cultivating a Taste for Composition."[71] Her classmate, Julia Beverly Whiting (?–1903), kept records that indicate something of the schooling that produced Jane's text. Julia, whose papers also include a handwritten will leaving her trust account in Philadelphia to two unmarried sisters, was charged $68.78 for one quarter of instruction, including $.13 for a "Blank Book," $.20 for a "Parsing Book," $.38 for a Composition Book, and $.50 for McGuffey's Reader 12. She was charged $2.50 for an unspecified number of "Blank Books." Her 1856 report cards indicate that the discursive studies pervasive in academy curricula included reading ("Murray, McGuffey and others"), English grammar ("Syntax &c. Parsing, Comly/Various Authors"), elementary composition ("Parker"), advanced composition ("Selected Subjects"), poetical recitations ("Various Authors"), and rhetoric ("Blair"). She also regularly studied geography, history, natural philosophy, chemistry, physiology, mathematics, mental and written arithmetic, geology, French, and a miscellaneous studies in music, the U.S. Constitution, and German.[72]

Jane Thompson's essay on composition is one of a group entitled "Specimens of the Compositions of the pupils of the Alexandria female seminary selected and written by themselves, 1853 and 1858." This compilation included Gertrude Ashby's "He shall not die" (on Pocahontas saving the life of John Smith), and "Christmas"; Isabella Atkinson's "Soliloquy of a Canary Bird" and "Visit to Melrose Abbey"; and Mary McVeigh's "Advantages of a Good Education." After its discursive title, Thompson's essay begins with notable energy:

> Yes! young friends we have at length come to the conclusion that *there is* an advantage—yes, a great advantage, in cultivating while at school, a taste for composition—or in other words to learn to express our ideas on paper. But while I am writing this, methinks I hear some little girl say, "certainly, it brings to mind poor Job and his trials. Then again, I hear some other little girl console herself, when told to write a composition; well! this must be one of the ills schoolgirls are heir to." But excuse me, if I have judged to hastily, I really had forgotten that *this* is the "age of progress,["] and that the days are almost passed, when the name of "composition" was welcomed only by the school-girl with a groan or a sigh. Surely times have changed and in no respect more than in this particular. To write a composition has now become a delightful and easy task to the children of those who looked upon it in the light alluded to.

Jane specifies writing a document as the composition she intends here. She separates herself from her parents' generation, "those who looked upon" writing with the earlier, less delighted view of it as a formidable auxiliary to speech, the image that George Dabney's "Address" set about to revise. She lists the advantages of learning to compose, noting (with Hugh Blair) that "some persons possess the talent naturally":

> There is no little skill necessary to produce an interesting and nicely expressed letter—or even a note, or an invitation requires some little taste to be displayed and this everyone more or less is called upon to do. . . . Of course we do not all expect to become either authors or authoresses, yet it tends to cultivate the mind and teaches us to estimate intellectual labor. . . . Though our humble efforts may not increase the store of intellectual enjoyment, yet we hope that the time devoted to the exercise, will be like unto "bread cast upon the waters, to be found after many days."

This essay clearly displays traditional rhetorical forms taught in oratorical training for men. Like many treatises and speeches by women, it shows that classical forms of education were available to both sexes in entitled groups. Thompson's essay follows a standard pattern that demonstrates this female rhetorical skill: it provides the context of what most people think of composition, with allusions to Job and schoolgirl "ills," then distinguishes its argument for a distinctly modern recuperation of writing for young ladies, since "everyone more or less" must produce letters, notes, and invitations. Using the special deliberative topic of comparing past and present before listing the future advantages of embracing composition, Thompson's text is a pointed instance of advocacy for writing itself in the new discourse celebrating graphic production. Here, school writing is a bridge to a social context. It need not "increase the store of intellectual enjoyment," a cache of literary and historical capital that defined "classical" education. But composing joins practice, intellectual labor, canonical authorship, and social texts—letter, invitation, notes—the processes and products that, as Dabney's 1849 address implies, "everyone more or less" must now produce.

The new concept of education as intended to blend personal and public spheres and identities is highlighted in two essays in Maggie Palmer's 1859–1860 commonplace book: "Education" and "Letters." Both were written in her two years at the Western Female Institute in Staunton.[73] In her essay on the benefits of education, Palmer, like Thompson, divides her topic, here as youth versus age. But in either state one is bereft of society if unable to read:

> The boy, who has fooled away his time at school, feels the need of education, when he goes in to business, and how much the old and feeble man feels the need

SPELLING FROM THE N. Y. EXPOSITOR.   ERRORS SINCE LAST REPORT.

PENMANSHIP, WILLIAMS' SYSTEM.   PROGRESS. *Very Good*

Studies.	Text Books.	No. of perfect re-citations.	No. of recitations nearly per-fect.	No. of pretty good recitations.	No. of recitations considered failures.	No. of recitation absen t from.
Reading, - - - -	Murray, McGuffey and others.					
Geography, - - -	Smith, Pierson & Large Maps.					
Eng. Grammar, { Syntax, &c. / Parsing.	Comly. / Various Authors.			1		
History, ...	Parley, Markham & Taylor.					
Elementary Composition, -	Parker.					
Advanced Composition, - -	Selected Subjects.					
Natural Philosophy, - -	Phelps, Comstock & Parker.	34	0	0	0	0
Chemistry, . . .	Phelps, Comstock & Youman.	21	0	0	0	0
Physiology, - - - -	Taylor, Comstock & Hooker.					
Rhetoric, & Composition	Blair.	13	0	0	0	0
Astronomy, - - - -	Olmsted.					
Moral Philosophy, - -	Abercrombie.					
Mental Arithmetic, - -	Colburn.					
Written Arithmetic, - -	Davies and Greenleaf.	29	5	0	0	0
Mathematics, - - -	Algebra —	12	1	0	0	0
Geology, - - - -	St. John & Loomis.			1		
Poetical Recitations, - -	Various Authors.					
French, - - -	Verb, Gram. Comas.		Does	Very Well		
Drawing, - - -	Music	Does	Very Well			
Miscellaneous, - - -	German	Do.	Do.			

Since *9th* mo. *16th* this Pupil has attended *0 0* Sessions of School, been absent from *0* Sessions, and late *0* times. She has, during the same period, received *0* marks for disorder, *0* for prompting others in the class, *0* for idleness, and *0* for minor deviations from her duty.

Marks for neatness in her wardrobe *47*. Marks for carelessness *0*

ALEXANDRIA, VA., *11th* MO., *10th* 1856.   **JAMES S. HALLOWELL.**

NOTE—In addition to the above, all the Pupils are required to write monthly letters, for inspection, which are returned to them after the errors are corrected.

Julia Beverly Whiting, report card from the Alexandria Female Seminary, 1856. MssID3545a, 962–67.

of it, when he is too old to work. How much pleasure it would afford him to get down his Bible and read in his lonely hours but Alas! he is doomed to sit down and hold his hands for he has no kind friend to read or talk to him. He was not allowed the privilege of going to school when he was young.

Palmer is rhetorically ready for counterarguments. The essay details how all other amusements will eventually fail:

But then he could find some other way to amuse himself when he is old and feeble he is obliged to retire from every thing and be confined to his home. Perhaps with no companion who might render his last days happy. His children are grown up, and have left him and he has no one to cheer him. Oh! how pleasant it would be for him, if he could now read. He could make many a long hour seem the shorter.

Palmer's equation of this cure-all, reading, with sociability is recast in her essay about the benefits of correspondence. There, writing maintains strong family connections with children away from home:

LETTERS

How it cheers the poor school girl when away from home to receive a letter written by the dear hand of a father, mother, brother or sister and learn that they are enjoying good health or that they will come to see us soon (ye!) When the mail comes we all gather around the one that goes to get it and eagerly enquire "is there a letter for me". And if there is none how soon our countenances fall and the first thing we say is, "well I believe they are sick at home or something is the matter or they certainly would write to me". But if there is one you will see us go away to some neglected corner to peruse it and if there is good news in it we will be happy all day. But sometimes we get bad news and so we almost wish he had gotten no letter a tall.

Imagining dire results from seeming good fortune was a common topic for composing school compositions.

An extensive group of essays by Bettie (Martha Elizabeth) Coons (1839–1863), of "North Cliff" in Culpepper, are part of a larger family collection. It includes report cards and essays by her brother, Henry Wilkins Coons, written at Richmond College, letters from him while in the army from 1859 to 1862, and exercises in Latin, dated 1859, by another brother, George Dallas Coons.[74] Bettie, attending the Richmond Female Institute in 1858–1859, kept notes on lectures on English history and on John Burrows's lectures on religion. Her essays are titled "Nature," "Description of my Schoolmate," "Bridewood Flowers," "Music," "A Dream," "Summer Dreams," "Life and the Seasons." She also copied and composed poems titled "Saints Rest," "I never can forget thee," "Right Rev'd Sir," "An Evening Reverie," and her own "The Old Potomac State." Like Maggie Palmer, Bettie uses the common topic of opposition, arguing that a savage enjoys advantages if he is, through ignorance, spared the troubles of an educated capitalist. She astutely equates education with social arrangements:

THE DISADVANTAGES OF EDUCATION

Would we not have been much happier if we had never been educated.

For then all mankind would be upon a level, neither all our wants much the same, for we would labor only to obtain the [?] necessities of life, each one having no desire beyond this.

Education has a tendency to create within us the spirit of emulation; which viewed in one is a curse; that is a desire to excell, merely for the sake of excelling, and this has brought much trouble into the world and has perhaps much more in store.

Let us for a moment compair the condition of an educated white man, with that of a savage. Upon the brow of the former may be seen marks of trouble, and perplexing thoughts. Perhaps he is trying to solve some problem, or plotting some [?] that he may grow rich faster than his neighbour, or how he shall [?] that he may obtain a finer house, and live in more style; or it may be that he is ambitious to immortalize his name; become some distinguished character. Upon his cheek we see no rosy tint of health, for night, after night his lamp burns low while he is perplexing his mind over his books. But now let us look at the savage, who knows of no better condition than his own.

How happy he seems, his troubles are few. His whole appearance speaks at once of his health, strength and happiness. Yes the educated man has a right to envy the condition of the savage.[75]

It may amaze us that at fifteen, just before the outbreak of the Civil War, Bettie Coons wrote so easily, and seemingly brutally, about envying a "savage" antithesis of her "educated white man." It is most likely, however, that this "savage" was featured in her reading about Indians, a favorite figure in Rousseauistic visions of a primal state characterized by the "health, strength, and happiness" of the "noble savage." This trope also circulates in the narrative construction of young Frederick Douglass, who felt, if only briefly, that "learning to read had been a curse." "I envied my fellow-slaves for their stupidity. . . . Any thing, no matter what, to get rid of thinking! It was this everlasting thinking of my condition that tormented me."[76] Sharing the hope of self-preservation through ignorance, if not relative depths of feeling and analysis, these two entirely separate examples of nineteenth-century common wisdom demonstrate the cultural power of commonplace *doxa* circulated across a society. Coons's "Schooldays," dated May 27, 1858, also hints of a parallel desire to return to preschooled freedom. But it relies on another commonplace logic whose boundaries assimilate gender and race:

> Schooldays are the most important, and if we would but think so the happiest period of our lives; for on them, and the subsequent use we make of them, depends not only our future position in society, but our happiness here, and hereafter.
>
> There are few of us I fear who appreciate them as we ought, for instead of studying hard, and trying to improve we too often wish them were at an end, that we might be "free" as we deem it from all things necessarily incumbent upon us as schoolgirls.

This essay reiterates common but revealing themes in many other school texts. It uses the trope of personal "possession" of one's education and its attainments as property to be reviewed with satisfaction. It equally assumes that the goal of schooling is the sociability associated with both attending school and writing. But in addition, Coons, like Dabney, suggests that writing may become a way of life itself, bringing distinction and fulfilling the ambition for fame that is, in his speech, colonized for the private lives of writers:

> At the end of each session is it not pleasant to look back and see what progress we have made in our studies? and then there is pleasure in trying to [?] others in our various employments; also and we know not, but that by studying now, we may at some future day become distinguished writers, and thus immortalize our names.

Coons's essays also suggest how writing was scrutinized by academy teachers. At the bottom of another, research-based essay, "Inarticulate sounds by animals and man," a teacher's comments (not unfamiliar) are preserved: "Don't make periods like commas. Your sentences are too long. All this page has only two." Bettie's discussion of language rigorously distinguishes among animal noises that are "inarticulate to us," two classes of inarticulate human sounds, "natural and required" (interjections), and a third category, articulate "spoken language," which is either "a divine or human institution." Choosing the divine side of this further division of her topic, Coons presciently embeds in her nineteenth-century religious explanation of the origins of speech a hypothesis, similar to one circulating among linguists today, that "there was only one language or rather all nations spoke the same language until after the building of the town of Babel." Preserved also is a typical student protestation; she closes with a simple plea for teacherly forbearance: "I would like to write more on this subject but ignorance prevents."

Coons's plea suggests that students were self-conscious about making compositions, creating documents. Apparently expected to "develop" their topics, they write with an honest, scrupulous sense of inadequacy in the face of stringent protocols like those prescribed in Barbour's "Directions for Writing." A similar self-deprecation is found in an essay entitled "Amusements" by Mary Jefferson Randolph (1803–1876). The essay, recorded in the commonplace book she kept at school in Richmond in 1826, begins simply, "My ideas respecting this subject are very indistinct."[77]

Most preserved school assignments include essays *about* composition, language, and notably about the shift away from spoken to written forms of discourse. An example is "Printing," an essay by Allan Talbott (1843–1901), too young to go to war when he wrote in 1860–1861. His pieces, written at the Virginia Military Institute in Lexington, address topics to be expected in any school archive—"College Life," "Comparison Between City and Country Life," "Beauties of Nature." But others are especially suited to a military education ("The plough share and the sword," "Drunkenness," "The worth of a thing is best known by its want," "Lying," "The Soldier," and "Honesty is the Best Policy"). In still other essays ("Dissolution," "The Union," "King Cotton," "Delays are dangerous," "Be sure you are right and then go ahead"), Talbott appears to be working toward a logical yet loyal perspective on his state's political situation on the brink of secession. Between the draft and final preservations of "Dissolution," he changes his original partisan conclusion to a more complicated and qualified, and less direct, position, noting that skillful rhetoric can be used to support antithetical arguments:

[Draft]

Therefore we conclude that although a dissolution may be lamentable on account of the evils which we may occasionally expect to follow in its wake, still will be beneficial as the only method whereby the long practiced principle of slavery may be protected.

[Final version]

But although the source from whence dissolution has arisen [the slavery question] may be protected with selfish motives and hence still this does not prohibit the conclusion that, dissolution itself is right under the circumstances, provided it be constitutional and will fully meet the urgencies of the times. As to the former of these, the constitution affords arguments for either party; and as to the latter we contend that it is the only remedy that will possibly satisfy the demands of the South since that Republicanism, having once gained the ascendancy, will in all probability administer the government in a manner detrimental to Southern interests.[78]

As his essay "Printing" also suggests, almost all of Talbott's writing assignments—with the exception of a timeless piece, "Which is the Most Injurious to Mankind, Lawyers or Doctors"—brought him to address the "present state of society," which he portrays as entirely out of hand:

PRINTING.

Printing is one of the greatest arts ever invented by man. No one can too highly appreciate the magic power of the Press, or too deeply deprecate its abuses. No course of reading is better calculated to show the present state of society than the perusal of the various newspapers of the day. The variety and quality, size and quantity, have increased to a mighty fold. We have the political party sheets some of whose editors are often goaded by demagogues, to the most disgraceful venality; assailing persons; placing party interest above public good. This is an evil that editors and author's can, and should correct in all of their works, for the use of printing was never intended for the abuse of the public. Their whole aim should be to enlighten and improve mankind, and to avoid all publication calculated to produce ill blood, or lead to erroneous conclusions. The object of printing was to give to man an opportunity to improve his mind, but we too often see it abused by men who have nothing to do but to slander each other, because they belong to another party.

Let every sheet issued from the Press be a bright and shining light, to guide us in the path of wisdom and virtue, which is the only path of safety.

Allan Talbott.
Jan 18th 1861

Talbott accurately assumes that the power of printing lies in the "Press," which managed to inflame both southern and northern prejudices that innocent purity might transcend. His lopsided connection between "wisdom and virtue" and "safety" suggests a prediction that the use of "one of the greatest arts ever invented"—printing—could create new, divided "publics." But what strikes us with equal force in this essay and others is that Talbott assumes, evidently with his teachers' concurrence, that his school writing should take an authoritative position on a matter of immediate political urgency. The "dread reality" of "dissolution," repeated in his dire account of misuses of the press, clearly dominates his interpretive framing of common topics in unconsciously intense language. Composition thus served Talbott, as education would also serve him, in a vexed local context that prevented delicate quotations from crumbling like ancient paper exposed to the light. In this exactly attuned narrative, however, motives for school writing are not yet left unmarked in abstract assumptions about "education." They remain vivid reasons that split available subject positions in more than one discursive space.

How Hard It Is to Be "a Critic"!

School writing about literary reading and the possibilities of literary authorship retains Talbott's practical, "applied" sense of participation in simultaneously discursive and civic purposes. Even in examples from the late nineteenth century, school essays do not reflect a canon or an institution's agenda. Asa D. Watkins (1833–1902) attended Hampden-Sydney College after teaching English literature and language at Hoge Academy in Blackstone. He kept records of his academic performance, including a Greek language exam written in 1894; report cards, 1881–1883; later notes on the occupations of Hampden-Sydney's class of 1894; and miscellaneous essays. These essays include "The Eagle," "My Christmas Hollidays," "Compensation," "Thoughts on Reading Thanatopsis," "Titus Livius," a long essay on teaching entitled "Literature in the Public Schools" (to be discussed), and a character sketch of a family slave, "Polly," interspersed with dialect. ("She is a regular negro, with no modern improvements.") He later submitted this piece to the *Southern Magazine*.[79] Watkins's report cards comment on his uneven performance in Latin, Greek, and mathematics, but state finally, in June 1893, "[He] has done well in his studies, especially so in Moral Philosophy, Bible Studies and English. He has also attained Excellence as a writer and . . . he will make his mark in this direction. His character and conduct as a gentleman meet our highest approval."

Watkins's writing particularly reveals how a relatively new discursive position was constructed as a precisely academic literary gentility, which Ian Hunter explains as an internal, bifurcated self-monitor. In Watkins's "A First Attempt," he remarks: "How hard it is to be 'a critic'! The world seems to expect more of the 'critic' than of other writers, and probably it is the world's weakness in requiring a critic to shew her how and what to think that is inherited by the world's children individually who find it so hard to be independent in thought and judgment." The preface to his "attempt to dissect a few clauses in . . . Wm. D. Howell's *An Imperative Duty*" lists and identifies rhetorical figures (such as hyperbole), and applies now puzzling critical principles to Howells's language: "'Olney *got back* to Boston'—he deliberately chooses *got back* in preference to the Latin derivative *returned*. Do not rhetoricians warn us, however, against the word—*get*?" The mixture of rhetorical and critical discourses in this exercise reveal how literary study in Watkins's time was still a purposefully overdetermined activity, home to many sorts of expertise. But *critic* is a specifically textual identity, a new discursive possibility. Watkins embeds it in an equally tentative and newly self-conscious role: *writer*. Agency here belongs to a vague "world," which demands instruction for a unified, yet individual, knowledge of what its "children" are to think. Nonetheless, "rhetoricians" still define literary figures and hold sway in preferring one linguistic choice over another. For Watkins, the "critic," the "world," and "children" (whom we assume are his former and potential students) are only tentatively demarcated categories.

Another Watkins essay, "On Composition," tacitly constructs a privileged canon of vernacular literary discourse. But it highlights the ancient and continuing view in rhetorical education that literature is useful as "models" for speakers, not as objects of aesthetic appreciation or analysis. The essay also self-consciously assumes a newly imagined appropriate position for a teacher/critic, instructing a writer who is, in turn, a critic. It negotiates a relationship between fame and an imagined student's more limited, ordinary originality, coming down firmly against the idea Harold Bloom expressed as an "anxiety of influence":

> Tennyson in speaking of Shakespeare says, "He saw through his own soul."
>
> If those trying to get their style from the author whom they most admire would consider this witticism, they could probably study the Masters of English with better effect. Truly, Shakespeare "saw through his own soul" and reflected its clear depths in his writings. In his work he poured out his soul, and we who find pleasure in the untainted stream preceding thence know that its source is pure. Therefore you who must follow Shakespeare, do it in this way: abandon all attempts to make your thoughts, your writings, conform to any chosen model; give up the model itself; stop trying to see through Shakespeare's soul and turn your gaze upon your own. You can fathom your little well of thought, for it is not as deep as that of your idol, and when you know yourself thoroughly, then you are prepared to write your own thoughts in a style that must be entirely your own. Had Shakespeare copied Homer, where would be the Prince of English Poets? Had Milton aped Shakespeare who could be edified by *Paradise Lost*? Each has his own sphere, and consequently, can fill the room of no one else; but each one of us can make what is in his small space, perfect.
>
> Many a jewel is no larger than a pin head, but is, nevertheless, flawless and a gem in every sense. What prevents our aiming to make our composition so? I believe that our compositions and magazines are so poor because we are afraid to aim high; we are afraid to advance our own ideas therefore have nothing original while originality is the very thing wanted. The world does not want another Shakespere, another Byron, another writer that she has already. Therefore each must stand for himself, though it certainly takes some courage to face what we have written, to see that our foolish sentiments have been scrutinized and that mistakes have become glaring red blotches to stare us out of countenance.
>
> However, let those who laugh at the poor grass-hopper so earnestly, consider-

ing the flight of eagles, remember that many a little insect has flown up towards
the stars, how far it matters not.

Asa D. Watkins.

For Watkins, the "Masters of English" are to be emulated, despite the inequality between Shakespeare's "well of thought" and that of his readers. "In
a style that must be entirely [one's] own," "each one of us," he emphasizes,
can perfect our own compositions if we aim for originality. The "poor quality" of the compositions and magazines that Watkins deplores can be improved by advancing not rhetorical history but "our own ideas." As a teacher,
he encouraged high-quality classroom writing and vernacular campus publications like the one that George Dabney's address praised as local sites of
fame.

Nonetheless, as in school essays by women, Watkins is self-conscious
about his lowly status as a student. The "courage to face what we have written" as "foolish sentiments" and "glaring red blotches" must accompany any
attempt at writing. Working out his status as a writer, a teacher, and a potential contributor to campus publications, Watkins's essay shifts among
these subject positions. Like Maggie Palmer and Bettie Coons, he closes his
composition by framing "serious" consideration of authorship, suggesting
growing restraints on increasingly evaluated nineteenth-century students. In
his polite and self-protective closing demur, he is not even a limited emula-
tor of Tennyson, Shakespeare, and Byron, his "eagles."

Watkins invoked this scrutinized subjectivity, the specifically "student"
writer, both at a later date and as an older writer than William Ellzey Harrison, whose undated essay "On Compositions" is preserved in family papers
kept from 1802 to 1862.[80] The essay, captioned in another hand as "a specimen of Will Harrison's composition," is brief and humorous:

> Writing compositions may be indeed very useful but is one of the most difficult
> tasks that can be given to a school boy.
> He first sits down to write without even having thought of a subject.
> He at last selects one, and writing a half dozen lines gets up in despair throws
> aside his pen scrates his head and determines that he cant write about any thing.
> He then goes to play and something occurs to his mind abut which he thinks
> that he can certainly write.
> He sits down again but after writing three or four lines gets up much more
> quickly than he sat down. He now sits down for the third time, *determined* to
> write, and after an hour's hard work succeeds in finishing a dozen lines and imag-
> ines that he has immortalized himself; but alas!! after reading it he finds two or
> three mistakes in every line.

On Compositions

Writing compositions may be indeed very useful but it is one of the most difficult tasks that can be given to a school boy.

He first sits down to write without even having thought of a subject.

He at last selects one, and writing a half dozen lines gets up in despair throws aside his pen scratches his head avid determines that he cant write about any thing.

He then goes to play and Something occurs to his mind about which he thinks that he can certainly write. He sits down again but after writing three or four lines gets up much more quickly than he sat down. He now sits down for the third time, determined, to write, and after an hour's hard work succeeds in finishing a dozen lines and imagines that he has immortalized himself but alas? after reading it he finds two or three mistakes in every line.

After these several disappointments he thinks just as I do. that writing compositions is a very troublesome business and therefore ought to be abolished.

Your's Resp't William Harrison

"On Compositions" by William Harrison, with a circled "Bill" in his hand under his signature. MssiH2485e, 125–26. Reprinted by permission of the Virginia Historical Society.

After these several disappointments he thinks just as I do, that writing compositions is a very troublesome business and therefore ought to be abolished.

Yours Respectfully,
William Ellzey Harrison

The humor of young Harrison's self-righteousness is visually embedded in a physical format that offers yet another guide to students' compositions about writing, mapping the social space they inhabited before writing was institutionalized as the social property of schools. It is written in a large, obviously schooled, hand, in one- and two-sentence paragraphs, and signed with a great flourish, "Yours Respectfully, William Harrison," under which, in the same hand, is a decoratively circled "Bill." Harrison, like his peers, put his name on what we now call "his paper." But the visual impact of his formal signature and its diminutive is strikingly different from the name at the top of the page, or on the back, that marks current student texts as institutional productions, property of an educational state apparatus.

It first appears that in his mounting frustration Harrison forgot that he was not writing a letter to his father asking to be rescued or, like parents suing a Vermont school district in 1859, complaining that writing compositions had no place in schools. Those parents argued that schools should teach how to think and speak quickly in public, not how to write in the enforced isolation called for by George Dabney but vividly denounced by Harrison.[81] As he says, Harrison was desperate. He might have confused the form of his essay with that of the letter, taught in many schools as "epistolary composition."

But neurotic fear, not yet a trope in his time, does not explain this example, or others. Jane Thompson and her fellow essayists at Alexandria Female Seminary, Maggie Palmer, Bettie Coons, Allan Talbott, and Asa Watkins (significantly later) all neatly sign their compositions, usually with a date beside or below the signature. No other composition in this collection closes with "Yours respectfully." But similarly dated and signed texts visually emphasize that school compositions were not impersonally formatted institutional documents. They were, as Kenneth Burke says of rhetoric, "always addressed."[82] Their imagined readers were not only teachers but, as their preservation alone shows, family members who owned a child's graphic achievements as a manifestation of Locke's proprietary and material property. Their signing shows how thoroughly these texts merged now demarcated genres, creating a blend of the formal essay and the letter. Composing them occupied a cultural space quite different from the one we now accept as properly initiative and marginal.

Honest Judgments

This bracketed cultural space of writing was not entirely enclosed in the (now denigrated) local schools in which students wrote. It was encompassed as well by a community gaze, a supplement to parental involvement that additionally protected students and provided evaluative audiences. For instance, Charles Minnigerode (1814–1894), minister of St. Paul's Protestant Episcopal Church in Richmond, wrote on June 17, 1881, to John Henry Powell, a teacher at the Richmond Female Seminary, pronouncing the winner of an essay competition. Minnigerode's letter not only reveals the ease with which young women accepted competition and standards by which their writing achieved exemplary status.[83] It also enacts the highly supportive stance of an extracurricular yet pedagogically informed teacher, a judge who clearly writes for more than one reader:[84]

My Dear Mr. Powell
You have done me the honour to ask me to act as umpire among four essays written by young ladies—members of your school. But I confess, the task put upon me, is one not easily accomplished. I can but say, that all of these are worth of high commendation; and that I was surprised, to find such [?] thoughts and [?] of diction in all. It would be easier for me to hold four prizes in my hand, than one.

Upon careful examination of all, I find that there are two which it might not be so difficult to designate as superior to the rest. . . . I cannot be too explicit in speaking my satisfaction with all, and the good, sound sense abounding in them. But the essays on the writing [of?] compositions, and that "on Solomon" seem to me, to be decidedly the best.

To pass an unbiased judgment between these two, is a very difficult task. The first is so fresh, natural, sprightly and brilliant, that it is difficult to put it out of your hand and not re-reading it again and again. . . . To judge between this and the essay "on Solomon" is so difficult because of the vast difference of the subjects—so that it might be said, comparison was almost out of the question. But as only one can be first, I feel constrained, to answer (as far as my judgment can go) the prize to the ripe and scholarly production of the writer "on Solomon." The writer must have studied very hard, and spent many days, weeks or months on its preparation; and the manner in which the material is worked up, and the [?] are researched; the thoughtfulness pervading it all, the surprising insight into motives, and what I might call "the genetic" treatment—going from causes to effects, and resting the results upon solid premises—this evidence of a very studious, a very mature, cultivated, thoughtful and correct mind—which in my opinion should endow it as the . . . best essay laid before me.

Of course, I am utterly ignorant of the persons who wrote any of these essays; and I have endeavored to abstract my mind from the subject, merely to speak of the treatment and composition. My heart turns toward the essay writer of the two other essays in admiration and with astonishment at the sound views they proposed. But being called upon merely to judge of them as "compositions": after having tried to consider everything & do so most kindly and without bias: I must conclude with this as my honest judgment, that the essay on "Solomon" is the one to which I would award the first rank.

Very respectfully,
Chs. Minnigerode

17 June 1881

Minnigerode indicates that he is aware of more than appreciative standards and correctness, even in the process of judging himself to be an ad hoc Solomon who must select one of two choices he has winnowed from four candidates. He praises the winner's complexity, research, and insight but insists that he has focused on the texts themselves, "abstracting" even his own thoughts on these two topics to distance these texts from their writers, of whom he scrupulously disavows knowledge. Minnigerode addresses writing *as* writing, and compositions as productions that, like an aesthetic "literature," can possess anonymous and intrinsic qualities.

Here, as throughout this body of work, the ownership of shifting positions for authorship is more complicated than first appears. Minnegerode's public acknowledgment of student texts bringing fame to self, community, and family circumscribes a still preinstitutionalized discursive space in which school writing remains a matter for family judgments. Writing in April 1890 to his son, Fairfax, at Yale, Burton Norvell Harrison (1839–1904) begins:

My dear Son:
Your typewriter has finished the job after several writings of it and it seems to follow you[r] ms and your directions. He says, strangely enough that your [handwriting?] is not always calligraphy or even legible. But I think he has done very well, and have paid him two dollars for his pains. His blue ribbon is a touch beyond the vulgar and may have a very deadly effect on the areopagus.[85]

Harrison follows with detailed comments on his son's composition:

You deserve great credit for the honest and persistent work you did in assembling the materials and I think you have made the most of it in the line you took and with the keynote you struck. . . . You are quite right to label the essay with the exact title proposed [and?] I agree with you that your treatment of it is the best practicable within the limits allowed.

Mother has read the essay, Harrison says.

[She] thinks it rather stiff but I tell her that is a characteristic of a young essayist, is expected by the judges in such a case, like this, and is to be considered as possibly to be not only read but spoken and for which latter use it is better than a more fluent and playful style.

By this reference to "judges" and his earlier praise of adhering to "the exact title proposed," Harrison appears to be describing an essay submitted for special evaluation, perhaps in a school contest or a competition held in an extracurricular vernacular debate and literary society. In closing, Harrison warns, "Don't make any more changes unless you consider them necessary and a decided improvement. If you do make any changes, send the whole thing back to be retyped."

By 1890 it was possible to hire a typist to tap out a son's contest essay in the ubiquitous blue ribbon of the time. But what is more important (and usually overlooked in histories that treat composition instruction as solely an institutional practice), it is difficult to imagine that an entitled son's education in 1890 would be conducted only by new professionals. Social historians often interpret the exercise of cultural functions like education in terms of their location, whether carried out at home or in newly organized public spaces. But the families whose texts are examined here still participated in the family-centered and decidedly fathered education defined in 1671 by Governor Berkeley, who envisioned "every man according to his ability instructing his children." Like many other fathers, as letters to sons show, Burton Harrison in 1890 would not leave a child in a writing competition to his own devices or those of his professors. (See chapter 6.) As Jane Thompson wrote in 1853, education provided a union of family, civil, intellectual, and moral exercise. She assumed her school readers' interest in family views, social duties, and biblical knowledge in her exemplary essay, just as the young and unskilled Will Harrison assumed he might ask for the "abolishment" of composition with the authority of a citizen, not just a pupil. Formal lessons in writing, like all education, belonged to the dominant family unit, where parents met their responsibility to provide for their children.

The Harrisons' interventions in their son's writing process—their analysis, supportive comments, implied suggestions, and the production of the document itself—might be taken now as unwarranted outside aid, even a form of plagiarism. Current educational ideology mandates that school exercises are to be negotiated between the school and the student, as tokens of exchange between Hunter's student-teacher couple. This erotic dyad makes family participation taboo, excluding as well more than token acknowledgment or judgments from a "real" community like the one shared by Charles Minnigerode and Powell. Nor do currently sanctioned institutional occasions for writing invite working out immediate and locally contested opinions about civic conflict, to position their writers as actors in political events. Contemporary students rarely voice their civic ownership of the press, noted in Allan Talbott's essay. Like histories that assume a timeless separation between public and the private spheres, assigned writing now typically bifurcates the student. To enact its technology of the self, that is, composition teaching assumes a split between *expression* of inner perceptions and personal values and abstract *argument* using the universalized, public, expert voice, the "neutral exposition" that I. A. Richards attributes to print culture in *The Philosophy of Rhetoric*.[86] Both categories limit appropriate student discourse, making it either an evaluative or a self-revealing mechanism, an operation in Hunter's social technology that has only institutional consequences. But the writing of earlier students like Jane Thompson and Burton Harrison organized another discursive economy of proprietary involvement.

Those with a different image of "school writing" often fail to consider the evidence from the content, physical presentation, and public disposition of such writing. Nonetheless, each shows that writing in school was emerging as a publicly held trust. In the new prominence given to writing lessons documented by Dabney and others, school writing actively contributed to the society inhabited by its learners. These texts, now displayed in archives as possessions of remarkable families, were originally family property, signs of access to the culture they symbolized. But "cultural capital" (the controlling metaphor in Pierre Bourdieu's study of class formation in modern France) was not always a trope.[87] On this evidence at least, newly prominent nineteenth-century school lessons in writing activate the prerogatives of the established family unit. A fledgling state institution, *the* common school, replaced the many and various sites of teaching and learning in the early republic. But this form of schooling only slowly and unevenly came to dominate bourgeois culture and to have exclusive possession (in all senses) of the written language of a populace. That literate "mass" now occupies only the subject position for "student writers"; they are less mobile contributors to fewer discourses. These texts, on the contrary, recognize the writer's subjectivity as shifting easily between home and its supplements, among primary units of civil society and loosely joined hegemonic webs. As a temporary place of socialization and perhaps of struggles with topics for writing, formal schooling circulated dominant *doxa* as the servant of family values, not their source.

Home Improvements

Culture as Pedagogy

The mis-improvement of youthful days is more than the mere loss of time.
Figure to yourself the loss that the year would sustain were the spring taken
away; such a loss as they sustain who trifle in youth.

VIRGINIA ELIZA PRICE, commonplace book, 1849–1851

Among the relatively privileged group whose commonplace books survive in
this collection, school texts and comments on writing instruction only partially depict a larger cultural process designed to transmit family power.
Other accounts of pedagogic interactions and often surprising educational
tenets dictating the positions of both parents and children make it clear that
the early American family was an expansive, affiliative unit from which children were launched in multiple ways. But commonplace book records of
that system in which culture and pedagogy were identical terms do not describe what we think of as home schooling. That term implies transferring
the expertise and institutional arrangements for learning to a household, for
the sake of necessity, convenience, or a self-isolating strategy of instruction.
A resident tutor, like Philip Fithian, employed by the prominent Carter
family in eastern Virginia, does not exemplify the detached professional "I"
whose gaze on students produced more modern commonplace educational
cultures.[1] Instead, accounts of schooling in early Virginia shelter traditional
doxa in their reflections on learning. They characterize pedagogy as part of
the undifferentiated tenor of any family relationship. In a biology extended
by an almost Nietzschean will to improve, supposedly essential ties of affection were the result of acquired developmental affiliations, but rarely appear
to have motivated them. On this evidence, that is, many interactions with
adults during a child's maturation formed and re-formed primary, deeply
held social responsibilities. Those community-building family duties later

came to characterize interactions between teachers and students in state-sponsored mass education.

Social contacts at school also extended the biological family, appropriating into its genetic economy all of the content, many of the events, and some of the people encountered in actual schooling and its discursive representations. These extensions worked through the identification between propriety and property outlined earlier. They were constituted in relational metaphors that now seem embarrassingly clichéd, commonplaces that appropriate people and events into retained, collective, family identities. An entire social system was hereby constituted as an educational project, just as educational projects were imagined as social systems. Affiliation, not credentials, assured the collective improvement of a propertied class throughout a discursive era that collapsed its demarcated chronological periods into an always present tense of material and graphic "keeping."

This chapter highlights narrative preservations of culture-as-pedagogy to show how such proprietary family investments in children simultaneously enacted a reproductive process and extended a family's "property," in both a material and an intangible sense. It begins with an exemplary text, Anna Blanton McClure's dictated account of her attendance at boarding school, to suggest the importance of reading such accounts in light of the purposes for which they were written, not as sound bites or data for traditional and gender histories. The chapter then presents circulating dominant principles of educational responsibility, which in this collection often emphasized different curricula for boys and girls. Two accounts of home teaching are also included: a quasi-public/private narrative of the fairy-tale family history of Virginia's Governor Littleton Tazewell and a case study by Rachel Mordecai presented as an experiment in rearing her half sister Eliza. The chapter closes with texts that depict conflicts between this customary pedagogic culture and the emerging industrial and state interests that resulted in mass education. Particularly in Samuel Simpson's angry recollections of his own lessons and predictions of much worse public mass schooling to come, "the children of the commonwealth" in the 1880s are seen as deprived imitations of those who once gained from pointedly intended "home improvements."

"Being Dead, Yet Speaketh": Re-Reading Education

Remembering her attendance at the Misses Carrington's Select School for Young Ladies in 1882, Anna Blanton McClure (1868–?) emphasizes the expansiveness that schooling brought her—not primarily as its practical or intellectual result, but as a memory that sustained her lifetime project of forming an identity. In a memoir dictated to her daughter in the 1930s, McClure recalls traveling to school, visiting friends, and her conduct in the society of the Misses Carrington. She merges the often flat categories in later social history—family, teachers, and lessons. McClure's brother, Diell, physically bridges her progress in and out of these domains, while her Latin teacher is simultaneously a family friend, a sometime escort, and a teacher whose shifts within these identities also mark her new situation.

> There was no railroad within 25 miles from Burkesville to Clarksville. . . . So my brother Diell Blanton drove me 80 miles in a buggy. . . . After reaching Sunnyside and meeting Misses Emily, Agnes, Mildred and Belle and Mrs. Carrington, there arose to greet us Mr. Alf Graham. My brother told "The Ladies" the only mistake they made was to have Alf teach Latin and math instead of him. In June both had graduated at Hampden Sydney College. . . . Mr. Graham escorted me around several times during the week there, but when I became his pupil, it was very different.[2]

McClure highlights her memories of experiences shared with friends from home like Minnie Watkins, with new girls, and with her teachers. She remembers special meals with extraordinary food that regularly reenacted rituals at home:

> The girls who were at school were Minnie Watkins, Janie Carrington, Hallie Brooks of So. Boston, and girl from N. Car. and also Petersburg. One Easter a girl's mother from N. C. sent her carriage up to driver her daughter, Misses Mildred and Belle and myself to her home to spend a few days. I had seen pound cake before but this time I saw about 10 different kinds at once . . . to do honor to her daughters teachers, her table service was perfection. . . . No one could have a more excellent table service than we always had every day. . . . Each one's birthday was celebrated with an extra fine dinner and a large banquet of hot house flowers from the pit. (1–2)

Describing her life after graduation in 1882, which included teaching school in Missouri with Diell, McClure's narrative emphasizes how important it was to cement educationally acquired affiliations and how writing served that purpose:

> We three drew up a written contract—the first one to marry should receive a silver cup and table linen and the other two should be bridesmaid and bridesgroom. So Mr. Eddie and Emmie filled their contract. . . . Mr. Morton and Minnie came also. . . . I wished much for my dear Ladies but there were no railroad conveniences at that time. . . . I have recently received LONG letters from Minnie Morton. We have had 50 years of continued correspondence. Misses Mildred and Miss Belle and sometimes Miss Emily wrote to me as long as they

lived, especially Miss Belle. I have her exquisite letter of sympathy after our fire in Missouri. I often read it. (3)

This discursive fit among school, relatives, and a larger society suggests that McClure's education took place under the purview of a metaphoric family. That group intervened in her life in concrete ways, as do the surrogate families described in many other accounts. The memoir's closing reference to "the happiest years of [her] life" at Sunnyside school notes how important teachers were as model parents: "'The Ladies' left an indelible impress upon the girls under their care, and I believe those of us who have children tried to raise them with those ideals of religion and education. 'Being dead, yet speaketh'" (3–4).

This commonplace biblical ending exemplifies the gathering and recirculation that motivates such a composition. In her daughter's second-hand transcription, McClure writes multiple possibilities, encounters with reformed and novel identities that she accumulates and obviously endows beyond her daughter's generation, in a memory of "education." Her journeys with her brother to school, and later with schoolmates and teachers, thematize the movement away from home through particular material and social geographies that she would not have known without the interval of schooling. This actual and figurative travel gathers resources as she relives, and thereby transmits, a series of experiential acquisitions. As she recalls the long distances traveled to school, she also narrates her brother's education and expertise and their later partnership; her account of their arrival transforms Diell's school friend Graham into a sometime escort and Latin teacher. Because her account is meant to preserve experience, McClure emphasizes the identities and origins of her schoolmates and teachers, not personal details that would undermine this entirely local yet entirely public form.

McClure's text also enhances these old and new affiliations. Ceremonial meals described as family occasions, ostentatious productions of pound cake, and the imposition of a binding written contract all signify forms of ritual comfort, nurturance, and self-consciousness about the quality of relationships. But material sustenance in models for homemaking and interfamilial socialization is not the primary gain. McClure reveals to her daughter, as to us, the source of her best images of motherhood, teachers whose precepts she imitated. Literate interactions with them are bonds, possibly brought to mind and highlighted by a tacit demand for self-consciousness as she makes a text with her daughter. Outside and within this story, writing is figured as a medium for important relationships in which community is imagined around a life story, with a disarming acuteness. Writing is a commitment, as the contract with her friends reveals; it demands that she and her readers stay connected. The "exquisite," frequently remembered letter of sympathy from her teacher is a primary example of this connection, as she says in a voice no one could "author": "I read it often."

This memory highlights what we often take to be a gendered social responsibility for writing letters to maintain kinship relations. But McClure hereby reiterates the surrogate mothering relationship that is bequeathed to her daughter and her reading progeny. *Education* hereby constructs McClure not as a state-certified production, but as an enhanced, improved, enduring site of multiple subject positions, a proprietor of principles, experience, and identities that her writing bestows upon others. This endowment is also, of course, an expectation of literate behavior that is realized by the production of this narrative, which she caps self-reflexively with a reference to "ideals of religion and education." The dead that speak here easily carry the burden of education as an affiliative acquisition.

It is possible, of course, to read this text very differently, as data for interpretive historical claims about schooling, the status of women, and nineteenth-century female psychology. But texts should not be reduced to documentation, as in the new historicism; an archive demands attention on its own terms. For instance, like John Purdie's account (chapter 2), histories of education often demean "ladies' academies" like the Misses Carrington's School, ascribing to them only a focus on friendship, domestic skills, cookery, and courtship, all of which McClure's account includes. Assuming that "real" education means patriarchal rigor, discipline, and competition, data gatherers could find evidence in McClure's text of strict socialization into domestic values scarcely altered by a few years of schooling away from home with the Misses Carrington.[3] Alternately, these vivid recollections might be taken as evidence of the sentiments of many female slaveholders, whose rigidly regulated and constricted years of household drudgery imprisoned even a privileged woman after such brief periods of relative freedom.[4] Similarly, McClure's text might fit Elizabeth Fox-Genovese's description of girls from plantation households who attended academies where "the governing intention remained that of easing young women gracefully into the responsibilities of their station."[5] But following historians like Suzanne Lebstock, we notice a measure of self-determined accomplishment in McClure's teaching experience in Missouri, her partnership with her brother, and her cheerfully enforced contract with her friends.[6] All show how often and how successfully women availed themselves of equity law to establish separate estates.

From yet another perspective, one might emphasize, with Carroll Smith-Rosenberg and others, the intensity of support in female relationships, scrutinizing McClure's vividly recalled shared travels, visits, and intimacy with other women, including a fifty-year-long correspondence, and the models of motherhood that female teachers provided in lieu of academic prowess.[7] Smith-Rosenberg stresses that late nineteenth-century women at formerly coeducational university-level schools took on male-coded attitudes in creating their own world. Yet McClure's contemporaneous but discursively earlier self-identifications do not support that position. McClure's text, like any transcribed historical document, can provide such examples for master narratives of gender only if we ignore why and how it was written.

Unraveling the cultural work that these inscriptions intend to accomplish helps to keep the purposes of such extracurricular writing visible outside many interpretive frameworks that assure its erasure. Home records of education are not simple accounts of acquiring cultural capital in settings where learning was a "form of visible luxury" or "like tea drinking, part of a symbolic culture of regulated luxury," in Michael Warner's analysis of the southern gentry.[8] They display instead processes by which exemplary doctrines and fortunate practices depended on class positions but never limited the implications of those positions to a merely genial surface. Warner does not notice, that is, that schools were common places to form affiliations that maintained acquisitive power relations, as were the practices that recirculated them. Both power and its practices depended on class entitlements, but they were never limited to trivial ceremonies.

"The Whole Universe Is a Social System": Commonplace Educational Principles

"That Machine Which Men Call Society"

As Stephanie Coontz says in her history of the American family, "the family is both a place and an idea" in which we "conceptualize ourselves in relation to the social structure."[9] Although Coontz clearly fixes the social structure above family, its representations in commonplace books powerfully cement otherwise fluid relations connecting relatives, teachers, and schools to an ongoing process of family acquisition. Diverse statements about education place it firmly on local (if not always household) ground. Learning may be remembered as a formative activity undertaken away from home, as in McClure's account, or treated as a topic in discussions of family responsibilities. But in any setting, *education* clearly implies an extension of *relationships*. It is a cultural property on a sliding compass of social bonds, not a specific curriculum or vocational preparation.

This emphasis is clear in the commencement address by Mary Virginia Early (Brown, ?–1864), delivered at the Buckingham Female Collegiate Institute in 1842, which details why females and males should have an equal education and celebrates the accomplishments of her classmates under the idealized tutelage of the institute. Early portrays the continuation of this schooling as both continued self-development and relationships to be appropriated into her family on her return home. Identified at the top of this text as the "Daughter of Bishop Early," Mary Virginia begins with a lengthy statement of her version of social contract theory, emphasizing that in any machine each part must work and be kept in order by its imagined Engineer.

> Our purpose at present is to consider one of the springs of that machine which men call Society, to investigate its design which has been misunderstood & misapplied to so that it does not perform its intended office & to suggest means by which it may be repaired & the whole *machine* thus made to act as it was intended. *Woman* has never since the Fall been allowed to fulfill the destiny for which she was created, although of late Christianity has done much for her, & will ultimately restore her to her first state. She has been in some ages and countries, considered as a mere drudge, & while men have wondered at the deplorable condition of Society, they have not considered that the main spring was out of order.[10]

In examples familiar to any feminist reader, Early catalogues the mistreatment of women common in various countries:

> Various have been the opinions entertained in the minds of men concerning the Destiny of woman, & as various have been the duties she has been called upon to perform. Even now in some pagan countries, she is yoked to the plough & used as a beast of burden, or treated as a slave, denied the duties and privileges of a free and intelligent agent. In Carpagia her beauty transforms her from a slave to a toy, & she is treated with more care and tenderness. In *China*, her diminutive features are admired, but in neither of these contries is she taught (nor is it probably *believed*) that she is possessed of a mind capable of availing herself of the improvements and advantages of the 19th Century. Even the mention of her participating in the pleasures to be derived from Science and Literature causes her "*Lords*" to smile with incredulity and comtempt. In *Hindustan,* she is held in so little estimation that she is sacrificed on the funeral pile of her husbands or friends.
>
> But the progress of Civilization has developed the truth that *woman is possessed of mind,* & although the question is still agitated whether she is equal in mental ability to man, yet it is generally conceded that she is in some respects even *superior,* & that it never was intended that she should be degraded to the rank of a mere drudge & made to perform the tyranical exactions of the other sex, while man is revelling in dreams of imagined superiority, & indulging the reflection that—woman was made to be subordinate to him & fitted only for a servant's office. 'Tis not her destiny to be adorned as a doll, treated as a Toy, or to be the companion of a facetious coxcomb. *Woman* little understands her *own* des-

tiny, if she is content with such a place. Nor is it intended that she should nerve herself to march with heroic courage to the field of battle, or to face with un-blanched cheek the Cannon's roar, to scale with a Hannibal or a Bonaparte, the heights of mountains; to deluge with the blood of the enemy the retired and peaceful valley—nor was it intended that every woman should be a Cleopatra, . . . or a Joan of Arc. She would not usurp the province of the *"Lords of Creation"*! But she has a noble *destiny*, than which none can be nobler.

In Early's case, of course, this destiny is the benefits of her education at the institute. Early pleads for educational equality for women by flattering her country's *prosperity*, the central persuasive *topos* of the speech:

> For instructing her, schools must be provided, teachers furnished, & when the Community is brought to acknowledge her *influence*, & her importance in the scale of Being. Academies, Colleges, and Schools of every kind, & of sufficient number will be created. *It is an admitted principle that the state of Female Education in a country, is a sure criterion by which the prosperity of the country may be determined.* In no country, not even in Albion's Loastring Isle are the rights of Woman so strictly regarded as in *Columbia's Happy Land*—therefore she may be regarded as the most prosperous. (Emphasis added)

But this approach shifts. Early details the value of the school's parental "re-straints" on her, the excellence of her studies (which this well-formed rhetor-ical production is meant to demonstrate), and her classmates' accomplish-ments. She says simply, "The whole universe is a social system" in which family and school interact.

This dominant metaphor includes her classmates as a body, "sisters" she will miss after graduation but see again in heaven. Yet she looks forward to returning to "the family circle, to receive a Mother's tender care, a father's in-structions," which will extend the "sisterly attentions" she received from the academy's female teachers. In this entirely political theory, education, world sociology, and Christian values combine to foster the female's responsibility to blend learning into family relationships:

> Have you been liberally educated? Have you been surrounded not only by com-forts but even by the luxuries of life? Have you been admonished by a tender mother—Have you been blessed with the guardianship of a kind and judicious Father? Have you had the sympathy of dear friends in your petty trials; has your past life been unclouded with care and vexation—then remember that it is your *duty* and *privilege* to permit others to share in your cup of life—remember that you can, by a kind word, a look, or an action . . . wipe the tears from the Father-less and motherless, & render the most miserable and destitute happy in their poverty.

This language unifies family and the school as the place of "adopted Parents." It positions a child to enlarge the family circle by affiliations with strangers, acquired "relations." In this 1842 speech, in language that extends biology into distant settings, family feelings are equivalent to old school ties that bind strangers. Well into the nineteenth century, actual and acquired "families" constitute cultural pedagogies, whole "machines" of indigenous civic centers.

"Every Man Is Born for the Publick": Educational Doctrines

Educational doctrines also appear as the subtext of many conventional treatments of patriarchal duty, a duty frequently equated with ensuring that one's children acquire literacy as a social commodity. The title of Mary McVeigh's essay, "The Advantages of a Good Education," uses the word *advantage* in more than a comparative sense. This contribution to a selection of essays written by pupils at the Alexandria Female Academy in 1853 (discussed in chapter 2) portrays literacy in an adolescent version of the "intensive pious reflection" that Michael Warner reserves for New England sensibilities.[11] McVeigh's 1853 essay begins: "Education does not commence with the school, nor does it terminate with the University."[12] This earnestness persists, as McVeigh fixes the limits of personal property within education, in a turn that cautions against overgeneralizing the commonplace equation between schooling and "character":

> If a person has been well educated, he can place himself in any society whatever. . . . A good education is much more desirable than wealth, for the latter may be taken from us, but if we once possess a good education no one can deprive us of it. What is a more pleasant way to amuse ourselves after our daily labors are over, than to read some useful and interesting book, but if we were without education, we would be deprived of this pleasure; and many there are who are deprived of education, because they have not had the advantages which we possess. (26)

These class advantages are not, however, the metaphysically understood entitlements mentioned by Nick Carraway's father in *The Great Gatsby* when he reminds Nick that not everyone has had them. McVeigh's specifications, like those stated in other educational *doxa,* define profit from both school and self-instruction as a specific sort of responsible socialization:

> A well educated person can make himself agreeable in any situation in which he is placed, and the society of one is much more sought after than that of a person who is possessed of wealth. Wealth may descend to us from others but knowledge must be acquired by ourselves, and although we have to labor hard in order to obtain it, yet in the end we are doubly repaid for our trouble. (26)

These earnest, facile sentiments recirculate the cultural wisdom that equates the endowment of portable educational "wealth" with an explicit, codified family duty. McVeigh here recirculates familiar concepts of domestic responsibility for providing education; her views are both declarations of independence and confessions of avarice in framed moments of a cultural history that stretches our understanding of sentiment itself.

Almost a century earlier, Isaac Hite (1758–1836) and his descendants kept a commonplace book between 1776 and 1859. An entry for 1785 draws systematic principles of civil society close to proper relations between parents and children.[13] Like McVeigh's essay, Hite's record is one of many circulating sources of Mary Virginia Early's encompassing concept of the universe as a specifically social system. Hite's evidently copied statements of "common Rights" foreshadow this premise: *"All Mankind are one great Society* United under one supreme Lord & governed by common Laws" (13, emphasis added). It appears that Hite rigorously applied these laws, for his volume scrupulously notes the amounts he loaned to his children and whether they repaid them. His book documents such exchanges, along with familial principles that set precedents for commonplace language identifying the *advantages* that produced education as wealth to be deployed later.

Hite's rigorously organized document first lists "common Laws," which imply yet another of the ambiguous colonial definitions of privacy: "Every Man is born for the publick, & should neither maim nor distroy himself" (13). These laws, a list of seven that is headed "a few Instances," include injunctions against "monstrous Lusts, procuring Abortion," wastefulness, and keeping a "useful secret" (whose keeper may be compelled to "discover it upon a reasonable Compensation") (13). Next, the document itemizes (tellingly equated) "Economics or domestic Rights of Obligations," drawing a template for the eighteenth-century masculinist individual as a personality whose property and whose desiring "services" are codified marks of a socialized patriarchal identity:

> Such adult Persons as have a sufficient stock both of Wealth to support a Family in their [Comforts?] of Life, & of Prudence to govern it, [are] obliged to marry. . . . [It would] be dishonorable for one without a weighty Cause to decline his share of services requisite for the preservation of the human Race.
>
> The chief Articles of a Marriage Covenant are these; 1. That the Woman be faithful to the Man in [cohabiting] with no other, & that the Man be equally faithful to the Wife—2. The Persons wh. by a Union of Interest & Pursuits so consult the Prosperity of their Family, & *chiefly the Right Education of their children, & Improvement of their Condition, as they have Opportunity.* (14, emphasis added)

In other words, this manifesto for patriarchy says that the always "publick" man must marry, produce children, seek to improve their condition through education, and take every available "advantage," or "Opportunity," consulting family *prosperity* as a guide. These preserved principles, often noted as typical eighteenth-century social theory, were also the foundations for the continuing awareness of educational responsibility among citizens of the new republic, whose progeny, like Mary Virginia Early, continued to identity themselves collectively: "Mankind as a Body."

Women and Youth

The extent of circulated responsibility for educating children is startling. Two later examples codify expectations about gender education by detailing unfamiliar basics of a globally defined "good" education. An "Essay on the Education of Women and on Youth" (1822), unidentified in the Peyton family papers, explains the differences in education given to boys and girls.[14] But it considers this difference functionally, by reasoning that men need a greater variety of expert knowledge, if not more schooling. The essay highlights the purposefully united duties of both sexes, thereby again tying education to relational values, to how society "esteems" both sexes. The essay's commonplace explanation, that is, equates skills and professions as matters of family survival and improvement, not as essentially gendered or institutionally separated spheres.

The essay outlines the scope of comprehensive home education for young men and (separately) for young women, considering wealthy children and those of "the merchant, of the ordinary farmer, of the tradesman, and of many others."

> You ask me whether the education of male, or females should be superior? As I seem not to be able to espouse either side of the question exclusively, consistent with my real sentiments, I will only endeavour to give you my general opinion. I presume it would be by no means objectionable for [~~both sexes~~] either sex, should it be in their power, to attain to the highest pitch of learning known amongst us of the present day; that is, we would not, I suppose, less esteem, either a man or a woman, who was well skilled in all the arts and sciences now in use, as it would only tend to make them more useful, prepare them better to stand up under the adversities of fortune, and more clearly illustrate to them the infinite greatness and goodness of their creator. (5)

These premises are, of course, commonplaces based on deeply held principles about difference. For example, an English publication, *An Address on the Improvement of the Conditions of the Labouring Poor* (1852), argues that "children must be instructed according to their different ranks and the station they will probably fill in the graduated scale of society."[15] But this essay also details the relational values of education. It places individual attainments in categories of use, respect, and differentiated social associations, making a slip of the pen that verifies the endurance of colonial discourses even at midcentury:

> As the end of all education is to make us more useful, and more respectable, and the better fit us for the sphere of life in which we may probably move, and as there are many different conditions in life, we must take into consideration many different characters; first let us consider the son and the daughter of a wealthy gentleman, who can *afford* giving his children a liberal education. As this young man will be expected to associate with the first men of his country, and as there are no impediments in the way, he should certainly be instructed in all the elegant and useful acquirements which are customary in his country: and as the space of time in which he might be under his fathers direction would be entirely too short for the obtaining of such acquirements, I should consider him in duty bound as a man and as a [subject] citizen, to devote to them throughout his life what time he could spare from more pressing business; and not do as the youths of the present day, who make their own selfish interest, and the amassing of gold for themselves and their posterity, the summit of their ambition; or else spend in rioting and [drunkenness?] the fruits of their fathers labours. (5–6)

Like many letters from fathers that convey frustration to absent sons, the essay thematizes the responsible maintenance of family status through education, just as Mary Virginia Early did differently in addressing females.[16] The essayist's appalling matter-of-factness about the occupations of women from age five until death prescribes an even-spirited (and unfortunately realistic) allotment of time to useful activities:

> With regard to the young lady we must first take in view the time which she can with propriety devote to such occupations, and thus determine the extent to which she should aim. Every young lady in this country, (at least as far as I have been able to observe) from the time she is five years old to the day of her death, or at least as long as a capacitated nature will allow, [?] spend a certain portion of her time every day at her needle, or other domestick employments: and after marriage, (should she arrive at that state of bliss) her time is almost exclusively occupied with her household affairs and with concern about her family: it is therefore out of her power, *entirely,* to make those attainments, in the acquirement of which, few have succeeded, and many have devoted a laborious life. Since then she can with reason only aim at a part, this part should certainly be such as are more immediately necessary both for ornament and use. (6–7)

One assumes that the pointedly named *power* that young ladies and blissfully occupied wives are "out of" is to enjoy relaxed study of the classics, often also assumed to be the pastime of educated males. But the essay disabuses the reader of both assumptions by detailing the equally practical ideal male curriculum from which women are excluded:

> The military tackticks, therefore, mechanicks, navigation, surveying, surgery, anatomy, law, oratory, and many others would be entirely out of the question [for women], whereas the youth, above mentioned should aspire to at least the *greater* part of these. With the same ratio, if similarly situated, should I be inclined to consider the children of the merchant, of the ordinary farmer, of the tradesman, and of many others. (7)

The experience that this essay addresses in the content of its demanding curriculum for children of a Virginia planter is entirely situated in that agrarian system. Under a father's direction, children of both sexes need to be fitted for multiple and blended "spheres of life" in which further self-education is a duty. This language endows learning with simultaneously practical and socially resonant connotations that were later separated into gender-coded, public versus private, educational programs.

The essayist's view of women's separate needs can obscure how curricula relied on and fostered *functional* learning for both sexes. What was "immediately necessary" for young women was equivalent to the essay's representation of even the barest scope of study for young men, a "basic" list whose mastery is now unimaginable for either sex: "military tackticks, . . . mechanicks, navigation, surveying, surgery, anatomy, law, oratory, and many others." A male "should aspire to at least the *greater* part of these attainments" if he was to be an educationally "improved" supporter of "his fathers labors." This "~~subject~~/citizen" would indeed need skill in "the greater part" of this list before professionalization regulated these activities as sciences. A young woman's studies were pinioned by the needle she would wield throughout her life. Yet she was not to be deprived of the less physically demanding, spiritually portable classics and the intellectual attainments of "higher" education, at least not on principle. The separate spheres of this discourse thus preserve and improve a *mutual* division of labor within family life. They do not represent Puritan and later ideology about gender, but the needs of an eighteenth-century functional unit.[17]

"Trained as They Ought to Be: Hints to Parents"

Comments on the nature and content of family responsibilities in these texts identify parenting as a means of education, not as affective "child rearing." Many commonplace books express regard for parents, but few state precepts for them to follow as home teachers. One instance, however, was preserved by Blair Bolling, whose brother John was married to Thomas Jefferson's sister and whose uncle Robert's published *Anecdotes* (1769) set a precedent for Bolling's self-conscious authorship. Bolling's commonplace book, a "continuance of the memoir of the Bolling Family," includes pieces on "Female Character" and parental teaching.[18] It preserves the educational capital among his family's attainments. Bolling notes of his uncle Robert (described as "a faultless youth"):

> That nothing might be wanting to render his education complete, [he] was sent to England, and upon his return, studied Law under Mr Waller [described later], and after several love adventures, married Miss Mary, . . . which amiable lady, died at Jordans on the 2d day of May 1764. (5, 8)

But this offhand attitude about the amiable lady's death does not characterize Bolling's staid note on parental responsibility in August 1836. A brief piece on parental teaching, which he evidently composed, imagines the parent's power over children as almost absolute, certainly as an urgent duty:

> The most lasting impressions, either good or bad, in their tendency, are made upon the youthful mind; and demonstrates most forcibly the importance of guarding against the baleful effects of the latter; and clearly points out imperious duty, to inculcate the former, both by presept, and example; that our influence may be advantagiously ex[ecuted?].
>
> The parent or guardian is wofully mistaken if he supposes that he can indulg in evil propencities, and habits, and keep his ward free from them, by telling them not to follow his example.
>
> Human nature is imitative, and more certainly will follow example, than presept; therefore the error of the instructor is twofold, in its conciquences, because it not only exposes himself to the disapprobation of his God and conc[ie]nce but entices the inexperienced into the same predicament.
>
> If therefore you would have the young trained as they ought to be, and what you are (to a certain extent) bound to make him, by all means in your power set him a good example. (11)

This advice fulfills our suspicion that parents at all times have possessed the same book of monologues. It highlights the common wisdom that is circulated as a wise family's possession in many descriptions of educational processes. Writing of this "imperious duty," Bolling incorporates views held by nineteenth-century social authorities who recommended that parents train children in the duty and order necessary for public life "by engineering a 'cheerful subordination in the home.'"[19] But Bolling specifically focuses on the "father's labors" as educational patrimony, not on the mothering sensitivity that, as Mintz and other family historians claim, was relegated to the realm of female domesticity.

Immediately under this passage, Bolling records another bit of advice: "Hint to Parents." It cautions restraint about punishing children "lest they excite in their sencitive bosoms the feelings of disgust, by the betrayal of anger" (12). To forestall this excitation and instead "make a lasting and salutary impression," he prescribes a three-step method of speaking to children, which returns to the omnipresent relation between family and a wider society that is emphasized in all educational records:

> I would therefore earnestly recommend to Parents first to pronounce Filial instructions mildly and affectionately, and should that, not have the desired effect, then use firm and commanding language, should that fail also, then resort to punishment, to an extent only as is requisite to enforce implicit obedience, and the Parent who desists his efforts before he has gained his point, does his child a lasting injury—
>
> For those, unacquainted with the wholesom restraints of parental authority in youth, wile in manhood reluctintly yeald to those enforced by the laws of the country in which he lives for the common good of all. (13)

Bolling's compressed exposition presents pedagogy as a matter of persuasion across a spectrum in which a child's changes, "effects," will not depend on content or pedagogical method, but on mildness and affection, firmness and command, or situated punishments. All occur (if the adult is properly "restrained") as precisely the *language* of the parent/teacher. By connecting wholesome parental authority and "the laws of the country" as he closes, Bolling captures the interplay between family and socially contracted regulations. The language of "the fathers" is set in the parallel between relations to one's own children and the mature participants in a larger community.

A Hearth with a View: Learned Fairy Tale and Domestic Case Study

These commonplace doctrines and advice so far tell little of the actual content of home pedagogies and self-teachings, apart from the comprehensive list of domestic professions found in the essay on gendered education and Sextus Barbour's "Directions for Writing" examined in chapter 2. When a curriculum is specified, as in the following narratives, it becomes a textual memory like McClure's, a partner of specific affiliative relationships. Classical, literary, and even the most basic home lessons, at least as portrayed in these accounts, integrate filial attachment into family histories. These stories are instructive in two ways. They obviously provide rare details about the content and conduct of specific lessons. But primarily they preserve exemplary interactions. Idealized family relationships are a matter of highly textured home teaching in which subjectivities are formed in moments of persuasive statement. Verbal examples, what relatives *say,* are in fact what children learn.

Littleton Waller Tazewell, governor of Virginia, equated his late eighteenth-century education with his devotion to his maternal grandfather, Benjamin Waller (1714–1786), who raised him. (Waller was also Robert Bolling's mentor.) Tazewell describes Waller's education, and his own, at the hands of an extended family that over two generations followed the custom (mentioned earlier) of "putting out" children to surrogate parents. Jonathan Goldberg suggests that this practice "virtually operate[d] to redraw class lines," insofar as it treated children as commodities and increased the family's wealth.[20] In each case, the effect was to extend the opportunities of two generations of the Waller family.

At about the age of ten, Benjamin Waller (1714–1786) was taken from his family by a surrogate father, although his parents were not eager to part with him.[21] Tazewell tells how Waller, son of a "plain planter" who claimed the poet Edmund Waller as an ancestor, became the charge of John Carter, "then Secretary of the Colony." His account recasts this sudden intervention as a patriarchal fairy tale of opportunity, the result of Carter's perception of the promise and destiny of a special child. (This motif is repeated when the adult Waller, in turn, replaces Tazewell's father after his mother's death and displays him to his friend George Wythe, who becomes Tazewell's teacher.) In Tazewell's account of his grandfather's memories, a real chariot carries the young Waller away in a well-detailed narrative of transformation:

> When my grandfather was about ten years of age, John Carter Esq, the then Secretary of the Colony, a man of immense wealth, and whose office placed him in a situation inferior to none in the Colony, save only that of the Royal Governor himself, was occasionally detained at the house of old Mr Waller, by some difficulty he experienced in crossing the Mattapony river while making a journey from Williamsburg to his seat at [his plantation] Currito[wian] in the Northern neck.
>
> In the course of the evening my grandfather came in from school, and the Secretary either to amuse himself, or to please his host calling the little boy to him, began to question him and examine him upon the subject of his school studies. Struck with the quickness and correctness of the boy's replies and supposing that he had found a boy of uncommon parts, which would not probably be developed in his situation, for want of a proper education, the Secretary observed to old Mr Waller that he must give him that boy and he would make a man of him.

To this the old man assented very readily supposing however that the secretary was not in earnest. Mr. Carter therefore stated that he would return that way on a certain day and expressed a wish that the boy might be in readiness to accompany him on his return to Williamsburg. On the very day appointed the Secretary punctual to his promise, again came to Mr Wallers, he never having believed the Secretary to be serious and not supposing, therefore, that he ever would be called upon to comply with his promises, had done nothing toward getting his son ready to leave home, during the Secretary's absence, and so stated. Mr Carter was vexed at this and insisted upon taking my Grandfather with him as he was, this being at last consented to by his parents.

He was placed in the Secretary's chariot and carried by him to Williamsburg. Upon his arrival in Williamsburg, he was immediately placed by the Secretary in William and Mary College, where he remained a student for several years, during which he completed his college education, when he was between sixteen and seventeen years of age. (5–8)

Despite its seamless narrative shape, this story has obvious gaps that show how a cult of authenticity might prevent some factual stories from being told at all. We wonder why Waller's father never supposed Carter to have serious intentions in offering to educate the youth, how "vexed" Carter was, and how much resistance was contained in the consent given "at last." Even if one accepts that the elder Waller and his wife were only politely reluctant to "impose" on Carter, since they could in no way repay him, we wonder particularly about the accommodations for ten-year-old Benjamin at the College of William and Mary. The fairy tale works in this recorded inheritance, the only commonplace idiom that could credibly record it.

Nonetheless, Tazewell assures posterity that Waller's education included the verifying detail of studying "in the Secretary's office under the direction of a Mr Kempe, the clerk of the general Court" (9). When Waller was twenty, Carter also obtained permission from the widow of Sir John Randolph (a former attorney general) for Waller to use "her disceased husband's excellent law library . . . which he prosecuted indefatigably at every leisure moment when the business of the Secretary did not require his attention" (10). Tazewell comments that this education included honing the excellence of Waller's legal writing:

> The reputation of my grandfather as a lawyer was as high as any lawyer in Virginia of his day. He was called upon for more opinions than any other either before or since his time, and his opinions were always considered conclusive by all who saw them. I have seen many of them since I came to the bar. They were remarkable for their clearness and brevity, and all I ever saw, I thought unquestionably correct. (19)

Benjamin Waller prospered. In 1782, he emulated Carter by taking the young Tazewell from his widowed father and keeping him until his death at the age of seventy in 1786. While Tazewell visited his father every Sunday during these years, his affections and remembered education attached him entirely to his grandfather, who manifested a persistent will to "improve" him:

> My education had not been neglected before this, for I had been very regularly taught by my grandfather, than whom there was none better qualified to improve me, and my uncle Robert, who wrote a most excellent hand [and] taught me to write. In the year 1783 some private business calling Mr Brack[en?] to England [his teacher] he broke up his school, and I was again happily dependent upon my grandfather alone for my instruction. His mode of education was most excellent. (29)

As in many accounts of literacy education, *writing* here refers to handwriting, not composing discourse. Tazewell details how his grandfather's methods rely largely on recitation, casting his reading lessons as exercises and rigorous testing made pleasant by his grandfather's attention:

> Besides my customary lessons which I was made to recite to him twice a day, if any circumstances during our recitations or in the course of our convirsations together (for we were very seldom separated) upon which he could lay the foundation of any anecdote or story calculated to arouse my curiosity, as soon as he had excited my interest and attention to a high pitch, he affected to have forgotten some circumstance connected with his narrative, and I was sent to the study for some book to assist his memory, from this book I was made to read to him the whole account, in which he never failed to find numerous new stor[ies] to whet my curiosity and to produce an ardent desire to gratify it by continuing the reading of the book we had begun or something of alike kind. By such means I was induced to read with great attention the whole of the Bible, Plutarch's Lives, many treatises on Heathen Mythology, and large portions from the Greek and Roman Histories, as well as from the History of England, and many of the English poets, before I was twelve years old. These occupations gave no interruption to our regular studies which went on unceasingly, so that by the year 1784 I was well grounded in Latin, Syntax, had gone through the Colloquies of Corde[n]y and the dialogues of Erasmas, and could write a fair hand and understood sufficiently well the first rules of arithmetic. (30–32)

Home evaluations repeated, expanded, and validated school examinations within the simultaneously pedagogic and social community of men that Tazewell was being prepared to enter:

> Some months after this returning from school one evening to my grandfather, I found him sitting with Mr Wythe. They had been very intimate in their early

days, and altho my grandfather never went out then and Mr Wythe very rarely, yet he made it a point to see my grandfather once or twice a year, and to spend an afternoon with him, when I came in, Mr Wythe immediately recognised me and seeing my grandfather caress me, as he did he repeated to him with high eulogies the occurences of my examinations. Pleased to hear this account (which I had before told him) from Mr Wythe himself, my grandfather requested him to examine me again, and he did so. I was then studying Ceasor's Commentaries, and Mr Wythe taking the book from me, made me recite several passages and to accompany my recitations with an account of the circumstances introductory to the passages read. To these my grandfather added many questions relating to this portion of Roman History and to the ancient geography of the Roman Empire at that time. I answered all the questions and performed all that was required of me so intirely to Mr Wythes satisfaction that he observed to my grandfather with an appearance of great earnestness—

"Mr Waller this is a very clever boy, and when he has advanced a little further you must let me have him." To this my grandfather replyed with much feeling, "George" (for by this familiar appellation he always spoke to Mr Wythe) "this boy is the sole companion and the principal comfort of my old age, I feel that I cannot part with him while I live, but when I die if you will take him under your charge, I shall consider it the greatest and highest favor you can confer on each of us" Mr Wythe thereupon promptly answered, that he would do so, and the conversation of the old gentlemen was turned to other subjects. (33–34)

Clearly, the emphasis on memorization, like the value placed on memory by such detailed memoirs as Tazewell's, both signify how intimate relationships and retained information are mutual educational paths of acquisition. But as in the case of Carter's appropriation of Waller, displaying a child to an appreciative observer also implies that the child can be disposed of as property. (This may be why all children resist such occasions.) Tazewell's narrative of filial connection, friendship, and home displays of academic progress captures basic assumptions about socially superior educational endowments and appropriately "improving" curricula among upper-class families. Equally important, the texture of this memoir is woven from particular *discourses,* stories Tazewell remembers about youth. The classical languages and literature, arithmetic, and handwriting exercises that constituted his formal curriculum were ways of thinking that he also learned as authority, friendship, terms of address, and affection in a human curriculum of "memorized" relationships.

Tazewell's residence with Waller was interrupted when he broke his leg in 1785 on a Sunday visit to his father, causing a separation from his mentor more painful than the injury. But on their reunion, his lessons intensified:

I had no use of my left arm and lest I should sustain further injury in my situation from the heedless wildness of my numerous schoolfellows I was kept from school for sometime after I returned to my grandfather's house. My education was not neglected, however, during this interval my grandfather again took me under his care and instruction, and attended to me so well that when I again returned to school I found myself much in advance of my class. To my knowledge of the Greek and Latin languages I had added during my absence from school, some acquaintance with the French, which my grandfather perfectly understood. At this critical period of my life just as I had begun Cicero and Virgil in the Latin, and Homer and Xenophon in the Greek, I sustained the heaviest misfortune I had ever felt in the loss of my much revered grandfather, who died in May 1786 in His seventieth year. The shock I experienced in this calamity beat me to the earth, and I felt that I could never rise again. (35–38)

Setting aside for now this document's obvious interest as information about constructions of gender and male affiliations in the early republic, it is apparent that Tazewell's life between the age of twelve and seventeen encompassed what we now cast as formal education, here written as his family legacy of acquired social position and a genealogy that verified his credentials for public service. This textual inheritance displays family stories that are portrayed as identical to pedagogical practice, as they were in Socratic fatherly moments. Tazewell's frustraton that his grandfather died just when he was beginning to read Homer, like his earlier pride in performing for George Wythe under Waller's eye, exemplifies how family history is a domain of substantive learning. Tazewell's grandfather supervised home lessons that monitored not just his progress at school but schooling itself. This story of bonding across generations consequently reveals less about Tazewell's academic precociousness than about why the propertied classes were slow to support the less rigorous common schools—which were, by definition, never intended to enable their pupils to acquire radically improved social status. But this memoir of two generations of home studies reveals not only the disinterested leveling instituted by official instruction. In Tazewell's memoir, family-controlled advantages and opportunity are identical to nurturance, civic involvement, acquired prestige, and social relations among peers.

Neither copied doctrines nor family stories like these are written exclusively on lines of male inheritance. But the preponderance of male doctrinaire discourse and accounts of lessons for sons in these commonplace books suggests that, as inherited capital, they deserve detailed attention as a primary site for the transmission of patriarchal entitlements. Unlike later "domesticated," fully privatized households, these homes placed the responsibility for such transmission on fatherly supervision. (See chapter 6.)

The one detailed account of home lessons for a young girl, by Rachel Mordecai (1789–1838), balances on a fulcrum of social forces that are studiously effaced within the text. Rachel's account of teaching her half sister, Eliza (1809–1861), is beholden to the religious but not social separation created by her Judaism. We do not see Rachel's dissatisfaction and later attempt to leave her faith, the power exercised to prevent this by her husband and father, the ungendered regard for study and learning in this family and other Jewish families in the community, the frequent necessity for children of a dead mother to help a stepmother raise their siblings, or often unremarked relocations in the face of financial crisis. This last, a common occurrence, motivated Jacob Mordecai to move his family to Warrenton, North Carolina, where he opened the most rigorous school for young women in the South at this time. But Rachel never directly mentions these forces in her annual log of Eliza's progress from age six until she was eleven. Nonetheless, all of these social texts may unevenly contribute to Rachel's desire to record Eliza's progress as a tentative professional case study. They certainly inform its sanctioned focus on Eliza's "character."[22]

As an unmarried daughter and an educated woman, Rachel was well suited to oversee her half sister's education. Rachel corresponded with English novelist Maria Edgeworth for twenty-three years, and was, as Sheldon Hanft claims in his history of the Mordecai academy, the original for Edgeworth's protagonist in *Harrington*.[23] She helped to establish and taught in her father's school for girls in Warrenton, "the first successful school for women in the South which attempted to provide women with a solid academic education comparable to that given to men."[24] Rachel at twenty-seven took it upon herself systematically to tutor, nurture, and "improve" six-year-old Eliza, who occasionally also attended school classes. But Rachel's project is not surrogate mothering. Her journal portrays a relationship between a distanced teacher and a student, observer and experiment. Like a contemporary case study, it both tells a story in rhetorically selected details and persistently avoids or transforms suggestions of a psychological, "inner" dimension in the interactions between observer and subject. Its copious data about both the content and methods that are "applied" to Eliza offer unusual referents for current opinion about female education. It certainly reverses gender expectations that might assign female history to a realm of fairy-tale narratives like Tazewell's.

Rachel remarks early in her log that she integrated lessons into Eliza's daily activities, thereby bringing household routines into her framed narrative. Her language suggests the influence of European pedagogical ideas, particularly those of the Swiss writer, Johann Heinrich Pestalozzi (1745–1827). Pestalozzi, who observed peasant women teaching their children, viewed these interactions as emphatically *home* models, but they were later taken up by organized schools.[25] Rachel was evidently more comfortable than Pestalozzi about combining home and "public" settings for lessons. Her account clearly forecasts mass pedagogical systems that incorporated a child's immediate experiences into social, cognitive, and spiritual development.

In his account of Victorian families, Mintz argues that this educational aim derived from a nineteenth-century need to instill "a capacity for self-government within individuals . . . by internalizing norms of duty and responsibility."[26] Perhaps such internalized norms stimulated Eliza's fatal devotion as a nurse during the Civil War, which was cited as the cause of her death.[27] Rachel employed theories also prominent among influential Anglo-American educators,[28] as exemplified in the connections she makes among tasks, occupation, employment, and a marked reference to rewards:

> Eliza has never been taught any thing in play, neither have her studies ever been made tasks, tho forming regularly a part of each days occupation. To learn something new has been most of the "reward" for becoming perfect in any little study in which she might be engaged. To this arrangement may probably be attributed her being attached to all her employments. (4)

Nonetheless, it is Eliza's "attachments," not internalized self-discipline, that Rachel's pre-Pestalozzian pedagogy self-consciously counts as progress in both Eliza's development and her own. She writes this narrative, she says, for her "later gratification," setting this text in a specific genre, as Tazewell did in identifying his account as a memoir. But her different "nursery anecdote" adds discursive distance between the sisters, bracketing them as pupil and teacher. She persistently refers to herself as "R.," to "her sister" and "Eliza," rather than using pronouns, so that the account simultaneously displays filial attachment and imitates formalized pedagogy. Successes and failures for both pupil and teacher emphasize a didactic, not personal, narrative:

> It has long been my intention to commence writing juvenile, I should rather term them, "nursery anecdotes," of my little Eliza. Since three years of age, this child has been a constant source of delight to her whole family. Her earliest observations, fall of mind, and goodness, seemed worthy of memorial; but procrastination, alike the thief of time, and its events, has robbed me of all but a confused recollection of them. I will not however occasion myself future reproach by longer deferring, what in future years, should they be granted me, will be a source of gratification. (1)

But Rachel's pedagogical purposes go beyond mere "gratification" at producing a detailed record for future reference. Her quasi-experiment in applying formulaic pedagogic principles to Eliza has the age's parental purpose, making her *useful* through correction and lessons. Rachel persistently keeps a discursive distance, as in the following metaphorical transformation of Eliza into a flower referred to as "it":

> Should it seem good to the most High to suffer it [the "flower" of Eliza], and me, to continue on this great theatre of existence, I will watch over, and mark its daily progress, I will endeavour to destroy each canker that would enter its bosom to render it less sweet and lovely, and O! may I be rendered capable of forming the materials which nature has bountifully placed in my hands, may reason, combined with virtue, and nourished by education, form a character eminently fitted to discharge every duty of this life, and when called from this transitory state of being, worthy to open eternally in the presence of its Creator. (2)

After a double line in the center of this page, Rachel begins the entry for May 19, 1816, with a story of Eliza's generosity at age six with regard to a gift of the first strawberries of the season, "so few that no one would eat them." Eliza, inadvertently deprived of her share of this feast, learns an early lesson from Rachel about the rewards of her goodness:

> Just then the servant re-entered with half the strawberries saying that C. insisted upon R's taking them. R, ate a few, then called Eliza and gave her the rest, saying, "I give you these, my dear, with pleasure, because you were not discontented when you were deprived of them, you see goodness is always rewarded."
> E. No sister R[,] not always[,] you know.
> R: Not always in this way my dear, but always by the pleasure of feeling that it has done right.
> E: O yes, sister R. it always has that reward. Sister R if you please to eat some more of these strawberries. (3)

Later, when teaching the word *catalogue* by having Eliza list her favorite pleasures, Rachel rations her praise with a mind to its possible effect on Eliza's character, despite her conviction at this time of the child's precociousness. Eliza says, "'Oh! I like being a good girl' the best." Rachel notes her restrained response: "Her sister did not wish her to think that she had said any thing extraordinary. She therefore did not praise her, but merely said, 'I thought my dear that would be your choice'" (5).

Rachel's record of Eliza's education does not always provide such dialogic detail, but it does proceed systematically, logging year by year the content, "improvement," and methods she hopes for and, by and large, approves. Her chart of Eliza's and her own progress shows how inseparable that life ideal is from *written* progress.

On the 17th of August [1816] she was seven years old, and I am well pleased to reflect on the improvement she has made during the past twelve month. I must again regret that this record was not begun sooner, I might then have precisely ascertained what her progress has been. I will mark what is her present state of improvement with respect to her different occupations, that I may be better prepared for a similar examination, should we both be allowed life & health through another revolving year. (15)

These different occupations by the end of Eliza's sixth year included reading, "writing [making letters] without difficulty," writing "a very good large hand," and knowing "several pages of [French] nouns, which she pronounces & translates." In addition, Eliza had studied arithmetic ("knows the multiplication table well"), had begun geography ("commenced in June") so that she "knows the first principles, can find the latitude & longitude of places, & knows the boundaries, & chief cities & rivers in Europe, these she has learned entirely from the map." She had, like John Purdie (chapter 2) learned grammar, "by verbal instruction": "In Grammar, she understands the principles well, can tell with readiness any of the declinable parts of speech, comprehends the moods & tenses, & conjugates with facility, verbs either regular or irregular" (16). Music and the omnipresent needlework, which Eliza never really accepted as her lot, were her gendered studies. Rachel names fourteen ballads, waltzes, minuets, songs, marches, and sonatas that Eliza plays at this time and notes how writing and sewing become joined modes of fostering precision: "She sews plain work tolerably well, and has marked the large & small alphabet on a sampler" (17).

Given this base line, Rachel sporadically but carefully records Eliza's growth in dramatic episodes, noting both additional academic progress and achievements in developing named mental faculties and ethical powers. In her eighth and ninth years, Eliza demonstrated an understanding of ratios and proportions, began dancing lessons, and developed a sense of innate inclinations. Rachel worries, however, about what she calls "recollective memory":

Eliza's memory is very good as to retaining, but she has often shown herself deficient in that useful talent styled "recollective memory". When circumstances were recalled to her mind she knew them well but when it depended upon herself to think of something at a particular time, it was generally forgotten or neglected. Her sister, desirous to conquer this defect resolved to give her motives for recollecting which might occasionally rouse her dormant powers. R. happened to be reading the life of Peter the Great, & was one afternoon speaking to her brother [Thomas] of his uncommon character, & singular marriage. Eliza became interested, and begged to be told something about Peter the Great. "If you will remind me of it tonight, just before you go to bed, I will tell you what you want to know". Eliza ate her supper, talked & played: bed time came—Peter was not thought of—. Her sister [Rachel] went into the room where she was undressing, thinking thus to remind her of him, but recollection did not come. (37)

Later in Eliza's ninth year (February 9, 1817), Rachel began to note other "sources of uneasiness." She reports them in a developmental discourse that emphasizes, like European pedagogies of the time, the benefits of physical activity:

It is said that after 7 the age of infancy ceases, and the character & propensities of children begin gradually to unfold themselves. It is this reflection that has increased my anxiety, on viewing the errors which in the last few months have shown themselves. May Heaven grant to this beloved child a continuance of those amiable dispositions, which blessed her infancy, and promised so fair a progression.—

Eliza has never been an active child, but what used to seem steadiness, now seems to show a want of animation. When her sisters go to walk, she begs to stay behind, and if not permitted to do so, walks slowly at their side. In order to induce her to run & play in the open air, one or two of her little companions generally accompanied her, but even then, tho' she would run with them when bid to do so, it was evident that she obeyed rather from duty than inclination. Looking mean time pale, and thin, and frequently complaining, her sister thought it would be good exercise, to jump the rope for some time, regularly every day. In a few minutes she would complain of being tired, & her sister [Rachel], determined to give her a certain number of times to jump, hoping both to give her an idea of regularity, and to oblige her by indirect means, to take more exercise. She had learned to jump with some degree of ease & dexterity, so that she could accomplish her 600 turns of the rope in about a quarter of an hour. One morning her sister was above stairs when she heard Eliza counting & jumping in the passage below. "Forty nine, *fifty, sixty* one." (44)

Despite her sister's worries, Eliza showed an uncommon awareness of the eighteenth-century sublime and outstanding mastery of advanced categories of grammar. Eliza's grammatical analyses reveal how reading lessons were then conducted by recitation and grammatical parsing, not in ways intended to instill the values of a canon:

July 20th   Eliza was admiring the appearance of the clouds at sunset after a shower she said, "Sister R: I was walking in the garden the other evening and when I looked at the clouds I felt afraid, they looked so beautiful"—Was this or was it not, a first impression of sublimity? I should incline to answer in the affirmative.—

21st   In saying her parsing lesson, she met with the line "Whose days are dwindled" etc. & remarked, "are dwindled cannot be a *passive* verb for it never could have been *active*, O, I see! it is a neuter verb with just the passive form". I was pleased with the observation as it had escaped my notice & showed attention, & that she perfectly understood the *nature* of the three kinds of verb. In the next line "and Heaven will bless etc." she said "Heaven *is* a proper substantive, and yet we say *Heavens*, & that is not an *individual*, but stop, don't tell me, I know now—When we say *The Heavens*, we mean the same as the sky, or the clouds, but when we say *Heaven*, we mean that particular place." (45)

Rachel follows this evidence of sophistication with a comment linking Eliza's learning to her teaching. The didactic domestic space blends discursive positions that are a template for later institutional manifestations of a displaced student/teacher couple:

Those who feel interested in the education of children, may often receive from those children useful hints on the subject, & be taught the best means of correcting errors & of training both the mind & the morals. I have before mentioned Eliza's wish to attend in the school room. Tho' I could not consent to indulge her entirely, I have done so, so far, as allowing her to work in the afternoon with the other children & she is employed on a sampler . . . with another little girl. . . . When Eliza began she was so awkward & progressed so slowly that I more than once said to her, "Eliza I am afraid I shall be obliged to let you have off working on your sampler until you grow larger & handle your needle better". At last one day when we were alone she said; "Sister R if you would only *think* I could go on with my sampler, I *know* I could do it better, but when you say, I shall have to let it alone, it *discourages* me, & I cannot try so well". R. "If that is that case my dear, I will *think* that you can do it as well as any body, & I hope you will *convince* me I am not mistaken". I did not "discourage" E. any more and she immediately began to improve. (45)

Rachel makes careful note of Eliza's moral progress as well. In competition with another needleworker, Eliza confessed that she envied the praise accorded her, thereby occasioning Rachel's correction, praise for her candor, and a view of how reading includes moral development:

R. "You are right my dear to be so candid, & I love you for it; besides when you tell me truly what you feel, I can tell you better how to correct your faults. You recollect the story of "Envy & Emulation" in Evenings at Home, which I read to you some time ago, I wish you now to read it to yourself, and remember my dear, that *Envy* or the sorrow we feel at another's pleasure or praise, is not amiable & will make us very uncomfortable & unhappy—so we must try as much as we can to check it." E. "But I don't know how I *can* check it sister R." —R. "The best way I believe my dear, is, to keep in our mind that it is *wrong*, & when we feel it coming on, try to see for *ourselves* the good things for which any one is praised, and to endeavour to praise them too; after *trying* once or twice the task will become easier. (46)

Eliza further develops the attribute of kindness, again reinforced by an earlier reading lesson that merged nature with Rachel's nurture:

> August 8th—Eliza was repeating a poem in which a little worm complains of those, who among other cruelties practiced on his species, use them as baits for fish. E: "Fishing must be a very cruel amusement, you know it is cruel because it hurts the fish, & the worms too, that are used to catch them." This remark introduced a conversation of some length on the propriety of man's destroying animals for his own security and use. E recollected one of her sister's [Rachel] having told her, at the time she cried about the pigeon's being killed a story (contained in one of Goldsmith's Essays) of the situation in which the world would probably be if all animals were suffered to live. At last recurring to the first subject which her sister had forgotten, "think, said she, how far the poor little worm has led us!" (46)

As Eliza's tenth year begins (August 9, 1818), Rachel comments that her sister's "improvements have in most aspects equalled [her] wishes." Eliza evidently cooperated with Rachel's desire to harvest her progress in regular records by delivering a review of her daily conduct that also aided both her wayward "recollective memory" and reinforced a self-conscious habit of conscience. Here again, Rachel evaluates Eliza's demeanor in relationships, not her mastery of information. She emphasizes positive qualities in Eliza's character but notes bothersome personal habits that affected her mastery of formal lessons and her social acceptability:

> Not once in the whole year has an instance of the want of candour occurred, indeed in the account which she gives me every evening of her conduct through the day I not unfrequently find her "of herself a judge severe". She is much less heedless than she was some months since, and exerts herself to remember what she is told or requested to do. She is too averse to early rising, too apt to be dilatory in dressing, has a habit of laughing frequently which sometimes makes her silly, is acquiring a *stoop* of which I must endeavor to break her—and, here I believe ends the catalogue. (47)

On August 8, 1818, Rachel reviews the categories of study—grammar, arithmetic, language, dancing, and needlework—that she had demarcated three years earlier when Eliza turned seven. At this juncture, a better fit emerges between Eliza's learning and our expectations of children of her age. (Rachel did not number pages in later years, so quotations are dated.)

Of Grammar she has a remarkably correct idea for a child of her age has reviewed the small grammar several times & will begin to study the notes in the larger grammar (Murray's) this week. She parses very well and can generally supply with little difficulty any ellipses that may occur in parsing sentences in poetry.

In Geography, to which she is seldom otherwise than attentive, she has a good knowledge of the maps of all the countries in Europe, Asia, & Africa, & has studied the general maps of S.& N. America, with part of the United States with which she is now occupied. In the maps of the separate states commencing north, she has proceeded as far as Virginia.

Arithmetick, she is now reviewing, having proceeded as far as the rule of three. She prefers the compound rules to the simple ones, finding them equally easy & more amusing. She does but few sums, sometimes (if difficult) not more than one a day, but she is not allowed to proceed one step without understanding *why;* nor indeed does she ever wish it.

In [hand]writing her progress has been tolerable.

In French her sister is well pleased with her late attention & improvement. She reads it tolerably well & begins to translate a little.

Musick not entirely equal to what the last year promised. She is apt to forget former lessons and does not always play with animation or correctness.

Of work as I have before remarked, she is not sufficiently fond. She is now much pleased with her sampler, and will I trust, by degrees acquire the knowledge requisite of useful plain work, about which when I have more time to devote to her, I shall be more particular. Dancing she has been learning this year, but tho' she is very fond of it, she must be acknowledged to show more of agility than of grace.

Rachel annotates a list of the books Eliza had read during this year, with evaluations, the appropriate moral stake in her sister's maturing reading:

"Pictures of English & Grecian History" (merely read once) . . . Robinson Crusoe . . . "Rural Walks" (Charlotte Smith) not much liked, observations about it just & correct; Moral Tales (Edgeworth) in part, some not understood.[29] Admired the "Elegy in a Country Church yard," but could not understand it all . . . "William Tell" translated from the french of [?],[30] admired exceedingly . . . "Anecdotes of the Horse", a great favourite—"Adventures of a Donkey", not liked because not written naturally—opinion very correct. "Abridgement of Gulliver."

In October, Rachel's comments briefly turn to her sense of herself. Eliza's continuing development of concern for others is an explicit part of Rachel's curriculum, and her motives for this teaching are acknowledged as her own antipathy to falsity and distance.

The feelings that induce affectionate manners should be the spontaneous impulse of the heart; wherever they appear, they should be cherished and cultivated, but they should not be planted, & forced to grow, lest they degenerate into affected sensibility, perhaps into deceit. Eliza said that she had thought every day of asking brother T. how he felt, but that she heard every body else ask him so many questions about it, that she did not think it was worth while for her to. She was reminded that if she had felt as much interest as others she would not have waited till they had all made their enquiries, & that there were besides many little services that even a little girl like her might render to a sick person if she wished & sought occasion to do so. No more said on the subject. Eliza was much affected & shed tears on bidding her brother farewell—I remark this because I so much dread a coldness of character that it is a comfort to me to remark every gleam of amiable & natural feeling.

Rachel here also reveals that she is conducting this home teaching while aware of alternative public schools, perhaps like the Infant Schools for the poor that were popular in England after 1816 and were briefly a project of elite reformers in the Boston area in the 1830s.[31] The record tacitly acknowledges a concern about the advantages of collaborative over private learning:

It has been justly observed in favour of publick education that it affords the stimulant of emulation, which when properly regulated, accelerates the attainment of knowledge inspiring an eagerness to excel which almost involuntarily surmounts obstacles, scarcely taking time to reflect that they exist. This is an advantage of which the private pupil and domestick instructor experience the want. Without some frequently renewed stimulus to exertion, the human mind whether juvenile or adult becomes at times sensible of fatigue; is inert, & listless.

Continuing this new reference to educational discourses, Rachel tells how she has attempted to overcome listlessness in Eliza by adopting a method of behavior modification from a fellow teacher, a "friend . . . who is much interested in the success of a charity school." When she hears of a system of rewarding school children with tickets for good conduct, she proposes to try the practice:

Fully sensible that to combine pleasure with improvement is a great point gained in the arduous progress of regular daily instruction, I have always sought for rewards which might give a zest to the words of praise for successful application. [In the charity school] tickets for good behaviour, attention etc. were given to the children, that *seven* tickets entitled them to a *red* one, which procured them a reward of books, or something useful or agreeable. I determined to pursue a similar plan with my little sisters, & made them tickets on which are written, Early rising, study & work, bad habits overcome; etc. etc. they also have tickets on which are written the faults to which they are most liable, as, carelessness, heedlessness etc. & when these penalties are incurred two *good* tickets are to be forfeited. 7 good tickets obtain a red one on which is written—Reward—and the reward is then selected by themselves & if not unreasonable, is readily granted.

Rachel finds that teaching Eliza to appreciate her reward tickets stimulates both progress in lessons and good feelings.

On August 10, which "closed Eliza's eleventh year," Rachel's annual summary of progress remarks on how quickly Eliza is changing. Her comments on reading and "recollective memory" close with an assessment of Eliza's progress in specific subjects and of her mastery of the texts used to teach them:

> English Grammar—Syntax & part of prosody; Ouiseau's french grammar—In this branch I am glad to say she improves—she now reads easy books with pleasure, & translates with little difficulty; History. Snowdin's America. . . . History of Greece & England, a lesson every friday; Geography—reviewing the maps, & reading Guthrie; Arithmetick—reviewed Practice & has been over the preceding rules, as far as Reduction; Parsing in verse promiscuous; Reading lessons, Elegant Extracts, prose & verse; Alternately—a chapter in the Bible every day; Murray's grammatical Exercises; Progress in Musick satisfactory—and to the needle, rather less dislike than heretofore, but still great room for improvement.

A footnote to this passage reads: "With the volume of Exercises I gave Eliza the 'key' with a charge never to open it unless by my direction—Elmona has since asked me if I would not let sister Eliza open that book, that she had asked her just to raise the cover & she would not."

In listing books Eliza has read for the year, Rachel's account reveals more about how the pedagogic subject was embedded in standard, accepted principles of propriety that prevailed in this prominent Jewish family, even though "Christian" values are usually taken to be the exclusive sources of those values. She censors specific chapters of the Bible, probably the more purple Old Testament narratives, by telling her little sister that "tho' the Bible was all excellent, yet owing to the difference of time, and the change of manners since it was written, there were some passages which it was not now, necessary or agreeable to read." Ignoring childhood "reading levels," she lists twenty-seven books, including biographies of Pythagoras, David Rittenhouse, and Baron Frenck, and what appears to be preparation for a woman's future—"Officers Widow," "Merchants Widow," and "Clergymans Widow." The list includes standard fiction, including "parts of Arabian Nights," *Gulliver's Travels*, Percival's tales, "Popular Tales—Miss Edgeworth," "Castle Rackrent—Miss E.," and "Scott's Lay of the Last Mistrel." But, in a process that clearly included memorization, recitation, and some elementary commentary, Eliza also read "2 Vols. Elegant Extracts," "Sketch Book, 6 Numbers,"

"Search after Happiness—H. More," "Lady Montague's letters," "Edinburgh reviews," and "Telemachus." Her reading had a decidedly female, if not entirely feminist, character.

Eliza also attended the theater during this year, seeing "The lady of the Lake," and later hearing "Scott's beautiful poem, . . . tho' not capable of entering into all of its beauties." Rachel comments, "It is only within a few months that she has acquired a relish for poetry except of the simplest kind . . . and now as she becomes more capable of comprehending, she begins to admire it." Eliza was now "highly pleased" with "The Lay of the Last Minstrel," which she could not understand at the beginning of the year.

Rachel broke off her diary in December 1820, before her marriage into the Lazarus family, which is otherwise unremarked here. She describes Eliza's reaction to moving to a new home, with the approval of Rachel's fiancé, "the kind partner of [her] future years," and their "dear parents":

> December 9th—Eliza's 12th year will probably be marked by a considerable change in *her* situation, in consequence of that which is about to take place in her sister's. In deciding on this change, I could not for a moment think of separating myself from this child of my care, at least until her education should be nearer its completion, and her habits of mind more matured. . . . Previous trials having given ample proof of her discretion I did not hesitate to entrust her with the secret, informing her also that when I left home, she would accompany me. She showed such feelings as the intelligence ought to have inspired—blushed & wept. I asked her why? if she was sorry to have a new brother, or if she did not wish to go with me? She replied: "I don't know how I feel sister R. I am glad & sorry—I do want to go with you, but I cannot help crying to think of leaving all at home."

These excerpts greatly abridge Rachel's lovingly detailed account, but like the essay by a concerned teacher described below, this narrative obliquely draws not only on surrounding cultural forces, but on a number of commonly unremarked genres. Rachel's authorial gratification is never referred to as coming from the act of writing itself, which is also merely noted in Eliza's studies, not detailed as are her reading and progress in grammatical and "recollective memory" work. She did not encourage Eliza to write notes, keep a journal herself, or become a polite correspondent, at least not on this evidence. Rachel regretted not having started her account earlier because, we infer, she desired a full record of both Eliza's development and of her own pedagogical failures and successes. But she did not fetishize writing the document, nor its status *as* a text. Nor did her document become a biography that was later justified by Eliza's accomplishments, marked only by later family references to a handwritten translation from the French and her noble service to others before her death.[32]

Despite Eliza's early precociousness, she became only well educated, a family member obviously steeped in standard contemporary curricula. She was apparently not curious beyond its limits, at least not as the child portrayed here. She remained a "complete" moral, social, and "educated" being, but not markedly intellectual. She was, that is, the pointedly socialized subject desired by this educational process. Rachel compares Eliza to her siblings and playmates as their socialized partner, judging her growth within a collective identity, not by individually stunning scholastic achievements.

Consequently, Rachel Mordecai's detailed account highlights differences that are for us so obvious as to be overlooked. Its writing demarcates "pedagogy" as a discourse still within the keeping of familial educational processes as family property—although not exclusively so. Assuming responsibility for a sister's every lesson, in any family tradition, is a rarely documented process. In addition to exposing Eliza's formation as a desirable sister, and later as an upper-class Jewish wife and contributor to literary and public discourses, this account records specific curricula and progressive learning from both a teacher's and a student's perspective. For instance, it supplies a rare record of a child's returning to books that were at first too difficult, with pleasure in new understanding. It particularly depicts enacted family responsibility as a model contribution to a larger, collective didactic purpose.

But this text also reveals a historical difference within the always available subject positions of student and teacher. Rachel's authority as teacher, like Eliza's receptivity and resistance as student, derive from family relationships, which further stem from a family's traditions and the father's occupation as a schoolmaster. The difference, for instance, between Mordecai's and Tazewell's accounts is visible in Rachel's persistent avoidance of feeling, her discursive distance. But this distancing is an artifact of generic conventions whose subtexts are relational rather than cognitive or psychological. Eliza is not seen to develop mind or personality, but socialized abilities to fulfill Rachel's early stated sense of "every duty of this life." This focus on developing feeling, sensitivity, discrimination, and interactions might be taken as appropriate to two young females, but the results of this account are neither stylized womanhood nor a complicated "inner" life. Eliza and Rachel end by discussing relationships in a time of change, determined by precepts and conventions that people of model character display in social behavior. Like other records of educational doctrines and family stories of male learning, this account emphasizes developing a fitness for social interactions, not isolated interpretive perspectives.

Mordecai's record also disappoints the expectations of readers who want home stories to be seamless narratives. This is not an "I got up, I got dressed," bed-to-bed record or a classically plotted instructive tale, but an uneven insertion of remembered experience into both of these forms, which we now easily submerge in the constructed objectification of the case study. Remembered "typical" material is boxed, to use Walter Ong's term, in equally commonplace categories. It remains in the space of acquisition that characterizes commonplace self-education. As they construe multiple subject positions, these texts fluidly construct memory as a possession across the discursive generations that such property is meant to support. Consequently, these stories do not narrate private accounts of family doings, just as student essays on education, writing, the press, or literature are not precisely "public." All of these genres assimilate the newer instructional mode that teaches us, showing how ordinary writing purposefully develops new subject positions as exponents of a primary civil unit, the family.

Forced Into Position: The Children of the Commonwealth?

Until after the Civil War, these commonplace collections document the human objects of education as members of a whole society, an interconnected civic space constituted by shifting subjectivities, like those comprising Mary Virginia Early's familial "universe." In that world, affiliation remained the first source of training and, more important, of a blended socioeducational success. But when all children are acknowledged to deserve both institutional schooling and familial education after the Civil War, new surfaces of articulation emerge. In this later context, family collections began to incorporate discourses previously excluded, or included only as ceremonial connections to political, military, and religious institutions. These additions provide new images of education in the broad context of efforts to nationalize school curricula. Their surfaces reveal ambivalent attempts to resolve the place of the family among new economic and class arrangements.

The New Teacher's Troops

An 1880 essay on education headed only "Ann Eaght" (perhaps the author's name), preserved in the commonplace book of Georgia Screven Bryan Grinnan (1837–1912), is a discussion of education for children of all classes.[33] In its emphasized *now,* it portrays a gender-coded concern about basics of the domestic hearth whose mastery can foster later learning, there and elsewhere. The essay, apparently written by a teacher in an informal school, remarkably blends demarcated personal and public registers, blurring its generic status by compressing narrative "historical" anecdote, personal examples, and imagined vignettes in a polemical reflection. Its linguistic and substantive echoes of well-rehearsed *doxa* retain their distinctive imprint in this address to common history, family responsibility, economic-demographic change, social economies, child development and pedagogy, and domestic skills. But the essay also takes up these topics in the service of delineating new subject positions.

The essay begins by recalling how the need for more troops prompted the Confederate Cabinet ("during the last and gloomiest period of these Confederate States") to suggest drafting boys "at an earlier age than had previously been done." Quoting Jefferson Davis, who had disapproved of this emergency proposal to interrupt the "bright days of youth," the essay develops the conflict between social needs, new economic demands and occupational shifts after the war, and ideals of parenting and provisions for both public and home education (2).

But the striking novelty of this essay is to portray public and family interests as potentially contradictory, not mutual. It describes the "national increase of population" and the new practice of "pressing children into the places made vacant for failing men and women" (2). It complains of "any act which encourages children either boys or girls to be *forced into positions . . .* [in which] their further . . . development may be hindered. The degeneracy of the race must be the consequence" (2, emphasis added).

This forcing "into positions" becomes a trope linking the essay's first reference to military pressures, then industrial ones, and finally to restraining family forces. These energies in turn are used to contrast the subject positions available to a fortunate student and to an unfortunately situated "new student." Because of new economic divisions and the drain on the family caused by emerging occupational class ranks, families have a renewed responsiblity to maintain their children's education. But here, this maintenance is intended to set up a boundary around the family's social place, not to send children away from that place to a social or institutional source of expansion. Education should take place under the supervision of a nurturing teacher's subjectivity; "the kinder gender" should be responsible for child rearing (6). It insists that "laboring people" may be deprived if they avoid this responsibility.

> Children are left in the hands of their parents to control, educate, hire out to mine or factory etc.—until the age twenty one (& often only until able to resist) their parents and start a new life for themselves. The public school offers an opportunity (not compulsory) of education, but in a large majority of cases this only teaches the rudiments, and in fact to laboring people this is generally all that is needed. The few cases where unusual genius or energy are found, will work

their way to the front, and the many institutions of learning open to the public will afford them a chance to develop what [talent?] may have dictated at first. (3)

As it works through the obvious contradictions that qualify the concept of meritocracy, the essay interprets the well-documented economic changes of the later nineteenth century as changes in the tenor of discourse on education. An earlier, but now "foreign" family model is evoked in a nostalgia that highlights the falling away of parental responsibility:

> Each year the demand for trained labor in all departments increases and we may expect its continuance while the civilized world is making such demands on the manufactories for all that is needed in our present state of enlightenment. Thus the pressure is continued and the unscrupulous parent, edged in turn by poverty or love of money, condemn their children to toil in . . . factories or subterraneous mines, where dwarfed in size, and . . . in intelligence, they become mere pieces of machinery. . . . These children are to be trained to labor, the very machinery of civilization requires it, and unless they are well trained the age must retrograde. (4)

Against this picture of unfortunate parents "edged" by poverty and greed, once assigned to the unruly children of faithful parents, the essay compiles a civil discourse. New commonplace wisdom brandishes phrases like "demand for trained labor," "our present state of enlightenment," and "the very machinery of civilization"—the last an echo of Mary Virginia Early's conception of Newtonian, not industrial, "machinery" (chapter 2). This new conversation needs images from a better world. In that parallel universe, "the child of cultivated parents" is recalled as a striking contrast to one deprived of early home training.

Using examples presumably drawn from observation, the essay erects a Hogarthian opposition between visions of felicity and distress. One child, "under the loving care of a christian grandmother," could "take delicate stitches, of curious patterns, print, read, write, and enjoy many a well selected book" (4). This is, we assume, the daughter of the rich man described in a page added to the document. She is fortunately "positioned," having been "insensibly taught from . . . birth, many things which it would take years of laboring [after?] years to acquire; . . . at a comparatively early period [she] is placed under a governess or tutor and learns in a few months what it take years for the less fortunate [child] urchin in the back street to acquire at the public school" (7).

This exemplified ideal "stands" in contrast to a "[child] urchin" whose failings as a result of poor parenting were evident at about age nine, when she joined this teacher's "class of little girls to whom [she taught] sewing, knitting, and any thing for their general improvement" (5). Unlike her advantaged counterparts, the unimproved child "did not comprehend what a really straight line was, and could not be made to see the difference between it, and a curved or wavering one" (6). The essayist generalizes that this ignorance demonstrates a failure of discipline, here a beneficent force that would properly stamp what we now call early childhood development:

> The idea that to train any one thoroughly and with the greatest ease you have to begin early in life. . . . Observe these two children, one absolutely ignorant of what *labor* was. A foolishly indulgent mother had allowed it to spend its first decade in total idleness, with an idea that it was time enough for her to work; and postponing what she considered the evil day for her child had allowed it to spend as useless a life as the [fly] which flits in the sun shine. Yet she belonged to that class who must find employment, or seek refuge in an [alms] house—or in vice. The other child had almost imperceptibly attained a degree of knowledge and training, which if not acquired early would have taken many years . . . and was being prepared to fill the position in which [nature] had placed her. Still this had been done by constant care, attention, and office to the child with some weariness. (7)

This teacher clearly agrees with many others whose emerging sense of themselves as sources of a socially regulating gaze allows them to voice an increasingly codified expectation that the *primary* function of home training was to prepare children for a common school. For example, John J. Scherer (1830–1919), a Lutheran minister, lived and reluctantly taught school in Texas during the Civil War. In a sporadically kept diary (1850–1908), Scherer complains during a cold February rain that he has "a full school to day. Five new scholars yesterday. I have 2 or 3 boys that are troublesome. They show *the want of home training & parental authority.*"[34] As his language here and later indicates, this want of "home training" was not shown by a lack of good manners or of "reading readiness," but of substantial preparation for disciplined study. Later entries describing his devotion to his wife and many church offices suggest a characteristic good humor, but Scherer appears never to have been happy with his pupils, who seem to know nothing of the new subject position for those accepting a regulated "force." He remarks on January 27, 1862, "School has been unusually trying today; think it will not be so soon again: 'the Cross leads to the crown'" (15).

The "Ann Eaght" essay, in another genre no more or less public in its result than Scherer's journal, more reflexively sustains this emerging official discourse on the lacking public student by considering cases from other countries. It reinserts the family in its new educational discourse as a unit of changing society that is contrasted to idealized foreign practices. In distant places, parental training and authority equip workers for future tasks:

In Switzerland you will find an entire family engaged in carving wood, or making watches. The children are instructed by their parents at a very early period [~~and at an age when the generality of the human race is considered too young to entrusted with~~] each one will have his department assigned to him & understand and work at this delicate mechanism of a watch or clock, when his little contemporaries in other parts of the world, will believe they have attained the height of art in having learned to make a bow and arrow, or construct a bark boat to sail on a brook." (7–8)

The essay hereby reinforces the tradition of overriding family responsibility to educate children, but in a postwar, now openly and self-righteously "classed" world. It acknowledges differences within this world by alluding to practices in other nations and cultures: industrialized, agrarian, European, and naively portrayed ("primitive") Native American. New public schools for the poor will not produce genuine preparation for labor among this diverse population. Such preparation still depends on prior home teaching.

The essay's rhetorical strategies for defending these displaced but traditional Puritan family values show how commonplaces simultaneously constitute and generate *doxa*. In this later society, as in earlier republicanism, the text appropriates and reconfigures various cultural tropes in the service of maintaining family "position." But this generic opinion piece simultaneously contradicts and deploys the material on which it draws. It uses new publicly held phrases and images, exemplary personal observations, anecdotes of war, and stereotypes of other cultures. Its nostalgic and experimental cultural analyses fit shifting educational needs. In references to child development, to situated parental motives influenced by economic pressures, and to moral stratifications, it suggests that its writer was well aware of current persuasive strategies, common wisdom, and topical concerns. Each discursive strategy complains of, while accepting, the evolving cultural identification between education and common schooling. But we may miss this discursive work in mistaken attempts to find stable, familiar subject positions for *student, teacher, male, female, parent,* and *child*. In other words, this commonplace argument preceded and differs from later schooled writing processes. It does not reflect on change through a privatized inner perspective that is exposed to and assimilated by governing cultural pedagogies. Its reflections on new educational settings are not yet totalized by that *I,* but remain fragmented self-education-in-progress, a gathering and recirculation of individually held, but affiliative, property.

Preserve this for future reference S. Simpson

Edrington Pedigree (over)

John Catesby Edrington Jr. was killed in battle near "Malvern Hill," i.e. mortally wounded and died in Richmond Va. the day following in 1862, he was a member of the Va. 9th Cavalry and was burried in "Oak Grove" Cemetery south east of the City. Second Miss Sallie Bettie Edrington (Mrs. Seth R. Combs, Mother of Rev. S. R. Combs) died 1858 or 59. Third Miss Ella A. Edrington Mrs Col. S. Simpson, died at Fairfax C. H. Decbr. 20th 1880. Fourth Miss Mary Edrington, Miss Angelina Edrington, and Miss Fannie Daniel Edrington now living with their Mother at Myrtle Grove the old "Home Stead" in Stafford County Virginia.

By the marriage of J. C. Edr. the second, and Miss Golson there was one daughter who married Mr. Edwin Moncure, who resided at Clear Mount Stafford Co — they had several children Dr. Moncure, and John Moncure of Mississippi and Mrs. Agatha Glasscock, late of Clear Mount.

James Edrington married a Miss Withers, Charles Edrington Esqr. now of Fredericksburg Va. is the only surviving child of this marriage. Miss Angelina Edrington (the first) married Major Selden Brooke they had some six or more children Mrs Dr. Daniel (Miss Fenton Brooke) being one. Mr. Armat another. Mercer Brooke died many years ago at "Mill Vale" his Fathers residence. Capt. St. Brooke now Editor of the "Roanoke Leader" and two single sisters complete the list. Christopher Armat (or Armit) Esqr. who was the husband of the lady above named was a Baltimorean and brother of Thomas Armat a distinguished lawyer of Natchez Mississippi.

* See P. 101. Fol.

Fourth

Wounded July 24th Died July 26th, 1862

Single

· 5 ·

Page from Samuel Simpson's "Pedigree," kept in his commonplace book, 1879–1886. Pages are headed: "Preserve this for future reference," and "This autobiography has been written off hand and without any pretentions to style." Mss1ED745a384, sec. 39. Reprinted by permission of the Virginia Historical Society.

For Future Reference

That circulatory process also works in a commentary that blatantly insists on its status as a self-forming heritage. The commonplace book kept by Samuel Simpson (1815–?) is a series of what he terms *memoranda*. Dating from 1879 to 1886, it contains detailed genealogical notes and letters to family members and neighbors who might have information about his family's connection by marriage to the Washington family. The oldest male in the family is reported as saying that the "Washingtons were *'his ancestors' Overseers,'*" to which Simson adds, "which I presume arose from the fact that Edward Washington was Edward Barry's Agent and manager, I believe, and who afterwards married the widow Barry."[35] (She was Simpson's great-great grandmother.)

This large book also contains a year-by-year autobiographical account of Simpson's youth and travels, which he emphatically bequeaths to future generations, along with copies of his letters of opinion submitted to newspapers. Simpson's text "saves," in all meanings of the word, what was left of his tradition. Each page is headed with a large dark imperative, *"Preserve this for future reference."*

In its self-contradictory statements and self-conscious, uncertain use of various genres and discourses, Simpson's is a virtuoso performance. It suggests that we misinterpret contradictions within discursive formations of the subject if we first insist that a text is a unified product of a "personality" or of situated material circumstances. Simpson's demarcated private and public discourses on education, his journal for the future, and his late-century supplementary letter to a newspaper, all exemplify energtic resistance to being "forced into position" by schooling, which, it seems, he values only as a series of family relationships. Simpson preserves his educational and genetic history, as his remark about the Washingtons' status and his page headings show, to shore up his family heritage. He critiques new educational practices by specifically addressing their cultural ownership and, more particularly, by asking whether family or state may be presumed to "own" children. The text displays Simpson as a "subject of pedagogy," in Gregory Jay's phrase.[36] He writes as a "student" whose learning is produced by family, schooling, self-education and a new approach to history that conflicts with earlier positions. These largely unrevised, often long-winded accounts reward the patient reader because they demonstrate how acts of writing enable a writer to compose multiple subject positions.

Simpson's 1880 memoir of his earliest years establishes an identity between family relationships and social practices that constituted a gentleman's education. He was first exposed to the family lineage and educated in propriety by his grandmother's patrician conduct:

> My grandfather Stone died in the autumn of 1821; . . . on that Occasion some of the old apple and Peach brandies of which my Grandfather kept large store in his elegant cellar, was set out and one man by the name of Dyson Mills got a little too much and . . . became a little boisterous in the parlour, when my Grand Mother, who was a perfect Queen in manners and dignity of deportment, marched in to the room and said "If there is any person here who does not know how to behave himself, and forgets the proprieties of conduct, and the respect due the occasion and my house, he must leave"; and with a courtesy she turned and walked back to her own room. (51–52)

Entering school at age seven was the beginning of "trouble," problems detailed in numerous anecdotes. Simpson attended his brother's school for two years, where persuasive force was a fearsome matter of physical size and verbal volume:

> The following year 1822 began my first year of trouble, my brother Caleb Simpson opened a school about two miles south of my Father's house on my Father's wood land; . . . it was the first school ever started in that quarter and the families living on Occoquan [River] had a numerous uneducated progeny from adult size and age down to the six year olds, Male and Female. [Well they] largely from "six footers" and upwards, thirty year old boys, and strapping young women eighteen or twenty, and take it all in all it was the grandest school I ever knew, my brother was the best speller and definer I ever saw, [wrote?] a fair hand and was good at arithmetic, this was about the sum total of his qualifications added to which he was a rigid disciplinarian but a Tiger in passion when excited, and was one of the stoughtest men "to his inches" to be found, and his schollars big and little, feared him as they would the roaring of the lion, or the lions' whelp. (52)

As the crossed-out "well they" indicates, Simpson wrote as a voluble story-teller who checks his language in the interest of preserving graphic authority. He subdues this volubility by organizing his narration with inserted places, dates, and pointed evaluations. Like many other writers, he says he will omit anything he deems irrelevant to the record.[37]

> [Caleb] continued his school for two years and did good service thereby. the noticeable events of these two years if related would fill a good sized Volume, suffice it to say, some of my misery was at an end. For a while, I rested on my acquired [honors?]; several years after this [an old] gentleman from Stafford or [?], county came into the neighborhood and started a very good school. his name was "Peter Smith" to whom I went some what irregularly for two years, after Peter Smith Mr. Thomas Storke from Stafford set up near the Smith school and called it

"Windsor Forest," (because the land and house belonged to a Mr. Richard Windsor). (53)

Simpson's experience with Storke permits him to include a judgment on the character of "bad student," a perspective absent from most preinstitutional educational accounts. He remembers the fatal interference in his progress caused by Storke's son, displaying common wisdom to justify his otherwise questionable opinion of how Storke slowed his progress:

> Mr. Storke was a little old fogyish, though an average good teacher to whom I went some two years, and but for his stupid block head son "Langhorn" who was yoked with me in arithmetic I might have been benefited there by, but "Langhorn" was wholly incapable of comprehending the science of numbers, and sat with his slate before his face day in and day out for weeks, months and years, chewing his pencil, which was rarely one or under one inch long. The only sign of intellect displayed, was his ingenuity in flanking one in order to take from over my shoulder the figures from my slate, being under orders not to show him, while I was not allowed to go forward and report progress. The consequence was I sat inactive waiting the motions of Langhorn—for days and even weeks killing time. If there is an unpardonable sin, it is where the teacher yokes a bright boy with a dunce, and in effect makes two dunces where there need be but one, it is like putting the Ass before the swift courrier to regulate his pace. It is unpardonable, so my two years [?] amounted to but little, in that direction, in other branches some progress was made. (53)

Despite his limited lessons, Simpson invests this memory with a boost to his self-esteem, compensating for his scholarly deficiencies by highlighting his affection for his sister on their walks to school. Prefabricated language, what is "supposed to be," powerfully appropriates this interpolated account of brotherly love into a syntactically confusing but vivid antidote to his scholastic failures. This recollection of brotherly affection apparently came to him in the process of writing his account:

> To this teacher my little sister Jane S. C. Simpson (subsequently Mrs. Sipscomb) began to accompany me, the distance we had to walk both morning and evening was about 2 1/2 miles. *I will remember* my brotherly affections towards this little mild and placid sister was as tender and deliberate as a babe's is supposed to be. I would with great assidicity assist her over the streams and fenccs and when the weather was cold I would get her to walk near my side and put her little hands in my pockets to keep them warm. I *shall ever think well of my self* for my devotion to my little sister whom I never but once saw after she was grown, and that only for a few hours, in 1840. at my Fathers old place when I was passing through Virginia on my way from New Orleans to New York, thence to Europe and the East Indies. This poor Sister died in [Missouri] leaving a large number of children and

her husband a Widower many years past, Alas: how great was & is, my grief. (54, emphasis added)

Simpson's various school experiences are given a sense of progress in light of other personal relationships. In his next series of schools, he encounters another product of education away from home, his "first unsophisticated love." Again, the school (at least in memory) stimulates description of human and geographical relationships, not of codified learning from a distant "hill of science":

> My next attempt to climb "the hill of science" was under the tuition of Richard Burke who opened a school in my brothers old school house on my Fathers place, and afterwards on the "Ox Road" at a place better known by the name of "BrimStone" or "Brimstone hill". . . . Here came to school a girl by the name of Lewis with whom, though I was not then over 14 years old, began my first unsophisticated love, which hung to me for many years, and intensified as time went, up to my 17th year, or when I left the state, when "Mary Ann" got married and all ended well I hope. (54)

Like others, this narrative privileges a superior, independent self-education and defines formal schooling as but one site among many for learning, a place that has no primacy or total hold on the "improvement" of youth. Simpson echoes both John Purdie's vociferous assertion that he learned correct language before he attended school (chapter 2), and Littleton Tazewell's certainty that his grandfather's home tutelage cemented their mutual affection. Education, he says in closing, does not depend on and cannot greatly be hurt or helped by institutionalized lessons:

> In about my 16th year I went to school for a few months only to a Mr. John Sweeny, which ended the sum total of all the education i ever received at the regular schools, subsequently I obtained some private instruction. . . . Whatever else of knowledge and learning I have attained to, I acquired by private study, application and research. (55)

This dismissive finale stresses the independence from ordinary people and from ordinary public institutions that constructs this textual emblem of family pride.

The Commonwealth Cannot Bear Children

Given these attitudes, it is not surprising that Simpson included in his commonplace book a vivid letter to a newspaper complaining about newly common public education, addressed to "Mr. Edition" of Fairfax Courthouse and dated the year he wrote the memoir of his education, 1880. Given the many frustrations noted in his biographical sketch, evidently written to combat his fear of a dying family position, it is notable that he focuses on education in this source preserved "for future reference." Whatever his state of mind about other matters, he is appalled at what he calls "reversing the order of things" by making children the wards and responsibilities of the state in new public schools. His almost hysterical protests invoke all the foundational authorities he can muster to resist this shift. Doctrines of natural rights, economic necessity, legal precedent, and personal responsibility are figured rhetorically in maxims, exemplars from history, biblical quotation, epithets, and rhetorical questions, all mustered with energy that often results in garbled syntax. All of these commonplace devices convey his utter dismay at the prospect of a publicly controlled, undifferentiated school system. Meritocratically gained, well-disposed "tallents," he argues, will be overcome, not encouraged, by bureaucratic governance. The state, or the metaphoric commonwealth, cannot "bear" children.

This lengthy letter resists such enforced limits on subject positions with copious authorities intended to overwhelm the new cultural configuration with predictions of what "everyone knows" will be inevitable failure. Yet it promotes an equally vivid, if subtextual, awareness that new identities produced in common schools might benefit the common governance that Simpson wants desperately to preserve. The text struggles among commonplaces to find what will count, or be assumed, as the future common wealth (158–62):

Memoranda: "The Children of the Commonwealth"

A phrase common and flippant in many mouths these days, which by transposition means "The Commonwealth's Children"—things really hard to find and yet more difficult to establish by law. If it be the duty of the state to educate all the children within its limits under the idea that they belong to the state, and hence its duty and right—superior to that of the parent, who nevertheless is held to be in law responsible, as lawful guardian, for the conduct of his child during the whole period of minority, . . . as after twenty one (21) years they all become Free Citizens and free agents and are personally responsible for their whole conduct.

This assumption of ownership of all the minors of the state—within the limits of the state—is a dangerous assumption, it distroys, if fully carried out, the lawful control, to a large extent, of their natural guardians—which is, I repeat, a dangerous interference with long settled principles of natural rights, sanctioned by all well regulated conditions of human society in the ages of the past. If the state has a right to put in a claim to regulate the conduct and condition of the children over six years of age till they are twenty one, why not assert this claim earlier—say from the very first day of existence, and provide for the "Lying in" mother, and thereby relieve the overworked Father, (it may be) or the state may even go back of this and look after all the *Encient matrons* in the land and see that they are all well provided for so that their offspring may be strong and healthy, and in this way restore the Spartan age and custom of rearing *Helots* to till the soil of the *Paridee.*

In a country like America and under a Gov.ᵗ founded upon the consent of the goverened it is especially revolting to the Sense, as well as threatening to the safety of the state in thus reversing the order of things where the Gov.ᵗ asserts such control over public instruction, or dictates it to be done by any other power than the Father (or Mother) of all the children whatsoever; Any interference in this regard is to assert incompetency on the part of the people for self Gov.ᵗ If a state can do this, how much more the U.S. and then where are we? and what have we? a nation of dependents, like young birds in a nest all gaping and crying with open mouths to the Gov.ᵗ for food and aid; how long, in the name of common sense, will this people remain free and independent? How long, I ask, and who will answer me? and to begin it, is to carry it out; *Change;* and revolution will follow close upon the heels of the footsteps of such a system; I am told the people are too poor to bear the burden of tuition; this must be false, because the people pay it as it is with cost of collection super added, were it true that they are too poor, then who made them so? In a free country like this where industry is or ought to be, and is supposed to be, adequately rewarded how come it that the people are so poor, needy and dependent? It must be the effect of bad Gov.ᵗ It can be nothing else, and this public school system is a part of the maladministration: Far better would it be for the people not to be educated at all than to forfeit freedom for a *little learning* and *much poverty.* Too much Gov.ᵗ is a curse to any people, But just let the people go free and they will thrive! Thrift will procure Education, and Education in this way will produce self reliance, which latter is the source of Free institutions, the offspring of a Liberty loving [~~people and~~] sentiment among a progressive people. Public education puts the people in the power of the state, that is the Officers of the state, to be shaped for weal or woe as the inclination of the authorities, for the time being, may determine with a tendency to keep perpetual control, the longer the firmer, and finally slavery and the dark ages may set in under the delusive idea of light and good for the people who, all the while are being "goodwinked" to their own distruction.

It is not safe to say that in this advanced age of general intelligence and a free Press, *all is safe* but be not deceived thereby while the mass of mankind yet believe in *Fables* nothing is safe, and if there be any truth in the Maxim *"the price of liberty is eternal vigilance"* as the great Jefferson believed it was, then we can find no condition of perfect safety. We are certainly far from it where we are now. "Set him who thinketh he standeth take heed lest he fall", is an admonition applicable to all conditions and all ages of mankind.

July 30th 1880.

S. Simpson

Simpson's awareness that "fables" will destroy the society that his family memoir wants to preserve is prescient, forecasting how new myths of education would paradoxically relegate the family to the background of bourgeois nineteenth-century domesticity. The energy with which he pursues this counterdiscourse on the terrors of public schooling, if only in an editorial letter, might allow us to read it as trivial nostalgia and bombast. We might be relieved to see this text's almost total absorption of the discursive era that had enabled such failed upper-class independence, and dismiss its even slight retardation of public schools where we now teach "thesis sentences" and how to write "unified, coherent" compositions.[38] But dismissing Simpson's Althusserian view of the public school as an apparatus of the ideological state is perhaps too easy. Ordinary writing, at least in this instance, sustains both preinstitutional schooling and the shifting subject positions that have preserved objections to later official public opinions.

The power of this sort of writing as a process is fully realized in "Supplement to Memoranda, July 30, 1880," which Simpson inserted on unnumbered loose sheets at the end of this volume. It first reverses the memorandum's argument by openly supporting the establishment of public schools, then undermines this reversal. A new, refreshed subjectivity emerges here, as Simpson's concern becomes not danger to the family from public schools, but their quality. The "Supplement" reiterates meritocratic principles, digresses on school piano lessons—or failed piano lessons—that Purdie also complained of, and finally states explicitly how making language can relieve tensions, alleviating "diseased" confusion.

The supplement engages myriad sources and competing interests, particularly the conflict between tradition and a need for charity in a new state order. In demonstrating that "all Mankind are not the same," Simpson projects a palpably calmer view of education that nourishes differences—in social status, professions, and individual needs. Public education becomes a "system we can't get away from or do without," thus susceptible to "improvements."

The "Supplement" occasionally loses its own logic, despite its closing words, "therefore, this brief will argue," which may indicate that he decided it should precede the editorial letter. But the logic of an act of writing remains clear: perspectives unfold as Simpson writes and are finally convincing only at the end. It is again worth reading the entirety of this process to understand this text as a self-administered writing pedagogy, a "free write" in which inscription is a self-persuading action, subject to change. In addition, a self-named supplement has obvious theoretical connotations that make it an appropriate example of ordinary writing as a self-educational practice.

Simpson speaks to that purpose with a force that uncovers this usually invisible but commonplace process of cultural formation.

SUPPLEMENT

All history and human tradition from the earliest ages of the race to the present time if we except the last twenty five years, show that it has been an accepted truism that there is such a faculty as individual talent—or peculiar adaptation of personal idiosyncrasy which has hitherto been, and ought always to be, allowed to influence in the choice of occupation and profession, and hence the world has often, in its past history, been electrified, as it were, by the brilliant display of individual ability, surpassing all contemporaries, becoming distinguished in their sphere of action and classed among the rare men of genius, instances of this sort might be adduced in conspicuous numbers were it necessary. While mankind has often been greatly benefited by the observance of this important principle in human nature, in the adaptation of individual peculiarities to the persuits of life. Yet of late years, instead of striving to make the rule universal, or as nearly so as possible, just the opposite obtains, and modern views and practice seem to have settled under the belief that all mankind are just the same, and are as much alike as two black-eyed peas—color and other radical differences going for nothing, and the only real difference consists in opportunities and education, [and?] hence the effort to educate all just alike etc. as though that [were?] all that is needed to fit all for the highest of the varied professions and duties of life. This is, in my opinion, a radically dangerous *error,* that must eventually injure the race and defeat its general welfare. Alongside of the better practice we have witnessed too many instances of this grave error, all the way down to our day, so much so we may ask, How few do we see who have made *Law* their profession that are fit for it, and what a travesty upon the name of Doctor of Medicine and Surgery are the majority of those who are set up for practice, in this our time, afflicting every community in the land with their malpractice. While the preachers even *are ground out,* at the Theological Seminaries, *to order,* (though I see no great harm that can grow out of this mode of filling the Pulpits, as it is a matter of form at best, the age of witchcraft and persecution having happily measurably passed). How few again are the Mechanics who have any *"turn"* (tallent) for their trade and the country is filled with mere *"botchers",* in consequence of which the country people are badly served. How few of the children are blessed with musical tallent yet all the girls are learning to strum on the Piano, to the exclusion of all other Instruments regardless of tastes or gifts, and too often loosing thereby both money and time to become indifferent, but persistent, performers in company.

Then again the public school system, *which in a general way I am greatly in favor of,* it seems to me is defective, as at present established wherein all children are taught alike and in the same branches, with no chance for the brighter youths to go above and beyond their less gifted fellows. This defect must be looked at by our Legislation and remedied, or we shall soon have a community consisting of common place qualifications unsuited to the higher spheres of official, professional, to say nothing of scientific, efficiency, constituting a Nation, very soon to be looked upon as we now erroneously perhaps look upon the Chinese Nation and people, "*All the Same*".

"Equal justice and political rights to all", does not mean equal capacities and abilities [by a jugful], to acquire equal stations and distinctions, not *by a* [jugful] *ship load,* it simply lays no embargo on any, from mans stand point, as no human institution can correct incurable natural defects in [?] charity alone can relieve the needy, and in certain cases may even "minister to a [mind?] diseas'd:

> Pluck from the memory of rooted sorrow;
> Raize out the written troubles of the brain;
> And, with some sweet oblivious antidote,
> Cleanse the stuff'd bosom of that perilous stuff,
> Which weighs upon the heart.

The Public School System needs enlarging in as much as it has supplanted the private schools of the country to a very large extent, rendering it next to impossible for the latter to exist for the want of adequate patronage, the former named being none so thoroughly established as a system that we can't get away from it or do without, few would, and hence the impunitive necessity of its enlargement by the legislative provision [establishing] for graded schools in every county of the state, so as to make it a complete educational system. If this cannot be accomplished it would be best to abandon the entire system and the sooner this is done the better.

Some classical technicalities of geological, chemical and botanical sciences and their respective nomenclatures ought to be taught, or supplied in some way or we shall have no competent Drugist Clerks, no [amateur?] geologists, nor botanists or ornithologists-horticulturalists and naturalists of any sort, it is not every boy who would show any aptness in this way, not perhaps 10% of the whole mass, but that 10% is always more important and absolutely necessary for the benefit & well being of mankind than all the remaining 90% outside of actual laboring classes. Therefore this in brief will show the pressing necessity of the higher grade of schools, in each and every county in the state, to supply this obvious need and fitting the community to be, to some extent at least, self sustaining, at all events greatly strengthened. (Emphasis added)

From his memory of school as "trouble" when he was seven to this writing to "raize out the written troubles of the brain" caused by the prospect of public education, Simpson's account struggles with class differences, intraclass aptitudes and merit, and the paradox of meritocracy within supposed democracy. In each contradiction, his texts sustain a multiplicity of positions that work out beliefs around *quality*. They measure how well or how poorly education creates an affiliated group of contributors to a whole system, *not* how it fosters a particular sensibility suitable for informed but self-isolating consciousness, a goal diametrically opposed to Dabney's hopes for institutionalized literacy in 1849 (chapter 2). In grudgingly accepting public schools as a possible source of beneficial mass education, Simpson would favor a curriculum we now designate vocational. But for him, practicality is essential to the survival of an interdependent culture that produces more than "common place qualifications." We witness here, consequently, a change in the definition of *commonplace.* Simpson's texts reveal a tentative encounter with new institutions that will value centralized monitors of and interventions in the education of a populace made "All the Same."

These reflections, with other accounts of education, suggests that historicized counterdiscourses inside privileged, if not public, writing indicate resistance that forcefully shaped changes in the powerful *doxa* sustaining both education and the family. They demonstrate how education was figured in ways that Ian Hunter describes as *identical to* subject formation. Both in self-educational writing practices and in their preserved content, living memories of learning repeatedly place both subject and citizen under erasure. Commonplace texts process education as a relationship among people, not as visions of superior lessons. *Education* thus preserves an unstable subjectivity that is partially anchored by acquiring and deploying, digesting and recirculating, commonplace cultural goods.

PART II · True Biases

"A Defective and Naturally Bad System"

I could write a book on it [slavery], having seen it in all its horrid deformity, not so much perhaps from individual depravity, but from a defective and naturally bad system, and the wrong feelings and notions it engendered.

Samuel Simpson, commonplace book

Introduction: True Biases

Indigenous writing asserts a difference within the dour category of *literacy*. Such writing, that is, reproduces and modifies commonplaces that simultaneously contain and liberate current categories applied to literate practices, in a cultural process that continues well after those categories are installed. Inscribed *doxa* shows that experience is always discursively mediated, but also constitutes it in repetitions and differences. This doctrinaire tradition produces accountable fictions of stabilized subjectivities, as "characters" that are invested with a Lockean labor of inscription. It thus also becomes an ancestor of modern views of cultural reproduction that focus on transmitted identity.

The following three chapters push this argument further by analyzing how commonplace texts deploy formal and informal gender precepts, how they critique unfortunate assignments of gender to purposes for writing, and how they transmit patriarchal identity among males as an Enlightenment *individual/universal*. To do so, these chapters imitate a common technique for finding the true bias of a piece of fabric, here a figure for how the commonplace material of ordinary writing configures inevitably partisan categories. To find the true bias, one first locates vertical and horizontal threads, then follows an oblique angle 45 degrees from the straight.

Finding a true bias, in cloth as in discourse, does not serve the same end as mapping a field by placing its elements on a preexisting grid. Fabric hanging on the bias has an oblique tension in its drape, just as the biases that determine a text's ambivalent "substance" (or, lack of substance, if one seeks to assign to it essential gender qualities) also produce a tension.

Finding a true bias, as reader or seamstress, allows us to move across the straight lines of analytic categories that make material intelligible, while simultaneously rejecting them to design a path through their neatly arranged but often useless absolutes. Making self-educational ordinary writing visible as a gendered and ungendered practice allows us to dismiss categories of analysis that obscure the natural "fall" of its substance and to speculate on how it both covers up and reveals prior texts. Looking for true biases uncovers traditions that resist and would deform their current cultural representations as hegemonic common sense.

The chapters in part II thus set aside many forms of identity politics to focus on how supposedly fixed subject positions in circulated *doxa* are written and assumed only provisionally. They do not search for essential personal qualities or biographical-historical data that enable the illusion of fixed categories of female or male gender and "universal" standards of conduct and value. They instead critique those old certainties by making visible common practices that are precedents for both categorical certainty and Stuart Hall's "family man" in the epigraph to chapter 4. Formal prescriptions for patriarchal conduct, like local realizations and retreats from them show the inaccuracy of applying modern categories to texts whose formative processes were differently grounded.

T. J. Jackson Lears observes that today "the ideal of authentic self-expression, of faithfulness to some inwardly felt or outwardly observed sense of the real, has fallen on hard times."[1] He suggests that no consideration of circulated doctrines, gendered genres, or patriarchal identity in ordinary writing can accurately take these formations to be "inauthentic" or to be written cynically, from a "role" merely tried out for social or material gain by a self who is centered entirely otherwise. In these volumes, hopeful prescriptions for invincible character, functional texts, and patriarchal responsibility for "correct" behavior are simultaneously "real" and entirely provisional. Reading across the biases of vertically classed and horizontally gendered categories, we see how ordinary writing manifests mobile subjectivities that take "authentic" writerly actions that are as yet not authored in a modernist sense. Personally compiled but never entirely private recollections of commonplace propriety bolster subject positions, refiguring and thereby revitalizing their powers of self-possession and reproduction.

Differences within these powers are not conflicts between authenticity and simulation, but between their repetition of commonplace conventions and their varied specificity. Texts on gender, that is, repeatedly overestimate and vividly underestimate their fleeting yet entirely consequential cultural power. Gender is thus a fabric of topics, not a speaking voice. It is always mobile, ambiguously reproduced, and modified. Gender-as-voice, consequently, is woven into gender-as-topos. It reproduces common topics in formal rhetoric and may now ground composition theory, but here it shows how one "finds a voice" not in biological or cultural identity, but within the commonplaces that one is addressing and being addressed by.

· 4 ·

The Class on Gender

> The uncritical forms of the modern family, the patterns of sexual domi-
> nance, the disciplining of pleasure, the reinforcement of the habits of social
> conformity are some of the key ways in which the political movements of
> the left have remained deeply conservative and traditionalist at their cul-
> tural core. The tiny "family man" is still hiding away in the heads of many
> of our most illustrious "street-fighting" militants.
>
> STUART HALL, "Crisis and Renewal on the Left"

The Class on Gender: "The Fault Was Mine"

Stable configurations of gender, in theory and in social practice, obviously
have more sexy results than hiding a body of *doxa* we do not see. Gender
boundaries, whether assumed to be functional or essential demarcations,
pointedly obscure class prejudice. They especially hide insults leveled at
groups of people to acutely demean the corpus of their language—their
speech, reading, and writing. Thus otherwise inconsequential writing habits
that enable gender category formations and put the class status of inhab-
itants of these categories in doubt are also the commonplaces of that status.
Writing gender, that is, is a literate diversion that symbolically enacts entitlement. Ordinary writing organizes gender to fund the exchange of its ready
sexual currency for yet another cultural property, discursive assurances of
class superiority. Of course, both this diversionary practice and its often surprising content must be learned, modified, and redeployed, through practices and textual substance that rank males above females to create a difference within a larger, always tentative, class unity. This class identity is taught
in commonplace practices that enact a particular Lockean labor, the discursive work needed to acquire the property that is propriety.

   The most authoritative source for that coded propriety is conduct literature, usually understood as fulfilling the needs of an always new middle class
in response to changing economic and social opportunities. However, conduct literature also belongs to the domain of formal rhetoric and its literary

examples, which regulate what can be thought in the limits recognized as it displays acceptable varieties of social and moral behavior. Traditional lessons in verbalizing appearances—for instance, the *ainos,* or slave talk voiced by animals in Aesop—teaches how to acknowledge status difference when addressing one's master.[1] Rhetoric, that is, has prescribed and exemplified a highly ritualized indirection in speech, a template for usage hovering between Jane Austen and Henry James. Its precepts precede legislated regulations of physical appearance and social interactions that maintain social ranks. Thus common practices, including the "soft" speech of women of gentle status, have historically displaced rhetorical training and sumptuary laws as sites for circumscribing and containing human desires.

Conduct literature has therefore been preserved and circulated to prescribe local family traditions that males and females use to fit themselves quite literally—in language—into self-conscious ways to maintain their relative class positions. At least before the Civil War, conduct literature was circulated as "home improvement," a mode of literate education in families for whom formal schooling was not a master text but an ancillary gloss on "character" shaped by parents. Conduct lessons in family-supported settings addressed gender categories as fixed ideals, especially by adding in regional seminaries and academies a curriculum that openly specified cultural expectations for women and men.

Constituting a Lady

The commonplace book kept by Mary Jefferson Randolph (1803–1876) includes school essays whose titles allude to a rhetorically schooled focus on appearances: "On the proper deportment in Church," "Amusements," and "Revenge."[2] One of these essays on deportment verifies how class and gender are equated in this academic context:

THE DEPORTMENT PRINCIPLES AND MANNERS THAT CONSTITUTE A LADY

A real lady should have an easy deportment, soft and gentle manner, good temper, a kind and compassionate heart and humanity towards every thing. You never see a well bred person hollowing [howling?] and [bawling] though the streets or [?] but always mild and gentle as a lady should be. If she has good principles, she will be beloved by everyone, if she has soft and gentle manners, she will be admired wherever she goes, and if she has an easy deportment she will be admired likewise. Some persons think if they are rich they are ladies, but riches and finery never make the lady. In my opinion an easy deportment, soft and gentle manners, and good principles, are the truest mark of a well bred lady.

Mary Randolph, Richmond Virginia 1826

This essay suggests that Randolph's school and its assigned writing paid more than casual attention to teaching its pupils how to behave, specifically as ladies. Yet in writing about "real" ladies, Randolph places herself at a remove from this identity, even if her obvious injunction against bawling through the streets reminds us of the *Book of the Courtier*'s advice to avoid eating with one's sword. To this youthful interpreter, that is, a lady is too "high" an identity to be immediately realized, yet at a standard only marginally above common examples of déclassé forms of behavior.

Like school notes and outlines of treatises on eighteenth- and nineteenth-century moral philosophy, this composition equates ladylike behavior to having good effects on others. Some females, but not others, will be well received because they have mastered the fifth domain of rhetoric, "delivery." Its elocutionary gestures are finally philosophized as the "dispositions" in conduct literature and moral philosophy, where they are assigned categories of human feeling. An elaborate organizational taxonomy of human qualities is also explicit in other students' notes on "abstract and mental sciences."[3] But for Mary Randolph, "good principles" directly evoke an audience's love; "soft and gentle manners" evoke admiration. A lady's "mild and gentle" nature is equated with modulating her tone of voice, to avoid "bawling through the streets," which a "well bred person" does not do. In other words, a casual, unexcited self-presentation marks an elite class boundary, as Lucy Butler notes in her journal (chapter 5), praising the deportment of a "Miss Harden who, though she is an overseer's daughter, seems to have as much refinement and has as easy manners as any lady that I know." Learning to be a lady involves acquiring behavior that is identifable even to strangers, if only by making it clear that one will not raise one's voice.

The dire consequences of failing to acquire uniformly self-effacing and self-announcing behavior—or worse, displaying opposite behavior—are spelled out in an 1836 family essay by Blair Bolling. Its inconsistent spellings and syntactic lapses suggest not only that it may be his draft, but also that its implications are too horrendous to spell out directly.

ON FEMALE CHARACTER

So high is the standard of Female character for virtue and refinement established in public Estimation and so vigilantly is their deportment toward the other sex watched by the serious that it is difficult to designate a point beyond which they may venture with impunity, in their intercourse with men.

Even the sancity of engagement has been escerted [asserted?] against the innocent and unsuspecing, by the artful and fallacious and has too often caused them to mourn to late, the utter impractibility of retracing their steps.

Hence, altho shielded as females [they?] are sometimes induced to concider themselves by this solemn pledge of mutual affection, and led to receive the disceptive lure bestowed in form of tokens of Love. How bitterly has the once immaculate fair one, been caused to mourn the humiliation of [~~her~~] condition, which a more prudent course would have protected her against.

How unnecessary, as well as improper is it, therefore for one to place herself in a situation, the concequences of which may blast her happiness, and her most sanguine anticipations realised, can be no more than in imperfect enjoyment of the more solid happiness of the married state.[4]

This decidedly oblique advice by a male recalls Bolling's statements about parenting in a similarly didactic register, his description of a father's "imperious duty" to set examples for children (chapter 3). The essay's opening, "So high is the standard," tells a great deal about the gaze of patriarchal universals, the scrutiny of "the serious" who are the unmarked judges of female conduct. Females are held to such circumspection "that it is difficult to designate a point beyond which they may venture with impunity in their intercourse with men." This father figure elaborates his pithy assessment with allusions that are difficult to decipher, even in the overlapped commonplaces of Christian suffering, feminine vulnerability, mourning, and the gender-neutral condition of human failing. Evidently, even the period of engagement before marriage in which a woman was allowed some freedom in social intercourse with men could be turned, by the "artful and fallacious," against the "innocent and unsuspecting." Bolling appears to say, that is, that an engaged girl, who by definition has been offered both purification and safety in marriage, can lose both that contracted form of social salvation and her chance at others by having her assumed willingness to renounce all other associations turned on her. Accepting "the disceptive lure bestowed in tokens of Love" that should save her could instead destroy her happiness. It is no wonder that the essay's last paragraph self-destructs "the imperfect enjoyment of the more solid happiness of the married state."

Sharp Eyes: Anguish Unspeakable

Here and elsewhere, paternal concern for female reputation protected a social identity whose value could be gauged in material terms. But a great deal of intercourse between young females and males did occur, as recorded in many letters and diaries, and its danger to a girl's reputation was not diminished by the ease of such interactions. A letter enclosed in David Meade's 1869 commonplace book closes with this request, "Let me ask one thing: destroy this note as soon as you are familiar with its contents, and still another, let this be the last allusion to this painful affair that will ever pass between us—Goodnight."[5] But its writer, now known only as "F. A. B.," was not safe from the damage to her reputation that this appeal was intended to forestall. The letter, written in the blush of apprehension of some danger she thinks she has brought on herself, does not fully explain why its writer secretly met its recipient, perhaps Meade, or say what she wanted to discuss at their meeting. Nor do we know how the letter was transmitted; it may have been slipped under a door at a household party. But its language, including attention to rules of argument, reveals more than F. A. B.'s acquaintance with the universal judgments that Bolling evoked to circumscribe female character. The "sharp eyes" cast on these unidentified lovers belong to more than chaperones at one gala:

Sunday Night Nov 14th 186[1?]

Ten minutes ago I parted from you, leaving unsaid what I would have given much for you to hear. The [?] to say it was oweing to two causes, either of which is amply sufficient: I name them in the order of their occurrence to my mind, rather than in the order of their merit. First: because the time offered for the interview was of too short duration to admit of somewhat lengthy theme. Second because it was a matter of such extreme delicacy, that I could not trust myself to speak on it. My heart is rended with anguish unspeakable- Anguish and remorse. I am ready to die with shame & with self disgust. I feel that no furnace can [expiate?] my sin, no tears of self-reproach can wash away my corroding offence. *I blame you not: both of us yielded to a temptation which was cast in the way; as it were & which neither saught, but the fault was mine.* Truely, there has been error in what I have done, and it has won me bitter wages, which I will go and spend, far from the scene of its occurrence. There is yet another thing that adds pain to this keen torture; & that is the thought that that good man of whome I am so unworthy & who trusts me so implicitly is deceived in a measure. I cannot lash myself too much; self inflicted torture is the most severe but I deserve it all.

My dear love, the knowledge that I have fallen in your esteem is grief insupportable. If I did not love you devotedly I should never feel so. You have assured me that my weakness has made me dearer to you: believe me you are self deceived: that is your true nobility of soul leads you to think do, but, I have lost in your heart of hearts that respect & esteem upon which the trust love is based. I trusted you as I would heaven, Dear heart, faithful friend preserve my faith sacredly. May you never know the pang that tears *my* heart! For my sake if you love me, do not appear so depressed. Sharp eyes are upon you & me as well. Treat me as you hitherto have done, and make an effort, as I do to appear gay, though I "bear a laden breast."

This letter's handwriting is not its only clue that a female wrote it. Whatever transgression is at issue, its writer's persistent attempts to take the blame show that she knows well on whom a larger judgment would fall. Her avowed trust in her correspondent is an illocutionary act that hopes to *make* him trustworthy, but as her readers now, we can infer he was not. "Art and fallaciousness" may have determined his responses, and despite (or because of) her concern for his welfare, he may have blasted her happiness. Each of these commonplaces constructs a slightly skewed intimacy, conveyed in the simultaneously formal and hysterical tone of this note. As she says, "I deserve it all."

But these speculations do not justify making the stakes in this untold story entirely psychological. It could be that the indiscretion at issue was pecuniary, not sexual, or that it had to do with a gesture or verbal slip that undermined firm preexisting arrangements for either lover's "happiness." This writer fears, that is, the consequences to her publicly regulated "character" and "esteem," not primarily to her emotional state.

Both sexes bore the burden of regulated gender assignments. Many texts monitor gentlemen in their exchanges with females. Their hints about how a category for universals is articulated make it clear that both ladies and men had to acquire a deportment that determined material gain, not just social success in manners.

A Man of Appearances

Lessons for young men on how to behave are overlooked in descriptions of their formal school curricula, despite the intense attention paid in classical lessons and assigned literature to examples of correct behavior by famous, heroic, and courageous models. But these lessons did more to accomplish the social purposes of schooling males than is found in later, purportedly democratic schooling. The classical curriculum for young men contained models of behavior whose imitation would connect boys to reproductive but purportedly disembodied models and to "history." Thus attending academies and universities marked one as a member of a class, not just as a graduate.[6] Nor were being learned and achieving class standing assumed to be equivalent. Bookishness interfered with a more highly valued companionship that affirms a man's social aptitude and character (See chapter 5).

Nancy Armstrong and Leonard Tennenhouse observe in *The Ideology of Conduct* that if in other cultures kinship relations are "one and the same as political relations, then we must also assume that whatever it is that makes certain objects of sexual exchange more valuable than others also provides the basis of political authority."[7] An unidentified, undated essay on the manners of a gentleman in the commonplace book kept by Alfred Byrne Horner (1861–1934) describes this "whatever it is" in detail. It is explicitly not bookishness, for as this essay says, "The reading of the new characters is more your business now than the reading of twenty old books—showish and shining people always get the better of all others though ever so solid."[8] To fulfill a fixed gender identity, a *character,* is to get the better of others by managing an idealized subjectivity that is articulated in evaluative social norms applied to both males and females. These lessons in doubly meant "class markers" promote stable gender identities, yet do not strictly divide them; they prescribe the same qualities for a gentleman as for a desirable lady. And for both, signs of character and gender determine class status. The essay conveys directions for acquiring these sexually homologous traits in amazing Chesterfieldian detail, clearly imagining them as providing access to wealth.

As its allusions to Pope and Swift indicate, the cultural assumptions underlying this probably published essay (including directions on how to speak to a king by practicing on one's footman) were hardly current by the time Horner copied or imitated it. But considering the regular production of valued males by conduct literature across the centuries, the essay cannot be thought of as dated in Horner's time. It is an undiminished example in an ongoing process by which gendered advantage is learned and circulated, its first-person intimacy bringing the process home:

> Mankind as [I?] have often told you are more governed by appearances than by realities and with regard to opinion one had better be really rough and hard with the appearance of gentleness and softness than just the reverse. Few people have penetration enough to discover[,] attention enough to observe, or even concern enough to examine beyond the exterior. [T]hey take their notions from the surface and go no deeper; they commend as the gentlest and best natured man in the world, that man who has the most engaging exterior manner though possibly they have been but once in his company—An air[,] a tone of voice[,] a composure of countenance to mildness and softness which are all easily acquired do the business and without further examination. . . .
>
> Do not therefore trust to appearances and outside yourself—but *pay other piople with them* because you may be sure that nine in ten of mankind do and ever will trust them. This is by no means criminal nor blameable simulation if not used with an ill intention. I am by no means blamable in desiring to have other peoples good word[,] good will and afection if I do not mean to abuse them. (Emphasis added.)

Giving blunt advice on how to read the "character" of others, the essay esteems a social self: "friendships—they keep hatred within bounds" (1). It is applicable to both sexes in the pursuit of a negotiable identity, strongly recommending, for instance, that a young man turn to a woman to monitor his self-presentations: "Desire some women to tell you of any little awkwardness that they observe in your carriage, they are the best judges in those things and if they are satisfied the men will be so too" (5). The essay hereby reveals where qualities taken to demarcate gender meet, in class-marked cross-sexual interests. It offers specific information about how gender can be stabilized to form this class identity. Learning to behave, that is, exclusively involves regulating a specific form of self-presentation that confers class.

The essay explains qualities in a gentleman that are usually taken to mark only ladies as objects of desire, even if their sexuality is constrained by patriarchal authority. It instructs men in regulation of their bodies as well as modulation of their language. Like Mary Jefferson Randolph's school composition on ladylike deportment, the essay blurs the categories of class and gender, especially in its opposition of gentility and shame:

> More people stand and walk than sit genteely. Awkward ill bred people being ashamed commonly sit bolt upright and stiff—others, too negligent and easy which is ungraceful and ill-bred unless when the familiarity is extreme but a man of fashion makes himself easy, and appears so, by leaning gracefully instead of lolling about; and by varying those easy attitudes, instead of that stiff immobility of bashful boobs. (1)

Posture is not the only way to show flexibility. The essay figuratively applies ease of carriage to other forms of refinement. Again, it addresses both males and females in its encouragement to acquire a "person" that is a sign of educational advantages:

> You cannot conceive how advantageous a good air, genteel motions, and ingaging address are, *not only among women, but among men,* and even in the course of business; they fascinate the affections, they steal a preference, they play about the heart till they engage it—I know a man and so do you, who, without a grain of merit, knowledge, or talents, has raised himself millions of degrees above his level, singly by a good air, and engaging manners. (1–2, emphasis added)

Favor equally depends, as a matter of principle, on formal regulation of one's language. Here, gentlemen are encouraged to achieve an elegant speaking style:

> But as you would please[,] persuade[,] and prevail in speaking it must be by the ornimental parts of oratory. Make them therefore habitual to you, and resolve never to say the most common things to your footman but in the best words you can find and with the best utterance. . . . Talk well upon the subject you talk upon and the most trifling frivolous subjects will still give a man of parts an opertunity of showing them. (2, 4)

As the influential *Ladies Book* magazine put these principles in 1831, "To converse well is of more importance in every-day life than to write well." This social tenet is elaborated with common rhetorical advice: "But [speaking and writing] are both *talents or acquirements of inestimable value, the possession* of one of which need in no instance exclude that of the other. On the contrary, if properly cultivated, they are mutual promoters."[9]

The advice to youth in Horner's commonplace book brings the categories of men and women together, but it commodifies women further by placing them in a decidedly patriarchal realm of desire. Young men of parts are directed to use women not only to improve their deportment and to provide access to fashionable circles. They must also remember, for instance, that in business, "*masters are like mistresses:* whatever services they may be indebted to you for they cease to love you when you cease to be agreeable" (15). While maintaining the cross-gendered tenor of this advice, the essay slips from generalities to explain specifically how to attract women:

> To be liked by women you must be esteemed by men and to please men you must be agreeable to women. Vanity is unquestionably the ruling passion of women, and it is much flattered by the attentions of a man—who is generally esteemed by men. When his merit has recieved the stamp of thier approbation, women make it current that is to say put him in fashion. On the other hand if a man has not received the last polish from women, be may be estimable among men but will not be amiable. The concurrence of the two sexes is as necessary to the perfection of our being as the formation of it. Go among women with the good qualities of your sex and you will acquire from them the softness and graces of thiers. Men will then add affection to the esteem which they before had for you. Women are the only refiners of the merit of men, it is true they cannot add weight but they polish and give luster to it. Force, [?] attention, tender looks, and passionate [?] on your side, will produce some irresolute wishes at least on her side and whenever the lightest wish arises, the rest will soon follow. (3–4)

Here a "character" for highly gendered women partially undercuts its own prejudice against them by always *applying* the uses of their ladylike identity, and by doing so in a discourse that equally commodifies young men. The essay, that is, explicitly identifies contact with women as a way to produce advantages in dealing with other men, not just as a resource for manners. Contact with females in this desired class is not taken for granted. It requires work to increase a male's "esteem" in the eyes of other men, heightening it to the higher exponent of "affection," which results from making a good show.

Nonetheless, the essay makes it obvious that female company is to be cultivated. It curiously combines the advantages like those that the young Boswell wanted from meeting both low women and great men like Samuel

Johnson: "Frequent those people and be glad but not proud of frequenting them, never boast of it as a proof of your own merit, nor insult, in a manner, other companies by telling them affectedly what M&F [?] were talking of the other day; as I have known people to do here with regard to Pope and Swift who had never been twice in company with either" (4).

These anachronistic literary allusions make us pause until we recall that it is not the origin, but the circulation of such dogma in an ordinary collection that identifies assumable subject positions. The politics of gender and its production of class currency had a specific usefulness for Horner's local acquisition of a blended class and gender ideology. The essay's main concern, to prepare young men for success in business, was certainly an appropriate topic in the postwar South. The last twenty pages of the fragment explicitly explain how a youth with ambition and no entitlements could shape his character to converse and have business dealings with equals, superiors, and inferiors. Repeatedly, this Addisonian advice recommends attendance at court sessions to observe successful manners in operation where judicial formality modulates passion: "The good breeding which alone can be acquired at courts are not the showish trifles only which people call or think them. They are a solid good; they prevent a good deal of mischief; they create, adorn and strengthen" (17). In every particular, then, the essay treats social encounters as means of self-education. It notes differences between what is necessary for a youth and the privileges that age will bring. "Sloth and indolence are pernicious and unbecoming in a young fellow; let them be your resource forty years hence at soonest" (19).

A New Wife

Educational texts preparing males to be men of business and social affairs may have been cross-gendered like this one, but they in no way discounted the sexual division of social labor or offset the need to fit females for their distinct occupation as wives. Commonplace gender *doxa* details the subjectivity of a successful wife—a social, not private or "natural" identity. Wives occupy a mature identity that is realized in their behavior and discursive practices—appropriate reading and writing. Women must consequently approach this way of living with either "wisdom and virtue" or "improvidence." Addressing this subject, again relying on the balanced parallels characteristic of eighteenth-century style, a fragmentary letter was recopied to assure its survival and labeled only "copied from paper in Welly [Wellington] chest."[10] Intended perhaps as a model for epistolary greetings to a betrothed or newly wed woman, it conversationally describes a female's progress from person to woman to wife.

You have just entered into that state which is replete with happiness or misery. The issue depends on that precedent amiable, uniform conduct which wisdom & virtue so strongly recommend on the one hand or on that improvidence which a want of affection or passion may prompt on the other.

The letter was written to "ensure all that happiness" that might be possible in "the union of virtuous persons." The author writes, "How can I render you a higher service than by presenting you with that advice which the warmest affections suggest—my experience as well as my solicitude, my fond hope of seeing you happy and beloved." The letter-essay prepares the recipient for both this happiness and the formidable achievement of remaining beloved. The author outlines a typical formal program of conduct and modulation of temperament, common topics in many conduct books for women from the late eighteenth century on:[11]

> You possess a good heart and good understanding. You are allied to a man of honor and of talents and of an open generous disposition. You have therefore in your own power all the essential ingredients of domestic happiness. If you now see clearly the path from which you will resolve never to deviate; our conduct is often the result of whim or caprice often such as will give us many a pang unless we see beforehand what is always the most praiseworthy and the most essential to happiness.

Further dividing the path to follow into "rules," the letter lays out maxims that demand the same emotional control advocated elsewhere for both young men and maidens. Anger, impatience, or any opposition may "stop his attachment," which will thereby subject the new wife to untold (the silence on this point very telling) marks of disaffection. As does Book II of Aristotle's *Rhetoric*, the letter identifies belittling behavior as a source of male shame that will destroy affection:

> I will call your attention to a few primary rules of conduct from which a virtuous wife one who has the sense & the goodness to endeavour to promote mutual happiness & to render the matrimonial state a feast of the purest affection, will never depart from—The first maxim which you should impress most [dutifully?] upon your mind is never to attempt to controul your husband by opposition or any other [?] of anger. A man of sense, of prudence, of [space] feelings cannot and will not bear an opposition of any kind which is attended with an angry look or expression the current of his affections is suddenly stoped his attachment is weakened he begins to feel a mortification the most pungent in being made little in his own eyes and be assured the wife who once excites those sentiments in the heart of her husband will never regain the high ground which she might have retained—when he marries her if he be a good man he expects from her smiles & not frowns he expects to find her and who is not to controul him not to take

from him the freedom of acting as his own judgement shall direct but one that will place such confidence in him as he believes that his own prudence is his best guide—Little things which in reality are mere trifles in themselves often produce bickerings and even quarrels never permit them to be a subject of dispute. Yield them with pleasure with a smile of affection. Be assured one difference outweighs them all a thousand times. a difference in reallity with your husband ought to be considered as the greatest calamity, as one that is to be most studiously guarded against. It is a demon which must never be permitted to enter a habitation whose all should be peace unimpaired, confidence, and heartfelt affection.

The letter reinforces these warnings, emphasizing that wives have a great deal to lose by "allowing" quarrels to occur.[12] The letter specifies the foolishness of risking the loss of a husband's affection in view of the trouble it will cause an "idle and silly" complainer:

> Besides what can a woman gain by her opposition or her differences. But she loses everything, she loses her husbands respects for her virtues, she loses his love and with that a prospect of future happiness. She creates her own misery and then utters idle and silly complaints but utters them in vain. The love of a husband can only be retained by the high opinions which he has of his wife's goodness of heart, her amiable disposition, of the sweetness of her temper, of her prudence and her love of him—let nothing upon any occasion ever lessen that opinion on the contrary it should augment every day. [H]e should have much more reason to admire her for those excellent qualities which will cast a lustre over a virtuous woman when her personal attractions are no more.

If beauty must fade, a wife's skillful management of an invariably acquiescent identity need not. To provide specific advice, the letter exposes traps in which a wife may catch herself. It specifies what to do when a man is away from home longer than expected, brings unannounced company home to dinner, or indulges in any other potentially disagreeable prerogative. In all cases, cheerful acceptance preserves a wife's safety and enhances the good reputation required by propriety:

> Has your husband staid out longer that you expected? When he returns receive him as the partner of your heart—has he disappointed you in something that you expected [?], never evince discontent receive his apology with cheerfulness. Does he invite company without informing you of it or bring home a friend whatever may be your repast, however scanty, it may be, however impossible to add to it, receive them with a pleasing countenance, adorn your table with a cheerfulness, give to your husband and to your company a hearty welcome, it will more than compensate every deficiency it will evince love for your husband, goodness in yourself—and that politeness of manners, which acts as the most powerful charm, it will give to the plainest fare a zest superior to all that luxury can boast,

never be discontented upon any occasion of this nature if apologies as silly people often think be necessary your husband will make them or an ingeneous wife will with good humor banter her husband for giving his friends so indifferent a repast.

The letter further specifies the purpose of its saccharine pointers. It explains that a family's success, counted as possessions and reputation, depends on a wife's support of her husband. In particular, deploying the class-marked character of a *wife* ironically involves effacing her awareness of class status:

> In the next place as your husbands success in his possessions will depend upon his popularity and as the manners of a wife have a little influence in extending or lessening the respect & esteem of others for her husband you should take care to be affable to the poorest as well as to the rich—a reserved haughtiness is a sure indication of a weak mind and an unfeeling heart—

Clearly, the wife in question is also to be a manager, with the copious duties that fell to the relatively autonomous planter's wife (chapter 5). She needs cooperative servants who will respond favorably to her own self-management by managing their own, further enslaved, identities:

> With respect to your servants teach them to respect and to love you whilst you expect from them a reasonable discharge of their respective duties. Never tease yourself or them by scolding, it has no other effect but to render them discontented or impertinent. Admonish them with a calm firmness[;] if that mode will not produce the desired effect let them be moderately corrected.

It is notable that this restrained management style was expected of upper-class slaveholders specifically to identify their class standing. The letter does not, that is, argue for humane or religiously motivated attitudes toward human chattel, if "servants" here means slaves. The essay advises wives not to acknowledge power relations over people whom they in any case only infrequently owned or paid themselves.

In a final segment, the letter focuses on mental training, the basis for all of these forms of behavior. In this particular context, commonplace advice about reading is given a significant spin. It promotes reading specifically to maintain a social identity. By avoiding novels and plays, and instead reading the great (masculine) deeds of universalized history portrayed in "geography, poetry, moral essays, biography, travels, sermons and other well written religious productions," the wife will acquire a mental disposition that supports her work:

> Cultivate your mind by the perusal of those books which instruct whilst they amuse. Do not devote much of your time to novels. There are a few which may

be useful in improving & giving a higher [plane?] to our moral sensibility but in general they tend to vitiate the taste and produce no substantial intellectual food—Most plays has the same consequence they are not friendly to that delicacy which is one of the monuments of a female character—History, geography, poetry, moral essays, biography, travels, sermons and other well written religious productions will not fail to enlarge your understanding to render you a more agreeable companion and to exalt your virtue it is sacrificed to her passions whose voice and not that of her God is her only governing principle—a woman devoid of rational ideas of religion has no security for her virtue. Besides in those hours of calamity to which families must be exposed, where will she find a support of it be not in her just reflections upon that all ruling Providence which governs the universe & all things there.

This copied letter was left unfinished, ending with "mutual politeness . . . ," it is an educational document, not a gratuitous reiteration of mindlessly gendered, repressive requirements for women in marriage. A recipient might have wished for more such advice to avoid becoming one of the many wives who were beaten, deprived, infected with venereal disease, and displaced by mistresses and illegitimate children, all without legal recourse.[13] The essay instructed a wife in how she might escape "misery," but she will not escape it automatically. To do so, she needs this particular, important education that is circulated among women. Modulating one's disapproval, skillfully managing servants, and avoiding the influence of harmful reading that would stimulate rebellion or encourage idiosyncrasies were necessary but at times insufficient tools against what was often a legally sanctioned personal disaster for women.

But assuming the position of a wife was not the same as achieving *womanhood*. Nor was becoming a *husband,* a subject position ignored in much conduct literature, precisely equal to becoming a *man,* although Issac Hite's "laws" state that a socially adequate man must marry (chapter 3). As these doctrines tacitly admit, and as a great many records of emotionally intimate marriages in this period further emphasize, females and males did not occupy these positions in fixed ways. They borrowed them as versions of propriety, applicable in specific situations to which these discursive conventions applied. This articulation of desirability pointedly addresses the "new" wife, a female whose success after entering a defined social, legal, and economic class status did not go without these advisory sayings. Until the era of privatized domesticity honored the wifely role by casting it as a natural fulfillment of a woman's psychological and biological essence, a class-identified wife entered only a social construction site.

The Expedience of Misogyny: Base Lines

Other ways to articulate gender identity, and less polite ones, have also been common in attempts to stabilize social constructions such as *wife*. Peter Stallybrass and Allon White suggest that common lewdness reflects a "constitutive ambivalence" about fixed, especially privileged, identities.[14] In their words,

> The "top" attempts to reject and eliminate the "bottom" for reasons of prestige and status, only to discover, not only that it is in some way frequently dependent upon that low-Other . . . but also that the top *includes* that low symbolically, as the primary eroticized constituent of its own fantasy life. The result is a mobile, conflicted fusion of power, fear and desire in the construction of subjectivity.[15]

Of course, for Enlightenment sensibilities, this "top" and "low" were mind and body, human versus animalistic identity. Many attempted to suppress all public references to the body by either sex. A German immigrant, Frederick Williams (1800–1877), was one of few who were apparently comfortable in both cross-gendered and physical discourses that were relatively free of the prurience of a few native Virginia accounts. As a merchant sea captain, Williams recorded detailed notes on each of his voyages between Norfolk and European ports, including the antics of passengers and his wife. For instance, he describes, with delicacy, frankness, and good humor, the births of three children to two mothers during a storm at sea:

> On the 5 of November, 1830 in a Severe Storm. One of the Female Passengers was good and well delivered of a Boy Child. Another of the Passengers at the same time was delivered of a Boy. The Husband overjoyed came to inform me of it and asked for a bottle wine which was given to him. When he went forward. Which was with great difficulty as *he labored very hard*. When he handed the Bottle wine down in the between decks. They told him from below, that his wife had had another One a girl Child. *The good man came right up and told me that his wife had had a nother one. and that he must have another bottle of wine. which was quickly given him. and he hurried forwards with all haste. No doubt to put a stop to it,* but he evidently fell on decks, rolling from side to side but saved his bottle wine. so that in one hour in a heavy storm 3 children were born all good and well *and no doubt that the rolling and laboring of the vesel assisted Nature a great deel,* for they all arrived safe in the U. States on the 9th of November.[16]

Patriarchal Rage?

Another example of the fantasies of the "top" preserves as a cultural legacy otherwise unspoken but intentionally transgressive bases for gendered identity. Thomas Massie (1783–1864) recorded jokes and street stories he heard on a trip to San Francisco in 1854 and elsewhere. His commonplace book also includes purported anecdotes about John Charles Fremont, Thomas Jefferson, James Madison, and Thomas Mann Randolph, among others.[17] As Kenneth Lockridge remarks in his study of the commonplace books of William Byrd and Thomas Jefferson, misogyny is a long and dishonorable tradition, visible in the recorded fears of politically marginal men like Byrd, as well as in works by Swift, Pope, and Jefferson. Lockridge argues that in this male folklore, circulated from the *Malleus Maleficarum* (1484) on, "self-fear and social and political alienation were combined . . . into a portrait of pervasive horror whose name, or at least whose central metaphor, was woman."[18] Agreeing with Foucault, Lockridge identifies as confessional texts both Byrd's detailing of the frailty of female character and the female body and Jefferson's scrupulously cited literary examples of the perceived annihilating qualities of female power. Lockridge finds these examples personally horrific, despite their seeming literary displacement of the personal, precisely because the privacy of the commonplace textual setting in which they were inscribed shows that "this is private rage, not public play."[19]

Less surprised feminist readers may question Lockridge's belief that the public realm is not a "private" male one, especially for those men whose cultural memory is constructed by commonplace networks. It is not obvious, despite Lockridge's psychologizing, that males *must* imitate patriarchal models but fear failure, nor that they must always attribute to females their own inadequacies.[20] Nor can the historically situated, newly gendered male *citizen* constructed in France's revolution and exported to others be counted as always a victim of an oedipal essence. *Citizen,* like *woman,* was an assumable, temporarily held position in discourse, certainly in its initial circulation. Nonetheless, Lockridge claims that well before and after the period he surveys, "not only marginal and anomalous elites, but also established ones faced with the feminization of marginal and central areas of public life, were prone to misogyny, and to a nervous masculinization of power."[21]

This situated nervousness would better explain Thomas Massie's recirculated misogynistic anecdotes, especially his stories about powerful leaders, were it not true that even in stable times men have fantasized absolute power over women. In commonplace networks, such tales maintain racist, regional, and antifemale prejudice as an obverse articulation of "conduct." They account for customs that lie outside codes of behavior that uphold honor and reciprocity, while simultaneously underlining the power relations and desires that constitute those values.

From such transgressions, we learn what the assumption of fixed social identities, especially those of wife and husband, allow respite *from*. Perhaps Massie's anecdotes emphasize marriage because he was a bachelor; perhaps he shared Jefferson's suspicion of powerful wives and mothers.[22] But stories that can't be told in polite company also situate the teller beneath respectability, in a sewer more odious each time its well-established conventions are realized. For instance, Massie records the following account of President Madison, a representative of the highest patriarchal status, in an anecdote that shows class and gender prejudice in Massachusetts:

> Dr. Massie, (my uncle) mentioned today, in conversation, a singular anicdote communicated to him by J. Madison then Ex-President of the U.S. J. M. stated that one of the most singular circumstances attending his service of President, was the fact, that whilst in office, he repeatedly recieved letters from young unmarried ladies, stating that they were with child! The singular fact he could not account for, except by referring the act to a species of temporary insanity on the part of girls, who had thought so much of marriage, and so ardently desired it as to impair their minds, and make them really beleive they possessed that which they so much desired.[23]

Massie continues this characterization of the female desperation for sex, and for the wedlock that would make it respectable, by confirming the next remembrance as his own experience. Women's avaricious passions are proved, that is, both by the authority of James Madison and by "fact":

> The same subject brought to his recollection the historical fact that the women (doubtless the old maids) of a certain town in Massachusetts petitioned the Legislature of the State to make it lawful for white women to marry negro men. Soon after this a petition to the same effect was sent by the women of Boston to the Legislature, which body was ultimately so harrassed that they finnally granted the prayer of the petitioners; notwithstanding the earnest remonstrances of the "colored ladies" of Massechusetts, who complained bitterly [that their?] black lovers would leave them all, so soon as the liberty was given them of marrying white women. The white women, however, gained their cause, and it is now, and has been for a long time, lawful for a negro to marry a white woman in the puritanical state of Massechusets. (1)

Interracial marriages were not legal in Virginia, although they did occur as locally accepted formal arrangements and in informal, sometimes scandalous alliances. The more obvious point of this story is, however, traditional regional competition between males. The chief patriarch of Virginia is imagined as bewildered by the behavior of degenerate puritanical northerners, the

failings of "the sex," and subhuman African Americans. But the use of females as prizes in a competition between males is an old theme. After the
English civil war, for instance, female radicals claimed to be pregnant by the
politicized Christ of the Second Coming. James Madison may have received
such letters, perhaps written for similar political reasons, but their politics
cannot be deduced from Massie's account. Women, that is, have traditionally
deployed their bodies politically, in one instance stripping to the waist in
Whitehall to protest a sermon, an event excoriated in David Brown's *The
Naked Woman* (1652).[24] It is thus possible that many jokes about the fathers
of their country had political origins in female practices that misogynist
blasts attempted to neutralize—as a result, of course, effectively suppressing
a history of female protest.

Massie obviously does not reflect on these anecdotes as I have. He appears
to think of them as expressions of the propriety and morality of the dominant culture. Their circulation, that is, is usually coded without reference to
politics, as was Samuel Simpson's note (chapter 3) that "yet at my Mother's
breast," he was "shown a servant woman's breast which I looked at for some
time, and pinched with my little hand, but finally declined."[25] Simpson
shares with Massie an exploratory prerogative that is taken to be equal to
nursing women writing about their sore nipples in other accounts.[26] But
Massie much less decorously also records how a woman invites a judge to her
home to swear to the paternity of her bastard children, repeating the story in
the interest of revealing "improvements" in his time:

> May 25th.   Breakfast. W. Boyd acted as commissioner yesterday, at the elec-
> tion at Massie's Mills for Sherriff [?]. He stated that whilst on the bench, a rather
> good looking woman came up in the midst of the crowd, and spoke to W. Cof-
> fee, the magistrate[,] telling him to come to her house, on a certain day, as she
> "had business for him." When the woman had gone away W. B. asked Coffee
> what bussiness the girl had with him. He answered that she had a couple of bas-
> tard children whom she had heretofore neglected to swear to their supposed
> fathers, and that she needed him, at her house, as a magestrate for that purpose.
> Dr. Massie remarked that such occurrences were now very uncommon, in com-
> parison with what they used to be—that the morals of Nelson Co. had under-
> gone, in the last 50 years, a most wonderful change for the better: that when he
> was a young man, it would have been a difficult matter to find a young unmar-
> ried girl, of the lower classes, who had not, at least one bastard child; and many of
> them from 3 to 6. And yet this did not, in those days, prevent them from getting
> husbands, such as they must have been. (5–6)

In this view, female independence had been successfully tamed, to the degree
it existed at all among the imagined "low" in these stories, who often could

not afford to keep legal households. These "husbands, such as they must have been" either married the mothers of their children or took on legal responsibility for families that were not their own. But male transgressions against patriarchal opinion, like female transgressions against wifely subject positions to which they had no economic access, are marked in these anecdotes as infractions of sexual, not class, mores. The change in morals that Massie's uncle perceived probably resulted from a temporary improvement in the economy, so that writing a supposed new puritanism as an essential change in the desires of the lower class celebrates a new will to obey the expensive requirements for middle-class marriage. Massie continues the anecdote with another sly particular:

> He mentioned the case of two young girls who lived on [Lye?] River, which was both amusing and [?]. They were large enough to go to parties, but had never gone till one day a stout country fellow riding by to a wedding in the neighborhood offered to take them both with him upon his horse—one before and one behind. The old folk consented, and the horse groaned away under his heavy load. The three danced all night and went home in the morning—and, just nine months afterwards each of them had a child. (6)

Class prejudices are here turned against country people, whom Massie elsewhere calls of "limited intellect." The interest of this geographical determinism is its assumption that two country girls were ignorant of proper behavior, especially after receiving the consent of the old folk. As Nancy Armstrong suggests about British attempts to reform morality in the working classes rather than the middle classes, these girls are portrayed as "at once promiscuous and insufficiently gendered."[27] They obviously are denied the status of "young women," which is unavailable to their class, and the "manners" that would prevent the story of their fun-filled fall from being told (although obviously would not prevent its occurrence).

But prejudice against females extends beyond commonly derided lower-class and rural subjects. Massie also tells a seemingly harmless story of a female cousin's entry into a specific gender status. He evidently records the incident in the interest of reforming the female craving for marriage that President Madison encountered:

> My cousin Juliet Boyd [Juliet Anna Massie Boyd], when a young girl, was exceedingly beautiful and vivacious. Just before she quit school, under Tom [?]—the most sarcastic of men— . . . in Richmond, at the house of [Jay] E. Heath, where a party of ladies and gentlemen were collected Together. Cousin Juliet said—"Now, Papa, the school will soon be over, and when I get home to Nelson you must give me a *turning out party*." Ans. "You wish it to be known that you are in the market. Very well! I stick up a sign at the gate—"A goose for sale." (6)

Young girls associated with men fairly freely, but this story again shows that they did so at their peril, placing themselves under observations meant to keep them, precisely, in line. In this "character," Massie claims, Julia is a frivolous and beautiful—therefore prized—family possession. Her father articulates her status as merchandise from his position, alluding to a material exchange that will occur whether he posts a sign or gives a coming-out party. But this truth about the economic basis of a father's attention to a daughter's future is displaced onto Juliet, who is hereby also accused of being overly aggressive about it. A later anecdote that employs the trope of lost virtue tacitly contrasts cousin Juliet's implied aggressiveness with the "delicacy" of women of an earlier time, equally determined to marry:

> May. 31. *Early days of Va.* The conversation turning, this evening on the subject of the delicacy and fastidiousness of Virginia ladies, at the present day, Dr. M. said he wondered what the women of the revolution would think of them if they could rise from their graves. "I recosent the following, as an authentic account of those days. It was when Augusta County extended almost to the Ohio river, and settlements were very few and far between. A young gentleman and young Lady, who lived in [T]ygarts Valley, not far from the present city of Wheeling wished to get married, and there being no preachers in their part of the country, they [?] to come to Staunton to have the marriaje ceremony performed. The bridegroom brought a young man along with him as attendant, or waiter, with whom he quarrelled when the party had got within some 30 miles of Staunton. From a quarrel they went to fighting when the bridegroom got so badly flogged he could proceed no farther. The bride complained bitterly of this conduct towards her intended, when the attendant told her that rather than she should be disappointed in getting a husband after riding so far he himself would proceed on with her to Staunton and marry her. *The young Lady said his conduct was very gentlemanly, and she would accept of his offer;* and accordingly, leaving her first-intended in bed, they proceeded to Staunton and were married. On their return, the wounded man, being sufficiently recovered to travel, joined the party and returned home a bachelor still. (13–16, emphasis added)

Of course, for this bride's "delicacy and fastidiousness" to be manifest, she must, like the females in all these stories, be determined to marry a gentleman or a lower-class substitute. But this woman's "leaving her first-intended in bed" and marrying another man is praised in the interest of making a nostalgic comparison between "Early Virginia" women and later examples. Massie rearticulates the positive values implicit in all such counter-representations of a moral society: A socially sanctioned identity is far preferable to a psychological state of desire.

Circulations of this social *doxa* regularly include references to acts of artic-ulation. Proper language links relative evaluations of human states, the chief purpose for Massie's anecdotes, to relative evaluations of discourses where those states are located. He comments, for instance, "Wm. M.—speaking of the old testament, remarked that it was a pity that policy had required, that such a tissue of *absurdities and vulgarities,* should be stuck on to the New Testament, which was, on the contrary *the most perfect system of morality* with which the world had ever been [blessed]" (3, emphasis added). Storytelling also turns on nominalist precision in definitions, as in Massie's account of a falling-out between his uncle and the son of one of his peers:

> When Dr. M. was member of the [Virginia] Legislature, he was, at times, pretty severe upon that body. On one occasion, in the presence of [?] Macon, son of Gen. Na[b]. Macon . . . generally thought almost an idiot, the Dr. said the Leg-islature was composed of one half fools, and the other half knaves. "Well, Doctor, which do you belong to?" asked young Macon, who has since then not occupied so high a place in the Dr.'s esteem as formerly. (10–11)

Another story directly describes a common prejudice against those whom gentlemen imagine to be non-native speakers:

> *California Legislature*   Walking one day with Edward Stanly in the streets of San Francisco he [?] was accosted by a Spanish gentleman, who spoke to him, a short time, in bad English. When we passed on, W. S. remarked that "That man, a handsome fellow, was Don Juan Castillo, a native of California, and now a member of the Cal. Legistature. At the opening of the present session he at-tempted to make a speech in English, and committed many rediculous blunders. Among others—the subject under discussion being the election of a chaplain to the house—Castillo spoke in opposition to the whole business, and concluded by saying he did so because it was "all d———n nonsense". When told of the im-propriety of his language he respectfully apologised, by saying that he was sorry he had committed a rudeness; but as he had learnt his words from Americans they should not object to hearing them. (11–13)

The male, universal moral of this story is situated in complex power rela-tions that, here and elsewhere, specifically figure foreign versus native and grammatically correct versus improper language. But these relatively infor-mal anecdotes indicate the power of commonplace othering. These conduits for male identity and upper-class male privilege to judge females and others, like their formal didactic counterparts in the abstractions preserved in essays such as those entitled "Youth" and "A New Wife," turn on negative differences from an assumed universal standard. This imagined universal is, at bottom, the linguistic substance of male gendering.

These storytellers of course knew this. Massie's record includes a final example that serves as a cautionary tale. It is a lengthy Chaucerian story of a community's revenge on an unfaithful husband "notoriously in the habit of visiting a certain girl of an all-obliging disposition who lived alone in a cabin, in the woods, some miles away from the village." The villagers, who stealthily put his saddle up a tree, ever afterward tell of "how finally Old S. got home late, and how cunning a lie (being a strict Methodist) he contrived to relieve the suspicions and uneasiness of poor good Mrs. G. And what a wonderful reformation took place in Old S. which lasted several long weeks" (19). This last entry reasserts the power of commonplace stories and of the further repetitions that make their tropes familiar to us. The tale concludes: "All these points the tellers of this famous anecdote, in Nelson [County], dilate upon with much gusto. Old S. he is now dead, but that tale will last as long as his memory endures" (19).

Gender as Discourse

The Character of superficial is by no means applicable to the whole Sex. Like all other general Rules, this one has some exceptions.

CONRAD M. SPEECE to POLLY HANNA, January 9, 1791

If I were a man, no such thought would dare enter my mind, but I, being merely a woman, must sit still, and with my weak sisters, for fear of doing aught unwomanly, and see 7000 men surrender as they did at Donelson, a deed that women would have blushed to own, and a deed that makes us weep to feel that such men are our countrymen.

LUCY WOOD BUTLER, journal, 1861

Within every society, each social agent is inscribed in a multiplicity of social relations . . . that determine positionality or subject positions, and every social agent is therefore the locus of many subject positions; . . . each subject position is itself the locus of multiple possible constructions, according to the different discourses that can construct that position.

CHANTAL MOUFFE, "Hegemony and New Political Subjects"

Gender as an Assumable Loan

Many literary theorists, women's historians, and feminist rhetoricians properly take accepted categories for men and women, which are written only provisionally by the gender *doxa* discussed in chapter 4, to be damaging classifications of human beings. But to include gender as a useful category of analysis in textual professions that already stratify their textual objects of study, these scholars often accept and strategically essentialize these categories. To do our professional work, that is, it is convenient to agree to separate male "universal" or "public" discourses and their privileged cultural work from female texts and activities that have only recently been retrieved from oblivion. I have been arguing instead that all branches of humanistic study would benefit from reexamining such modernist categories in light of evidence that shows how the circulation of commonplaces in indigenous writing helped establish those categories, but in ways that simultaneously flatter and deform the purposes and outcomes of textual practices.

The gender *doxa* discussed in chapter 4, for instance, never articulates the categories of men and women apart from its primary purpose, to manage anxieties about class standing. The broader consequences of deploying these categories to regulate social interactions are certainly overwhelming, in political, economic, and human results. But the discursive strategy of essentializing gender by making it a coherent first cause never entirely works, nor was it meant to. Certainly gender as a category never absolutely opposes the larger system without which it cannot exist as a category and never marks individuals in ways irrelevant to their status within that system. But circulations of stable gender identities also never entirely support that larger system. Both off-color stories and the social "laws" that produce serious advice on gendered characters always operate with the self-irony of any citation. They are written as one of many branches of cultural pedagogy, in a self-educative practice that in this case is a sign of contact with and deference to society, but not of simple binaries within it.

Chapters 5 and 6 continue this critique of the categories of men and women and their frequent political uses to privilege "universals" that shore up class-coded access to patriarchal entitlements as against "gender," a limitation assigned to supposedly lesser and supposedly monolithic female interests and covertly to other marginal demands. These commonplace texts show emerging uses of the subject position of the "tasteful" individual/universal in the late eighteenth century and later. Power resided in this personalized male identity, which postrevolutionary societies understood from many sources but made natural through widespread schooling in the new rhetoric of interpretation written by Hugh Blair. These chapters emphasize that this emerging essential category retained a great deal of flexibility, as did its increasingly needed binary opposite, woman. These chapters analyze the genres exemplified in this collection of commonplace texts to show that the cultural work they accomplish is largely irrelevant to fixed gender categories, if not to sex, class, race, or other forms of discrimination.

Gender polarities are largely difficult to verify in these genres, whose necessary cause was not sex, but access to literacy. That access through various kinds of male and female schooling does fix limits on the purposes and results of these texts, but it does so much less often and much less rigidly than we have been schooled to expect. As I emphasize in this chapter, access to schooling for women was much more extensive than most people now think, with the result that women wrote for purposes we often assume they would not take up and with much more substantial cultural results than are visible when their discursive labor is assigned to "women's work."[1] Males, on the other hand, participate across all the generic categories in this collection, equally taking up supposedly only domestic and only public purposes for writing.

It is important to gloss this argument by noting that neither females nor males write gender identity to express an inner, privatized self. The "voices" or psychological dispositions that modern analysts impose on both sexes from a post-Freudian perspective are, on this evidence, precisely post-Freudian.[2] Levels of visible or hidden essential consciousness are never at issue in this writing until the end of the nineteenth century. It does, however, display the verbal elocutionary gestures that were taught in rhetoric and moral philosophy as signs of persuasive feeling and that are now mistaken in historical texts for internal self-awareness. Stable gender identities and the psychological states associated with them are indeed deployed in these texts to reinforce the arguments of legal, civic, and class desires. But they are a means to achieve rhetorical authority, a tactic that may muster anger in a female diatribe against Lincoln or invoke fatuousness in a grandfather's actually stern advice to his favorite descendant. Gender-marked statements that we take to be projections of seldom shown inner feelings in the past are better understood under the rubric of rhetorical training, which prescribed appropriate discursive emotions in war, in property arrangements such as marriage, and in other crucial moments of social self-consciousness. These statements appear most often to anchor identity and explain actions taken or hoped for in liminal situations.

This is to emphasize that gender was only one of many subject positions available to those with the social credit needed to borrow it, and it was taken up provisionally, not as an absolute purchase on an identity. It was an assumable loan, a discourse that could amplify or diminish many generic conventions. As many others have said in support of similar critiques of gender categories, they have offered an unevenly adopted functional system, often ignored but as often enforced or resisted for political and social gain.[3] The influence of these categories on modern textual studies needs to be modified by reevaluating ordinary writing. These and other records of the instability of established but always provisionally deployed subject positions demonstrate how neither (the categories) "woman" or "man" can, or are always intended to, achieve the cultural work we too easily attribute to them.

Genders and Genres: Spheres of Literate Practice

Mindful of what Linda Kerber calls "the Rousseauistic assumption that the world of women is separate from the empire of men," we find unassailable evidence that traditional differences in schooling for boys and girls curtailed the number and limited the quality of texts written by females. But this observation usually ignores class-coded stratifications of the availability of writing instruction.[4] When class issues are introduced into analyses of gender, we learn more about how texts by women participate in a civic consensus—not about sexuality, but about domination. It becomes clear, for instance, that the general claim that females were deprived of schooling is a biased inference drawn by historians of literacy who lump vocational training programs required of nonelite males with elite forms of male education. But both males and females of the elite wrote in an oratorical context on topics of professional and civic importance, and both address them equally. It is common, but inaccurate, to assert that some genres, topics, and purposes were the exclusive property of one or the other sex. The imagined "educated" populace was not separated from an "uneducated" opposite that included women.

"A Far Greater Proportion of Young Women"

Presuppositions about female ignorance should be stringently qualified. Could unified gender identity and lack of schooling have produced, for instance, the 1901 commonplace book of Lila Hardaway Meade Valentine (1865–1921), containing her forty-nine pages devoted to "beauty" and "socialism"?[5] This mix of writing about gender and politics, foreshadowed in Lucy Butler's many commonplace books (to be discussed later), was the product of a culture overlooked in more recent formations of gender prejudice. Modern biases are fortified by the many accounts, already described, of women's exclusion from education. Many histories cite the separate educational settings for girls and boys (see chapter 2). But the place where one is educated is of little importance to ordinary writers, now or in the past. The content of these volumes raises significant doubts about categorical expectations for the relative mass, types, and functions of writing undertaken by either females or males.

The ability to write was fairly evenly distributed among the children of professional and planter families in Virginia well before public schooling was available. There were at least six academies in Essex County during the nineteenth century; the school attended by Lucy Yates Wellford Gray graduated over 800 females from 1820 to 1860.[6] Lynne Templeton Brickley suggests that this small county was not unique: "It appears that a far greater proportion of young women attended academies in the 1790 to 1830 period than the proportion of young men who attended academies and college."[7] Cathy N. Davidson extends this claim: "Figures for the 1850 census indicate an impressive rate of literacy among whites: an almost identical rate for both white men and women [in New England] of over 90 percent."[8]

Of course, in these commonplace books, one cannot easily identify by sex the source of passages written by many hands over many generations. But archivists at the Virginia Historical Society assign authorship in ways that suggest that literacy was distributed between males and females in proportion to the commonwealth's changing politics and resources. For the last half of the eighteenth century, only about 5 percent of the volumes in the collection can with certainty be attributed to females. But about 40 percent of books begun between 1800 and 1840, and 38 percent of those begun between 1841 and 1880, are attributed to females. (Books catalogued as "unidentified author" are excluded from the totals from which these percentages are calculated; see chapter 1.) The Virginia census reported a drop in illiteracy from 79 to 20 percent among all free adults between 1840 and 1850, so it appears that literacy education among the elite was fairly consistently shared between the sexes in the period.[9] At least five of the books in this collection were kept by both males and females. But the scrawls, drawings, handwriting exercises, and mature annotations in many other books were apparently added indiscriminately by writers of both sexes. Many volumes indicate that anyone in a household might use a family book as a paper source or less casually set about to annotate the family's accumulation of its collective memory.

This evidence, although based on a single (necessarily partial) manuscript collection, weakens the claim that literacy was assigned to males only, or that males kept it as their exclusive proprietary property. Nor do the apparent purposes for which these books were kept suggest that commonplace volumes belong to separately gendered discursive spheres, even when a scribe's sex is easy enough to ascertain. Accounts and work records, slave records, diaries, miscellaneous lists, copies of documents, prescriptions, recipes, and correspondence were written by both men and women. (School compositions are treated in chapter 2). Exemplary texts in these categories contradict or only partially fulfill expectations established later by more stable (and consequently more immediately negotiable) concepts of gender. With notable exceptions, these genres are divided between the sexes in proportion to the gender breakdown of the entire collection. Most important, when we look for typical, gender-marked uses of inscription—"public" versus "private" content, displays of sentiment, or formal versus vernacular patterns of composition—it is difficult to find differences that endorse common assumptions about even those genres whose gender-biased construction is typically admitted. Discursive conventions appear to limit the cultural content in many genres of textual property, but gender does not.

With the exception of Mary Virginia Early's commencement address (chapter 3), public speeches in this collection were written by men. But even the masculine expectations for that oratorical genre can be modified if one compares speeches to unpublished political essays by females, like the "Ann Eaght" commentary on education (chapter 3), Lucy Butler's polemics about cowardice and her disgusted comments on Lincoln's paternalism (to be examined later), Jennie Stephenson's published memoir of the Civil War (chapter 7), or Lila Valentine's discussion of socialism. The six addresses copied into commonplace books in this collection are found in volumes kept by men. They include an 1817 address by John Mason (1796–1820) to the Franklinian Society at William and Mary College,[10] a record of two speeches delivered by John Rutherfoord (1825–1866) before the House of Delegates on the removal of free colored people from the commonwealth (1853) and on the banking policy of Virginia (1856),[11] and notes in a commonplace book kept from 1722 to 1729 by an unidentified author on sermons preached in England.[12] The last is the only record of public oratory that evidently was not kept as a copy by its author.

"Their Minds and Feelings"

Common interpretations of gender differences do not generally apply in these texts, whether they seek to account for relations between the public and the private spheres, differential access to information and material for stylistic imitation, or the alleged muting of women's voices. This last characterization of a structure of female feeling contends that sporadically secretive writers of either sex recognized twentieth-century discourses on intimate feelings but did not always choose to articulate them. But the Freudian master narrative of the human psyche came later. In these texts, it is not reticence or inhibition that excludes "minds and feelings," thus making them "neither self-reflective nor self-revealing," in Harriet Blodget's words.[13] Like the feelings of any writer, as R. S. Neale says of the writing of history, they cannot be understood "as other than specific to class, time and place, or apart from . . . historical location."[14]

In this historical location, that is, both males and females deployed rhetorical conventions that portray them as the multiply socialized subjectivities that Chantal Mouffe theorizes. Few writers of either sex used written language to vary the conventional self-educative content that verified their personal propriety. The daily jottings of events and accounts that constituted "experience," like narratives developed in journals and letters, show the transformation of "events" into property that became proprietary "address," shaped both by genre and by rhetorical conventions of elocution. When such writings expressed feeling, it is obvious that eighteenth-century American rhetorical treatises like that of immigrant Joseph Priestly were at work.

Priestly promoted figurative language as a specific way to enliven print. As Jay Fliegleman says, Priestly and contemporaneous rhetorical theorists organized the "sincere" but not bombastic political discourse of early American federalism, which operated not with the ideal of realizing thoughts and feelings through appropriate elocutionary gestures, but to display *"the experiencing of* those thoughts and feelings."[15] The range of conventional expression of emotions did not, of course, diminish with this federalist "sincerity." Both the understated affect of Conrad Speece's letter to Polly Hanna (to be discussed later) and the energy of Samuel Simpson's pronouncements on any topic verify that emotional registers that are taken to be natural feelings in specific sites have accumulated over time, not absolutely changed. A range of expression is always greater than the designation *commonplace* implies, as Tazewell's memoir of his grandfather demonstrates in its moving yet generic memorial (see chapter 3).

Nonetheless, this writing does not include accounts whose unsullied authenticity reassures analysts that current modes of pleasure and pain dominated, or were repressed in, the repertoires of either sex at this time. Instead, these writers construct experience discursively, in particular relations between their memories of verifiable events and a situated understanding of the "reality" of feelings. As Kathleen Woodward explains, in some cultures the acknowledged reality of feeling exists only *externally,* in a space between people who may simply forget feelings when separated from their stimuli.[16] Obviously, an event, memory, and text are not essentially joined but culturally linked in strategies of inscription that enact specific purposes. As Joan Scott points out about all historical sources, we can take as a principle that they are never transparent but coded in myriad conventions and made to *"count as experience,"* not in "self-evident nor straightforward [but] always contested, always therefore political" ways.[17]

The otherwise easily dismissed lists, notes, and other genres described here, that is, enact a politics of acquisition. They are more open about how these writers determined what "counts" as experience than may appear to later eyes. Similarly, both sexes participate in counterdiscourses that are realized as irony, singular interests, dissatisfaction with the state of the world much like Lucy Butler's, or open satisfaction with its gendered inequities, as seen in Thomas Massie's lewd jokes about the privileges of a decidedly class-coded sexism (see chapter 4).

Keeping Tracks: Accounts, Work Records, and Slavery

Genres that keep track of property and labor recast conventional accounting formats as memories. But they in turn portray memory itself as a conventional format. Formal records of daily events and transactions were aids to immediate recollection, sources of verification. But they also made new property, by gathering, codifying, and transmitting otherwise perfunctory data, in visible attempts to teach family history to the future. They allow others to reflect on "facts," to acknowledge and form subsequent purposeful plans, and to reenact earlier dispositions of property and labor. Their unstable gendering, a comment on the sexual politics of these texts, offers a number of surprises.

As expected, most records pertaining to money, wages, and interactions with slaves are found in commonplace books attributed to men. Of the ninety-six volumes that contain accounts and work records, seventy-four (or 77 percent) were kept by males, sixteen by females. Three of the remaining six, by unidentified authors, concern male occupations. But sixteen of the seventy-four records of accounts and work written by men are by the same author; therefore, of the writers involved in keeping such records, 28 percent were female. Women often recorded the household's material acquisitions, indebtedness to neighbors, and expenses. Landonia Randolph Minor (1830–1912) kept a list headed "Mama's Indebtedness" that listed debts and gifts to her mother after the death of her father, Robert Dabney Minor.[18]

"How Disposed . . . "

Slave records, a stark subgenre of accounts, are similarly distributed among the nineteen volumes in which they appear. Five women recorded the births and deaths of slaves and regularly accounted for clothing and food apportioned to them. Twelve men, two of whom kept such records in two volumes, compiled similar accounts. But further gender differentiation appears in the content of these lists. With the exception of two men who list clothing supplied (in one instance) and slave deaths (in another), men recorded only the names or births of slaves. Isaac Hite's "memorandum" has lists of "negroes their ages," kept in 1790, 1792, 1800, 1808, 1827, 1841, and 1848. It is identical in form to his list of "names of my horses / age when folded / how disposed."[19] These lists clearly illustrate writing designed to account for possessions whose status changed over time. Nine of the nineteen volumes containing slave records were begun in the eighteenth century. Only one, evidently begun in view of closing such an account, was kept in the later nineteenth century, beginning in 1863.

Twenty-nine percent of the keepers of slave records were female, a proportion close to that for all records kept by women in the nineteenth century. But the involvement of women in clothing and feeding slaves, duties that belonged to their usual oversight of household economy, demonstrates a different relation to this human property. For instance, the shared volume of Jane Frances Page and Jane Byrd Walker at Castle Hill, Cobham, and Turkey Hill (1802–1845), lists clothing and food for Negro slaves along with other records like a recipe for pickled walnuts (transcribed below). In "A List of People that have had Clothes at Barnwell P[lantation]," and "A List of People that have had Clothes at Mountain Plantation," both divided into "Men and Women" and marked off as in a ledger, these women recorded against the slaves' names those who received coats, "Jacketts, Shifts, stockings, Shoes, Hats, [and] blanketts." In addition, this accounting records: "August 8 sent 10 lb cotton," "I owe 16 sent Wm M. of [?] Fresh meat for Wm. [Rlow?]" and similar marks of significant exchanges that appear to have involved slaves.[20] Elizabeth Fox-Genovese says that slaveholding women "overwhelmingly . . . supported slavery and its constraints as the necessary price for their own privileged position."[21] She also suggests, however, that the burdens borne by mistresses of plantations might be compared to the disempowerment of slaves. Neither judgment is entirely applicable to the ethics of these writers, judging from their commonplace books. Nor does Fox-Genovese speculate on how these women may have learned *from* African women's indigenous cultural traditions, including their economic customs.

"My Opinion of the Slaverat Was Not Favorable"

Writing by both females and males suggests ambivalence about slaveholding, particularly in its late "cotton culture" domestic version, which partially endorsed immediately prior republican beliefs that slavery was both wrong and doomed. This ambivalence is visible most often as a subtext in correspondence about the war. Yet a vividly direct objection to slavery, written long after the war, in 1886, is Samuel Simpson's summation, a statement much like his letter about public schools (see chapter 3). In accounting for his actions in 1838, he explains his reasons for passively upholding slavery in the face of horrors he witnessed as a result of both slavery and the decimation of Native American populations.[22] This text exemplifies a different sort of "slave record" and exhibits a rare clarity about the injustice of all racist and nationalistic invasions:

> [1838] I was truly glad of an opportunity to get away from a country afflicted with worthless money, and constantly undergoing political and financial revolution, and great commotion arising from the institution of Negro Slavery, which latter I had seen much of in the cotton states of the South, and was a good deal disgusted with it, but having been born and raised in the belief that slavery was of Divine origin, and was religiously right, my faith and my interest readily squared with this abomination, feeling deeply implicated, I will not enter upon details, in

this part of my narrative, that came under my personal observation, "but could a tale unfold that would harrow up the soul."

The Northern people claim great credit for the part they took in freeing the Negroes, they seem to forget the great wrong they perpetrated upon innocent people by robbing them of their property. They seem too, to forget the huge wrong they have sanctioned in robbing the Indian of all the lands of this continent, they appear to have no grams of conscience about that, especially as the aboriginal tribes have dwindled under oppression and wrong and the Sword, to an insignificant number. Yet it may be within the possibilities of the unchangable laws of nature—out of this remant might arise a host that shall in the long course of years reinhabit the lands of their Fathers, who can tell what may happen; what may come to pass; But to all appearances the poor Indian is likely to perish out of existence on this wide domain of continent.[23]

Simpson characterizes as "slaverats" the planters opening new cotton plantations in the frontier South, to whom his more established family felt superior. His views articulate an infrequently glimpsed counterhegemony based on a felt superiority to his peers and Yankee nationalism, if not on antiracism:

My opinion of the Southern planter, ("Slaverat"), in those days was not very favorable, they were an overbearing tyrannical set as unfriendly to the poor man as ever lived on Earth, with a few exceptions, there was nothing to be admired in their habits and manners. They were never satisfied with getting. They, the Masters, had about the same feeling for their slaves as they had for their horses, mules, and oxen, and that was measured by their market value alone, indeed in some cases the life of a slave appeared to be held far below market value for I have known 20 or 30 valuable Negroes male and female to be burried within a few months, worth say $25,000, for the want of a Doctor's attendance and medicine that would not have cost one fourth of that amount.

Simpson explains how this "waste" typically occurred. His record of a complex mixture of ignorance and concern is probably more accurate about these horrors than Harriet Beecher Stowe's portrayal of Simon Legree's oversight of a Louisiana plantation. The fictionalized malice of Legree in *Uncle Tom's Cabin* is less devastating to read than the banal facts:

The custom was in settling new farms to send some 40— 50— or 75 hands under an unlettered Overseer, with a medicine chest full of drugs into the "Swamps", uncleared lands, there to hew out and erect a "Negro quarter", fell trees and cut *cane*, and open a cotton plantation. Drinking swamp water, grinding their own meal on hand mills, and eating salt pork, with no vegetables, or other change of diet, for the first year at least. The result was, and as might have been expected, great mortality among the colored people. An extensive grave yard was [to be seen] among the most noticeable features of all new farms. Calomel and Jallap and other poisonous drugs were given in astonishing quantities to the sick by the Overseers, while aiming to do good, they really did incalculable harm, and killed many valuable slaves. Poor things they had no volition, but were obliged to swallow the death potion when presented to their lips by the hand of ignorance; I will not however [longer] dwell longer upon this unpleasant feature of a past condition which no longer exists among us. I could write a book on it, having seen it in all its horrid deformity, not so much perhaps from individual depravity, but from a defective and naturally bad system, and the wrong feelings and notions it engendered. Poor creatures, I am heartily glad they are Free.[24]

Simpson's paternalism toward the "poor creatures" clearly locates this text in the dominant class whose passing he celebrates, but his language also offers an exceptional negative self-assessment of a writer and of his peers. It articulates the force of culture struggling against resistances within it in ways rarely visible before such resistance became conventional in dominant discourse. This particular slave record, unique among these texts, vividly reveals what is *not* said in any of these accounts of slave management. Simpson hereby highlights the perpetual "wrongness" of the commonplace, its constant spin away from the predictable. He produces a compelling deconstructive juxtaposition of nature and nurture in a system that entirely misunderstands both.

Daily Acquisition

Simpson's "Memoranda" may appear to be a journal in the modern, self-expressive conception of the genre, but its sententious tone betrays its stated didactic purpose: to create a civil family history. Similarly, the designation *diary*, applied by the Historical Society's archivists, refers to another pointedly "addressed" form that preserved temporal property in the form of daily records. Diaries were often notes kept while traveling, to store information about expenses, lodging, and distances traveled over a day as an indigenous AAA guide. Most travel notes and other daily expense accounts were kept by males. Of the seventeen commonplace books in which they appear, fourteen were kept by men, including Samuel Simpson's autobiography and travel records. Other examples are two volumes by Frederick Williams (discussed in chapter 4), a German émigré and merchant sea captain who recorded the weather on each voyage and the ship's cargo and passengers in a detailed autobiographical account.[25] Other diaries by men describe school attendance, ministerial service, and other travels. Two include data on service in the Confederate Navy by Robert Dabney Minor (whose death occasioned his daughter's accounts of "Mama's Indebtedness") and Alexander

Payne's (1837–1893) service in the Confederate Army and imprisonment at Old Capitol Prison, Washington, D.C.[26]

But the designated keepers of these books were not always authors of the diaries contained in them. The commonplace book of Susan Hancock Lee Gordon Thornton (1792–1867), dated 1860, contains the diary of William Harrison Shover written between August 8 and 20, 1845, while serving in the army at Fort McHenry, Maryland, and in 1846 in Corpus Christi, Texas.[27] William Rust Baskervill's volume containing his accounts also includes the 1833–1872 diaries of Sallie P. Turner Alexander, handwritten on blank pages of 1833–1872 editions of John Warrock's *Virginia and North Carolina Almanac*.[28] Alexander often tipped in additional blank pages on which she listed debts, assets, daily work, and family exchanges:

> "*1833:* I received $2 of Dunnon, $2 of Kent [?]; 7th received from Brutus 50 lbs [?] for minding . . . youngest [?] oats; celery seed; 9th planted potatoes; 11th sowed peas; 16 finished 2 pieces of cloth; . . . commenced soap; 13th Erasmus returned to me; 26th. John born, son of Lizzy; 14th. Erasmus left the house; April: 21st. James T. Alexander was Baptised by Mr. Steel at Col Coleman's in Halifax; November 3rd, "Caroline's child born"
>
>   *1845:* Plantation 6 turkeys, 2 Goblers, 20 hens, Geises [geese] 6; "Salem' 6 Turkeys, 1 gobler, 22 Guse, 16 hens; 8 Turkeys, 2 Goblers, Geese, 5 Ducks, 2 Drakes, Hen? 1 drake.
>
>   *1855:* January: Lilly, 6 turkey Hens, gobblers, Ducks Drakes, hens Roosters, Geese.
>
>   *1857:* Jan. 1, snow; 2d, more snow and children got sick. 8th, exceedingly cold—river impassable from running ice.[29]

William R. Bernard (1826–1881) and his wife shared a commonplace book between 1847 and 1850. It contains "enclosures": an appraisal list of the estate of William's father, John H. Bernard, in Caroline County, with an inventory of the estate, a list of its slaves, and his verses. However, William's part is primarily a series of small compositions, including chapters of what appears to be a children's novel. Jane Gay Robertson Bernard recorded recipes and kept a diary between 1848 and 1850.[30] Both Sallie Alexander's daily records and the Bernards' cross-gendered book, like other genres, indicate that men and women shared common purposes in keeping such books—to aid memory, mark legally significant dates and exchanges, and preserve work as a labor of notation.

The two diary accounts of travels by women are Carrie Lena Moffett's (1854–1898) extended record of her life as a student, teacher, and minister's wife in Kentucky from August 1871 to May 1898[31] and Josephine Dulles Horner Eppes's (?–1852) brief but detailed notes of gifts, letters home, and appointments on an trip to England in 1850.[32] Eppes's tiny (2 × 3 inch) book lists on its first pale blue page, "Items for Letters home." Details show how assiduously this traveler composed her correspondence: "English women, red cheeks bustles in window here; trimmed bonnets; street sweepers; Marino glue." Each item is crossed out, suggesting that Eppes used the list as the "material" of experience, an expendable resource to aid memory. On the back of the book, she practiced spelling "duly / dully / duly," writing "no" and "dull" next to these experiments. Eppes later lists "letters received," and on a facing page, "letters written," a conventional accounting system for correspondence found in numerous letter books—for example, in the commonplace book of lawyer Timothy Chandler (1761–1831).[33] Eppes's final page contains a list of "presents to take home," including "plate," "French testament for Paull," and "little umbrella for Sid Paull."

Thirty-six commonplace books (by thirty-two authors, ten of them women) contain other evidence of compulsive writing, lists that verify the acquisition of experiences, possessions, and what were termed "connections" with others. The lists by women include a student roster of a French class, students at the University of Virginia in 1830–1831, clothing and linen, agricultural equipment and livestock, supplies for hospital beds, and books presumably owned by the writer.

Scoring: Reading and Dating

Three other remarkable itemized lists among those kept by women raise intriguing questions about gendered genres, particularly about the actual rather than figurative "coding" of acquisitions as possessions with specific genders. The first is a fifty-six-page list of the books read each year by Maria DeRieux (1762–1826) from 1806 to 1823. This accomplishment, noted in her obituary, indicates that to be a "woman of letters," if taken to mean a reader, was to assume a specific gender identity. DeRieux's obituary celebrates her literary acquisitions: "Died—Yesterday (at the residence of her son-in-law, Mr. John A. Lancaster,) after a short but painful illness, Mrs. Maria M[artini]. DeRieux. This lady was greatly admired by those who had the pleasure of her acquaintance, for her extensive literary *acquirements*."[34] DeRieux's list reveals yet another version of the equation between *property*, as her counted volumes, and *propriety*, a socialized, public identity as an accomplished individual. DeRieux read approximately 1,120 volumes in seventeen years, or about sixty-six a year, most of them fiction. In 1814, for instance, she lists "Tristram Shandy, Gt." and "Modern Times." Her 1820 list cites "Women or pour et contre" and "Hesitation or to marry or not to Marry, 2 vols." In 1822 she read "Memoirs of Napoleon Bonaparte" and "Dictionary & Memoirs of

Eminent Persons, 8 vols." She included the magazines "Town & Country; Ladies Book" and notes her reading while in North Carolina, Petersburg, and Richmond, evidently finding ample reading material wherever she was. As a female born in 1762, she apparently took this accomplishment seriously enough to communicate its significance to those who knew her; we may wonder about her pastimes before 1806.

In 1875, Susan Elizabeth Roy Carter (1833–1902) recorded a common joke about such reading: "'Are you fond of novels?' 'Yes.' 'Have you ever read "Ten Thousand a Year?"' 'No, never in all my life!'"[35] Susan Carter shared a book, which covers 1875–1879, with Thomas Nelson Carter, who contributed flirtatious verse, and with Juliet Roy Carter Lee. In addition to Thomas Carter's verses and copies of songs, including "Old Black Joe," the volume contains a peripheral example of a list that exemplifies the parlor games played by youths of both sexes, a "magic Table—To find a Lady's age." Its columns list yearly dates and numbers that indicate age in relation to birth year.

The second remarkable list is a multiply organized inventory of people who visited and were known by Ida Spooner Lownes (1819–1889). In 1840, at age twenty-one, she recorded the names of participants in her social life at school and later, in Petersburg. The first page of this volume centers "Scrap Book, Petersburg," "Ida Spooner," and "Virginian." Subsequent pages have separately headed sections for "gentlemen visiting her in Petersburg, Va"; "Names of my Boarding School Mates at Philadelphia, new Haven," and "names of the Girls I have [waited?] on." The names of girls are paired with names of young men with whom they may have danced or whom Lownes may have chaperoned.[36] Above the first list of young men, she self-consciously wrote, "The names of all the gentlemen who have called on me in Petersburg since I left school," leaving a space in a column on the right for their hometowns. Early in the list, most are from her hometown, Petersburg. But the list includes other visitors from afar:

> Cpt Ramsey, Fredericksburg; Wellington Gordon, Mr. Cutcher, Ben Minor; Bob Hart, Baltimore; Mr. Mitchell, Judge Hanson, Mr. Kennedy; Mr. Conkling, New York; Jonas Thompson, Mr. Waller; Ralph Cordes, Mobile with Mr. Hutchenson, Robert Smith, Mr. Jeffries, Mr. Johnson, Dr. Palmly, Mr. Palmly, all Mobile; Mr. Powel, Pontitec, Missis.; Mr. Riley, Norfolk; Mr. T. Morton, Farmville, Va, Mr. Warnick, Farmville; Henry Shipwith, Staunton [Va.], Wm Shipwith, Amelia [Va.]; Judge Wiltherson, Louisville; Dr. Stith, Brunswich, Va; also Dr. Beasley, Dr. Lewis, Mr. Levis; Wm Gurley, Southhampton [Va.], with Frank Ridley, Robert Ridley, Sam Douglas, Mr. Crump, Susex, Va. With Mr. Chambliss, Dr. Blow.

In its entirety, the list contains over 283 names, impressive by any standard. The dates and alphabetical ordering of the list suggest that these young men stopped to visit and were accounted for as they traveled in groups after graduation or for professional purposes, for Petersburg was a convenient midpoint on many itineraries. But Lownes records them in a way that suggests Tennessee Williams's "gentlemen callers," an accumulation of acknowledgments by men whose distant geographic origins verify her sophistication.

Lownes's friends at boarding school covered an equally wide geographic range. Her list of "Names of my Boarding School Mates" again emphasizes the city of origin of her acquaintances, listed in a column to the right. She distinguishes her thirty-eight Philadelphia schoolmates from the ten from New Haven, named in a small corner on the top of one page. All of the New Haven friends are from New York, but the next page lists Philadelphia schoolmates from "Buffalo, Maine, Providence, Walingford Conn.; Rochester, N.Y.; Lyons; Columbus, Ohio; Hillsboro, Ohio; the West Indies, and Mobile." In the next column are names of girls from Washington, New Orleans (3), Louisville (4), Lexington (3), Nashville (1), Florence, Alabama (2), Augusta, (1), Charleston (2), North Carolina (3), Richmond (1), Petersburg (2), Norfolk (1), Smithfield (1); Rockhedge, Virginia, (1); Boynton, Virginia (1), Delaware (1), York (1), South America (1); Augusta (1), Philadelphia (1), Natchez (1), and Trenton (1). Obviously, she was "connected" to friends throughout the East and from other countries.

After the twentieth-century publication of *Mary Chestnutt's Civil War,* *Gone with the Wind,* and *Scarlett,* we might plausibly infer that Ida Spooner ("as she was") was a "belle." But the prominence given to geography in these lists equally suggests that she was scoring not just her social station as a female, but a young woman's excitement at access to distant places. Both lists show that young women might be well traveled, actually and vicariously, in ways that their later discursive imprisonment as "angels in the house" might lead us to overlook. Like Anna Blanton McClure (see chapter 3) and many others, Lownes reinstated such connections as personal and family property for which gender does not sufficiently account.

Gender relations may, however, explain the last example of remarkable lists. Anne Page Friend (1860–1882) at age nineteen recorded in Hampden-Sydney, Virginia, the "Escorts provided by students of the Union Theological Seminary, Richmond."[37] Her 3 × 5 inch book, with "Forget Me Not" embossed on its cover, contains her name and the date, January 4, 1879, on the flyleaf, over "'Engagements.' January" in boldface. Friend apparently first supplied a format for experiences, organizing in ink the days of the week, names of the school recitations ("Rhetoricals") she would attend, and "Mr. ———," then adding the names of her escorts in pencil:

The names of all the
Rolling, Robertson. Petersburg
Frank, Robertson. " "
Frederick Robertson. " "
Dunlop Osborne " "
John G. Rainey " "
Richard Burkett " "
Laurence Smith " "
Wm, Cannon " "
Posy, Robertson. " "
James, McCulloch " "
C, Fisher " "
Montgomery Lynch " "
John Dodson " "
Geni Morton. " "
Robert Field. " "
Tom, Wallace " "
Dr, Wallace. " "
Waverly Journs. " "
Wm Meitens " "
Mr Mordecai Jr " "
James McNichol " "

gentlemen who have
Dunlop Williams. Peters-
John Williams. " "
Wm Armistead. " "
Wm Hinton " "
James Pope. " "
Henry Baskerville. " "
James Hamilton. " "
Wm G. Colquhoun " "
David Mingo " "
Dr Beckwith " "
Mr Bartlett " "
Nat Harrison " "
Ben Vaughan " "
Jaby Smith " "
Marcus Armistead " "
Albert Aiken " "
Wm Page " "
Mr Randolphe " "
Wm Johnson " "
John Sharpe " "
Dr Spencer " "

called on me in Peters
Mr Deveraux Petersburg
Mr Franks " "
Chas Campbell " "
Moses Paul " "
Josephus Hurt " "
Chas Cabniss " "
Capt. Ramsey Fredericks-
burg
Willington Gordon. " "
Mr Crutcher. " "
Ben Minor " "
Bob Hart. Baltimore
Mr Mitchell. " "
Judge Hanson. " "
Mr Kennedy " "
Mr Conkling. New York
Jonas Thompson. " "
Mr Waller. " "
Ralph Cooles. Mobile.
Mr Hutchenson. " "
Robert Smith. " "
Mr Jeffries " "

burg since I left School.
Mr Johnson Mobile
Dr Palmby " "
Mr Palmby " "
Mr Powell, Pontotoc. Missis-
Mr Riley Norfolk
Mr T. Morton. Farmville Va
Mr Warmuck " "
Henry Shipwith. Staunton
Wm Shipwith. Amelia
Judge Wilkinson. Louisville
Dr Heath. Brunswick Va
Dr Brasley " "
Dr Lewis " "
Mr Lewis " "
Wm Eyrley. Southampton Co
Frank Ridley. " "
Robert Ridley. " "
Sam Douglas. " "
Mr Crump Sussex Va
Mr Chambliss " "
Dr Blow. " "

Sundays:
  1st Mr.
  2nd. Mr.
  3rd, Mr.
  4th. Mr.

Wednesdays [same list, repeated]
Rhetoricals
  1st. Mr. Campbell H.
  2nd. Mr. [left blank]

This format is reiterated for February, with "Campbell" named again. In March, she adds the category "Debates," and in April lists Sundays, Wednesdays, and "Seminary Commencement." In May and June, only Sundays are listed, with Campbell as the only name. After Commencement, on Monday night, spaces are provided for graduation celebrations on "Tuesday night, Wednesday. morning, Wednesday Night, and Thursday Morning." Friend reversed her book, turning it upside down to begin a new demarcation. Here, the same lists appear from October to February, with an Intermediate Celebration appearing again. In March, she adds "Debate" again; April repeats "Seminary Commencement." In December 1879, eleven months after beginning her record, Friend began listing "Walks," numbering them in ink on two pages and adding names of her escorts in pencil. In January 1880, she began the list again in the same form.

These notations offer a rare view of the content, organization, and publicity of the theological seminary's curriculum, as they do of Anne Friend's projected hopes, if not entirely successful accumulation, of encounters with escorts. The poignancy of this memorial to the last years of her brief life, not its status as a record of conquests, perhaps explains its retention as a significant family property. But any view of her and her family's purposes must also note the absolute *neatness* of Friend's record, a scrupulous schedule of planned attendance at the seminary's declamations, debates, and ceremonies.

· 6 ·

(Facing page) Page from 1840 commonplace book of Ida Spooner Lownes (1819–1889), headed, "The names of all the gentlemen who have called on me in Petersburg since I left school." Mss5L9547, 1, Virginia Historical Society. Reprinted by permission of Richard T. Wilson III.

Attending school events with a male escort was not unusual. Asa Dupuy Watkins, recording a speaker's first sentence at an "Intermediate" celebration at Hampden-Sydney College, verifies the mixed group in attendance:

> This celebration will long be remembered for the length of the time consumed by the speakers and for the large number of beautiful ladies present" was the remark with which, on the night of the twentieth, the last speaker opened his address: and all the people expressed their agreement with applause; for both ladies and gentlemen were certainly conscious of the former's beauty, and on that very account were particularly anxious to get away and to speak privately with each other about the matter.[38]

These memorial lists demonstrate an earlier form of American acquisitiveness, an overwhelming, relentless compulsion to keep catalogues, yet one innocent of positivist relations to *value*.

"Redeem the Time, for the Days Are Short"

A midcentury plantation woman's diary further elaborates the form and content of accounting for a writer's time. Rebecca Anne Dulany (1828–1858) compiled events in her family's daily life and travels, provision of seasonal clothing for slaves, medical treatments for herself and others, and her three-year decline toward death from tuberculosis at age thirty. Married at nineteen to Richard H. Dulany, her first cousin, Rebecca gave birth to the last of five children in 1856 and died two years later. A typescript copy of her diary reveals how she blended motherhood, management, a desire for "systematic" regulation of her days, and what she refers to as "literary pursuits" in a regular record. Reading this account entry-by-entry highlights the distinction between imposed expectations about "historical" female activities and Rebecca Dulany's own self-educational purpose for writing.

MARCH 4TH, 1855—WELBOURNE HALL. JOURNAL OF REBECCA A. DULANY.

> Sat. A bright and balmy morning. Busy as a bee in the earlier part of the day, sorting clothes, looking over house linen, superintending the weekly scouring, scrubbing, etc.
>
> Richard arrived about noon from the State Agriculture Fair in Richmond. Mary indisposed with bad cold and hoarse voice.
>
> Monday 6th—Mary's cold still keeping me anxious. Went to Upperville in the closed carriage. . . . Found Ed Carr's child with convulsions. Gave it an emetic and a hot bath and sent for Dr. Leith.
>
> Ed's child better tonight. My children have an influenza. After tea read for an hour or two. Sent the baby upstairs to sleep with Margaret Moriarity; took John in my room. Went to bed with toothache.

March.
Sundays.
1st Mr. Cummins
2nd Mr. Venable.
3rd Mr. Woods. 2
4th Mr. White 1

Wednesdays.
1st Mr. Moore 2
2nd Mr. Summerell
3rd Mr. Stokes
4th Mr. Wardlaw.
5th Mr. Stewart

Rhetoricals.
1st Mr. Wardlaw
2nd Mr. Grayhill.

Debate.
Mr. Martin.

April.
Sundays.
1st Mr. Wardlaw.
2nd Mr. Venable.
3rd Mr. Moore.
4th Mr. Woods.

Wednesdays.
1st Mr. Wardlaw
2nd Mr. Walton
3rd Mr.
4th Mr.

Rhetoricals.
Mr. Wardlaw.

Seminary Commencement.
Tuesday night Mr. Moore
Wednesday morning Mr. Wardlaw
Wednesday night Wardlaw

• 7 •

Pages from calendar kept by Anne Page Friend (1860–1882), listing "Rhetoricals" and "Debate" with the names of students of the Union Theological Seminary, Richmond, who escorted her to public rhetorical exercises. Mss1B6117a124, 17. Reprinted by permission of the Virginia Historical Society.

Thursday 9th—Confined To my bed with pain in my limbs and breast. Weather still beautiful, but colds prevailing very generally.

Friday 10th. Windy and cold. Passed the day upstairs, working, reading, & writing. The new Rosewood bedstead with two easy chairs for my room arrived today.

Tuesday 27th. After breakfast, sorted and arranged in the Store room a supply of the Groceries. Opened a barrel of flour and one of sugar. Measured 90 yds. of cotton for the Servants' shirts; and gave out the requisite number of buttons; and quantity of thread, cotton, etc.

Sunday, April 2. Bertha died in childbed—baby living.

Spring at last. Warm, balmy. Father gone to New York. Hal [a brother] to Philadelphia for wedding clothes.[39]

Rebecca also reflects on this busy schedule, indicating how writing is a way to account for herself and improve her days. She applies time-management principles (with reservations about their potential for success) to fulfill the variety of domestic, maternal, religious, literary, and physically realized subjectivities she demands of herself:

Feel much dissatisfied with the manner in which my time passes. So many evenings come, when in looking over the day, I am compelled to say "nothing attempted, nothing done"—Alas! Lay wake late last night, forming the following plan for the more systematic arrangement of my hours: [listing follows] Rise at six/ Prayers and breakfast at 7/ Children's' Chatechism and religion reading until 9/ Household affairs till 12/ Work in the nursery till 1/ Dress and dine at 2/ Profitable reading till 5/ Exercise, and tea and 7/ Read papers and magazines, or work, till 10.

I shall try this plan for one week—but I am subject to so many interruptions from my dear little children that it is hard to keep up any thing like systems.

As the record continues, the call of her failing body increasingly displaces her other identities:

Sunday, May 6. a week yesterday since Richard left for New York. Miss Margaret has been with me since, and we have been visiting, gardening, riding about, etc. Children all well and happy and bright—Dear little ones. it is the springtime of life with them, and they feel an entire sympathy with the freshness and gladness of Nature's Spring.

March 8th, 1856. Give out today all the women's and children's summer clothes, except Jane's two babys. I still owe old Charlotte a calico also; and Nancy is yet to be provided for. Gave out to Priscilla 15 yds. of cotton for Alred, Clifford and Charley—Cutt out six shirts for Ariana, 2 for Charles Bingham, 2 for Dan Brooks, 2 for Richard Thomas—Cut out 6 for Sarah Peters, 2 for Garner, 2 for Molly, 2 for Lewis—Cutt out 6 for Ellen Jackson, 2 for Ed Miles, 2 for Dick Miles, 2 for Armistead.

February 10, 1857—Welbourne Hall   Feel better than for a week.

Less unhappy about my lungs, though I put some turpentine on my breast—Counted out the clotes. Richard left for Richmond. I should be quite well and strong now if it were not for my constant anxiety about my health—Oh for a cheerful and contented spirit. My precious children all well and merry.

March 2nd, 1857—Bitter cold day . . . rode up to church with Richard in his buggy—felt a little afraid of his pretty little black mare.

I have been rather indisposed today and continue to cough a little. My side still hurts me occasionally when I draw a long breath, cough, etc. Oh that God would grant me a heart entirely resigned to His will. I do long and pray for life and health.

This self-educational text repays careful attention. It obviously confirms typical accounts of the difficult lives of plantation mistresses.[40] Yet it does not represent Rebecca Dulany as circumscribed nor as submissive to external pressures to overwork. It portrays complete, autonomous responsibility for superintending a large number of people and attending to their material needs, in discourses of social and intellectual life, labor management, and parenting. Dulany is not a later bourgeois housewife whose constructed "domestic sphere" created a discursive bubble around all of these domains. She expertly and independently applies medical remedies, modern "scientific" time management, and the important sewing skills so often mentioned (and often rejected) as an educational necessity for females. She visits, receives visitors, and makes family connections with the social expertise prescribed by upper-class conduct literature. In addition, her account alludes to religious texts, regular reading, and a Rousseauistic view of children's affinity for nature. It offhandedly inscribes the conventional formats for accounting, keeping weather records, and marking life crises, found in diaries by both men and women. Rebecca Dulany's journal realizes intersections among various codes. Like others, it both highlights and effaces gender as that category appears in, or is irrelevant to, commonplace doings. Yet it reasserts another relationship: between the commonplace and mortality. Each of her activities mediates between death and the everyday, between purposes for living and pressing, always social, time. Her record is not, that is, a specifically feminine submission to the will of God, but an indigenous philosophical investigation of existential realities.

Official Crises: Certificates of Conflict

Official and semiofficial documents placed in commonplace books for safe-keeping do not overtly mark gender, although they often affect and fix social identities and property. Of the fifteen copies of documents in this collection, three are in commonplace books attributed to women, and one is in the book of an unidentified compiler that includes an affidavit of Sally Johnson.[41] One of these volumes, the 1885–1886 commonplace book kept by Anne Lee Peyton (1836–1919), contains a copy of an affidavit by Dr. Frederick Homer. The book kept by John Peyton Dulany (1785–1878), Richard Dulany's father, contains a copy of an affidavit (discussed later) concerning activities of the Army of the Potomac at Rebecca Dulany's home, Welbourne Plantation, in Loudon County. Other volumes include maps, a census report, autographs, two wills (of Sarah Cornelia Jones and Thomas Pannell), family coats of arms, and copies of published or prepared obituaries. One of these obituaries honors Maria DeRieux's life of letters; the other three memorialize men.

"A Confirmed Maniac"

Among such ordinary documents, affidavits are probably least familiar. But they often contain legal particulars in which gender assignments are decisive. An example is the 1827 petition to the Virginia General Assembly by Mrs. Mary Howard to sell approximately 700 acres of land owned by her husband, Joseph Howard. She is joined in her petition by her children and their spouses: Jane S. Howard, Richard H. Howard, William Howard, Ann Howard Littlepage, Douglas Muir, and Maria Howard Muir. This petition is accompanied by affidavits of Dr. William H. Henning, Jacob Michaux, Thomas Miller, and William Wathall.[42] All testify, as the petition does, that Joseph Howard is insane.

Howard's land "was devised to him by his Father and two slaves, the one male about forty years of age, and other a female about fifty with a small portion of perishable property which is the whole of his Estate." His wife's petition reveals both legal protections for Howard's civil liberties and how women and children might seek to achieve legal credibility. It details Joseph's infirmity, to which each affidavit attests:

> That the said Joseph is now about sixty six years of age but notwithstanding his confirmed lunacy, is yet in the enjoyment of seeming good health and is likely to live for many years. That from the great length of his derangement there is not the slightest ground to hope that he will ever be restored, but on the contrary is evidently growing worse, each successive year.

As a wonderful sidelong glance at a certain masculine idea of social life, William Henning's affidavit affirms,

> I have been acquainted with Joseph Howard for the last 10 or 11 years and have always considered him a confirmed maniac: indeed I have never seen him enjoy a lu-

cid interval during all that time and I have seen him very frequently. March 13 1837
Wm. H. Henning

The petition accompanying this testimony further explains that the entire family plans to emigrate to Missouri, taking Joseph with them, and begs permission to sell land he owns legally, despite his mental condition. Joseph's absolute right over property and its disposition can be set aside only by both his wife's and other potential heirs' concern for the entire family's welfare.

The Howards carried out extensive textual research before writing this petition and collecting affidavits. The family habit of preserving statements and agreements is evident in their collective commonplace book, begun in 1765 and started again by Joseph in 1803 and in 1804 by his son William, who wrote from the back of the book forward. William included, for instance, agreements with overseers about pay: "For the Year 1809 have agreed with Sherwood Boscomon as to Overseer Viz 1. he is to have 8 1/2 part of Tobo [tobacco]; H. B. Corn. 10 1/2 of grain"; and later, "Memorandum agreed with Henry Adcock as an overseer for the year 1809 Viz.: He is to have 9th part of all that's made & hand the plough Horses are to be put under him; allow him 500 weight of port 8 Barrl corn & a milk cow & find [?] winter. Some cows of provender enough if not he is to furnish it himself." Here also, family genealogical records are formatted as documents:

MEMORANDUM:

The Sons of Col Allen Howard Virgil Wm. & Jn. were born as followeth
    Wm. Howard was born March 13th 1736 . . .
    William Howard Carter the Son of Wm. Carter & Jane His Wife was born the 3rd day of Novem 1809 being a Locust year. . . .

William also penned a "Memorandum of the fishing hand wrought at Dog Island in year 1808," with a daily diary that lists names, including his own, and the "hands" of the catch.

But the Howards' book also gathers the warrant for their later petition to the Assembly, a copy of information concerning the legal implications of lunacy. This document spells out the legal situation of the "Ideot," the senile, drunkards, and others with legally defined deficits:

Nov 17th 1809

The following is an extract from the "Clerks Magazine" written by Harry Toulmin, Secretary of Kentucky on Wills. Viz.: "A mad or Lunatic person during the time of insanity of mind cannot make a will of land or goods; but such an one as hath his lucid interval, fear or calm intermysions, may during the time of such quietings & freedom of mind make his will, it will be good"

"Who also an Idiot, i.e., such an one as cannot number twenty, or tell of what age he is, or the like cannot make a will, or dispose of his land, or goods, & although he makes a will, reasonable & sensible will, yet it is Void"—& If he goes on

"So also an old man that by reason of his great age is childish again, or so forgetful that he forgets his own Name cannot make a will for a will made by such an one is Void—So it is with drunkards,—It is understood that for a man to make a will, must be of a disposing & *reasonable mind*

Look & see on the other side respecting Deeds—from Toulmin[:]

A man that is drunk may give or grant, do have & make by deed as any other man may do: or as he himself when he is fresh & sober may do. This deed will in Law be as binding on him, & all others made at the time, as at any other time—

To the making of a good deed, it is requested (among other things) that he who makes it, when he does it, has his reason & understanding: and therefore, if a man void of reason, & that wants common understanding and that is either born so, & has been so, then been so from his birth, who is called Ideot as Nativitate [?], or one that is born with understanding, & becomes accidentally so, such as we call a Lunatic or mad person be so always, or at Certain seasons & by fits, that has his lucid Intervals, if any such person when he is in this case, Shall do anything [?] or [recovery?], or enter into a cognisance & this will good to bind him & all others . . . so that the Law in this is that all acts done by one of insane memory are good against himself, but Voidable by his Heirs, Ex. & Such as to have his Estate after his Death.

Howard's faithful copying of this legal information particularly demonstrates needs that create the range of necessary studies for "women and youth" discussed in chapter 3. This writing stores for later use a connection between legal discourse and, in this case, a generational tragedy. It is a portable source text for writing the petition and evidently determines the diction and emphases in the details given in the affidavits attached to it.

A Lunatic in Jail and Other Follies

Public reactions to particular human states and the source texts that shape these responses are illustrated in Timothy Chandler's (1761–1831) interest in the unusual events of 1821–1823, a record that shows how "lunacy" was named and treated in criminal behavior. Chandler regularly recorded such news, exposing community practices in extraordinary situations:

On Sunday the 28th of Nov. Thos Hacket Jr. in a fit of Lunacy . . . cut of his riding horses ears, and then cut his throat; he was put in Jail to undergo a trial for Luncy: but he found means to make his escape: & was suffer'd to run at large until Tuesday the 2nd. day of December: *when without having the fear of God before him; or in other words being a Lunatic;* he killed his own mother and a negro woman: he was again sent to Jail: on Monday the 13th December came on his trial before the County Court: and after a laborious trial of 10 hours he was remanded to Jail for further trial before the Circuit Court to be held next May. Wm. Carter [L?] Stephenson, was his council. and acquited himself with Credit in defending him—May Term. Again came on the trial of Thos. Hacket in the Grand Jury found a true bill, the said Hacket was tried by a Jury of 12 men as to the state of his mind & was unanamous of an opinion that he was a lunatic; & was again remanded to Jail.

Chandler kept a faithful account of Hackett's progress, or lack of it. But he also notes other criminal activities and local responses to them:

At this Court John Hamm a free man of Colour was sentenced to 2 years imprisonment in the Jail & Penitentiary house for aiding & receiving stolen corn from a slave.

Fall Term Superior Court: Thomas Hacketts minds still deranged & therefore was not brought out.

Spring following still derangement

1821 January 19th. Mr Matthew Campbell had his leg broke and ancle dislocated: in attempting to suppress a riot———

In consequence of the above accident Mr. Campbell was confined to his home four months. . . .

1821 Spring & Fall Term; Thos. Hacket's derangement on Lunacy still continuing & he remains in Jail. Hacket at last sent to the Lunitic hospital & soon died.

Fall term of the Superior Court 1821. At this session John Gilman and Wm. Reid wer found guilty of the wilful murder of Jane Coats: & sentenced to be hung on the 7th day of December.

Chandler recounts the outcome of this judgment in a journalistic report of the public hanging it prescribed. His staccato narrative blends class markers with legal discourse:

John Gillman and William Reid late of the County of Caroline Labourers, who stand convicted of Murder in the first degree, were again led to the bar, in custody of the sheriff of this County, and therefrom it being demanded of them, if any thing they had or knew to say why the Court, here to Judgment and execution against them of and upon the premises, should not progress; they said they had nothing but what they had before said; Therefore it is Considered by the court, that they be hanged by the neck until they be dead, and that execution of this Judgment, be made and due upon them the said John Gillman and William Reid, by the sheriff of the county or his legally qualified deputies, on Friday the 7th day of December next, between the hours of ten in the morning and four in the afternoon of that day of the usual plan of execution.

(on Dec 7th, Gillman was hanged at about 3pm; 3,000 people were there. Re prieve from the Governor was read to put off Reid until "next Friday 14th. On that day, Reid was hung by the neck until he was dead" "in the presence of many County people.")[43]

This record gives the appearance of notes made by an ambulance-chasing solicitor. But such diary notes were a typical form of self-education, attending to court actions that inform Chandler's profession. He followed the suggestion found in conduct literature to attend judicial sessions, where mingled strong feeling and restraining social codes educate males in universal propriety. (See chapter 6.) He made an equally faithful record of the burning of the Virginia penitentiary and its aftermath in 1819–1821,[44] and noted the appearance of a comet "of considerable magnitude" on July 4, 1819: "I [think] it is as [splendid] as the comet of 1811. It may be seen again in the morning at two o'clock.—disappear'd about the first of August."[45] Chandler clearly treasured and made treasure of extraordinary particularities—cutting a horse's throat, killing one's mother, trafficking with slaves in stolen property, a hanging, and celestial appearances—to own the unusual.

"A Gentleman and an Officer"

Yet another unusual circumstance motivated a family affidavit claiming reparations for damages during the Dulany family's experience of the Civil War. John Peyton Dulany's affidavit (kept and copied in 1935 by Julia Beverley Whiting) draws on legal commonplaces, a gentleman's *doxa,* to narrate the incursion of Union troops into Welbourne, the family home. John Dulany here performs a patriarchal duty, keeping family property in fact and in memory. His document layers discursive materials, assuming an injured perspective more vividly than could a conventionally unified personal essay. It merges legal affirmation with detailed narrative and dramatic renderings in a document describing events whose adjudication is unknown.

STATEMENT

[At left margin:] In *Aunt Julie's writing*
I, John Peyton Dulany of the county of Loudon in the State of Virginia make the following statement, which I wish to be considered as if made upon oath. I am upwards of seventy years of age, and have lived in the county of Loudon for the last forty years. My family now consists of five grand-children, the oldest twelve years old, their teacher Mr. Wiedmeyer a citizen of Switzerland, two nieces Miss Herbert and Mrs. Wans, and the servants. I have an only son Richard Henry Dulany who is forty years old and is now with the Confederate Army: I have never in any way taken part in the present war, never in any way approved of Secession and did not vote for the Secession of the State of Virginia.[46]

This formal introduction pointedly notes members of the family, its retainers, and dutiful educational provisions, all of which mark a household with standing. It scrupulously notes the education of servants and the quite relevant absence of Dulany's grown son, away serving in the Confederate Army the father claims to reject. John Dulany next narrates the invasion by northern troops, of which he complains, calling the strategy of living off the land "robbery." In its emulation of judicial depositions, this plea first portrays a civil interaction between gentlemen, then in increasingly excited language moves to its crisis, the violent invasion of the family home. The document ignores the resistance near Welbourne by Mosby's rangers, the Confederate guerrilla unit of local men who blended into the community after their raids in civilian clothing.

> About the last of March Co. [Gary?] of the United States Army occupied the town of Middleburg with his command (about four miles from my residence) A short time after my house was surrounded about twelve o'clock at night by a body of armed soldiers, I suppose some thirty or forty. I got out of bed, went to the door and asked what was wanted; one of the person spoke and announced himself as Captain [Gallier?] of Col. Gary's command sent to search my house for my son Richard H. Dulany. I assured him that my son was not in the house or so far as I had any reason to believe in the neighborhood. He expressed his regret not withstanding my assurance at having [to] search the house, but he must obey orders. I told him certainly, I know that. Captain [Gallier] then came in, and went through the house. I am glad to state that throughout Capt. [Gallier] behaved like a gentleman and an officer. I offered to have some supper prepared for him and his men, he said that the men would like something to eat, which was accordingly prepared for them. On or about the sixteenth of April, Col. Gary having removed his camp as I am told to . . . about seven or eight miles from my house another armed party of soldiers came to my house with two officers who announced themselves as Capt. McCabe, Lieut. Laws, that they were acting under the orders of Col. Gary, and came to take horses. I asked to see their authority, they would not show any but said if I chose I could go see Col. Gary and ask him. They then went to the stables, took my riding mare, a very valuable animal and my two carriage horses that cost me seven hundred dollars; returned to the house and talked a good deal. On their leaving I told them that I protested against their taking of my property and that I considered it robbery. On leaving the farm the carriage horses got away from the men and returned. . . . On or about the twenty-eighth of April, Capt. McCabe and Lieut. Laws came to my house with an armed body of soldiers, stationed a guard around the house placed me and the teacher Mr. Wiedmeyer the only two white male adults about the house under arrest; went to my storeroom broke open the lock took out nearly all the tea, coffee, sugar, wine whiskey etc. that I had for my family use and then approached by my niece Miss Herbert and told that the key of the storeroom would

be sent for if wanted, Capt. McCabe in a most insolent manner told her he would not wait for the key and broke the lock. Capt. McCabe and Lieut. Laws then went upstairs and as I am informed by Miss Herbert and Miss [?] and verily believed searched the rooms upstairs to the [?], opening trunks and wardrobes where there was nothing but clothes and ladies' dresses and when requested by Miss Herbert not to open a particular trunk, she telling them that it contained nothing but some articles and clothes which had belonged to Mrs. Dulany before her death, they refused her request, opened the trunk and scattered the contents about.[47]

This plotted movement unfolds from an obviously strained visit between two gentlemen who represent householding and military apparatus, and who present their relevant credentials to each other. It ends with a symbolic rape of the family women—the soldiers' invasion of trunks and wardrobes and handling their dresses. The heinousness of these acts, Dulany assumes, is evident in his definition of them as *robbery*, the word that regularly coded the entire federal action against the South as a crime against human and material property rights. (See Samuel Simpson's protests discussed earlier). In the heat of this violence, another adult white male, perhaps not a full-time resident at Welbourne, comes to light:

During the whole of this scene I am assured by my niece Miss Herbert, Capt. McCabe's language and gestures were most insolent and threatening to her; at one time telling her that she should be arrested and sent to Washington, at another time crying out to the men below to fire the house etc. Capt. McCabe went to my gardiner (who is a white man) and I am told by him and verily believe, cursed and abused him with my servants, drew his sword threatening if he did not tell him where I had put my bacon he would cut his head off. He then had the house where I had put the bacon broken open, took what he wanted, I do not know how much but a large quantity not leaving me enough for my family's use, and then ordered dinner for his men, called them into my dining room where the men dined after which they left, Capt. McCabe taking with him in a wagon and a horse cart, my bacon, four or five demi-Johns of whiskey, a trunk with the clothes of one of my granddaughters, a gold snuff box a [?] tumbler and [?] of the wardrobes and the rooms up stairs. During this scene Lieut. Laws commanded me to give up my letters and private correspondence. I told him that I had none, but if I had I would [?] to give them.

[At left margin:] *Aunt Julia's own statement:* "This is all of my Grandfather's statement that I have found among my Mother's papers. J. B. W."[48]

Again, this account describes outrages by Union troops without mentioning the troops' strategic and practical reasons for taking food, for threatening anyone likely to join Mosby's guerrillas, or for appropriating correspondence that might contain useful military intelligence. As Julia Whiting notes, we have no more of the statement than this, nor a date. We can only conjecture about how this family drama was played out or whether Dulany requested the reparations sometimes granted after the war. But Dulany imagines these "scenes," as he says, as a factual literature in which the initial civility of enemy "gentlemen" becomes dehumanized and, at the least, subtextually "unmanly." Attacking family retainers, like cursing and intruding on symbolic private female spaces, is a breach of another man's patriarchal authority, a ready-to-hand discourse of convenience in this accusation. The document becomes, like many others written after the war, a family's discursive acquisition, its retained honor in legal action against material losses. It balances lost property against moral gain in civilian memories of maintaining patriarchal propriety, the identity of a gentleman. In that identity, the invisiblity and omnipresence of gender emerges, if only in Dulany's shifts of tone.

Yet Dulany does not psychologize the people or fictionalize the events that this statement portrays in the manner adopted by later, more notably "authored," accounts of the war (see chapter 7). The legal conventions of this consequential but homemade discourse perforate compartments that later officially separated military from private domains. John Dulany's affidavit thus offers a glimpse of patriarchy *in situ*. Its assumptions about the human and material content of family "holdings" and about the codification of interactions between enemies, like its Old Testament insistence on "what is fair," place it in the discourse of specific local commonplaces.

Household *Pharmakons*

Prescriptions and recipes in commonplace books may appear too trivial to include as evidence that disengages gender from purposes for writing. But these texts are especially effective ways to problematize fixed assignments of gender, both as a category for actions by the polarized sexes and as the privilege granted to male discourses that are treated as public statements, in Foucault's constitutive sense. In this collection, only two of the sixteen books containing medicinal prescriptions were kept by females. Among the entries by males, Hugh Blair Grigsby's startling list of remedies for deafness and Joseph Dupuy's prescriptions for "the care of persons, cattle, horses, and crops" in his 1810–1865 commonplace book exemplify the relatively mechanical application of potions to an unfortunately *dis*embodied knowledge of the human organism.[49] This "science" appears to have entailed applying one remedy to an undifferentiated assortment of bodies. Equally intriguing are "directions" written by Edwin Gray (1743–1790) in his diary for 1778, kept in blank spaces in David Rittenhouse's *Virginia Almanack* for that year. The

back of the book contains printed almanac information like that in Sallie Alexander's many yearly volumes. With this printed material, Gray records
"Directions for boiling salt," followed by "A short and easy method of making very fine Epsom, or purging salt."[50] He also includes "A green Ointment
to cure a Wound," a recipe followed by printed directions for horse traders to
discover a horse's age: "You must remember that a Horse, when he has all his
Teeth hath just 40; that is, 24 Grinders, 12 on each Side, 6 above and 6 below."

Recipes in commonplace books are more evenly distributed between volumes kept by men and women. Of the eighteen books containing recipes,
eight were kept by men, one by William and Jane Bernard, sharing the same
volume by writing in it from different directions.[51] Of these, four either contain recipes entered by a woman or do not identify who wrote them. Among
these recipes are Joseph Dupuy's formula for paint and William Howard's
record of the lamentable Joseph Howard's recipes for molasses, beer, and dye,
with his prescriptions for medicines.[52]

Recipes kept by women are often instructions for preparing one dish, but
may be more elaborately constructed cookbooks. In contrast to contemporary recipes for novice cooks, these sketchy instructions indicate relative proportions of ingredients, not absolute quantities. They may be annotated with
remarks such as "Good," "The best Yeast ever made, Mrs. Wormley,"[53] or
with possessive cautions, as in the commonplace book that Jane Page and
Jane Nelson kept from 1802 to 1845: "Plese take care of this receipt."[54] The
recipe here for pickled walnuts contains a note to Page revealing that walnuts
were a form of currency, here traded for potatoes, that linked neighboring
household economies:

> Put your Walnuts in strong Salt and Water, let them remain for fifteen days.
> Shrifting the brine on the seventh day, and then wash the walnuts in fresh water
> for two or three hours changing the water several times—then take a course towel
> and wipe the fur off the walnuts clean—Rench them out in fresh water. lay the
> walnuts on something & let the water drip from them, so as to have as little water
> in the pot as possible—
>
> Count your walnuts and put them close in the pot, for every hundred wal-
> nuts—half pint mustard seed—Black pepper 1/2 ounce, all spice 1/2 ounce—
> cloves 1/4 oz—mace 1/4 oz[—] Two or three horse raddish roots
>
> Two or three whole onions, put in the pot, Pound all the spices together, put
> them in the Vinegar the stronger the better, Boil it well, and put it hot on the
> walnuts when in the pot. Tye something close around the top of the jarr—that all
> the strength may remain in the pot—set it away so it may be used in a few
> months.

Think the walnuts are rather two yong, the last of next week would be better time to gether them. I [?] cant get any more hear. You had better sent to the creek, perhaps you may get some there. Dr. Page will oblige by giveing me a peck of potatoes.

With respect, yours
R. Gamlilee [?]

Unless we understand food preparation to be inherent in female biology and distinguish it from supplying other provisions like medicine and household preparations, food recipes are not a female specialty. Before female domesticity was a widely published discourse, recipes were written and circulated without reference to the math anxiety later imagined for and imposed on females. For example, a late eighteenth- and nineteenth-century compilation by Marianna Russell Speace Hunter contains sketchy plans for making cakes and a salve:

SPONGE CAKE

This is the best recipe for th sponge cake.

Put your eggs in one scale & as much sugar as will balance them in the other. Then take half the weight of the sugar, in flour. After beating the eggs w[ith] sugar light, a little before putting it in the oven add the flour.

Salve for risings [?]

Take cedar berries and leaves pound them very fine, the [birds?] of [mullin?], green plantain, comfrey leaves, or roots, and life everlasting, beef [?] & mutton suet, or tallow. pound all the herbs and put them all on to [?] with water which you must put in proportion to the quantity you wish to make. Stew it till al the juice has stewed out of the herbs, then strain it tho' a cloth into water before using it, put it in a [big?] metal skillet with some spirit and let it stan till al the spirit is stewed away.

to make Cake

1 pound sugar 1 Pound of Eggs by weight. three quanities of a pound of flour. Beat the yoks and whites separately in the ingrediets will [?] then season it to your taste with [?] or Spirits of Lemon [?][55]

More than one such compilation requires its reader to understand algebraic concepts and to negotiate kitchens and household pharmacies without exact measuring or modern cooking devices, in places where men and women were equally skilled or unskilled and equally vulnerable to the results.

Co-Respondence

Many historians treat the copious correspondences of nineteenth-century women and men as sources of autobiographical expression and historical data. But accounts of correspondence among literate people often overlook how letters serve many of the purposes identified here, especially when they were pointedly preserved in family records. Steven M. Stowe is unusual in acknowledging how letter writing, and hence language itself, is a site for conducting, in their totality, affairs of honor, courtship, and rituals around coming of age: "Letters often were the very substance of relationships, otherwise strained by distance, gender differences, or emotion. Such letters existed as a bond and a commentary on the bond."[56] But Stowe neglects the additional significance of keeping these texts long after their initial exchange, thereby preserving relationships that extend the family's provenance and elaborate its collected memory.

Female Manners: The Whole Sex?

Of the twenty commonplace books that contain letters that had been sent or copies of them (as distinct from many other letter books containing first drafts), nine were kept by males, five by females, and one (the Bernard commonplace book) shared by husband and wife. One is unidentified.

Obviously, correspondence was not socially assigned only to women or to men, although the content of letters did vary by gender. Some letters, as Stowe says of the correspondence that enacted (or prevented) dueling, *are* gender. The earliest letter in this collection, evidently part of an ongoing exchange, both comments on and pursues a courtship almost entirely on the basis of establishing and then critiquing a discourse on appropriate gender identities. In 1791 Conrad M. Speece (1776–1836) began a letter to "Miss Polly Hanna daughter of Matthew Hanna of Lexington, Virginia" in the space of polite "letters" of another sort, writing as an essayist reflecting on the topic of female manners.

Liberty Hall—9 Jan'y 1791

> Madam
> [In] your last and very acceptable favour you made some judicious observation on female manners. Will you accept of a few reflections from me on the same interesting subject. I do confess myself but badly qualified to unfold the various principles and springs of action in the human mind; much less can I pretend to discover and lay open those delicate feelings and peculiar dispositions which exist in the breasts of the fair. I have a few conjectural thoughts however I do entertain and shall not scruple to submit them to the inspection of my amiable friend. Where ever I am wrong her candour will excuse. If I am right my opinion will be confirmed by her approbation.[57]

Speece clearly attempts to keep to this subject. But as the letter unfolds, so does his personal interest in persuading Polly Hanna of points that he casts as academic inferences. By advocating women's elevation, he reverses the positions we might assume the two correspondents would occupy in a discussion of the relative "seriousness" of women:

> You observe that "the Fair Sex are superficial themselves and their works bear the same aspect." This charge which you so candidly acknowledge has I believe, been frequently advanced. The fact I shall attempt to account for, after just observing that the Character of superficial is by no means applicable to the whole Sex. Like all other general Rules, this one has some exceptions. The Fair Sex are not at all deficient in natural Genius. Their desire of Knowledge is generally strong and when rightly directed is after productive of the most pleasing Effects. In short they are capable of high advance in Knowledge and great Refinement of Taste. Witness among many others the learned Madam Bacier an eminent Critic in the ancient languages and the pious Mrs. Rowe so justly celebrated for the Brilliancy of her Imagination and the Beauty of her Composition. And without looking farther for Examples I do not hesitate to say that I am a witness of at least one living Instance of Genius and Improvement which fully confirms the above Observations. Pray don't suspect my sincerity when I tell you I mean my fair Friend and Correspondent. (1)

Ironically, Polly's learning and lack of superficiality, which must have been evident in the letter Speece now answers, caused her to take the negative side in this debate on the potential of the "Fair Sex." Speece reasons further about the causes of women's general reputation, explicitly saying that education, not nature, determines the behaviors assigned to men and women:

> I suppose therefore that the Superficial Manners of the Fair Sex are not owing, in any considerable degree to any original Peculiarity in their Constitution but rather to *what I shall call their Education.* I take it for granted (permit me to speak my opinion freely if I am wrong I cheerfully submit to your Correction) I take it for granted I say that the first notion which takes possession of their young minds is, that it must be their chief business in life to render themselves agreeable to the other Sex. *How this Rule of Conduct is first infused I shall not pretend to determine. It may perhaps owe its origin to the Instruction of Parents, and perhaps in a still greater degree to the Influence of example.* But supposing it fixed as a Rule in the young breasts of the Fair it becomes an Enquiry what are the Qualifications necessary to render them agreeable? And here I freely acknowledge, (and I must speak it to the shame of our Sex) that the most of men are more pleased with a brilliant external appearance and a Vast flow of Loquacity which, by the by, generally passes for excellent Wit, than with the superior qualifications of solid Sense, and Improvement in Knowledge. I am sorry to observe that even Gentle men of considerable Knowledge frequently discover too great a Regard for excessive Polish of Behavior and Gaiety of appearance. (1, emphasis added)

Speece hereby agrees with Hanna's point, that most women are superficial. But he de-essentializes this quality, correlating it with their education, in the interest of placing her in a specific socialized "Character . . . Friend and Correspondent." We might take his case to be mere personal flattery constructed on the backs of other women. But Speece assumes that gendered subject positions, including loquacity that is mistaken for "Wit" and a gay demeanor, are as readily learned from purposeful lessons, or "infused," as are "Imagination," ancient languages, and brilliant composition. He assumes that gender positions are learned and taught in a family and by example. He also reasons that a learned vapidity has its purposes:

> If these observations are just it will be easy to discover why the fair Sex pay so great attention to external Qualifications, to the Neglect of mental Improvement. They imagine that these are the means of rendering them the objects of Esteem, of admiration, of Love; and therefore they willingly spend their time and Thoughts as you will observe in grasping after the fashions and endeavoring to possess all those little arts so much admired. and this must be the case so long as the Fair make it their main Business to please the other Sex and so long as we manifest that we admire them for these qualifications more than for substantial Knowledge, Modest Diffidence and Piety. (1–2)

For Speece, such gendered behavior might as easily be learned otherwise. We might speculate on how a culture whose women need "Knowledge, Modest Diffidence and Piety" to gain male esteem would mount its advertising campaigns. But more important, Speece sensibly takes it for granted that young women must be accepted by men if they are to enter the sustaining settings that men control. This economy goes without saying. Yet he emphasizes that Hanna would take a place with him in a differently constructed gender education:

> Surely a reform in the Manners of both Sexes is much to be wished for. I think it can never be attained in a great Degree without a greater Sense of Religion and a conscientious regard to the practical Duties which it inculcates. Yet let it not be thought that I am an Enemy to a good appearance or to elegance and dignity of Deportment. These Qualities are truly amiable in both sexes where not carried to excess. I only censure that immoderate pursuit of more valuable attainments. I don't wish any man, much less would I enjoin it on a lady to become a mere Book Worm. (2)

In imagining her as part of this gendered economy, Speece compliments Hanna, noticing her ability to remain conventionally attractive while also serving in the characters of Friend, Correspondent, and Knowledgeably Diffident and Piously Sensible commodity, all of whom Speece praises. The fate worse than spinsterhood *and* bachelorhood that he projects is to become a "mere Book Worm," unable moderately to pursue two "Characters" at once. He ends, in fact, by expanding on this warning:

> Such persons [bookworms] are seldom agreeable or improving Companions. I am Sensible that without a practical acquaintance with men and Manners the greatest Scholar must make *an awk[w]ard figure in public life.* No particular attainment should be sought after to the exclusion of others which are necessary. Too great Inattention is the Cause of Ignorance; excessive Bookishness often produces Pedantry, and of these two extremes I think the latter as disagreeable as the former. Here as well as in every other Case the middle Way is best. (2, emphasis added)

Here, Speece's own composition becomes less "brilliant" than at first. He appears in these relatively staccato directives to be carried away from the topic of female gender, to write in haste, or perhaps to moderate his own studious proclivities by pursuing the quality assigned to culturally valuable males, the ability to achieve civic presence as a participant in community affairs. The strategy of his postscript is more humble and interactive, a way to keep the epistolary medium of this relationship alive, but equally to show us the always active autodidacticism of ordinary writing:

> I freely send you my Remarks and earnestly request yours whenever you discover anything erroneous in my Letters. If you can write between this time and Thursday Evening you shall receive a Line or two more before the end of the Week; and I shall also have a farther proof of the value you entertain for our Correspondence. (2)

Speece moves here from the position of teacher to that of a pupil. He asks Hanna to correct him, to show her "valuing" of their interaction, alluding to the common practice of writing letters to improve epistolary composition.

This tutorial relationship, usually ignored in historical analyses of correspondence, accounts for many otherwise opaque or seemingly irrelevant comments in letters that are not otherwise about writing. As in one-sided corrections of youthful language in fathers' letters to sons, Speece's invitation to correct his language remarkably empowers Hanna, placing her in a direct line of patriarchal power over discourse. (See chapter 6.) The letter's close, like its opening references to this correspondence as an occasion for evaluative responses, equally shows how this ongoing education enacts a courtship. Language about assuming gendered positions itself works "improvements" in Speece that he wants Hanna to supply. Candor is highly valued here, at least the candor that is possible in a thin intellectual exchange between potential mates. With somewhat heavy-handed syllogistic reasoning and delicately executed ingratiation, Speece also "educates" Hanna, clarifying his requirements for *a* woman. In that process, this text reveals the variability and instability of the gender positions from which it borrows to make more than one point in this local mode of instruction.

Lines Across Battlefields
"Unmanly Fears"

Obviously, standard history demonstrates how both men and women were deeply affected by the Civil War. But few treatments of this period attend directly to how gender was itself refigured during and after this drastic rearrangement of American cultures. The war itself appears to have heightened a consciousness of gender, as though its trials and deprivations called on people to assume crisply outlined positions that might support their comments on the conflict in which the legitimacy of their culture was at stake. War makes crucial the "manly" and "womanly" identities that are later fondly recounted as the personalities of heroes and heroines.[58] For instance, the commonplace book kept from 1865 to 1871 by an unidentified writer contains a letter from John Yates Beall written shortly before he was executed for spying. A note attatched to it says only, "J. Y. Beall acct. master brought here [?] 2nd was caught in the U.S. [?] and uniformed; can be tried as a spy."[59] Beall's brief farewell letter adopts conventions of religious discourse to construct a needed "manhood" that appears to comfort him in this situation:

> Dear Paul. I thank you for your encouraging words and kind offer—I wish to see you [before?] I leave. I am not depressed [?] indeed go in hopes [?] *or yield to unmanly fears.*
>
> For many years, I have believed in God and [?] sometimes [pray?] earnestly to prepare for that day which I look upon earth no more. I know that my Redeemer liveth.
>
> I do [?] thank you [?] sustain me when I am called on to go over the dark [river?].
>
> Do you remember "How firm a foundation" and the promise "the soul, that to Jesus has [borne?] reposith"? Give my kindest so far as to my former roommates. Truly yr. friend/
>
> T. Y. Beall

The letter is annotated, "Executed at Columbus, NY, Feb. 27th, 1865." Together with this now blurry, penciled preservation in this small, worn book are addresses, relatively flat notations of accounts listing names and totaling the sums next to them, and a record of a trip from Jackson, Mississippi, to Charlotte, North Carolina, with a list of distances (at the time perhaps strategic) from Augusta to Atlanta and to West Point [Virginia?], with amounts spent and indications of travel time in adjoining columns. But the keeper of this book also included stark comments on the waste of Beall's death. Along with a list of orders to fire a weapon—"Silence / Body / Loose / Prime / Point / Ready / Fire," which is glossed with "Save vent & sponge / Load with [carbine?] Load shot or shell/Run out" is recorded Edmund Burke's opinion fitting both warring causes:

> "This eminent criterion," said Burke in his great speach on reform in 1780 "for distinguishing a [prudent?] government from a [?] and imprudent one, was this: well to know the best time and manner of yeilding what it is impossible to keep." It was the want of this wisdom that involved this country in all the horrors of civil war.

Beall, Atkinson, and thousands of others figure manhood as a shield against fear that may be forged from religious wisdom and other trusted common-place wisdom like Burke's. John Edrington, a brother of Samuel Simpson's wife, Ella, wrote to his sisters at home soon after joining the Confederate Army, in which he died after three months. He characterizes one of his first battles through the authority of a Yankee enemy, who judges that John's comrade "fought like a man."[60]

> April 28, 1863, My Dear Sisters,
> I take the oportunity of letting you know how I am and where I am. . . . I can tell you my dear sisters I never exprienced "God"ding [?] before untill the last few weeks. It is a very hard life Picketing. yesterday [?] we have had to run from two yankees [twice?]. the last time [seemed?] a very serious one the Yankees were in sight charging on us at full speed. They numbered about one thousand Cavalry. We retreated first above Falmouth and remained all night by our [?] until just be-fore day and then we were drawn up in line of battle to wait the [offices?] of the enemy. We remained in that place nerly an hour [line missing in fold of paper] enemy were not long making their appearance They came down the road with a perfect rush but poor fellows they must [with?] over there match. the first charge they [?] and in great order but when they came again it was a perfect yell but poor fellows many of them maid there last charge for our men plaid havock with them. it is said we killed and wounded upwards of [sixty?] men and twenty or thirty horses. We had one of our men wounded, Mr. Isaac [C?] had has arm broken in our retreat and four taken prisoner among the number was Mat Nor-man poor fellow he was on picket to watch the approach of the enemy. Those that wer with him had to run for their lives over fence and diches but Mat's Horse fell down with him but before the Yankees tuck him he killed a first Lt. The yankeys say themselves he fought like a man, we also had one killed but by our own men.

Of course, Edrington's commonplaces are *so* common that it may appear redundant to remark on them. The deaths of young men habitually evoke familiar and pitiable verbal gestures of comfort, as in a letter informing the family of Thomas Jones's accidental death by drowning while with his company in the West a decade before the war. Jones's immediate superior (unidentified) wrote to "Dr Miller," his brother-in-law, on July 24, 1853:

> Camp on the Rio Grande, below [Requosale?] S. Boundary [?]
>
> Dear sir:
>
> It is my most painful duty, a duty which this Night [3rd?] I would cheerfully yeild to some other and better qualified hands to pen this letter & I take the liberty of making you the medium of communicating the sad intelligence to . . .
>
> Last evening on our return from that day's survey of the Rio Grande the small boat containing my young and lamented friend, two [?] and myself was capsized by a squall & alas Thos W. Jones after an ineffectual struggle to regain the shore sank to rise no more. He was thus cut off in the [bloom] & spring of life by the hand of Providence.[61]

In view of the fluid quality of other highly gendered moments, these references to manliness recall Dulany's charge that federal soldiers abandoned the category of "gentleman" by violating his home. All suggest that gender is not only a convenient trope in this discursive exigency, but a refuge from events too overwhelming to meet without rigorous expectations for appropriate behavior. "Act *like* a man," that is, precisely states its own advantages.

Woman Warriors

Figures of womanhood constructed in and by the war are equally embedded in the commonplace *doxa* brought to bear in extreme situations and, we may imagine, were retained to glorify surrender. Lucy Wood Butler (1841–?), for instance, kept a commonplace book and copies of letters to her husband, Ward Butler, in which she translated womanhood into a discursive warrior-like stance. Friday, November 15, 1861, was the day after Lucy's twentieth birthday, which she celebrated with friends in a common entertainment, performing tableaux from familiar literature and art works. This description of "playing Shakespeare" shows how war defined all of her and her friends' "characters."

> We spent the day in agreeable conversation and the evening in games and tableaux. The games were only introduced between the scenes. Betty made a beautiful Imogene. Lizzie impersonated Lady Percy, with Mr. Strange as Hotspur, and he really bears a striking resemblance to Harry as he appears in one of the Famington pictures, but *it was an unfortunate remark of mine that it was appropriate*

for Mr. Strange to take that character as nothing would induce him to fight for his country but a good office and an easy time. Nannie looked sweet as a novice, and Cousin Lou made a fine Lady Abbess. Lydia and I both appeared in the same scenes that we did some years ago at home.[62]

Such entertainments occurred often. As Lawrence Levine notes, Shakespearean plays and other popular dramatic entertainments were appropriated into a postwar "highbrow" discourse later, in the nationalizing process of characterizing the bourgeoisie.[63] A note among Butler's papers describes another program of tableaux; "Magic Mirror; The Duenna; from Peveril of the Peak; from David Copperfield (David suddenly appears at his Aunt's house); the Coquette (showing favor to one and then another lover); Getting in a scrape and getting out; auld Robin Grey; Feast of Roses (Nourmahal brings Namouns the flowers to weave the magic wreath)."[64] Butler connects the homemade wartime birthday "act" to roles she had played at home, before her marriage to Ward Butler, who is serving in Florida.

Lucy wrote to her husband frequently in the character of wife, always addressing him as "Mr. Butler" in letters but in her journal naming him "Ward" and "Waddy." An annotation on her papers by another hand explains how this formality eventually pained her: "Though she talked about him seldom, she once told me, with tears in her eyes, when she was an old, old lady, that she wished she had been able to call Mr. Butler by his first name as he begged her to, but it did not seem proper to her at the time."[65] We do not know how Samuel Simpson's wife, Ella, referred to her husband in his presence, but in letters to her father he was "Col. Simpson."[66] Clearly the subject position of "wife" is at least partially hidden by treatments of these women as only "plantation mistresses," in their "households."[67] Both of those terms only tacitly acknowledge how women also entered a socialized, not privatized, identity. Lucy Butler's appellations for her husband (like Charles Friend's references to his wife as "Madame Friend" in his daughter's memoir; see chapter 7) show how marriage entailed shifting, unstable identities, not a coherent self-definition. Fixing one's place in this relationship, especially to view it as intimacy within social proprieties, was no easier or more common than always defining oneself as an entitled "husband," as patriarchal letters demonstrate (chapter 6). Acquiring versions of either label was the result, of course, of elaborate courtship arrangements conducted primarily in letters between a young man and woman and between their parents, exchanges that educated the couple about the identities to be acquired in marriage.[68] Butler's difficulty with this propriety is especially revealing against her easy use of her husband's first name in what she referred to as "this rather desultory diary of mine."[69]

Butler's journal writing, true to the genre's conventional self-recording purpose, refrains from unfettered confessions like the regret she expressed much later to her amanuensis with "tears in her eyes." Like Rebecca Dulany's journal (discussed earlier), Lucy Butler's journal constructs daily encounters in a socialized genre, here as letters to a female friend, which Lucy may have undertaken as self-assigned daily compositions. Her diary entries portray her as a public commentator who, in this instance speaking quite precisely as a woman, had little good to say about either her country*men* or their enemies. Her judgment on the cowardice of Confederate soldiers, for example, confidently treats gender as a specifically discursive category:

> And now that treachery and cowardice seem to have arisen in our land, hope is dying out, and we have brought ourselves to look the worst bravely in the face, and think of what we shall do when the Yankee tyrant reigns supreme, and grinds us to dust by insult and wrong. If I were a man, no such thought would dare enter my mind, but I, being merely a woman, must sit still, and with my weak sisters, for fear of doing aught unwomanly, and see 7000 men surrender as they did at Donelson, *a deed that women would have blushed to own, and a deed that makes us weep to feel that such men are our countrymen. . . . Pure cowardice would be enough to make <u>men</u> fight now for if we do not win, what would life be:* a useless burthen when honour, happiness, wealth are gone, and disgrace and oppression descend upon us.[70]

Like Conrad Speece's reasoning about women's character choices, Lucy Butler figures her feelings in syllogistic logic. She sarcastically "proves" that cowardice in battle is too brave a way to bring about pain, which future defeat would, and did, mean. But she also assumes that manhood and womanhood are fixed and opposing identities in wartime, simultaneously undoing both categories by refusing to be bound "as a woman" to hers.[71]

This "desultory diary," 180 typescript copied pages of entries that Lucy Butler signed as mock letters to herself, features such angry reactions to the behavior of men on both sides of the war. But it also depicts commonplace literary and domestic activities as other sources for the "mistress" she would become in her own home. In July 1862, soon after her husband came home on leave, she contracted typhoid fever. Smallpox was rampant near their home in Staunton and in the army, so "he remained until the first of November before he could be vaccinated."[72] While riding with a cousin and a paroled prisoner of war soon after this visit, she stopped to call on a neighbor. The diary's record of their encounter asserts class as an identity category, but as in other judgments Lucy immediately sets aside fixed opinions based on a categorical expectation:

We were received by Miss Harden who, though she is an overseer's daughter, seems to have as much refinement and has as easy manners as any lady that I know. She asked us into a very nice comfortably furnished parlor. There was quite a bond of sympathy between us as we all had short hair [cut when one suffered from fever]. (141)

This habit of setting aside constructed social categories (except in maintaining a verbal distance from her husband) may stem from Lucy's admiration of religious writings, which she read regularly and critically in the month after Ward returned to his unit. In an entry for November 19, 1862, she notes: "Nannie and I read Kingsleys Sermons this morning as we do every night for we are much interested in the subject and style, and are ready to proclaim Kingsley and his school as great reformers who throw aside the semblance of things and arrive at the very truth itself." She adds:

Then I read D'Aubingne's German Reformation until Major Dick Whitehead came hobbling in on his crutches with Miss Kate. . . . Nannie read one of our favourite Sermons to Aunt Lucy and her children, and we have now retired to our own room . . . for then we will resume our German, at least Nannie will assist me in that study, and our Carlyle's Frederick the Great which we are reading together, and DeQuincy, and I will commence making half a Dozen Soldier's shirts. (143)

Butler again mentions this mixture of needlework and reading, indicating that earlier doctrines recommending that a "women's education" should focus on duty to the needle were only partially observed. She obviously takes continuing self-education to be an equal duty, if a much more pleasant one: "I succeeded in finishing my six shirts last week in spite of my numerous interruptions, but it was at the sacrifice of all my literary pursuits, and by means of hard work that I accomplished the task" (147). Nonetheless, the touchstone by which she evaluates the war is her assumed identity in female "manhood":

Lincoln's late message surpasses in stupidity any of his or any other man's former production. Surely he is the great wonder of the age and will be preserved in Barnum's museum. *It seems almost incredible that any one calling himself a man should have concocted such a collection of absurdities.* The object of this document seems to be to do away with the bad effects of his emancipation proclamation which was to go into effect the first of January but I suppose the democratic elections have frightened the poor imbecile. He now declares that he has discovered a plan that will at once restore the union, satisfy his abolition friends, and in truth, bring peace on earth and good will toward men.

His brilliant scheme is as follows: On the immediate return of all disloyal

States . . . such States shall emancipate all slaves during the following thirty-six years, and he will indemnify them (the slave holders) by taxes raised chiefly amongst themselves. How magnanimous of him! (144–45, emphasis added)

Bringing these feelings home, she mingles her responses with those of other southerners that sardonically figure themselves as "children" of a tyrannical father:

Who can resist so generaous an offer? Why none, of course not. We will be but glad to run back to him and tell him how sorry we are for being such naughty children, that we never really meant to disobey and resist him, we were only playing. . . . He will find a glorious name on the pages of history with Nero and Caligula . . . preserved by his magnificent wekness and infamy. (147–48)

Here again, Lucy Butler's diary gives gender categories their force and simultaneously critiques them, using popular irony and satire. She declares that "to be a man," intended to mean either *male* or *human,* is an identity more available to her than to Lincoln. She resists not only this enemy, but also the infantilization that she and her region are being invited to accept by the trope of biological unity and "fatherhood" found in Lincoln's Gettysburg Address and similar appeals. As the war worsened, however, on May 7, 1863, Lucy acknowledged her childlike response to minor troubles, but unfixes that identity with humor:

Mr Earle has just been here with Betty, but Mother would not let me go down to see him, so I consoled myself with a cry for I am becoming very babyish. . . .

We have just recovered this morning from a second panic for we had a worse one yesterday than ever, and I would not be surprised if we had another before night. I hope not, for it is very fatiguing, and the poor old ladies, I am sure, are tired of putting away in a safe place their plate consisting of spoons. (177)

Her sudden tears and "panic" are played against images of the "poor old ladies" of the family, as befits a woman who insists on "being a man" about the war. As in other female reactions to the war, this text codes feelings not as core expression, but as they are portrayed in tableaux, the literary productions that emotions often were. These feelings are already circulated subjectivities, ways to figure anger, unusual identification across class boundaries, and fear.

As suggested by Rachel Mordecai's account of her sister Eliza's reluctance to ply the needle (chapter 3), by Rebecca Dulany's preference for child care over household duties, and by Lucy Butler's resentment at having to make six shirts at the cost of "literary pursuits," it is difficult to find angels of domesticity in these documents. However, the closing part of a letter from Julia Dulany to Miss Adeli La Roche (copied by Julia Whiting along with John Dulany's war "Statement") emphasizes that it was class entitlements, not gendered drudgery, that limited the range of female subject positions deployed by these women in response to manual labor.[73] Having returned to Richland Plantation after a visit to Welbourne, Julia Dulany certainly projects a cautious relation to the work expected of "ladies" while family "servants," she says ironically, are "visiting their Northern friends." Her letter distances her from discourses of a drudgery she has not been prepared to articulate, translating them into comic scenes for a friend, real-life tableaux in which she and other family members take parts while confronting new necessities:

> If I tell you any more of my life at Welbourne I shall leave no space for a sketch of my proceedings here, which are much more prosaic. As our servants are now visiting their Northern friends we are obliged to divide their work. How you would laugh to see Nina and myself at the spring she ironing away as if for dear life and I up to my elbows in the wash tub. I am quite proud of my proficiency in the useful arts. Just imagine getting up early in the morning and travelling to the spring with a bag of clothes on my back almost large enough to put you in. Dear little guy makes the fire helps to fill the tub, before breakfast all the boys jackets are washed. Mama sends me my breakfast which I take à l'Irlandaise seated on a barrel and shortly after Nina who has cooked breakfast joins me we work on together, she ironing, I washing. By the time the boys pants are finished my knuckles & wrists are minus a good deal of skin. Nevertheless we go on very cheerfully until a great steamer looms up grandly on the river when we become a little vindictive & almost feel in a state to profit by [Fuseli's?] advice to his wife [presumably, to leave]. At six o'clock we leave off work sometimes with the ironing complete sometimes not Nina & I take Rose, Neville, Guy Dulany Baby's & our own washing. Mary has the dining room to attend to Hester our little African assists Mama with the cooking & washing when she has not a chill. I am head nurse & superintend some of the childrens studies. (7–8)

Like John Dulany, Julia takes military actions personally, if not as personal insults. She concisely describes her family's danger:

> Father is now entirely helpless and much of Mama's time is of course taken up in nursing him, of course his disease is much aggravated by the deprevations committed by the Yankees. Not long since a steamer sent men ashore who killed our fine [left blank] a calf & some hogs & having thus supplied their mess left us. We had not recovered from our indignation at this when their cavalry made a descent upon the mill and carried off all our wheat there. Our great misfortune though is the unhealthiness of the climate. There is not a day in the week that some one is not laid up with chills and fever. Oh for one breath of mountain air. We have heard nothing from our friends in the army since the battle of Gettysburg & it is only by Yankee papers that we know some of our friends have fallen
>
> With love . . . (9)

Dulany clearly perceives this home collective as a domestic imitation of military assignments, which in turn have traditionally imitated functional divisions of labor in the sexual disposition of work. She does not say that she expects this slapstick washing and ironing to be temporary duty, but she clearly controls it, and the emotional temptations and deprivations in force, by portraying events with informative humor derived from literary conventions.

The opening of this letter is missing, so according to Julia Whiting's note it is only "Part of a letter written by Aunt Julia during the Civil War. Beginning of letter missing." But the remaining passages show that taking on servants' duties in no way circumscribed Julia with a conventional gender identity. Like Lincoln, Dulany rewrites war on the family, uniting this trope with actions that emphasize her conservative, not combative, cause. We do not know from the following fragment whether the dead youth discovered as if asleep is a federal soldier, but his colors make no difference to the tenor of Dulany's reaction. Having "nothing to give a clue to his identity," she imagines him as part of her family:

> . . . sleeping, his pockets had been rifled so we could find nothing to give a clue to his identity. We sent home one of the boys for a servant while we kept watch by the body. Mr [left blank] superintended them and we had him buried beneath an old tulip tree. There was something so inexpressibly sad to me in the whole, to us who stood by his grave the thought was ever present that such might so soon be the fate of our own brothers and dear ones who day by day are exposed to the dangers of battle. Even while we were giving this soldier a soldier's grave almost on the very spot where he had fallen the wreaths of smoke that rose on the mountain showed that his comrades were still waging the fight, and among them how many of our own.[74]

Again like John Dulany's affidavit, Julia's letter portrays the meanness of this backyard war in a literary register. It translates a particular raw event into a respectable property, a text of family memory demonstrating propriety of person. That propriety is not gendered in her or her companions' responses to the stark fact of this doorstep death.

Gender as a Useful Category of Analysis

As many of these texts demonstrate, females are not sole proprietors of affection in close relationships. Nor is affectionate gender *doxa* always sexually interested, despite the subtext of Speece's letter to Polly Hanna. Writing to his granddaughter from his seat in Congress in February 1823, John Taylor (1753–1824) both indulges her and, by directly addressing gender construction, playfully ridicules more than one sacred cow: the new Constitution, clothing as a mark of gender, and the muted but culturally instructive flirtatiousness with which the economy of patriarchy conducted itself to educate the young in such relationships:

Miss Lucy T. Taylor, Elmwood Academy, Essex county, Va.

Washington, February 2, 1823

You do not like [?], nor dolls, nor needles, suppose I buy you a pair of breeches, and attempt, if it is not unconstitutional, to procure a federal law, for transforming these emblems of power to the fair sex. What success might you not expect as a foreign minister if you should cultivate your talents, when, young as you are, you have already so ably negotiated, to open the purse of a close fisted old fellow, and extract five whole dollars, for the extravagant purpose of buying a ring. Perhaps the vanity of exhibiting the beautiful Virginian [?] adorn, presented to me by a lady of your acquaintance, Mary Lane, lurked among my motives for wasting this huge sum of hard money, but if you reckoned upon this trait of my character, it is as proud of our performed skill in [compiling?] all circumstances, which might contribute to the attainment of your object.

You ask me for all the news from Congress, and though it is not good, like that you have given me from elmwood academy about your studies, you shall have all. . . .

Thus my dear grand child you have all the news at this place, from a spectator, who laughs, laments, and shudders, when he contemplates the follies and vices of human nature, to which both you and himself are exposed. You may extract from it a moral, which would be extremely useful to you in your passage through life. If great men, matured by age and experience, are subject to be imposed upon by knaves, and to be led astray by bad passions, how careful ought a young girl to be, in improving her mind, and watching over her actions, for the purposes of detecting imposture, preserving her innocence, and securing her happiness both in this world and the next. Farewell.

Your affectionate grandfather, John Taylor.[75]

This translated conduct book advice draws on familiar literary models for improving the young members of a family, but does so, again, "otherwise." Taylor addresses a grandchild who rejected dolls and especially the dreaded needle—a commonplace choice.[76] He imagines her as a transgressor, both with "breeches" and the power of a foreign minister, thus playfully encouraging Lucy to develop a sense of herself negotiating public acts. In this letter, Taylor is simultaneously an ambassador of patriarchy and on recess from its "serious" demands. He reveals how a member of the relatively new Congress in this turbulent republican era perceived its ongoing titrations of self-interest.

Taylor here assumes the character of a spectator, the entitled polite observer of Addison and Steele's *Spectator* papers, often imitated models of epistolary style. His gently mocking pride in his granddaughter becomes relatively serious conduct book advice at the end of his balanced rhetorical disposition of the letter's three topics—an exchange of relatively new federal "hard cash" for her ring, the Congress's passions, and finally how both topics are relevant to future regulation of her whims. Confessing his indulgence of her as weakness, he identifies its cause as her success at school. But he invites her to identify with a different wisdom, cautioning her, as many young men are cautioned, against her "passions." In a balanced, Johnsonian parallel that compares "great men" to "a young girl," Taylor compares her whims to those of the Congress. He offers the advice perpetually given to young women, the same advice given by Conrad Speece and others, to "be careful," to improve her mind, and to avoid pretense. Taylor wants her, that is, to preserve an innocence that is obviously both a sexual and a character trait, the "good nature" encouraged by conventional eighteenth-century fiction. Remembering Fielding's *Joseph Andrews* and *Tom Jones,* it is difficult to assess this letter as only, or even as primarily, advice that reproduces the submissiveness that females were commonly expected to display.

As shown in the next chapter, which concerns how fathers circulated patriarchal commonplaces to sons, the subject position that warrants my flat generalization about submissiveness has its own precedents in ordinary writing. This supposed universal vision is especially common in correspondence designed to teach young men the requirements of the transcendent universal subject position now absorbed by academic discourse. Both well-worn doctrines about the acquisition of gender and letters from fathers to sons carry this constitutively coherent identity. But commonplaces attempt to educate *both* young women and men in "characters" of textual correctness that signify that paradoxically individual/universal *mankind.* This cross-gendered education further problematizes the category of gender as a tool of analysis. It reveals the unstable and bigendered quality of the paternalism expected of young men, an entitlement that itself crosses the categorical lines that formalism, but not commonplace practice, wants to keep separate as parallel inscriptions of gender.

· 6 ·

Learning to Spell Patriarchy

Fathers and Sons

I request you to <u>practice</u> <u>this</u>. . . . Lay down a rule for all these things in your writing for the future, and persevere, for when a person is illegible either in reading or writing, they never profit by anything on earth they undertake, they are like the dog in the manger, grasp at shadows and lose the substances they must have grasped at. Of this I have had total assurance in many instances of my life.

　　　　CHARLES MORTIMER, letter to JACK MORTIMER, 1787

How is it that we might ground a theory or politics in a speech situation or subject position which is "universal," when the very category of the universal has only begun to be exposed for its own highly ethnocentric biases? How many "universalities" are there and to what extent is cultural conflict understandable as the clashing of a set of presumed and intransigent "universalities"?

　　　　JUDITH M. BUTLER, "Contingent Foundations"

Culture is just that: the regimen that bodies pass through; the reduction of randomness, impulse, forgetfulness; the domestication of an animal, as Nietzsche claimed, to the point where it can make, and hold to, a promise.

　　　　FRIEDRICH A. KITTLER, *Discourse Networks: 1800/1900*

"For Your Own Good"

In the constructed social character of woman or wife, a female whose class status gave access to these identities in eighteenth- and nineteenth-century America had some protection from social and legal traditions that offered her almost none. She might, that is, wholly and irrefutably own the propriety granted through a gendered class identity, to claim a specific collective individuality. But equally circumscribed identities for males—youth, rogue, husband—instead only supplemented a larger discursive system that also allowed males to identify with universal mankind. It is clear that females could not often escape, legally or socially, identities that sustained that specific universal economy. But it is less obvious what the imagined universality of patriarchal manhood required of male children. How have the keepers of "mankind" reproduced this endowed position, entitling males to more than material property and functional places in society?

A patriarchal "character" is not, of course, an actual element of the Western alphabet, at least not beyond Hegel's tacit equation of grammar lessons with an "alphabet of the spirit itself."[1] Yet in letters from fathers to sons at school, we find a discrete form of gender education that has two arresting features. First, they specifically name earned patriarchal *identity* as a father's provision for a son's future. But more significantly, they explicitly connect this identity to literacy. Epistolary directions regulate young men's reading and demand (always absent) perfection in their writing. Unlike academy and university teachers, who scored work numerically or wrote sparse but charitable comments on the school writing of both female and male students, fathers caustically focused on minor lapses. Their express purpose was to link their son's graphic errors to moral faults and social mistakes.

It is not an absence of professional expertise, for example, that prevents current teachers from assuming the tone of a Hampden-Sydney College instructor who noted on Philip Southall Blanton's essay, "Public Celebrations": "Very well done. Be careful to guard against what may be called a wordy style. You are in the more danger on this point because you have a very ready command of language."[2] But earlier writing teachers were not, as they are now, charged with maintaining ranked cultural positions once bequeathed to pupils through the hands of fathers whose corrections teachers now trace.

This endowment of an identity category maintained a young man's class status, thereby marking a difference within its claims on transcendence. It fostered the same systematic exclusions that sustain local or diffuse pecking orders even now. This system also constructed *woman* negatively, in terms of what she does not do and cannot be, in various subject positions that ladies and others *would* not, as proper women, occupy. Lucy Butler must declare a vacation from this womanhood to protest that she and her "weak sisters" blush and weep at the cowardice of men, as Julia Dulany must vacate Confederate patriotic womanhood in her sorrowful account of burying a fallen soldier at Welbourne. In exceptional cases, men delivered this category to females, as in John Taylor's letter to his granddaughter about Congress. (See chapter 5.) But "mankind" never invites a female to assume a patriarchal position entirely within universal individualism, no matter what her class.

Similarly, professional accounts of texts often set aside the obvious ways in which designated Others occupy many values constructed as universal. Women's history often characterizes female schooling by its absence of "classical" topics or by contrasting a privileged woman's drudgery to equally taxing, but respected, masculine labor. Other selective professional traditions ignore the extensive education and relative comfort enjoyed by many women of the privileged class across history. Henry Louis Gates argues in addition that, like women, slaves—or servants, or Africans—and other groups figured racially have been known through a supposedly total absence of literacy, a lack that moves them, both historically and generally, outside "humankind."[3] Despite ample evidence that women and minorities often had better schooling than lower-class white males, both groups are represented as suffering from an educational lacuna. In addition, lower-class Anglo-American writing does not receive attention that emphasizes its positive articulation of and resistance to low social status. But lower-class workers in the seventeenth century, characterized by Richard Beale Davis as "poor rustic indentured servants, hungry and frightened," could write "genuinely tragic letters" after the 1622 massacre in Virginia.[4] American critical traditions rarely acknowledge the basic yet productive education given to these and other nonslave, non-African servants. Often, African-American and white "folk" cultures achieve credibility only when they are named "oral traditions," a quasi-anthropological category that overlooks both their literate participation in extensive textualities and their ordinary discourses.[5] By such exclusion, textual scholars reiterate, even if inadvertently and in a "liberal" tradition, categorical norms that sustain the idea of universal standards and their uses to rank texts.

Women, African Americans, and lower-class writers are not, of course, only abstract categories. They are people whose exclusion from the prerogatives of universal "mankind" make the consequences of exclusionary definitions of transcendent "nature" all too clear. But discrimination, while its results are entirely real, always takes its warrants from gender, racial, and class systems in re-formed theory and from cultural pedagogies that designate the texts of those outside entitlement as examples of the Other.

The literacy work of the Fathers grounds this textual identity politics in commonplace evaluations, recirculated now in interpretive judgments on the relative quality of texts. Belief in a hierarchy of quality, of course, echoes the religious concept of transcendence, the elevation invented to assure that "mankind" will endure as the specific beneficiary of a higher power. It may seem obvious that a constructed equality between dominant, special men and God manufactures many forms of relative evaluation that secularize transcendence. But just as the transmission of membership in universality is hidden in common places, the means by which culture maintains the exclusionary force of equating sacred texts with selected secular texts is hidden in "educated" common sense about their interpretation.

In the specific commonplaces that attend fathers' conveyances of patriarchy to their sons, generalized, formal gender *doxa* blends with local, informal interactions. Transcendence is written on the pulse and close to the bones that embody entitlements. The important subgenre of correspondence from fathers to sons includes a powerful cant language about writing in the steady gaze of transcendent judgment that warns against torn underwear and sloth. These letters are not artifacts of stylistic virtuosity, despite the wide publication of Lord Chesterfield's letters to Philip Stanhope, his bastard son. Nonetheless, these fathers write to their sons in the skillful register that perpetuates "mankind" as a category, precisely by frequently redrawing the plane on which vivid emotional sympathy for sons meets absolute standards for the quality of their writing and reading.

These letters consequently realize a foundational bequest to sons from their fathers, precisely by focusing on graphic propriety. Good spelling, a deceptively humble sign of the universal subject's control over language, accesses not just traditional aids to reading, but the *logos* of superior interpretive status. "Education" is a great deal more in this discourse than the lessons of a schoolmaster. The father is the source who "finishes" the son, making him and his language (unlike a daughter and hers) desirable not only to one man, to family, or even to God. Sons receive, that is, membership in the even higher perduring abstract category of *standing,* which guarantees acceptance in all lesser categories. They do so by learning the esoteric conventions of written language.

These paternal letters, like the letters of language they so often mention, educate the son in multiple ways. By communicating information, they demonstrate that fathers and sons in these families often exchanged affectionate, exclusionary "man talk." This closeness is always a mentorship, an affiliation like the one described in Littleton Waller Tazewell's memoir of his grandfather, who had himself been adopted by a benevolent mentor. Tazewell substituted this mentor for his biological father, describing the model who was dedicated to assuring his academic, social, and professional superiority. His record of this affectionate supervision was one of Tazewell's credentials, textual evidence of inheriting a dominant class identity. Like Blair Bolling, another male keeper of forefathers in both genealogical and discursive traditions, Tazewell testifies to having been "improved." These biographies, like the letters treated here, assume that older men were equipped to prepare male youths for society in a far more urgent mentoring than is imagined between generations today. (See chapter 3.)

That supervisory dimension is displayed in various ways. Although sons' responses are rarely preserved in this collection, they appear to have answered the fathers' constant questions (often unacceptably) regarding their spending of both the father's money and the time it bought them. Fathers send advice, oversee school lessons, and intervene in them, thereby portraying both paternal concern and its later relocation in academic advisors and the domesticated, feminized teacher of middle-class literacy. This group of patriarchs are not the uninvolved fathers often projected by social historians, but strict executors of their duty to improve children of both sexes.

If Virginia fathers represented in this collection became unimportant in an educationally privatized home, or secondary to Mother, it was after the Civil War, when they suddenly grew silent in anguish over their inability to educate children (chapter 7). Mass-schooled "respectability" only slowly replaced patriarchal entitlements and respect for them, perhaps because in Virginia, class stratifications based on property endured so long.[6] The "idea of fatherhood" that, according to Mary Ryan, had "seemed almost to wither away" by midcentury in Oneida, New York, appears to have retained a great deal of juice in this place and class.[7] This is exemplified in Landonia Randolph Minor's record of her widowed mother's debts and "A sketch of Papa's Life while in the United States Navy." She closes that list of his achievements with often imitated praise: "April on the 22nd 1861 Lieut Minor resigned his commission in the United States Navy, & joined his fortunes with those of the 'Confederacy of Southern States' '& his children rise up & call him wise & bless him.'"[8] These fathers also themselves apply and encourage what Ryan calls the "waft of sentimentality that blew through nineteenth-century culture,"[9] as shown in Minor's sketch and Jennie Stephenson's essay, "My Father's Household" (chapter 7). The endurance of such paternal feeling is evident in 1890 in Burton Harrison's letter to his son at Yale, discussing the typing and content of a contest essay (chapter 2). But Harrison's concern is only one confirmation of enduring fatherly affection for sons in elite transmissions of both practical and sentimental patriarchy. Many fathers affectionately offer technical information about business, for instance, apparently yearning for acceptance of their useful precepts. And all insist that their extraordinary concern with literate excellence is "for your own good."

"Fatal Consequences"
"I Rely on Your Goodness: With Gratitude and Esteem"

The concern with forming acceptable statements in early Virginia, Richard Davis says, was a "good" with precedents in rhetorical conduct traditions, where skilled correspondence is a mark of status. Conduct books joined social graces, epistolary effectiveness, and formal rhetoric in a universalized propriety. Similarly, scribal prowess, a version of oratorical power, was transmitted in the many "manuals for epistolarians" owned by colonial Virginians.[10] Davis uncovers in the letters of colonists the medieval epistolary rhetoric taught in these manuals; in turn, letters transmitted it to descendants who imitated the "Epistle Invective" and the "Epistle Accusatory" explained in Angel Day's *English Secretarie* (1592). Davis offers many examples of the vernacular textual tradition behind the belief that letters must be shaped to display propriety: J. Hill's *The English Secretarie; or a Speedy Help to Learning* (1486); *The Young Secretary's Guide* (1687?), and *The Young Clerk's Guide*, a later version. Hill's *Young Secretary's Guide* "included illustrations of how to compose one's will, or gave 'a Letter of Attorney from a Husband to a Wife upon a Voyage,' or a letter from 'A Wife to her Husband in Foreigne Parts.'" Many early Virginians owned this volume, and even "purely personal epistles were quite clearly composed under a strong consciousness of rhetorical rules."[11] Later nineteenth-century home libraries might include *Gay's Standard Encyclopeaedia and Self-Educator,* which published similar model letters, rules of composition, and sample texts.[12]

The continuity of this strong awareness of epistolary rhetoric is confirmed in an example from what may have been a copious correspondence between a guardian and his ward, an exchange entirely at odds with that guardian's letters to his own renegade son. Writing in 1788 from Eton to Ralph Wormeley (who had also attended Eton), John Tayloe (1771–1826) reveals both the absolute legal proprietorship of a guardian over a ward and the rhetorical prowess needed to manage it. Tayloe also exposes details about the English curricula that schooled early planters (chapter 2).

> Eton, 28th January, 1788
>
> Dear Sir:
> I shall ever esteem myself to be obligated in the highest degree to you for the opportunity I now enjoy of gaining the blessings of a good education, which, however unsuccessful my endavour may prove, shall not be lost by want of applicaiton on my part—as well as for your having placed me under the inestimable directions of the Major. And believe me, that the hope of rendering myself worthy of your esteem and future intimacy both excites and supports my application at school as well as house; in the latter of which situations we are by no means idle, as there the Major insists on our making good the deficiencies of Eton. the last holydays we were kept closely to the French language under an excellent master.[13]

His formal address shows that Tayloe perceived himself to have been "placed" under both Wormeley and his tutor, "the Major." A later letter from Wormeley to his eldest son Warner shows that Tayloe might know that his diligence over the holidays would please his guardian. The letter incidentally explains that French language instruction, frequently demeaned as only an item in female curricula, was equally demanded of boys to make up for a perceived deficiency in classical studies. As shown in many references in student writing, knowledge of French had business as well as social value. In 1839, before launching into the social system of the universe portrayed in her commencement address, Mary Virginia Early wrote a composition entitled "The advantages arising from the study of the French Language." It reads:

> It may be of considerable benefit, for should one of us be so fortunate, as to be permitted by the divine will of Providence, to cross the broad expanse of the Boundless Atlantic, and land on the shores of the European Continent in safety, we should undoubtedly desire to be prepared to converse readily with those into whose society we may chance to be.[14]

Again, the bizarre landing imagined here—foot on shore and French ready-to-mouth—demonstrates a commonplace obsession with getting all things "right."

Boys at Eton were not entirely without female influences. In his letter Tayloe explains, "We are very happy in our tutor and dame—the latter of whom is Miss Davis who is the sister of Dr. Davis, and lives at the bottom of the lane and in the same house where Dr. Davis lived in your day." But the primary purpose of Tayloe's letter is to connect with Wormeley's desires for him, in the interest of persuading his guardian to allow him to leave Eton as soon as possible. We learn more of the standard course of upper-class education from his request:

> I am extremely sorry, my dear sir, to find, by your letter to the Major . . . that you design to keep me three years longer at school, at the end of which period I shall be nearly of age. I am freely sensible of the great superiority of your judgement and of your good intentions towards me; but as it is now the general system for boys to leave school at the age of eighteen, I have hitherto flattered myself that at that age I should be removed to a situation where useful and real knowledge is to be acquired, which can not be obtained here. And for the adoption of my removal to the University at the age of eighteen, I am the more anxious, in order that my education may be completed by the time I shall be of age, when I am at present determined to return immediately to my native country—my attachment to which, I trust, will never be shaken.
>
> At the age of eighteen I shall have been better than six mo[n]ths in the fifth form, and it shall be my constant endeavour to become sufficenctly grounded in classical knowledge to pursue that line of study with full effect at the University, when should any pecuniary inconvenience arise from the embarrassments of the estate, I shall most readily accommodate myself to the allowance that you may

think proper to make me, however circumscribed it may be. My hope of so early a return to Virginia must depend on the earliest completion of my education. I rely on your goodness to excuse the liberty I have taken; and I hope that you will believe, however unsuccessful my wishes on the above subject may prove, that I shall ever remain, with gratitude and esteem,

Your aff. friend and servant, John Tayloe

Tayloe's later success as a wealthy state senator was apparently well deserved, on the basis of rhetorical aptitude alone. The delicate pleading of this persuasive composition may also have been matched by Tayloe's control of its surface features (which have been normalized for its publication in the *Etonian*). The above text, that is, offers no record of youthful spelling or word choices that fathers, especially Wormeley, monitored with amazing (at times puzzling) zeal. But Tayloe's argument was successful. In 1792, his twenty-first year, he returned to Virginia after attending St. John's College, Cambridge. The brevity of his acquisition of "useful and real knowledge" in classical study was common at the time as well as later, as Hugh Blair Grigsby's brief attendance at Yale also suggests (chapter 4).

"Ruined Forever"

Ralph Wormeley (1744–1806) had been at Eton from 1757 to 1762. His great-grandfather, Ralph Wormeley, Esq., entered Oriel College in 1665 and may have been the first Virginian to attend Oxford. Consequently, Wormeley's letters to his son Warner, when he was a scholar-apprentice in London at age fifteen, were written in a tradition of family expectations for achievement and deference, to which his ward Tayloe obviously contributed. But Wormeley's eleven preserved letters to Warner, and a twelfth from his mother, written from 1801 to 1805, are a chronicle of unhappiness on both sides. They negatively expose the joined expectations of behavior and language that constructed patriarchy.[15]

Wormeley's letters establish the repeated topics of fathers' letters to sons. He begins with a reminder that it is a duty of children to write to their parents. He responds to a letter just received (or complains of the absence of one), sends greetings to the schoolmaster, offers advice, and comments on local and political events. As is also conventional, he closes with an advisory salutation. Wormeley wrote from his plantation, Rosegill, but also from another family seat in Mt. Airy. Here, he notes the value of being in the company of a lady, a point noted in Alfred Horner's commonplace advice for "Youth," quietly adding that familiarity has limits.

Rosegill 16 December, 1801

Dear Warner—

I wrote to you since my return from the upper country, soon after I got home, your letter of the 9 of September arrived. it gave me pleasure to hear that Mr. Reeves was married, (though he never was so familiar as to mention it to me) because I am sure it will advance his happiness and because, you will have an opportunity to exercise [?] by your attentions to a Lady, when you are in the house with her, and never isolate the laws of good manners and decorum, either in language or gesture, under such a check, or in her company. When men or boys associate only with men or boys, they are very prone to lay aside, [their?] exterior good manners, and grow blunt[,] loud, and confidant instead of polite, muted, and diffident; negligent too in dress and persons: I request you to be correct and chaste in both; too neat you cannot be, and in dress cannot be too polished if it be easy and free from affectation.

Wormeley's most important concern is not dress, but his will to place Warner in his class, among his peers, by directing the primary matter of this advanced schooling, his reading and composition. Confirming the importance of "epistolary composition," he stringently notes graphic and spelling errors in his son's letters. He recommends the standard grammar (Lowth) and models for imitation from Addison, Steele, and Johnson:

But all of this is secondary to education and utility and though secondary, not [?]: I am concerned to observe to you, that you do not write, . . . either as to language or orthography, as I expected you would from the opportunities yo have enjoyed.

Of the stile of your letter of the 9th of september I will say nothing, but your wrong spellng of the local adverb <u>here</u>, which you confounded with the verb <u>to hear</u>, is such a gross error, that a youth of your age, who has been at a grammar school, ought not to have committed. Lord Chesterfield tells his son that he knew a nobleman . . . who was [shunned?] all his life for writing ["]upon the hole,["] instead of whole—Study English grammar, [?] & [Bishop] Lowth, after these Harris's Hermes. read epistolary compositions, and the writing of Addison & Johnson, especially, the Rambler; read also the Adventurer, as to French, it must be cultivated, by knowing it well enough to read, and translate English to French, grammatically, you may soon be going to France speak it well. Chambaud's is the best grammar—I think it probable when you get into the Counting house, that Mr. Reeves may want to send an agent to France on business, you may then if you approve yourself, trustworthy, be employed.

In closing, however, Wormeley makes the important connection between this particular advice and the *universal* happiness his son will derive from following it:

Let me frequently hear from you, my dear child; and I intreat you, as well for your future advantages in your future vocation, as for your own happiness through life, to apply to your scholastic pursuits and not only to the school but every [?] task, but also to read our best authors out of school for your own amusement and imprvement: cultivate first your mind, and afterwards your heart: becoming morals, manners, and religion will make a man respectable in *all* the walks of life; *without* those, he never can be held, in *any*—. . . make my Respects to Mr. Reeves, & inform me as to the lady whom he married—

Yours most affectionately, Ralph Wormeley.[16]

There is, of course, a discursive story here. Wormeley's letter moves from local paternity over Warner's last letter to assuming the authority of a Chesterfield, bringing to bear not only rules of courtesy and wisdom about women, but class universals in grammar lessons, textual models, and the practicality of mastering French. Additionally, if less directly, he shows expectations for Warner's future livelihood, emphasizing that the son must be employable.

In April 1802, Wormeley rejects Warner's request to take a country holiday with stringent reminders of the dangers of the soft life of pleasure that John Tayloe was denied by his tutor. Deploying common narratives of "character" against the "propriety of character" he wants Warner to acquire, Wormeley describes the dangers of a country visit:

Mr. Reeves did right in putting his negative on your going down into Yorkshire; no doubt he will either shew you or communicate to you what were my sentiments on that occasion: too high a relish for pleasant congenial company has been the ruin of thousands of easy=minded youths; Men [wedded?] to no profession, of liberal education, of open heartedness, of agreeable manners, and of indepependant fortunes are generally of the above description; and tho' they do not [?] in scholasicity to excess . . . yet of rural amusements and diversions they take commonly a large share, and of the pleasures of the table to an extent only limited by propriety to character, and considerations of health and constitution—in the morning hounds, parties, and guns; at four o'clock agreeable parties at dinner, & in the evening, whist or loo, this routine a little interupted by [?] or Balls—such courses will never do for you, who must be devoted to business, must be a man of business, or, must be a vagabond through life—do you think the last Lord Mayor of London, Sr. William Staines [?] would have turned out such a valuable citizen as he is, if, in his days of boyhood, he had been indulged in making parties into Yorkshire to enjoy the pleasures and spirits of the field, and the festivities of the convivial board—his modest answer to the thanks of the court of Aldermende pleased me much—"I spring from *nothing*, what I Am, I am by the blessing of God on my endeavours"—or words to that effect. This generally will be the case, God will assist the endeavours of those, who, by sobriety, industry, & prudence in their different walks of life, pray for and merit her assistance. I very much approve of your being permitted to accompany Mr. Reeves & her Lady in the summer to any of the watering places, these are wholesome relaxations, and here you may improve your manners.[17]

Wormeley clearly aligns himself with humanists in their debate against aristocrats about education. He applauds self-made republicanism by opposing sport, dance, hunting, and other Renaissance alternatives to "serious" textual self-elevation (chapter 1). In view of his family's Virginia entitlements, we can imagine Warner's difficulty accepting that he must climb as had the low-born mayor of London. But Wormeley's puritanical work ethic and fear of Warner becoming a "vagabond" must prevail. To assure this, he emphasizes epistolary duty between a father and son in a meticulously detailed accusation:

Your letter of the 18th. of January I received last week; you give a most curious [reason?] for not replying to my letter, namely, "that you had been for some time expecting *ano*ther from me'" whereas, you had no right to reckon on this, until *I* heard *from you;* however, I did write to you some time in the winter, and trust, you have received the letter, to which I desire you not to postpone your reply. in expectation of hearing from me.

Scrupulous attention to the timing of letters was a necessary concern in the absence of a regular mail service. But Wormeley's source of irritation was that he suspected his son of postponing replies and obscuring his reluctance to write. As seen in Charles Mortimer's letters to his son Jack in Philadelphia (1785–1789)—discussed later in this chapter—writing well and often was not only a mark of a son's filial piety in a mentoring relationship. Letters from a child were needed so that they might be corrected.

Wormeley divides what he calls "primary" education, attention to business, from secondary academic pursuits, again demanding from Warner a rigorous self-discipline he did not possess:

Your education is to begin when you enter [Mr. Beverly's] counting house; your primary duties will be to be performed here; but secondary must not be neglected; whenever you are not at the desk, you must be employed in cultivating your mind—you must read the best books, history ancient & modern—Moral essays & epistolary writing; French must never be neglected—at nineteen be taught to fence & I will have you taught the manual exercise, for evey citizen here must be a Militia man—*Your reading, writing, and French must never supercede business, your proper business,* but this may be done, and other matters not neglected; except, at your meals, and what time is necessary to employ about your person, to the neatness and cleanliness of which, I beg your attention, never be idle; have always a book in your hand or in your pocket, the best antidote to vanity & vice.

As he regularly does, Wormeley cites as authority the behavior of prominent male models, encouraging Warner to emulate their self-deprivation. He recommends the practice of Bishop Andrews, who spent *his* holidays each year learning a new language and "lost *no time*" in mindless relaxation. His emotional stake in Warner's turning out well is clear: "You see, my dear child, my extreme anxiety for your welfare, judge what will be my mortification, if you disappoint me."

A year later, Wormeley wrote again, reiterating much the same advice, repeating the same disappointments, and restating how personally he took Warner's success or failure. Concern about Warner's precise language is again entirely enmeshed in his vision of his son's future, here tied to bringing an end to slavery:

Rosegill, 16 May, 1803

Dear Warner
Your letter of the 7th of March and the 15th I have received, is your first you acknowledge to have received several of mine, and then say, though you have written to me six at least, yet not one answer has been given to any: how contradictory! I have written to you most frequently & am sorry to find you *so little improved—in your mother[']s letter which by no means pleased me, I find you do not know the difference between <u>accepted</u> & <u>excepted</u>, and use the latter word, instead of the former. in your's to me you have this word <u>ecnegaralable</u> advice, <u>there</u> <u>is</u> <u>no</u> <u>such</u> <u>word.</u>* Then you are on the object of money, and increase of allowance. I have written over and over again, that I would allow you one hundred and fifty pounds per annum, and that is more than I can afford, and that you ought to spend. I sent you to London to try to make you a man of mercantaile business, that you may be enabled to live by your own exertions independent of lands and negores, foreseeing that this latter property is becoming less valuable by becoming daily more precarious.[18]

Wormeley appears to want to praise Warner, to give him "credit" in this patriarchal school for at least one feature of his writing, a "good hand." Handwriting becomes a trope for his desires to avoid Warner's "ruin." He also discusses details of business, including his son in reasoning about the politics of tobacco trade, thereby transmitting lore to the son he wants to "place" in this exchange. Again, he closes with a reference that shows the precariousness of sending letters across the Atlantic:

I give you credit for writing a good hand, I think it an acomplishment myself—I would wish you to do everything well, and therefore wish to keep you out of Virginia; if you come here, you are ruined forever—

I have not purchased any tobacco, the price here so much exceeding Mr. Reeves's limitation and every idea of the value of it in London: if, war take[s] place [torn page] which I do not think [it?] will, we shall be losers (or not gainers rather) by not having purchased, if it do not take place, we shall be gainers (or not be losers) by declining to purchase . . . a few weeks will decice this doubt, and I shall then act accordingly. . . .

I send this to Baltimore—my letters by the Ocean Capt Murray were lost with the vessel, which we are told has never been heared of—by that opportunity I wrote to you.

I am dear Warner
Your most affectionate Father
Ralph Wormeley

P.S. Let me know how you are employed when out of the Counting house.

These letters did actually accomplish business, involving sons in purchases and, in the case of Charles Mortimer's letters to Philadelphia, in transportation of household items. In another lengthy postscript labeled "Supplemental," Wormeley describes an active contemporary debate on prisons, management of debt, and the establishment of a public bureaucracy, all of which were prominent concerns before their regulation in the nineteenth century. Wormeley's interests fit his station as a merchant-landowner and show intimate knowledge of current ideas about the "preservation of morals by the prevention of crime." He recommends that Warner join this reading community:

> The respectable Mr. Colhoun [?] one of the magistrates of the City of London, whose "Treatise on the police" and also on the Police of the Thames" I have wrote a letter dated the 16th of Febary last, to Thos Eddy Esq, New York," on Police . . . [in] general "and" penitentiary hours," and "management of the poor," and "prison [?] of criminals" &e, &e, which Letter if published in London, I beg to recommend to your perusal—it has pointed out to me several publications, which I am anxious to get and to peruse—Those tracts, which relate to the preservation of morals, by the prevention of crime, are most to my purpose—"his observations and Public House." "duty of a Constable"- "Reports of the Select Committee on Finance"—"Mr. Goatham"s & vols on penitentiary punishments." also "Annual Reports of the Penitentiary House in Dosshire [Dorsetshire?]"—on confinement of poor persons for civil debts, by James Nield Esq." Thse are the various tracts I want, some you will and some you will not get, unless Mr. Reeves could procure them by the means of his kinsman Wm. Reeves.

Two months later, Wormeley engaged in the only equal exchange contained in this correspondence, acknowledging that Warner had accurately assessed "Rules" of tobacco dealings. The repeated theme of sending and receiving letters frames this momentary rapprochement in a description of an exchange of letters lost with a ship that sank. Here, Wormeley's profiteering activities become visible as he discusses manipulating prices and favoring friends in wartime:

1803, July 23

Dear Warner

You complain in your leter of the 14th of May, which I received a week ago, of my not writing to you; my letters have miscarried, expecially that by the Ocean Capt: Murray, the vessel is lost I am afraid and every creature perished.

Your golden rules for the purchase of tobacco are very good ones, and such as I have endeavoured to observe; certainly better not purchase than purchace indifferent or bad tobacco. I have always shipt in order to get the tobacco to London before October; . . . The year before, the William & John lay a month at Norfolk & Hampton [R]oads. . . . How I shall now be able to secure freight is very problematical. . . .

If the war should raise the price of flour, I will try to send Mr. Reeves 100 barrels in the winter, & if I can procure freight, & the price will encourage it, I will consign 750 bushels of yellow Indian corn to Mr. Herbert at Lisbon.

I have written to Mr. Reeves on the subject of speculation. My impression is, that the war will not last, and that there will be too much of hazard in purchasing at high prices, and incurring heavy expences of freight, insurance, [?] and then possibly obtaining only peace prices. . . . I wrote to you the other day by the two Generals, and sent you a parcel of the Virginia Gazettes. Send me the Times, though they may cost sixpence each, if Mr. Reeves take that paper he might read it, then it might be sent to me, dividing the cost of it, unless he chose it to file it.[19]

Such man-to-man equality did not last. A letter of September 1803 contains little but scorn, the commonplace criticism of this genre jumbled with personal abuse. It attacks Warner's lack of thrift, his childishness despite his adult stature, and his always faulty language. All demonstrate to the father his son's unwillingness to assume his rightful position:

If you do not make a greater progress in improvement than you have done; and if, moreover, you exceed (as you have done) the allowance you yourself stipulated, one hundred and fifty pounds per annum; I shall order you to Virginia next sumer as to the mode of dispensing it, I left it to Mr. Reeves, and care nothing as to the arrangement, provided, you did not exceed the sum. When I was at Cambridge (and a fellow [?]) my tutor paid my bills, and I got pocket money from him as I wanted it, and was content. *you are tall, and are in a stature perhaps manly, but I am sorry to say, in [?] you are a child. Where did you collect this elegant expression, "anyhow" pleasing; and again "anyhow" allow me: be content to get the money and thankful for it, whether dispensed [partially?], or, in larger sums. My own opinion is, that you are not fit to be trusted.* This however, I have left to Mr. Reeves, and let me beg of you, not to fill your letters with remonstrances against those very parents, which, have been settled by me, or left to Mr. Reeves discretion[20]

In February 1804, financial concerns push Wormeley to express further disappointments, to which he feels entitled as a patriarch concerned for his son's chances in a world that "in a few years" will reject slavery:

> Rosegill 17 February, 1804
>
> Dear Warner—
> The last letter I received from you was on the old theme of dealing out your allowance to you; & then too after having fixed the amount, according to your own calculation, I am given to understand, that, *that* will not suffice: more, I cannot afford, and if I could, would not allow. I am apprehensive your situation & pursuits will not turn to much account, nor answer my expectation; I do not know, but fear you want application, and, that you do not feel the inclination to be what I had at heart to make you: be it so: I have heard you wished to return, and to tell you the truth, as you do not live under Mr. Reeves' roof, unless, you can live upon your allowance, and are disposed to apply yourself most strictly to the duties of the Counting house, I give yo my permission to return next summer—this is a sad case for a youth of your age, with such examples as are exhibited here, but I am not sure, that London is preferable, certainly more expensive. "When the young man does not feel an ardent desire to reap every improvement, both the practical and intellectual, that the situation affords."[21]

Wormeley concludes this disheartening assessment by explaining why he nags Warner. He bluntly yet euphemistically predicts the economic future Warner will encounter, closing as he began by reminding his son that he expects him to fulfill one duty at least—to send a response:

> I repeat, that I fear, you are not activated by any such feelings. I wished to make you a merchant and to enable you thereby to get your living, as I may be disposed to divide my little fortune nearly equal among all [my] children; and as I see clearly, in a few years, that a certain species of property we now employ as laborers in our fields, will be no property at all. This, I have endeavoured to make yo understand, but, in vain! perhaps, it is not easy to make young persons see clearly, even when age and experience point the finger directly to the object.
>
> upon the receipt of this Letter let me hear from you; I desire you to import this letter to Mr. [Reeve?]

Lest we imagine this patriarchal scorching as the fixed "character" of this father, we must note its moderating coda, which expresses the "concern" that guides him:

P.S. I do not suppose I am angry—no—I am under the influence of concern, more than irritability: my eldest son is very nearly every thing I wish him not to be—he wants understanding—is deficient in manners—is idle, expensive, and addicted to low company—

Wormeley's last letter is more cheerful. It describes his reactions to the effect of Anglo-American politics on the tobacco trade and foresees economic changes that later replaced tobacco with cotton, further entrenching the slave economy whose demise he had prematurely predicted. In this relatively chatty letter, he makes no reference to Warner's failings. Instead, he mentions that a carpet he had ordered has arrived and his hope that Anglo-American relations will be repaired.

Nonetheless, the predicted worst case unfolds. The only other parental missive is from Warner's mother, Eleanor Tayloe Wormeley (1755?–1815), sister of Wormeley's ward, John Tayloe. Dated 1805, the letter makes a final plea to her son to undo the damage caused by his abrupt flight to South Carolina. Although her letter begins calmly and later mentions family health and visitors, its tone and frequent underlining convey anger and fearfulness both for her son and for his father's health.

Wormeley's letters mention that Eleanor separately corresponded with her son. His letters may have omitted family news because she wrote regularly of the domestic happiness that she identifies as her primary expectation in life.

March 9, 1805

My Dear Warner

Your letter of February 8th I received, and it always gives me pleasure to have a letter from you. I had heard of your safe arrival at Charles Town, and of your abrupt departure from England, this information we gained from your letter to your father, and with deep regret did *I* read it, as I had flattered myself your conduct would not have *worried* me, but *southed* our declining years, by *propriety* of conduct, and the most tender *affections*, you must my *dear ever dear* child, feel that I am not only an *affectionate* Mother, but a sincere friend to you, with deep concern do I tell you, you have highly displeased your father, as his letter of this day will show you I [?] as your *friend urge, entreat, and request*, you will come *immediately* to Rosegill, see your father, confess that you have greatly erred and by your confession, soften his resentment, never lose for a moment your respect, and *veneration* for him, for however *harsh* you may think him . . . [he] as a parent and husband is most highly to be valued. follow I beg you his mode of reasoning here, tho not agreeable to yourself and when you come [?] with me freely as your friend, and be assured I will [?] as one. at my time of life I look in this World to no happiness but domestic, what then must my present sufferings be, the uneasiness you have given, has caused a return of your father's complaint, which wears him down, how much then does it behove you to come immediately and *quiet* him, by respectfull attentions, I again urge it, . . . as your friend with *him* do not let the gaiety of Charles Town suffer this friendly letter to be unheeded, just follow my advice, by staying you dayly involve in debts, which in honour *you must pay,* if it ever be, not a *future* day, I shall *dayly* expect you, and not one moment more shall I enjoy till I see a happy reconciliation with you. Mr. Carter [?] . . . has spent some days here, he leaves us tomorrow, Mr. Gay [?] is in very low health, and also his daughter Miss Mary. I must now conclude, I write by candle light, and with my spectacles on, you will excuse bad writing, and [?] your brother desires his love, and esteem to you and your Sisters their love, [?] who *dearly* loves you, is very uneasy, your father is vastly fond of her, I now bid you adieu, with full confidence, of your following my advice and if you do not, I cannot answer for the fatal consequences to you. Hasten then my dear, to the embrace of an offended, but most affectionate and *tender* parent, and rely on the friendship of

> Your uneasy, but
> Affectionate Mother
> and Sincere Friend
> Eleanor Wormeley.[22]

Eleanor's attempt to mediate between son and father, the force of whose anger we have already seen, stresses that Warner must trust her to intercede for him. Although his father had threatened to divide his property equally among his children, Warner now risks greater disinheritance. In addition, he may be literally disowned, as indicated by this letter's reference to the debts he is incurring in Charleston and "must pay." By including greetings from Warner's brothers and sisters and the affection of one unidentified person who "*dearly* loves you" and of whom Wormeley is "very fond," the letter animates the concern of the entire family to stimulate in Warner a reciprocal concern about being cut off from not only money but also human resources.

But Eleanor emphasizes that she is Warner's "friend." Her *ethos* is not verified, as a later mother's might be, by shaming appeals to intimacy or her sacrifices for her son. She writes of a motherhood that parallels, but remains distinct from, both friendship and the patriarchal fatherhood realized by commonplaces of responsibility and power in Wormeley's letters. Her most telling appeal is her reference to the "declining years" of both parents. But her own, separate, "domestic happiness" is the only personal claim on guilt that she deploys, evidently quite honestly.

These letters together resuscitate the complex mix of intimacy and form calibrated by such transmissions of patriarchy. They embody family duty, an overdetermined cultural function that fits the episodic medium that contains it. They juxtapose almost infinitely distant and painfully intimate perspectives, in one vector for parental duty, especially in the crisis of Warner's bolting from his family's supervision of both his person and his cultural identity.

The precisely commonplace nature of this mingled duty becomes clear as Eleanor brings up the quality of her dimly illuminated writing. She too knows the issue at stake in Wormeley's seemingly inexplicable shifts from anger at Warner's profligate spending to sarcasm over his mistaken locutions and spellings. She excuses her "bad [hand]writing," which is perfectly regular but occasionally made illegible by attempts to darken many words. But this plea for pardon is not to forestall attacks on such lapses. It instead acknowledges shared standards that equate the propriety of written language with the universal category of identity that these standards support. Both parents, that is, understand that "good" texts are marks of "propriety of conduct," which Eleanor's letter so baldly identifies as the boundary around a much greater power.

The preservation of this correspondence may well be owed to the continuous prominence of this family, whatever its fortunes. Eleanor's warning about "fatal consequences" was realized. Wormeley died a year later, in 1806, at sixty-two; Eleanor lived until 1815, dying at sixty, outliving Warner, who died the year before at twenty-nine. In December 1807, after returning to Virginia, Warner had married Maria Carter Hall, of Fredericksburg; in 1814, shortly before his death, he married again.

The disappointment and mortification that Wormeley had feared were not imaginary embarrassments, despite Warner's appearance of domestic respectability. After his return to Virginia, Warner had continued in his bad habits. The letter book of General John Minor (1761–1816) includes two letters to Warner about his unpaid debts and one to Eleanor thanking her for paying an unrelated bill. In them, Warner might again hear Father recalling him to duty and demanding another sort of reply:

> Dec 19th, 1810
>
> Dear Warner
> It is most disagreable to me to remind a friend of disagreable matter, but duty compells me to do it now—You will recollect that the execution of Bogle [?] you has become due, and that you promised me it should be paid out of the sumes you received from your late contract, and that your note at Bank for which I was Indorser should also be paid the Execution has not been paid and I have lately been called on to Indorse another note: I have the Execution in my hands but shall keep it up untill I hear from you on both subjects, which I trust I shall do soon, and state particularly,
>
> J. Minor

Warner L. Wormeley Esqu, Hanover Town

December 22—[18]10

Dear Sir

I wrote to you by the last post concerning Bagles Claim and the note at Bank both of which you promised you would take up when you returned from Philadelphia. I hope to hear from you, on these subjects by the next post.

I now farther address you to request payment of those Debts you owe me as the representative of Doctor Spratt, to wit a stay Bond of you and your Brothers to Daniel McNaugthton, the other a Bond of you and your Brother to me or per statement below. I pray you pay these little matters and save me the pain of prosecuting you. You told me you were, or certainly would be before these times in funds.

J. Minor

Minor's letter to Eleanor in 1811 thanks her for paying the separate debt to the estate of Dr. George Spratt (for which he was probably the executor). It notes his own fatherly offices to a son just beginning a distant education, this time in Baltimore: "Dr French, and my self were both disappointed in not having the pleasure of Eating our dinner with you but we were called to Baltimore by Interesting business. that putting our Sons in St Marys College (Roman Catholick) but do not think that I mean to make John a Papist. Yet I hope he will gain much good information there."[23]

"Your Poor Sister"
Working Books

It is easy enough to dismiss a relationship between an evidently money-hungry and stiff Wormeley and his trivial son. Vexed paternity is hardly typical of commonplace patriarchy, especially in view of the apparently happy relationship between John Tayloe and the same patriarch. But all of these letters, between Wormeley and his ward, and between father and son, reflect a continuing effort (successful or not) to reproduce universal male identity. Another instance is transmitted in the dedicated copying of a grandfather's cultural legacy.

Mary Anne Fauntleroy Mortimer Randolph (?–1858) kept a commonplace book from 1851 to 1855 that serves as a case study of the active uses to which the genre was put in the households that patriarchal lessons maintained. One section of this multipurpose, multiply authored book opens on pages of recipes, drafts of letters, and a summary of a lecture on Christianity written by her son. But from the reverse direction, the same book contains the remains of 135 copied letters (numbered and dated December 20, 1785, to August 30, 1789) that her father, John Mortimer, received from his father,

Charles Mortimer, while serving as a scholar-apprentice in Philadelphia.

Mary Anne, and perhaps other female relatives, used the active part of this volume as a cookbook. It includes recipes labeled "for Black Cake, candy, Sally Lunne Cake, 'To make Orange Pudding,' Lemon Pudding, Mince Meat, Irish Potatoe Pudding, and '"For Wash Soap.'"[24] Two pages later follows an elliptical record of a lecture on the distinction between "private" and "authorized" revelation, in the hand of her son, Robert Randolph Jr.:

> Mr. Norton's introductory lecture to a course on evidences of Christianity delivered at [?] on [?] 31, 1849. A very fine lecture. I will endeavour to give an idea of it. Comenced by showing that the individual [?] belief in revelation . . . inappropriate to the pulpit & tho. it was a minister's province more particularly to proclaim that ten[et?] of the bible and that to their own power & the influences of the Holy spirit to produce effect those in certain. . . .
>
> Robt Randolph Jr. / Farquier County

Robert here also practices writing "Robt.," followed by "This 4th day of January 1851, Up to this day 38 turkeys." This list is followed by an accounting of "tea plates" and cups, followed on the next page by a draft in yet another hand of a letter of condolence on the loss of an unidentified child. Its beginning suggests that the writer had recourse to epistolary guides like those described earlier:

> How can I with Pen Ink and paper offer in any degree to my much beloved parent and family the true sympathy me and mine feel for her and hers or indicate in any other way at this late most melenchoy announcement to loss of such a child, wife Sister and the community in which she has won the love of so many can?

This draft continues for three pages, followed by two lists of numbers in yet another hand, one of which is dated November 20, 1854. Here, a child has turned the book upside down to sketch. The sketching is followed by another drafted condolence, addressed to "cousin Lou [?]."

These contents highlight the typical working status of this volume, a ready reference in cooking, a place for children and other family members to scribble, note, and record. It mingles inconsequential scrawls and appropriations of social and intellectual *doxa* with drafts of memorial family correspondence. All of these miscellaneous uses are typical in commonplace uses of bound blank books. But their actual significance is revealed by the time taken to copy 135 letters from Charles Mortimer, a physician, to his son John (whom he calls Jack). The book displays an economy of family inheritance that should lead to reassessments of the cultural importance assigned to seemingly only practical domestic texts.

Many of the letters in this book have been torn out, but it is evident from those remaining that Charles Mortimer, who in 1787 had "lived to Sixty," wrote to fulfill not only his duty as a citizen, but a commitment to his son, then nineteen. He mentions that two or three of his letters appear not to have arrived; however, Jack should answer the one he now writes. In 1788, the year in which John Tayloe wrote to Ralph Wormeley from Eton, Mortimer expects the same promptness in response that Wormeley demanded.

Charles Mortimer's letters also frequently mention a close relative, also named Charles, age thirty, who has come to little good and who is a burden on the family financially and socially. Jack, on the contrary, is happily apprenticed to Mr. Barclay, although in what business the letters do not specify. He is expected to complete his schooling with Barclay, which involved his studying liberal arts as well as business. There is, however, no mention that Barclay evaluated Jack for any qualities but those of negotiable "character."

Like others, this relationship between father and son was both intimate and exclusionary. Charles Mortimer confides in Jack the details of his debts and requests him to send particular items like wine, tea, shoes and stockings. He frequently asks Jack not to mention his own business matters or worries about money in Philadelphia, and similarly asks him not to write about topics that could upset his sister or mother in Virginia. In many ways, this correspondence embodies a practical friendship built on mutual trust and confidence. Mortimer's advancing age, coupled with health problems, which curtailed his medical service to the Revolution in 1781, may explain the urgency of his tone.[25] But this urgency was also, perhaps in view of the perceived failures of his kinsman, Charles Mortimer, an educational process, devoted to instilling identification with universal standards. Not only in matters of business and finance, but by direct warnings about Jack's sexual, matrimonial, and literate choices, Mortimer repeatedly asserts that he is "finishing" Jack. He explicitly states his hope of providing his son with the improvements necessary for success. As Mary Anne's copying and a few annotations on the letters tell us, he was successful.

Men, Money, and Marriage

Clearly, in the early Republic a father's most important source of power was pecuniary. Mortimer always frames his letters with affectionate greetings and includes in them opinions of the new government, complaints about the postal service versus conveyance by "opportunity," local news, political opinions, and details designed to direct and improve Jack's life. For instance, he unsuccessfully tries to have shirts made for Jack, as Jack does shoes for him, and particularly directs Jack's packing for trips home, evidently in view of freight charges. But Mortimer's most regular attention is given to his debts and Jack's expenses, although without the warranted insults of Ralph Wormeley's letters to his son in England. The following letter, the earliest one in this exchange, establishes this theme and other recurring concerns:

December 20th, 1785

Dear Jack:

I wrote you last week by Doctor Bond and sent you two Guineas by him sealed up to be delivered to Wm. Barclay and a letter to place the amount to my credit, as I was [in debt?] to him, contrary to my expctations when I sent the bill for your 20 in Currency. The bearer [is] W. Weedon [?] a whole ale merchant here, and a good kind man from Liverpoole.

You are in my debt several letters now, and must watch out for families of Gentlemen coming here, and have your letters ready to go by them as the stage conveys. . . . You must not mind the newspapers. I can see them here. Remember to write to Weedo[n], short and genteel, as he will shew your letters, and mention [?], and Billey Mercer also.

I am your affectinatly, C. Mortimer

Most of this correspondence addresses the space of separation between Philadelphia and Fredericksburg. But Mortimer also reports local events, linking them to Jack's potential choices in both off-hand and urgent advice. In the second copied letter, for instance, he warns against "the example of the distractions of Youth before you. Its Jimmy Porter, who for 12 months has been a [?] pupil [is now a?] ruined young buck, and the parents so blind and unfortunately and . . . not to see it. He was in a [?] house the other night, and stabbed a man. . . . He will I believe recover, therefore may get over the scrape." Later in this letter, Mortimer elaborates another negative example, connecting a local youth's folly of "passion" to Jack's future, although quickly saying he trusts his son. As always, money and sexual choices are entwined:

If you lay out your money in useful purposes, and not in evil bad company I should not be displeased. I will now give a striking example in a handsome youth that I had hopes of here. Its young Jeremy Allen, a good Scholar was bound to Somerville & mistook. He got in with an idle strumpet here who has deceived him, and he has gone off to the West Indies. What must be the situation of his aged parent who laboured hard to provide for him. This is the rock that youth first splits on, and which they never get over if they give way to passions before they are of age. I hope my dear you will consider of these matters, and not bring your aged parent to the grave with tears of sorrow, but I do not suspect you. Have sent ten Guineas by Doctor Bond to be delivered to Mr. Barclay.

The tone Mortimer intends—mixed fatherly nagging, encouragement, caution, and abiding worry—is established through the topoi of these early letters and related cautionary themes. For instance, in the third letter (July 4, 1786), we discover that Jack has tentatively broached a "venture" and that Mortimer tentatively supports it, calling on Barclay's authority for information. Mortimer emphasizes his continuous concern about Jack's expenses, a worry that, unlike Wormeley's, is persuasively based on his limited means. This letter additionally demonstrates Mortimer's ongoing monitoring of Jack's propriety in reminders to show concern for a fellow Virginian, Billy Mercer, and to thank the Barclays for inviting Jack's sister Nancy to visit.

> Dear Jack
> I received your letter regarding Billy Mercer that [post?] is filled. You mentioned a venture and that you might gain by it. Why do you not [enlighten] me. Explain and [tell me the?] probablilty of it with Mr. Barclay's advice and coment. then I might have answered you to the purpose on it, but not without his comment or knowledge of the matter.
> I hope before this date you have received the letters and ten Guineas sent by Doctor Thomas Bond by me to pay off your expenses too. I wish to hear from you on the [torn page] . . . I can get a bill, also wrote Mr. Barclay. You must be as Saving in your expenses . . . [?] to all the money I have by you is more than I expected but if you do not [waste?] it by any . . . foolish expenses I would be satisfied. We have been uneasy at your not mentioning always in your letters something about Mercer. How could you forget it, as we did hear he is in a bad state of health. I wrote you about him, and about your getting clothing for him if [he?] needs any. Nancy is . . . obliged to Mr. and Mrs. Barclay, but she could by no means leave her mother in her state of health. Send all our respectful thanks to the family. She will write to Mrs. Barclay. Watch every opportunity now of Gentlemen coming here to write by, and write to General Weedon by post about Mercer.
> Yours affectionatly, C. Mortimer.[26]

In September 1787, Mortimer directly addresses the dangers of sexually transmitted disease. He asks Jack to send him privately a pamphlet on the venereal infections that are rampant, he says, in Fredericksburg. Mortimer requests that Jack wrap the pamphlet in plain brown paper and refrain from mentioning the subject in letters that sister Nancy (he notes elsewhere) will read. But the letter also reveals a father's authorization of a son, proprietorship of his current and future "prospects," in both familial and spiritual forms.

> I want a small book . . . a treatise on the venereal [disorder?] by [?] Hunter, London. Send it . . . sealed up . . . in a piece of strong paper. It would shock you to see the instances here (but say nothing about it) of the youth of the town ruined positively by the fowl disease, and their constitutions destroyed. I hope it will be

a warning to you. for I should forever disown you, if you follow their practices, as it destroys soul and body and the generations to come; . . . such practices render young men for ever miserable so therefore take care of yourself, now is the time for [minding?] a good or admirable constitution . . . without which life is a burden. By observing this rule I have lived to Sixty without much painful disorders except the consequence of declining life. Do you the like, and save your soul as well as body.

C. Mortimer

This warning from Mortimer was written at the end of a family disaster, a potentially ruinous and scandalous deception of Jack's sister Nancy that had been uneasily resolved. The immediacy of that event may account for the highlighted anxiety with which Mortimer instructs Jack in the qualities expected of a successful patriarch, a state he has serious reasons to doubt Jack has achieved. A deception of the family, not merely of its daughter, explains much about Mortimer's later advice as well, for Jack's relation to patriarchal responsibility is permanently altered by the fate of his sister Nancy, who becomes, over time, only a character of melodrama, "your poor sister."

Mortimer first mentions Nancy and a Mr. Moffatt in July 1786, saying, "Your Sister thinks you neglect her as she has received no letter from you and she is a very discerning girl." He adds that Mr. Moffatt "goes to Philadelphia soon and we shall write by him to you." In the spring of 1787, Mortimer writes of Nancy's planned wedding to Moffatt, advising Jack not to attend because of the difficulties of travel. He is also concerned about both money and his gout, about which he had noted in February, "I have had my [fill?] of bleeding and blistering. . . . [Barclay] is young and can rally, but my worn out constitution is so much against me, *however if you do well and maintain a good character, I am satisfied*" (emphasis added). In writing about the wedding, Mortimer additionally links these topics to the ongoing theme of Jack's success, which will be achieved by appropriate reading and curbing his "passions," two remedies that are recommended again as Nancy's marriage story unfolds:

My dear Jack,
I thought it needless to make you [concerned?] about my illness which has been very severe this winter, and now have the gout. The extreme bad weather, and great [risk?] in stage travelling in bad roads, prevents my [requesting?] to Mr. Barclay for leave, that you might come to your Sister's wedding to Mr. Moffatt, who is a very industrious man in good business, and well liked and esteemed. You will make us your annual visit in May, I hope, I shall write to Mr. Barclay about it. *I hope you do not neglect your reading, as the only pleasure I have now in life is to see you appear sensible and fixed with a good character, persevering in virtue, good*

morals, and reading are the only thing, to attain all desirable ends. Do not lose the opportunity my Dear, for the passions being curbed between 17 and so will save you from all evils, and preserve your constitution . . . [?] easy & familiar, thereby become a happiness to us and all your friends. Nancy desires her love to you. Mr Moffatt wrote you. Yours affectionately. C. Mortimer. (Emphasis added)

Mortimer recapitulates this information in a letter written on March 22, 1786:

[I] wrote you a few days ago by mr. [?], which I hope you received. I then informed you of my recovering from a second disease this winter, and the gout going off, also of Nancy's marriage to Mr. Moffatt, who is much esteemed and liked by all parties. I shall expect you in May and that you will write us all by May Day.

Under this letter is written in another hand, "her age was 24 when married," followed by "My Sister was married on the 7th of this month to Mr. Thomas Moffatt of London, during my absence. J. M." Jack Mortimer annotated the manuscript letter himself, and his note was copied, with the additional annotation fixing Nancy's age.

These scrupulous markers do not, however, highlight nuptial pride. In June, soon after the wedding, Charles Mortimer wrote, "Your mother and Sister are well. Moffatt at Norfolk at present. I fear his affairs are in a bad way, [?] very uneasy." By the next month, in a letter that pointedly cautions his son about partnership in the venture Jack had proposed, buying lottery tickets, Mortimer hints at how Nancy's marriage may develop:

I told you to get a ticket in the third Class of the lottery, and Wm. Barclay to pay for it, that you may be there by entitled to a ticket in the 4th Class. *Have no partnership in it with any person.* Its my desire you would not mention your having any ticket to General Weedon. If those produce us fortune, have done with lotteries in future. We are well as yet. I *fear Moffatt[']s affairs are not in a good way which affects me much, but you need not in your letters take any notice of that matter, as I must shew them to your Sister. I shall never say anything more to you about reading. but remember what I last wrote you. without [?] and reading regularly with a desire to remember it, you will be despised in all good company as well as by me.* (Emphasis added)

Mortimer frequently returned to the topic of Jack's reading, as we will see. But Nancy's story of a family's failed "discernment" also becomes thematic. Moffatt's cover is blown. Writing in October of 1786, Mortimer reveals all:

I fear Moffatt between you and I has deceived us all, and not worth a shilling, you know he told you he had half the capital. its wrong, and I wish [they?] all may pay the debt, but say nothing about it. Poor Nancy I fear is unfortunate, tho she did not deserve it. However I will never possess him of any thing of hers.

Mortimer may protect Nancy's property, but he is not equal to supporting her for life if she does not have additional resources from a successful husband, as he increasingly makes clear to Jack. In November 1786, he writes more of Moffatt's deception, which he takes to have been a deception of *him*, the responsible parent, not solely the financially jilted daughter:

> I . . . have nothing to inform you of that can give you pleasure, as Moffatts affairs are as bad as they can be. *I can't in any mind ever forgive him for deceiving me and your poor Sister, who does not yet know the truth of matters.* . . . Shall be glad to hear what success you have in the lottery third class. Its a dangerous way of gaming, but am willing you should try your fortune, and afterward give out all such [dealings?]. *am glad to hear you will not require the master longer, pray don't lose one hour in reading modern History or you will never speak English or any other language.* [We?] are well thank God, and this has been a most healthy [season?] in these parts. . . . An attempt has been made by the rascally part of our assembly to emit paper money, and no fund for it, but they were overruled by a great Majority. (Emphases added)

Early in the following year, Mortimer explains how this deception will affect Nancy legally, and how Jack must prepare to support her by taking care to preserve his "character":

> I recd. your letter. [?] make me happy to see you [paid?] some way to advantage in my life time. *That you might be able to support your poor Sister, for on you she must I doubt depend, in case of my death, for if I put my estate in her right, Moffatt's credtors would seize it at least during her life and leave her destitute.* for both Hayman & he were in prison [bounds?], as all their effects here, by force of the creditors not coming in to a division [?] will not pay the debt by Lb.1000. and besides this Moffatt owes Haman his share of the Capital, [?] which I shall elucidate to you. *But I intend to put it out of his power or the creditors of Moffatt by my will, to insure my daughter if I can.* They must take the benefit of the insolvent and deliver up all they have and then leave prison, but still this does not [exonerate?] them if they here after have effects; . . . a man must have "[Pegasus's?] eyes" to be secure . . . there's no knowing what state partnerships may be in, therefore mentioned to you by [?] if you can find out their state. Tell my friend Mayland I have a particular reason for desiring you to ask him, if he knows any thing about that company I mentioned as he is in the courts. When we come here we will talk about it, then it will be time enough to ascertain those matters. by no means trust any thing to Mr. Barclay for a disagreement in your apprenticeship, might ruin your character. (Emphasis added)

A few months later, Mortimer further explains property law to Jack, with some relief that he did not at the time of the wedding have cash to give, for it would now belong to Moffatt's creditors:

Its a dangerous affair to engage with any unless we were certain of the state of their affairs before hand, it might be ruinous, therefore make all the inquiry [about a business venture] privately as you can, in the meantime, *this is evident from Moffatt's affairs, for had I £1000, at the time he married I might have given it, and it [~~might~~] would be all lost, and they not a shilling the better for it. This affair has almost destroyed my peace of mind, and the family's.* We shall talk over these matters when we [meet?]. I mentioned coffee to you, but <u>say</u> <u>nothing</u> <u>about</u> <u>it,</u> unless there is money there, which you will see when I am credited with the Bill sent. (Emphasis added)

The extent of these effects colors Mortimer's continuing concerns about money, entirely appropriate, given post-Revolution difficulties in procuring cash. On August 15, 1787, he again writes of money, health, and the continuing difficulty presented by Jack's culpable kinsman, Charles Mortimer, who wants to return to medical practice in India, having ruined his own life:

I wrote you by Mr. McAusland, and sent 10 Guineas to Mr. Barclay, and three to you, which I hope yo received. I know not when I may have as much again, having nothing to sell, no income by practice, no debts can I get in, therefore I see many difficulties. [?] the whole family to maintain and support, and Charles in distress by his whimsical manoevers, now very sick, that the whole has almost overcome my Spririts, at times . My constitution is gone, however God's will be done. *Do you continue, I beseech you, to maintain character. Study or read close, get acquainted with [?] business be assured my dear son, you will want those necessary aid in due time. I mean not to dispirit you, but to advise you with fatherly care.* Your mother and Sister are gone to Bullrun to see Mrs. Carter in a low state of health. (Emphasis added)

These letters do not reveal how Nancy's declining years were spent, but parallels between her financial jilting and Mortimer's advice to Jack are clear. Mortimer's burdens match those Jack now appears to face, as the father mentions immediately afterward a typical remonstrance about reading in December 1787:

I hope you read all leisure hours. one of my Sisters who married Mr. George Barclay is greatly distressed, owing to her husband being negligent, drinking man for many years past. those things with the dependence on me from every hand of my family here, even Charles, makes me miserable, for I can't get in more than supports my family, and I can't now go about to practice.

Mortimer trusts his son with money in immediate matters, as a letter of June 26, 1788, makes clear. But persisting examples of potential missteps prevail, here in detailing how Charles Mortimer met ruin, caused Mortimer to repudiate him, and became a negative example for young Jack. The intimate link of family to political virtues is equally apparent, as Mortimer frequently avers in connecting government to personal wickedness. But again, such failures in life are connected with failing to read:

> Having rec.d the enclosed draft, in discharge of a debt due to me by bond, I will place a confidence in you to receive it and keep it for your year[']s expensene, which with the balance of the former bill, is paying you forty-two pound our currency, that you may find any thing necessary for you, . . . and you have but ten months to stay. . . . *I wish you to look back and think only the repeated advice and requests I made to you not to lose two years . . . and to read. then ask your own breast, if you have done so. In English learning I insist upon it is equal to Latin or Greek, as most authors are translated, and [large blank left by copyist] you have neither read History or Geography. . . . Charles Mortimer has split upon the same rock by not taking my timely advice,* when he came over, to set down patiently and give his mind to the point. no he chose rather to dissipate it with gee gaw girls, company, and politicking, then running from one place to another, because he could not be content in any, the consequence a beggar at 30 & a heavy charge to me, but never again will I advance one shiling to him more. You are old enough now to think of thse matters, if, neglectd you'll never get over it . . . after 21 therefore mind your time [left blank by copyist]. Give my respects to Mr. Barclay, tell him our conversation has been vilent in argument on both sides, owning to the designing declamatory Democrats, who have debts, foreign and domestic to pay, a vanity to gratify, which they naver could accomplish in the Govt. [left blank by copyist]
>
> I trust in God we shall have more Justice, when the principles of good governement are taken out of the power of ignorant wicked men. (Emphasis added)

The force of identity between patriarchy and linguistic propriety remains to be exemplified, but Mortimer's directions to make choices better than Charles's "gee gaw girls" draw together his wishes for Jack, the family's last hope of success. On September 13, 1788, after detailing requirements for tea to be sent him, he brings up this matter as another general set of requirements. Jack must select a suitable wife:

> My tender anxiety for your felicity is great & as I am declining fast, I wish to see you fixed in life. *Therefore, I need scarcely tell you there is but one mode that you can succeed by from the situation of matters, that is by marrying a girl of considerable fortune. Youth my dear are . . . unfit to be captivated by handsome faces, as its called, but this is fallacious reasoning, and their ruin which they sorely regret forever. A girl of good character tho not handsome, if she loves the man and has [?] fortune to enable him to live, its in this only that they will find solid satisfaction.* Therefore my dear child [?] this be your constant idea, which will glean you from the rigid authority of old [age?] & keep you from the uncertain drudgery of youth and manhood, for trade is precarious, and can be carried on without capital, which I have not for I

can only live [?] & support my family without debt, and your unfortunate Sister. think Seriously my dear boy of these things, and *never think of [?] incumbering yourself without a considerable fortune if such can be met with.* This is my advice to you as a father and wise friend, C. Mortimer. (Emphasis added)

This was not Mortimer's last word—nor were these his words at all, but an ordinary commodification of the politics of marriage. Nor were they lost to eternity, as an 1850 writer's version of this commonplace shows in its restatement: "marrying a woman for her beauty, is like eating a bird for its singing."[27] Both show well enough that the value of a wife was not always figured as special qualities of character and responsiveness—as in later middle-class assignments of the emotional work of relationships. On March 30, 1789, Mortimer writes to ask how much cash Jack will require for a proposed trip to visit businesses in New York and Boston. He suspects, evidently after close reading, that the trip may also involve an "amour." On that subject he is simultaneously encouraging and cautionary, but direct about Jack's responsibilities:

> As to your visiting the trading towns. which will not be expensive. Before that is attempted other matters must be settled, and I can get you letters here to N. York, Boston &c. but first what will in cash answer those purposes? and whatever you wish to compleat this is our point. I perccive in your letter, you mention in the first instance, leaving that agreeable place, this is the first time you made use of these words in all your letters. be it so. secondly you give me a . . . sentence of agreeable consequence . . . *if it is any thing of the amour kind, this is the very point in which the happiness or misery of your life depends. and that of the family, for if you married [penniless?] . . . for* time able to support a house in my life time, you would ruin all. *If you married I confess it would give me great happiness to see you fixed in life, and I think that may be done here upon a certainty in the marriage line with a little prudence and management to answer all purposes. therefore do not risk speculations for times a real estate is the only certainty for you, as [I can?] maintain my family during life, and you your sister after my decease. Think purposely of these matters. and take care to do nothing risky which can never be remedied.* (Emphasis added)

Jack must not expect a material inheritance, but must situate himself well enough to meet his own needs and perhaps those of his sister. We can imagine Mary Anne Randolph's feelings as she copied these letters some fifty years later. But we cannot accurately imagine them as the same psychologized outrage at placing fortune first that we might expect from a current in-law of this practical man.

Correct Capitalization

As has been evident throughout, male-coded practicality must be learned and exercised precisely in the well-formed characters of the alphabet. Mortimer is clear that the "English language" will suffice for Jack, who is not receiving a classical university education. Repeatedly, he intervenes in Jack's writing processes, at a level of particularity that applies the same evaluative paradigm that mass schooling applied a century later to discursive (and cursive) practices. For instance, in the fall of 1786, Mortimer had explicitly dwelled on Jack's ability to write legibly, linking this skill to inscribing Mortimer's own name as a supporter of a museum:

> I know not what hand you will write for scarce two letters are alike for want of one thing. that is you so disjoint your Syllables and use so many capital letters, with heads & tails so long that it will never look well or connected, of this I have repeatedly complained to you in vain. Large letters should be at [real?] noun substantives, the beginning of lines, or the proper names of things. If you would observe these things, its immaterial which letters [?] the first or the last you mentioned, provided you can [write?] fluently, but your fourishes at top and bottom are abominable. . . . insert my name amongst [his?] subscribing in the next month vis, Doctor Charles Mortimer, Fredericksburg, Virginia or Charles Mortimer, D.D. I request you to <u>practice</u> <u>this</u> . . . they [Jack's letters?] are foolish, and lay down a rule for all these things in your writing for the future, and persevere, for when a person is [illegible?] either in reading or writing, they never profit by anything on earth they undertake, they are like the dog in the manger, grasp at shadows and lose the substances [they have grasped at?]. Of this I have had total assurance in many instances of my life.

As elsewhere, this language of correct capitalization immediately precedes the discourse of another "capitalization," in which perfectly legible handwriting is a graphic mark of transparent character. This way of explaining why it is necessary to be "direct" and "clear," holding core virtues associated with "manly" style since the time of Cicero, connects writing to profit. This attention to handwriting and character verifies the class position suggested by the scanty information available about Mortimer's life—his friendship with George Washington, his island plantation on the Rappahannock, and his many investments and connections.[28] He writes rules that govern a "capitalization" enlarged in the word's every connotation.

Like Ralph and Eleanor Wormeley, Mortimer enmeshes these rules in the propriety of self-representation that he demands of himself and fervently tries to instill in Jack. On April 21, 1788, he again makes his point: "Settle your account, and bring me Copy [of a bill] to this time. Why *will you ruin your hand writing, and make it worse with such foolish flourishes to the head and tails of your letters, and after signing your name. pray leave them off, and write easy*" (emphasis added). The patriarchal connection between these reproofs and the opinion of "mankind" is even clearer in a letter of June 8, 1788:

> I rec.d your letter from Alexandria which you forgot to put your name to. I hope this will meet you safe at Philadelphia, and *that you will this year or never read, then you will either make me happy or miserable,* for tho you may have forgot all Latin, yet English is attainable by constant reading, and I declare you can't speak that by the negligence of the many Sermons I have wrote you upon it, but I never after this say a syllable more on the subject, if you can't at 20 years, think you never will, *or ever gain the esteem of any person unless you apply more than you have, but will be secretly laughed at by all thinking people.* (Emphasis added)

Mortimer's language equates "esteem," "thinking people," and Jack's absorbed vernacular reading and correct writing. Status and universal regard depend on the ability to write well, even where writing appears to be only scribal skill. But Mortimer's idea of education is not so limited as his outrage at foppish script might suggest. As we have seen, he allows that Jack may become just as well educated by reading translations as from the Latin he apparently studied before going to Philadelphia. And he forgives Jack's spelling of "sargeant," saying that as a "military boy" (perhaps a member of a local militia) he probably has a received picture of that word. But again, he unites propriety, good character, and spelling, as is visible in the neglected transition immediately following:

> Try to get intimate with Wm . . . Eddy with you when [he] goes to Philadelphia, he will see you. Be modest in your deportment when you converse with him &c.
> Next time you write the word Surgeon as Chircirgeon, don't make Serjeant as you did in yours to me. I suppose because you are a military boy, you have the word Sergeant in your mind. We are well & wish you health.

Even more important, as Mortimer predictably explains to Jack, was the absolute necessity of good, constant, and remembered reading. To assure his character and thus his happiness, Jack must appear "sensible and fixed with a good character, persevering in virtue. *good morals, and reading* are [?] the only thing, to attain all desirable ends" (emphasis added). After Jack's visit home in 1786, where Mortimer certainly quizzed him, he wrote on June 26:

> It makes me miserable to find you have not read, and that affects my mind in a sensible degree all the time you was here. if you do not read and improve in English, particularly History, you can't be company agreeable to yourself or any other person, therefore unless you rise early this year, and apply close (for I well know you have leisure time enough), I shall not receive you another year, with any de

gree of pleasure or satisfaction, and I shall be negligent in as proportionable degree for your benefit.

He then makes another broken promise: "I shall never say anything more to you about reading. but remember what I last wrote you. without [?] and reading regularly with a desire to *remember* it, you will be despised in all good company as well as by me." On July 6, 1787, Mortimer sounds even harsher criticism on this topic, again linking the syllables of this grammar of patriarchy—writing, reading, language, and access to power—in the class entitlement assured by meeting standards:

> I find you can't, or will not leave off your flourishes in head and tail of your letters & round. . . . *This shall be upon my honor the last time, I will ever advise you. you are of age sufficient to know better. and I declare you will neither know to speak or write, even English in a year or two more unless you read. To which purpose has all I have been paying for French, Latin, Spanish to avail, when you can't speak German? or a word in English? You must think we are very weak not to perceive that you have misspent your time, and why [?:] its because you [have] will not read English.* mark it, think of it &c, it will certainly be your ruin, and destroy your peace of mind when I am no more. trifling boys here in the [state?] speak better than you, who never had a latin, French or other Grammar in hand. Therefore alter your plan before too late. read History, make notes upon it, think and digest them with industry. other wise its useless to suppose you will not be despised privately by all thinking men. I have said enough upon the subject for three years. (Emphasis added)

We are inclined, perhaps, to agree with Mortimer, as Jack must have been, that he had said enough on this subject. But these words remain audible, in tone and message, in later schooling that monitors the privatized families imagined at the time that public education was established. Now, however, such harsh words encourage silence and discourage class identification among students, overturning Mortimer's repeated standard, the opinion of one's equals. These warnings, like Mortimer's broken promises to forgo sermonizing, now only faintly recall a different, active patriarchy. Mortimer says: "Read day and night, that you may not in company appear a mere effigy of ignorance"; "For God's sake read modern history, as you will not write or speak good english otherwise, or write in any genteel style" (October 15, 1787); "Rise very early and read, or you will be ruined by a sluggish Custom" (August 27, 1788). Finally responding to these morsels, the copyist of these requirements records John Mortimer's own note attached to his father's advice of October 15, 1787—a pithy and telling, "accordingly, he did." The sons of such patriarchs, that is, took this advice, absorbing the patriarchal authority now deceptively depersonalized as "standards."

Father Teachers

The early republicanism of Wormeley's and Mortimer's letters swiftly yielded to other social subsystems that accumulated modes of schooling and extra-curricular literate practices. But these later subsystems rely on a different construction of language learning, the domain of "mother teachers." Such shifts suggest that fathers' involvement rapidly faded after biological repro-duction. As I have noted, this is the argument of social historians who ex-plain a feminized domestic sphere as more than a trope. In that view, the dif-fuse "erstwhile caste practices" that circulated commonplace paternity among this relatively elite populace changed rather suddenly. This story of a nine-teenth-century decline of fatherhood suggests that its reproductive discourse effectively wrote the letters of the fathers only until after the Civil War, when wage labor curtailed family status that had entitled planters and profes-sionals to own a social place and bequeath it to their sons. Nonetheless, neither patriarchy nor its reproduction across generations abated in the early nineteenth century, as we may infer from Mortimer's letters having been carefully copied into Mary Randolph's book in the 1850s. Responsible pater-nity has remained a topic and a textual agent that transmits "universal" stan-dards for creating texts and designating superior examples of secular textual-ity, if in increasingly diffuse ways.

Steven M. Stowe suggests that exemplary letters from the antebellum pe-riod uncover how fathers were "knitting intimate experience to family and social well being."[29] They also reveal "slice[s] of a family's biography, a narra-tive reconstructed from family letters to suggest how the rituals of manhood and womanhood were bent by the novelties and role preoccupations, even the silences, that make up the ordinary run of days" (162). Stowe's different-ly theorized examination of letters from parents to children in the 1830s and 1840s confirms the continuation of domestic patriarchal discourse. Fathers wrote that they were "vexed with care, worn with toil," when a son was "not prosecuting his studies with diligence" (179–80). In 1839, Louis Traveau, like Ralph Wormeley and Charles Mortimer, wrote to his son Augustin com-plaining of his inattention to errors: "You [say] you are very sorry that I am scolding you so often for your bad spelling and writing: I am, [I] assure you, double-sorry myself" (152).

But Stowe's inference that "the key word is continuity" (162) does not guarantee that this word unlocks doors that open only onto conflicts in sep-arate family plots. The story these preservations tell is not precisely a master narrative, or a narrative of masters. Its plot highlights neither a psychology of core sensibilities nor even personal biographies that end in death. Either framework, while providing historical data, obscures the recirculations of male identity at the heart of domestic tales, composed against the never achieved universal standards that equate language with conduct. Differences within this discursive subsystem confirm not Stowe's narrative continuity, but how circulating *doxa* rewrites tropes of manhood on a shifting commonplace corpus. An example of this different continuity is Robert Henley's letters to his son Thomas Henley at Bethany College.[30]

Three preserved letters from Robert Henley, a minister, to Thomas take up many of the same topics, and in much the same way, as Charles Mortimer's and Ralph Wormeley's letters of a half century earlier. Henley's language suggests that he might himself have received letters from these early republicans, for he advises his son on preventive health matters in the same tone (if without the same information) that Charles Mortimer used and declares that Thomas's poor grades will cause him the same "mortification" that Wormeley feared. Henley's language performs the familiar music of this sphere of universal standards, in which linguistic standards and behavioral protocols are interlaced:

> You are too careless my son in writing and worse in spelling. I notice in your letters instead of saying I am going you say agoing and I noticed in your last you wrote me you were studying Mathew "Matiuk" and many other mistakes. This looks bad in a Student of College, to be spelling so shockingly, and it is a habit which you should not get into. It becomes a fixed one. You should make an effort to write and Spell more correctly. Try and improve in this matter. I hope you will push your studies. It is my desire that you will not only graduate but graduate with honor to yourself. In order to do this you must improve your time. Your expenses are heavy—you should then be industrious. Be careful about the company you keep especially your roommate—*You must not have a bad boy with you.*

Yet Henley's proofs are obviously from a later time. He is willing, for instance, to compare Thomas's grades to those of his sister Carrie, at the same school, to her advantage. He also significantly brings into play the gaze of school evaluations, a topic not mentioned by others:

> The reports which I have received since your arrival at Bethany are the worst I have yet received. I had hoped after so long a vacation you would return and prosecute your studies with diligence. I am sorry to see such reports; on the last is *written* that you have been rather negligent—and their numbers are quite low. this mortified me very much—

Perhaps in a mood of post-Rousseau educational practices, Henley also details reasons for this mortification in an attempt to persuade rather than compel his son:

—because I see you have but three studies—Latin, Greek, & Philosophy. Now you should certainly get a higher number than 5. I am fully satisfied at your present rate of study you cannot graduate another year which would mortify me *exceedingly*; after 4 years study and *fifteen* Hundred dollars expenditures not to graduate is enough to mortify all your friends. Indeed you should graduate with the *first honor*. Let me urge you for your own sake as well as my own that you apply yourself closely and not trifle away your time. I have to stint myself in order to keep you and Caroline at school and supply your demands and I think you ought to *improve your time* and not be squandering my means which are so difficult to earn. I am sure a moment[']s reflection would convince you that you should be applying yourself and not to be thus idleing your time and taxing me to no purpose. I hope, my son, you will improve and take more studies and be more attentive. You know I have your interest at heart and feel great solicitude about your standing and success. I know in after life you will regret having neglected your studies. and you should remember that you will be dependent upon your own exertions for support and therefore you should prepare yourself for usefulness. Do, I entreat you, let your reports be much improved, and do not defer doing all you can so as not to be pushed too hard in the latter part of the session. (Emphasis added)

But Henley's persuasion uses different proofs. On November 21, 1851, he stressed his concern about the spiritual life of both his children, as a minister might be expected to do. His privileging of salvation over worldly wealth is certainly unique among these parental texts.

And my Son do not forget get your Bible. Unless you are a Christian you cannot be happy in time nor Eternity. Remember your Creator in the days of your youth. I feel much anxiety about you and your Sister on this Subject. I would rather see you both Christians than to see you possessors of all the wealth & honors of this world.

Henley may prefer salvation to wealth, but, like Mortimer, he is a practical man, convinced of pecuniary as well as spiritual virtue. His account of Thomas's future needs is less detailed than Mortimer's explanations, but may be taken as a reminder that he was himself beginning a new family after the death of the children's mother. Thomas will also need to marry and establish a household without his father's help, as he evidently did.[31] But the force of Henley's closing of this letter does not rely on those particulars. As in earlier letters, he threatens Thomas with loss of class status. He suggests that his son take up a trade, evidently as a sincere threat in light of further comparisons of Thomas to Carrie and his vivid reminder about a final evaluation:

I would either study or go to a *trade* of some kind. Your Sister is getting on very well with her studies—her reports are as good as they *can be* and why may yours not be as good. You have mind and health and all that is wanting is, *industry* and *attention* on your part. . . . Your Sister joins me in love to you. Try and improve your time and keep out of bad company and I hope my son you will not forget your Bible. You are old enough now to be a Christian. Remember (as Solomon says) they Creator in the days of thy youth before the evil days come. We have all to die and after this the judgement. The Christian is the happiest man in time and he will be happy in Eternity. The Savior has *died for you* and you should love and serve him.

Wormeley and Mortimer threatened their sons with poverty as forcefully as Henley pictures the pain of damnation, for both fates deprive a failed scholar of a Father's endowments. Additionally, either destiny may be imposed after failures that predict them—failures to read, to study, to spell correctly, and to write a good hand. But Henley and other fathers cast each of these linguistic dies of identity to win their sons' future productivity in society, not a particular kind of consciousness. The identity stakes in reading, spelling, and writing correctly, that is, still precede the hermeneutics of understanding that Frederick Kittler associates with the institution of the mother teacher. As David E. Wellbery explains this temporal shift,

> Hermeneutic understanding is not at all what human beings always do with written or spoken texts, it is not a foundational condition for the processing of significant marks. Rather, it is a contingent phenomenon within the evolution of discursive practices [that] rests on a host of preconditions such as alphabetization, the expansion of book production, the organization of the modern university, the emergence of the civil service; it presupposes specific forms of socialization, . . . a function of instructional practices and technologies.[32]

Before the institution of the self-interpretive realm of consciousness or its twin, technical understanding of secular texts, fathers' letters do not complain of a son's faulty understanding or warn against the very appearances they desire sons to perfect as useful attributes in civic systems.

The case I have been making has, of course, its own politics. These letters from fathers to sons, like other highly codified formal, but personally kept and transmitted gender *doxa,* do not prescribe the later identites that constituted undifferentiated masses within a national society, or mark "a membership card to a particular discursive fellowship."[33] The power of these letters is to convey paradoxically more encompassing and more limited gendered and "universal" identities, which in turn are accessed through slippery commonplaces that remain unstable and treacherous as categories of analysis. Their continuing force relies on the circulation, appropriation, and labor that are the self-fulfilling functions of ordinary writing itself. Letters to sons especially convey and retransmit universalized patriarchy by excluding *positive* references to its supposed opposites—nonmale, homosexual, openly class-marked, and racial identities.

I have attempted to push further valuable insights like Stowe's about the languages deployed to form courtship, dueling, and initiation rituals, specifically by exposing another textual ceremony that bears male children. Learning to spell patriarchy embeds hegemonic traces of elite paternity in persisting power relations, which are later written on the identities of "breadwinners" and domesticated yet male-bonded "dads." Exposing this persistence places the power of gender categories and patriarchal universal standards precisely in the domain of ordinary discourse.

· 7 ·

Coda—Fundamentals of Authorship
Rewriting Commonplace Desires

But at least I was industrious. . . . Neither was fine writing nor flight of
rhetoric wanting, for the spell of Ruskin was upon me. The reading of [my]
paper took nearly two hours. Few subjects in heaven or earth were left un-
touched. Yet I am not deriding these old days of second-hand work. . . .
They gave us the habit of expressing ourselves on paper; *they taught us not
to fear the sound of our own voices.*
                    ANNA B. McMAHOAN, 1873

Political, ideological, and cultural interests must be analyzed in terms of the
available institutions of their formation and deployment; and they must be
analyzed without recourse to the notion of a privileged set of interests.
                    IAN HUNTER, "Aesthetics and Cultural Studies"

By reflecting on authorship, criticism aspires not just to describe a literary
phenomenon; it also wishes to bring to light the conditions that make this
phenomenon possible and thinkable.
                    DAVID SAUNDERS and IAN HUNTER, "Lessons from the 'Literary'"

Bursts of rhetorically prescribed literary imitation fill many pages of this collection, preserving lines like those of a poem in an 1824–1885 commonplace
book kept by Eleanor Calhoun Harper: "Dancing, Flirting, Skimming along
/ Beautiful snow it can do nothing wrong."[1] In such exemplars, ordinary
nineteenth-century writing heroically undertook to further the American
and southern literatures that postrevolutionary publications everywhere insisted should be next on the American agenda. Literate people contributed
mightily to what George Dabney called a "poetry of hope," the unwritten literature that would move America beyond its "promising boyhood" to "wake
to ecstasy" (chapter 2). Those with surplus time wrote tirelessly, especially in
self-sponsored and formal curricula, fiction, essays, skillful letters, and enor-
mous amounts of poetry like Harper's. They wrote on a cusp between the ex-
tralegal "copy right" that gathered and redeployed commonplace materials

and a cultural will to contribute to an emerging self-referential aesthetic action that would endow to posterity a specifically American literary subjectivity. But these writers also took immediately consequential self-assigned positions in a socially constitutive authorship. In "text acts" distinguished from more familiar "speech acts" by the various purposes for which they were created, they registered neither entirely private nor entirely public cultural actions. In legal, personal, and other exigencies, they produced a particular local renovation of an authorship whose fundamentals lay in the commonplace textual traditions begun in Aristotelian rhetoric.

As Roger Chartier points out, the link between literary texts and assigned authorship is but one manifestation of Foucault's "author-function."[2] Textual possessiveness appeared well before publisher's rights were protected in the Enlightenment commodity authorship that Foucault describes. (See chapter 1.) At certain historical moments, including the period of changing positions of agrarian patriarchy in republican and later Virginia, otherwise bluntly imagined "conditions of production" for authorship are nuanced. We find a mode of writing that is neither literary nor fearful about the sound of its own voice.

Three exemplary texts in this productive space perform significant textual actions over assigned but not literary autographs. They demonstrate how circulated commonplace desires reformulate hegemony in crucial social moments. Each example pointedly shifts a patriarchal arrangement in a delicate modification of dominance that has superimposed personal and cultural results. These texts renovate specific relationships to the Father as well as to a particular person, enabling a child's consequential position in discourse as a self-authored, but not aesthetic, event.

The earliest example, an 1824 divorce petition to the Virginia Assembly, pits two sites of patriarchal governance over women against each other. Its rhetorical strategies effect the legal liberation of a wife by successfully deploying patriarchal commonplaces to separate one man, her husband, from the universal/individual identity endowed by Fathers whose textual correspondence to him becomes, in this case, entirely lost letters of *doxa*. The second text, a son's account of a father's death, records that crisis as a shaped "experience" that is represented in the standard gestures of eighteenth- and nineteenth-century elocutionary rhetoric. This account suggests that retained conventions of rhetorical eloquence, not a later and equally conventional discourse of interiorized emotions, make materially productive lost Fathers at least symbolically available to vulnerable children with discursive skills. Its theatrical conventions organize the transfer of entitlements among men. Finally, a published account of the cultural "course" taught to one family by the Civil War punctuates all the texts transcribed in this study by locating them in a period, an epoch now available only as a stylized memory. It displaces into nostalgia the force of the patriarchal universal standards transmitted in fathers' pedagogic letters to sons. This rearticulation of family history in locally published individual authorship successfully renovates the universal/individual, making it a different, powerfully internalized category of understanding, if not of action.

These three documents, written in 1824, 1854, and 1897, historically arrange values that have comprised the subplots of the commonplace since its formation as a margin on which cultural *doxa* regulates social consensus and is regulated by it. Desires once managed *in* rhetorical common topics by deceptively neutral structures of organization (for example, supposedly obvious comparisons and contrasts) are transformed across this history. As characters of renovated subjectivity, they become the conveniently hidden agendas of a modern unconscious, the "syntax" that Lacan describes as "like a language" (chapter 1).

Consequently, these texts tacitly forecast the waning of certain cultural functions of commonplace books. Finally endowing its writer's defeated father with a modern psychological reality, Jennie Stephenson's Civil War memoir especially shows how new American political arrangements would create bourgeois privacy as a differently common place. In that secluded location, emotions now cast as interior realities are imagined to be divorced from official discursive sites, which become the "impersonal" political exteriority of dominant public statements.

The power to categorize and fix identity thereby becomes a discourse that is not always on the fences traced by collective efforts to establish civic order. Assuming American discursive positions is finally a function of well-built differences between private and institutional obligations. Thus this commonplace familial genre contracts precisely when the historical social and economic outcomes it helped to produce are no longer available. On our side of this provisional boundary, making property and propriety as a textual activity becomes simple record keeping and keepsaking, in literal accounts for oneself and family *to* internalized capitalism.

Hence each of these texts comments on current pedagogic and critical conventions that they in fact warrant but that rarely acknowledge them. These texts make available a lost connection between self-sponsored local authorship and a hegemonic system that now reasserts family authority as mere literacy versus literary values, especially in a publicly owned American "composition." Institutionalized ways of measuring and evaluating initiative exercises forcefully symbolize relative judgments on human subjectivities. These mechanisms transmit along the wires of "correctness" the earlier social biases accomplished by constructions of gender and universals. That power of social classification even now energizes trivial lessons about formats that contain traces of this active, self-reproducing textual politics. The domestic unpleasantness, biological inevitability, and management of crises saluted in commonplace books is trivialized in bureaucratic management of courses in a disempowered vernacular.

These exemplary texts also symbolize another of this study's many intersections, now where easily accepted phrases—private versus public, cultural history, and the commonplace—might be renovated in light of a material history. The experiences of a writing subject, sources of such locally authored texts, need not be only subjectively experienced nor made meaningful by technical literary interpretation. As Gayatri Spivak suggests, we can still "make visible the assignment of subject positions," including ways of resisting, deploying, and revamping such assignments, especially those assigned by a universal, evaluative Mankind.[3] This continuing investigation of ordinary discursive moments that become publicly visible actions on behalf of private events and memories uncovers what Judith Butler calls sites of resignification.[4] Recognizing the range of entitlements to mobile identities held by nineteenth-century Virginians and others helps to explain resignification—repetition and difference—as the tenor of everyday life. These texts retheorize the mutuality of universal and local discourses, showing how it constructs consequential social situations. The subjectivities in play in these texts—that of a wife, a son, and a daughter of both a particular patriarch and of the South—demonstrate the political urgency of the cultural work of early writing in changing material circumstances.

Erasing Manhood: Authoring Divorce

A wife's choice between the common poles of happiness and misery of marriage did not depend on her power of positive or negative thinking. Instead, wives had explicit instruction from conduct traditions in how to manage that social positioning by dancing gracefully toward the only good in their irrevocable legal and social state: absolute deference to both husband and the larger social good in which a particular husband and legal union participated. In law and custom, assuming the "character" of a wife has been an absolute. For upper-class women, marriage brought advantages only through its cultural anchoring of their sexual identity in class privileges. Marriage involved, that is, magnanimous entitlements inside a discursively well-established character, if only scanty protection from material, physical, and emotional damage. Wifedom protected females specifically by placing their sexuality and intellect in the service of acquisitive patriarchy, in much the same way as identity in Mankind endowed particular male desires with the authority of God and country.

Thus the identity of wife entailed both service to a patriarchy manifested in legal and genealogical communities and entitlement to privileges designed to gain cooperation with a total system. In that context, the divorce petition of Evelina Gregory Roane (1804–1885) was a rare, successful attempt to turn one wife's service into culturally justified protected freedom.[5] The petition translates the privileges of a wife's identity, bestowed by her submission to matrimony, into their opposite. Evelina received the almost totally unavailable privilege of a legal remedy when this deference did not protect a woman. The petition was one of very few made by early Virginians to the state Assembly, which in the absence of legislation before 1836 was the only body that might grant a divorce. But the Assembly rarely even "accepted" (read) the few petitions that it did receive and granted divorces even less often; more commonly it allowed legal separations and writs preventing contact between spouses.

Whatever Evelina Roane's expectation of success as she wrote, her motives for the attempt were compelling. Her husband Newman beat and verbally abused her. He brought his long-time slave mistress and their child into the legally sanctioned home, forced Evelina to serve them, and favored the mistress's son over hers. Identical offenses were commonly cited in divorce petitions, usually without effect. But Newman had also punished Evelina for joining her family at a cousin's funeral.

The General Assembly responded swiftly and without qualification. It granted Evelina a divorce, the only one given to the three (out of sixteen) accepted petitioners in 1824. It also gave her custody of her child, in one of the two such actions ever taken against "natural" and "constitutional" rights of paternity. (In the other instance, over 100 men protested to the Assembly, reminding them that the *father* is "the Guardian and protector of his own Children.")[6] But the Assembly went further, taking the astounding step of erasing Newman Roane's connubial access to universal Mankind. Its decision, which in the absence of divorce legislation was necessarily realized as state law, specifically forbade Newman from remarrying. It thereby imposed not only a humiliating exclusion from the full divorce granted to Evelina, but an even more devastating denial of Roane's manly prerogatives. This extraordinary act may have contributed to his depression and unexpected death the following year. Evelina married three more times, protecting the substantial property acquired at the death of her second husband through trusts and prenuptial agreements. She died at eighty-one, a wealthy widow, and is buried with her parents at their home.

The question is obvious. How did this petition, albeit drafted with assistance from her lawyer brother-in-law, effect Evelina's rescue, which legal separation and writ might have provided? How did this text additionally result in her sovereignty over her child, control of his property, and an absolute and greater entitlement to social autonomy than granted her ex-husband? It is difficult to overemphasize how unusual these circumstances were, or to make clear how irrelevant to them were family wealth and connections, the favor of local legislators, or even and especially Newman's violence, adultery, and instability. The Roane family had advocated reconciliation because of their long friendship with Evelina's father, and yet certainly had done so despite it. They had equal access to wealth, connections, and influence. Many other abused women and their families shared these privileges in equally painful circumstances. But Evelina's petition prevailed.

Even a summary of this lengthy document shows that its success lay in its rhetorical virtuosity. Its particular strategy was to create conditions in which the fixed subject position assigned to Evelina as a wife *must* receive authorization to shift if she were to remain *within* patriarchal rule. As the petition says in the voice of its fictionalized third-person protagonist, Evelina relies on the rhetorical strategy that she identifies as "*internal evidence* sufficient to guide the judgment of this humane Assembly, she fondly hopes" (37, emphasis added). The petition's strategic arguments, not its facts, by turns persuasively state, complicate, and rearticulate the exclusively male access to universal prerogatives that form and judge "character." It thereby reforms, to her advantage, established lines of inheritance among patriarchal holders of these universal standards. Primarily, this petition represents Evelina as an impeccable wife, happily subservient to and dependent on "the more powerful Sex" (37). Against this perfect fit to that stabilized identity, she, as "one of a Sex too feeble for resistance," must nonetheless hurl her fate at the Assembly (37). Yet the petition also offers these "more powerful" readers the pleasure of gossip about this feeble character. It details Newman's love for and actions on behalf of his slave mistress, appealing to the prurient interest in scandal among men for whom sexual congress with slave women was, as Thomas Buckley says in his analysis of this document, "not out of the ordinary" (35).

But early in his marriage, Newman had also demonstrated—against Evelina's father—a rather abstractly portrayed but significant "stern rebuke of threatening anger" and "strong and violent sentiments of hatred and censure" (42). These very uncommon feelings, which the petition construes as antipatriarchal, are only a taste, but a decisive one, of the juicy violence against females the petition describes:

> He [said that he] would bring the [slave] mother and her children home; and not permit them to suffer any longer & spoke in strong terms of satisfaction of this negroe woman; but your Petitioner then only conceived the tale, as a refined invention to render her still more unhappy; In a few days, however, this negroe woman and two mulatto children were brought upon the plantation; They were received by her husband; . . . He now again acknowleged the children openly, and admitted the eldest to every act of famililar intercourse, of which its age was capable would take it upon his knee, and instruct it to abuse your unhappy supplicant, and place her under the most prohibitive & threatening injunction not to correct it. . . . This negroe woman was placed in an easy situation, made happy and cheerful in idleness. . . . Let it suffice however that her husband adopted this woman as the more eligible companion & wife; . . . [Evelina] was now frequently ordered to take the place of a servile domestic; she was forced by the authority of her husband to bring tubs of water from the spring and sent into the kitchen to cook the dinner & breakfast for his negroes who were at work in the field. (44)

This narrative offers not only such gossip-worthy scandal, but also the illusion of a credible, unified, and coherent story. It serves, that is, as a contribution to family histories whose interpretation would commonly assume that in this anecdote Evelina is a versatile univocal "author," a contributor to a faithful, discursively innocent account of chronological events. But in her report of being violently pummeled when she attended a family funeral, after Newman had denied her all family company and church attendance for months, the character maintained throughout the petition strategically places the constant pressure of a supplicating knee on the well-maintained "powers" of its legislative readers. When Evelina recalls how Newman's violence caused her miscarriage after she returned from the funeral, this self-characterization fulfills its readers' desires to witness climactic violence without being visibly implicated in its subtexts:

> She returned, home in the Evening—unconsious of the severe destiny which had been prepared for her; she was attended by the little girl who nursed her child and an old servant woman of her Father's— . . . observing her Father's woman, he [Newman] furiously rushed upon the feeble old woman, and with an axe gave some dangerous blows over the head—The axe was gotten from him by a young woman [who] attempted to get away—but he stopped her with his dogs, and then knocking her down, he stamped her body exclaiming with every effort, that he would kill her; . . . he then commenced *beating your Petitioner with the Stick from the earth* and making an effort to save the life of her infant gave it into the hands of one of the negroes; She sought the mercy of her husband with affrighted

humility implored him to spare her life, he replied that her fate was irrevocably sealed; . . . *the most horrible scene of violence was now again renewed with furious blows & imprecations, and your unhappy and exhausted Petitioner did not conceive how she could save her life untill prompted by Heavens preserving power,* she sought safety by flight. . . . She reached the house of a poor old widow, whose daughters supported her fainting strength; these poor females seemed alarmed at the thoughts of pursuit and one of them gave notice of her situation to the family of her married Sister. (57, emphasis added)

Lest the Assembly think that this is merely an ordinary and regrettable family beating, a form of violence countenanced in law and custom and not cause for action, the petition provides a summary of these horrors, to buttress its strategic appeal to the paternal responsibilities of patriarchs:

And Truth supports her in the assertion that her husband knew that her peculiar situation subjected her to an injury, as delicate as it is unpardonable, for no repentance can give back to the mother, that which a cruel event has forever expunged from the face of existence—Your hapless supplicant . . . speaks the sensibilities of a mother, not as one discussing the influence of municipal law, in fixing the grade of the crime. (58–59)

It is already clear where the petition places the wedge that would split the assemblymen from precedents in similar cases. An inescapable difference between Newman and proper family maintenance must divorce Evelina from this particular husband's domain and separate Newman Roane from his patriarchal identity. But the text's rhetorical coup is to rearticulate the unanchored position in which Evelina has been placed. She is not only placed in the "power of violence" that Buckley takes as his title, but stranded between one and another patriarchal order. The petition emphasizes the conflict between her father and husband, and extends the implication of that conflict: that the Assembly itself is, with Evelina's family rulers, on the legitimate side of a division between all of this wife's duty and a now illegitimately ruling husband. The petition hereby opens a gap *within* versions of the Mankind to which Evelina is willingly subject. It makes it imperative that the Assembly choose one side or another and that it claim this alignment in its action:

Can this honorable Body be ignorant of what must have been the sufferings of *the Daughter of affluence, and the child of early & constant parental love?* . . . She had descended from the height of affluent ease and comfort, to become the partner of the Son, of her Father's early and constant friend; *she thought she was honoring the noble sensibilties of that Ancient Family union but how sad was her disappointment! She had exchanged the fond endearments of her Fathers family,* and the tender & apprehensive care of her Mother, *for, not even the second place in the affections of a cruel husband!* (44, emphasis added)

The petition repeats this point, making it an undeniable conundrum for its readers, whose cultural homes were organized identically, on the principle of propriety as property. For the Assembly to deny her pleas would be to deny the entitlements of patriarchal society, whose universal standards the petition skillfully separates from the rights of one, quite common, "cruel husband." As the petition explains this breach, "The situation of your Petitioner under these circumstances, *was not that of a wife who could leave her Father and Mother and cling unto her husband,* on the contrary the conduct of that husband had made it a duty of self preservation, that his wife should seek the aid and protection of her relatives & *particularly her Father*" (55, emphasis added). She is asking, in sum, to be sent back to the *valid* patriarchal nurturance to which Newman, who has shunned its legitimate powers, provides no alternative. By mingling sanctified homes and those "outside," but particularly by preventing Evelina from seeing her father and causing her to lose a child as punishment for fulfilling her duty to her father's family at a funeral, Newman Roane has denied the legitimacy, in all senses, of his own class-coded patriarchy. If Evelina remains with him, she will be unprotected—not because she is *within* his power of violence, but because she is *outside* any access to a validated patriarchal identity.

The petition again presses this point in closing, deploying political images that increase the distance between the righteous "state" and the inescapable taint on Evelina's sanctioned wifely identity. The local circumstance of her husband's home cannot sustain patriarchy, for she must compete with the powers of the slave woman and her child. In this position, she must be both self-authored and self-authorized by her "personal" identification with Western, southern patriarchal universals. Only a legislated divorce will allow her to return to the absolute standards of a "General" Assembly. The petition itself concurrently enacts this divorce by detaching Evelina from Newman and his false imitation of patriarchal responsibility in his relationship with the slave woman. She welcomes the shift that he refuses, to licit patriarchal control, so she must abandon him and his parody of legitimate family arrangements. It is thus logically necessary that the Assembly legally relocate her identity by returning it to its place under the commonwealth's proper universal values and authority:

> Your unhappy Petitioner is supplicating the humane consideration, of that Tribunal of her Native State which combines in the important office of its administration, the powers of Legislator and Judge, is very sensible that she brings before them *a cause of high destiny and import to the well being of Social Man;* It is a subject which the early *piety and lofty chivalry of the christian world,* in tender consideration of the *sacred union of the Sexes under the holy ordinances of God,* consigned

to the exclusive Jurisdiction of Religion & Conscience; Then it was not, as it now stands under the free and happy institutions, established by American Genius & valour. (59, emphasis added)

As exponents of that most distant and abstract "Genius & valour," who legitimately stand in for God and conscience in the history of Virginia's white upper-class Social Men, the assemblymen are logically required by this argument to take Evelina under *their* protection and thus divorce her, absolutely, from Newman's. If they do not, she cannot be a Virginian.

Buckley argues that the Assembly's decision can be explained by historical circumstances, not those emphasized in this rhetorical analysis of the petition's self-authoring moves. But he does so in ways that reinforce that rhetorical explanation, deducing that the petition was granted because Newman repudiated "the mores of a society based on white supremacy and black slavery. . . . The most damaging charge against Roane . . . was that he had reversed the proper roles within a culture based on slavery" (35–36). But so had others, without this punishment. The cultural bias in relation to slavery could not be articulated, that is, unless prior entitlements had first called forth the so-called larger or deeper universal values under which racial hierarchies found their logic. It is valid to highlight the historical circumstance of slavery here and to look more carefully than is common for slavery's precise effects on *all* formal and informal patriarchal directives. They could never have been inscribed without ink concocted in African-American blood, the damaged identity that Evelina imposes on Newman's slave mistress and appropriates to write him off. But neither the Assembly's predisposition to keep firm the ground under slavery nor the credibility of the petition's supporting witnesses can entirely account for the petition's outcome. Evelina's document itself, its "internal evidence," manipulates conventional articulations of patriarchal rights. By establishing her as a "character" and placing her fate between father and husband, the petition makes conspicuous a potential conflict between the Assembly and its own patriarchal norms. It persuades its intended readers that honor demands a unique destruction of the claims on patriarchal identity of a man it recreates as the "mere" husband who is only rarely glimpsed in this class and time, a bent twig on the tree of Mankind. It thereby forces a persuasive rearticulation of patriarchy.

This petition is not only one of the few that succeeded, but also a rare example of a public appeal for permission to acknowledge and act on a transformed identity. Evelina's local authorship of renovated cultural prerogatives relies on the virtuosity available in eighteenth-century fictions like Richardson's *Clarissa,* which managed changed identities similarly by creating in readers a protective imperative that overcomes the prurience that stabilized hierarchical privileges. As Joan Scott argues, we can take as a principle that experiential accounts are never transparent, even for readers under orders from a hermeneutics of understanding.[7] Experience, that is, is always already coded in myriad conventions. The stylized cultural productivity of experiential discourse can enact a rhetoric of sincerity that protects its socially constructed deficiencies—gender, youth, potential for a tragic denouement, or changed class positions whose rankings are called into question by the power of judgmental perspectives to undo status.

In this specifically rhetorical view, this petition's persuasive power is not in its choices of "appropriate" slices of life, but in a categorically dispossessed wife's memory. This weapon, the discursive layers of past events that her allusions invoke, takes unassailable political action through discourse, using the signs of risk and release that accompany revealing confessions, thereby protecting them from classification as special pleas for sympathy, or for power. The supposed authenticity of such revelations, like the uncertain accuracy of remembered private moments, "witnesses" in more than the legal sense this document requires. The rhetorical training in evidence here certainly helps shore up the Enlightenment subject's unified rational consciousness by forming an emotional boundary around its conventional thoughtfulness and implied logic. Yet the binary hierarchy that divides legal from emotional principles can also be contextually reversed by depicting circumstances that credit and privilege "hidden" feelings. The petition employs emotion strategically, as a rhetorical proof that fits the class, time and place that will credit it.

Experience as Gesture: "As It Were He W'd Hold Up His Head to Die"

Certainly a specific emotional context is the topic of the second text, Philip Claiborne Gooch's account of his three-day death watch with his father. This record takes as its audience not a public group who must be persuaded to act on his behalf, but propriety itself. It imagines a rhetorically schooled reader who expects family crises to be cast in the discursive strategies readily available for conveying "experience." Commonplaces extend its intimate moments to community feeling by displaying feelings as gestures, the substance of rhetorical elocution, for the ancients the fifth rhetorical domain of "delivery."

Sons most often respond to the lessons of their fathers by rearticulating their universal standards for conduct. Few men portray the impact of a father on their lives unless in a family memoir, and even those scanty records of a father's home educational practices most often position the writer as a mature adult whose stance in Memory is given an imagined universal objectivity. The memoirs of Littleton Tazewell, Blair Bolling, and Samuel Simpson, for instance, all announce as their purpose the preservation of ancestral "character," a propriety bequeathed to them, but not through a father's modern "personality." Simpson, for instance, writes to a relative of his wife in 1885, enclosing paragraphs from his "Memoranda" for her comments, explaining, "I wish to leave something of a pedigree for those who come after me and not leave my children so completely in the dark, as to such things, as I was left, and had to hunt up for myself. I have matter enough for a small vol . . . 700 years of well defined pedigree."[8] Similarly, the benefit to John Fautleroy Mortimer of Charles Mortimer's lessons is visible only in the pithy notes on his father's letters (chapter 6) and perhaps as displaced opinions in his own minutes of the Fredericksburgh Philological Society's meetings. Those brief records in this collection convey theses and adages at the heart of father Mortimer's lessons—for instance, "A moral being is one who gives up personal good for absolute good."[9] Even without such sententious models from a father's teaching, the tone of self-assured connection to the universal also marks John Coles Rutherfoord's summary of his progress at the University of Virginia. Rutherfoord (1825–1866) began a summary of his life on July 10, 1852, obviously intending, like Samuel Simpson, to serve posterity. But Rutherfoord's account maintains what he calls a "European" superiority to institutions and to everyone in them:

> About the time, eight years ago, I left the University of Va. with the highest honors and the highest reputation. I was the only A.M.—and the first, under a [changed?] system which had increased manyfold, the difficulties of obtaining this degree. If I had equals, I had certainly met with no superiors among the students and young men with whom I had been associated during my collegiate career. . . .
>
> I had reason to entertain confidence in my own abilities. I had not only attained the highest academical honors; but I had also received by [?] the highest honors of the Principal debating society. I had [led?] the life of the European student. My irregular habits and frequent visitings of the [?] of the institution had caused me to be more than once be forcibly admonished by someone of the faculty, that they were acquainted with facts which rendered me amenable to the [possibility?] of expulsion. Id had the reputation of being [melancholy?] . . . and dispirited. . . .
>
> I was not unpracticed in composition, and I had cultivated the habit of extemporaneous speaking. I was only in my nineteenth year. I looked forward to my future life with confident anticipation of a high and distinguished career. I was ambitious and my ambition was of a high order, and the ideal which I proposed to myself was [that?] I proposed to [defend?] the function of the town un-

til I had thoroughly qualified myself. I proposed to defer my entrance into family [?] life until I was fully situated at the bar.[10]

Overtly expressing the now risible personality of entitled elitism, Rutherfoord's barely legible autobiography remains only a credential for confident authorship, a character entirely alphabetized but entirely divorced from discourse now construed as "experience."

Philip Gooch (1826?–1855), however, kept in his 1839–1846 commonplace book a very differently crafted chronicle.[11] His detailed diary, faithfully recorded from April 1844 to February 1845, accounts for his time at Airfield (his family home), at Concord Academy, and at the University of Virginia, where he began to study medicine in the autumn after his father's death. Evidently having taken on the project of recording every encounter, Gooch "persevered," as he says, mightily. His diary details each day's schedule, records his many minor illnesses, catalogues letters written and received, accounts for purchases (including a volume of Shakespeare), recalls many drunken evenings at parties and their aftermath, tells what and how much he ate and studied, and preserves encounters with dozens of friends. It portrays school pranks, an evening spent reading Shakespeare, the content and quality of lectures attended at both schools, his successes and failures in oral examinations, and disputes verging on violence toward university faculty who dared to enforce punishments or ask untimely questions about assigned reading.

Gooch took his own and others' reading and writing seriously throughout his brief life. While still at Airfield and Concord Academy, in preparation for medical studies, he offered a pithy review of Irving's "'History of the Far West' 2 vols," which he read in December 1843. Its first sentence is worthy of Dorothy Parker:

> I would not advise any body else to read it, who had anything else to do, or to read. it tells "in glorious talk" the exploits of a band of adventurers, under Capt. Bonneville, USA, but gives none of the valuable scientific information which it says was Capt B's object in the exploit. of course it is written in Washington Irvings smooth, easy, fluent, rich, elegant, edifying style, tho not equal to Astoria, because, for that (Astoria) old story gives Irving a young fortune.

Gooch later edited *The Stethoscope*, a medical journal published for only one year, which contains his equally confident pieces on "The Vapors" and on the anatomical position required to commit legally defined rape.[12]

"Nil Imp": Daily Themes

A month after beginning his private record, Gooch writes, "I have kept a *diary* (a great one it is too) now for a month, & I find it is a very poor business. I am a real old-maid fellow, but not just the fellow for this business. However, they say 'Persevere.'"[13] It is unclear how being an "old-maid fellow" shaped Gooch's belief that diaries are not for him, for he also assigned this label to a visiting Judge Irving from Wisconsin, whom he calls a "minor philosopher." But such quick assessments repeatedly place the events and people he notes in available object positions, under the gaze of what Gooch accepts as well-established judgments. Much like the young James Boswell, although certainly more telegraphically, Gooch compulsively notes such categorical responses to others. After his father's death and his matriculation at the university, his observations become absorbed with what "they say," in annotations that use "them" to stand in for the paternal authority of universal standards that he has lost. His diary rigorously notes reactions by family and by many adults and his peers at school.

But this journal primarily records self-monitoring assessments of how well he is doing as a student, a scholar, a friend, and a budding political activist. Voices heard only momentarily in his shorthand persistently tell not only what happens, but how it might be evaluated. Gooch's diary thereby demonstrates one way in which an imagined "common" perspective, a constructed *doxa*, might preserve a partially formed man when death severs his biological link to the fathers before him. If Evelina Roane was "placed in the power of violence" by patriarchal society, Gooch might be said to be desperately seeking his own relative place and that of others in father texts.

The opening account of the senior Gooch's death (discussed later) is immediately followed by letters to and from his family. Gooch receives despondent letters from his mother and twenty-three-year-old brother at Amherst and takes this older brother's direction to postpone leaving for Charlottesville until his return: "I must not go till he does &c &c. That he had made a speech at the raising of a Hickory pole" (185). But interactions with faculty members and school fellows provide most of the substance of his records. Typical entries show the intense energy he focused on and took from each day's events:

Nov '44 University

Friday 29th   Attended lecs but not questds Rec'd a letter from Ma—no news—Brother in Essex. All college alive & in fear or excitement about the action of the faculty on Daniells' supper last Sat night. Rumors & reports [rife?]—the members of the Law class met & Aylett Daniell & [name?] (com[mittee]) drafted a remonstrance to the faculty to mitigate or suspend their punishment of Coles who was caught tight a few nights since. Dissected, loafed & studied very well—.

University of Va Decr. '44

12th   Got up as usual at 9 o'c went to lecs. Corked [reprimanded]. Dr H on pathology—nil imp [nothing important]. Went to sleep soon got up after 12 o'c & got my Physiology & [Therapeutic?] & wrote to Waller Brock

13th   Nil imp—walked to town saw Dr Ned [?] at Vowles; at a dinner party drinking wine Mr Binford asked me to drink eggnogg had to refuse. [Gooch had taken a pledge of total abstinence.]

14th   Went to lecs & all hands got touched up by Dr Cabell for not being better prepared generally &c. After dinner went with Leitch to Colo[nel] Randolphs—(or rather Leitch & Galt went ahead & I arrived on uncle F's horse very soon afterwards. Found all very well—agreeable—not disappointed at all. Miss Adam's there & a very fine girl too. Colo[nel] not very agreeable until after supper.

Obviously, this glossary on his days emphatically judges them. "Nil imp" suggests its own deconstructive operation on so faithful an accounting for his time. All is either redemptively "improved" ("loafed & studied very well") or is not ("all hands got touched up"). In the continuation of this entry, Gooch describes seeing the plans made for the university by his hero, Thomas Jefferson. He is awed by Jefferson's epistolary prowess:

They went off & [got?] the original plans, draughts &c of this University made by Mr Jefferson with his pen & pencil which [the plans] were exactly as it now is. Also his Letter Memoranda—a book of large size containing a record of all letters rec'd that Mr J must have devoted 8 hours per diem to his correspondence. What an economist of time!!! Also a cane with gold head & gold [?] of unicorns [horns?] sent to Mr J by an incognitus—& it was left by him to Mr Madison who, of course, returned it to Colo[nel] R[andolph?] on his death. Spent a very agreeable night & got up on Sunday 15th & sat till [?] & we 3 returned—calling at the factory to see Miss Adams & Miss R, who had gone down to teach the children—no one went to church. Dined with R [O W ?] after dinner went to chapel to hear the ladies & O corked at bible lesson. Loafed extensively (till 1 o'c [or?] [S̶k̶i̶n̶n̶e̶r̶?]) & went to bed [?] & got up at 8 o'c. (134–36)

These few samples from 200 similar pages give a sense of Gooch's participatory verve, not only as a student of the college, but as a determined self-amanuensis. He obviously sees this process as a way to acquire two benefits: digging the ore of events to accumulate a character, and providing himself with the "material" that commonplace books apply to future needs. For instance, as directions for keeping commonplace books regularly recommended, he faithfully indexes his account of "Stealing a Subject"—a midnight graveyard raid to exhume a body for dissection that is reminiscent of both Dickens's *Tale of Two Cities* and a contemporary horror film. Gooch notes this reference in another typical self-assessing entry: "Friday 20th [December 1844] Got up about 1/4 past 7 & studied like a horse—fully prepared but was questioned in neither lecture. Unfortunate!!! Wrote a long letter to brother. . . . [Many?] fellows got leave of absence & are cutting out for Xmas. I found out that the subject I stole (see index "Stealing a Subject") was a murderer—broke jail in Rockingham—name "Watsh"—Harri . . ."

The prescribed index details this November adventure in much the same telegraphic form, noting the cooperation of a local coroner who is terrified of discovery. But momentarily, in one of the few well-formed sentences in the entire journal, this arcane tale connects a purloined cadaver to Gooch's unstated responses to his father's recent death:

> At 1/2 past 11 we hitch up & go around 7 round till we come to a hill & a branch where McK & Lewis stay with the cart, whilst G & I go to Uncles F's [?] they are waiting with hammer & nail claws. Dr. H & [?] start off immediately & get to the house send Garnett to bring the fellows up & bring the cart closer. Dr. & I go to work & draw nails till G & Lewis come in after hard work & hearing the squeaking of nails & other necessary noise we get off the lid. *Then all those reflections crossed our inexperienced minds.* We took him out & cut sticks for the cart. I take 1 leg, Dr. the other ther other 2 the arms—he was very heavy (170 lbs, I guess) but we [?] slapped him in the cart & Dr. G & I go back to replace lid & c. We all take a big rock & place them in well fix on the lid well take our tools sticks &c lock the door & cut sticks brought him along up and got to Diss. Room (Dr. H went home after putting him in cart) laid him on table as clock struck 1. Came to my room to wash. Some of my neighbors not yet asleep came in and laughed at us. (191–92, emphasis added)

Gooch clearly wants a private minute of his life, but the reader for this particular story, as for other daily entries and the very differently composed account of his father's death, is not solely an idealized self. As his identification with Jefferson as a writer suggests, Gooch trusts "posterity" to want to know what *he* has done. Fulfilling that request, he creates a dramatic rendition of his father's "passing."

"With Trembling Hands"

This narrative begins by depicting April 17, 1844, the day young Gooch is called for at Concord Academy to come home because of his father's fatal illness. From that moment of being hailed into manhood, Gooch's father's death is *his* story, a framed realization of narrative strategies that unfold conventionally in a classical five-part structure of setting, point of entrance, crisis, climax, and denouement. In the past tense, not the historical present of later journal entries, precise temporal demarcations create the fiction that

Gooch does not yet know the immediate future but makes prescient guesses about it. All of these strategies construct an active memorial not to Gooch's father, but to discourse itself—to an *awareness* of a father's death. Gooch's notification, Gooch's special knowledge from doctors, Gooch's constant vigil and refusal to call his mother from sleep, Gooch's identifications with his father's view of religion, and Gooch's final critique of hypocritical (and absent) mourners are, in his term, the *scene* of this occasion.

This authorship remains on a border between psychological disclosure and commonplace conventions. It is not entirely a functional record of events, as diaries in this genre usually are, but "an experience," a telling that relies on lessons from formal rhetoric to articulate crucial events. Even its poignant "he w'd hold up his head to die," which Gooch tellingly prefaces with "As it were," is a common stage direction, a two-dimensional realization of the fitting gesture and language for "the death moment" of a heroic father.

This is not to say, of course, that Gooch's father did *not* hold up his head at this moment. He too knew the discourse of illness and death, or at least we assume he did, considering his literate class position. It is, however, to wonder what a daughter might have written, or a wife—what discourse might have managed this event as memorable "experience" in a different emotional inheritance. Here, a vulnerable younger son deploys conventions that portray feelings to enclose an especially painful event, a death watch (itself a conventional phrase). These easily misrecognized rhetorical conventions and theatrical gestures, "expressions of grief," later become evidence of a self-reflexive and decidedly classed psychology in analogous texts. But Gooch knowingly places in discourse an event and its coded memory, which benefit precisely from textuality, not from that psychology. His account takes from elocution rather than consciousness the universal connections and propriety that dignify the father and cheer the son. He writes as a descendant who is suddenly responsible, not economically, but for a renegotiable family property.

· 8 ·

(Facing page) Page from the 1844 commonplace book of Philip Claiborne Gooch (1826?–1855), describing how he and his classmates at the University of Virginia obtained a cadaver for dissection in their medical studies. The page is headed "Stealing a Subject." MssIG5906a242. Reprinted by permission of the Virginia Historical Society.

From its outset, Gooch's narrative relies on familiar tropes, conventional topoi of being "called home," of marshaling hope, of last conversations and last wishes, of fatal visages, and of confused "arrangements." It begins, for instance, with the most commonplace "memory" of death, the premonition:

> On Thursday—17th of April 1844—a wet drizzley day. Mr Coleman took the boys in wagons, sulkeys , buggies, on horses &c and we all started for the Hunter dinner. Mr. Hunter, Morrell & Garnett having staid here the night before. I rode a colt & as I passed a sign-post at the Bull'ch which said—"To Richmond 50 ms"—I made the remark, "I wonder if c'dnot get home to-night" Not once dreaming of such a thing nor thinking about it again. (150)

Gooch at this moment hears a voice, a messenger of the fate that installs this account in self-consciously authored funereal language:

> I was talking when I heard Ben's voice *(the academy negro)* calling "Where is Mr Gooch," I immediately hailed him, & he placed in my hand a mail package which had endorsed on it, in Mr. W. A. Davis' hand writing, "The P.M. at Guinea's will please forward this to Concord by express mail, as Mr. Gooch's father is ill, & he is desired to come home." *With trembling hands* I opened the package, & *was thunder struck* when I percieved letters with black seals. After looking off for a few moments, *to prepare myself for the worst trial, I coolly looked over the package*, and found letters for Mr. Coleman & Pefram with black seals, and a small note without seal to myself. This I opened & read, from Mrs. Daniel *the painful information* that Pa was very sick & Ma desired me to come home immediately—this was dated the evening before, written with lead pencil. . . . I took Mr. Cs' letter to him & told him to read & *tell me without reserve*, its contents. . . . He gave me money & told me go any way I chose to R R, so I got the horse I rode & took Ben & went at full speed to Chesterfield depot—where I arrived in time & jumped aboard. Capt. Ben Danacott told me he had only heard that morning & he hoped he was not so sick &c. (151, emphasis added)

The trembling hands, painful information, and directions to speak "without reserve" all frame this event in a style that formally educated writers would later articulate more "personally." But Gooch honors these moments by constituting them in community discourse that endows them with all the powerful rhetorical force he can bring to bear (on) this painful and evidently sudden abandonment by his parent. These conventions in turn evoke in Gooch the memorializing local authorship that controls such melodrama.

Following these situated opening guidelines for its composition, the account is immediately embedded in the good wishes of others. His father, that is, becomes the object of the gaze of Gooch, his doctors, and of relatives and other well-wishers, all of whom are characters in Gooch's script. Even the dying father, the prominent patriarch of Goochland County who is never named, contributes to this tragedy of manners by voicing pleasure in Gooch's celebrity at school:

> My [?] Elliot Braxton met me at the depot & told me that Mrs. Rawlings & his father had just gone out in the carriage—that Dr. Braxton was at the Powhattan house, & I c'd hear from Dr. Clarke or him about Pa's case, while waiting for the horse. I saw the Dr. (B) and he told me not to wait but get his horse & go out. This kind offer I accepted, and got home early in the evening. I found my poor father quite sick, as I thought, but was relieved to see him not sicker. He seemed very much pleased to see me, & asked me if I was studying well at school. To which it gave me extreme pleasure to say "Yes." He was disposed to talk much to me—but the Drs. forbid it & I did not encourage it. I was with him till 9 or 10 o'clock when I had to go to bed, knowing I was so tired I c'd be of no service that night. Next morning I got up to breakfast—after a thorough rest & found Pa about the same. (152)

The expected visit from a doctor, not only a reality but a device that locates the narration in exterior opinion, is told with predictable stage directions. Their literary familiarity warrants his inference that if the doctors cannot tell that Gooch's father has *not* been bled, a death sentence is inevitable. That sentence is here a notable "plain index" that the doctor wordlessly pronounces:

> I sat with him most of the day & all that night, & sent for Dr. [Kennon?]—who came very soon. He went with me into the chamber & in his usual jocose way, re-marked as he entered the door—"Well Col. Why I am sorry to see you here cocked up on pillows"—his voice fell before the last words were out of his mouth. He went to the bed-side, spoke to him and looked at him, & returning to me asked when he was bled. I told him—not at all. *His countenance darkened immediately, and as a plain index told me—"he must die"—from that moment I was alarmed,* & found from Dr. Kennon's disturbed and restless looks & actions that there was but little hopes—& from Dr. Clarkes walking to & fro in the yard in the rain. I knew that a crisis was near. Then it was that I had more intense suffer-ing than even afterwords in the greatest grief. (152–53, emphasis added)

Again, this is decidedly the young Gooch's experience. We learn nothing of the nature of his father's illness, of his feelings, or of his opinions about his own health. In the son's understandably hopeful view, his father briefly im-proves. Despite this rally, he sinks again, into Gooch's language:

> Finding I w'd not go [to bed] he wanted to talk much asked for mama (who had been sleeping ever since evening, & I prevented her from being awaked, as she had taken no rest for a long time—& I feared the consequences)—I told him, & he seemed very glad to hear it. During the night he expressed a great desire to be

moved upstairs, where he "w'd not be in the way"—he told me to go & tell Mama to have it done, but I pursuaded him out of the notion & he was very quiet and seemingly easy. I thought he was very much better & was off too good cheer. (153–54)

The doctor visits again, finds Gooch's father smoking, and remarks that "he was the best friend & best neighbor but most unruly patient he had ever had" (154). But here again, this comment is translated into Gooch's acute consciousness: "I thought the Dr's spirits must have been improving—to joke so" (154). Gooch's father, however, has been playing his part. "He had during the two days before spoke to me much about the crops—plantation &c" (155). On a Sunday morning, he dies, in a "scene" Gooch calls "magnificent":

> Soon after he got in bed Mama went out into the garden for a few minutes, during which time Dr. Kennon & I were in the chamber, & I observed his weak look and called Dr. K's attention to it. He went to the bed-side & looked misery itself. I knew—tho' I did not want to know its meaning. I saw Mama coming & told Dr. K. he went to the door to stop her, but she coolly told him she would come—and she did. Meanwhile, according to the Dr.'s directions I sent for [?] Haxalls & Wallace who had rode down the plantation—they got there at the close of the scene—the most awful & distressing of all I had ever felt or seen—tho' a magnificent one.
>
> Dr. Kennon told me he was dying. I would not believe it, but got on the bed by his side and saw the perspiration rose from the pores of his skin. He was motionless, but when Mama held a spoon with nutriments and asked him to take it he opened his mouth and swallowed several spoon-fulls, but stoped & looked around and straightened his head, which was a little turned. He looked like anything but a dying man. His countenance was mild, serene, and most beautiful—clear and most intelligent; indeed more so than I had seen him for a long time. He looked perfectly happy & soon was. (155–56)

Taking its own next breath, the narrative immediately transforms father into a source of sententia. He utters precisely the wise saying a son would need at such a moment. In addition, Gooch's father now "proves" a wisdom that makes him superior to organized forms of religion, thereby becoming a hero who has died as a universalized Man, "as it were," pragmatically and symbolically holding up his head:

> Then he proved that his words were not idle when he said, He was tired of this world and was always ready to die—which he frequently said for years past. He proved to fanatics, that the *forms* & doctrines of their churches &c &c &c were vanities & follies of the world. He died without a struggle or motion, save raising his head as it w'd fall over on oneside. *As it were He w'd hold up his head to die.* (156, emphasis added)

In this moment of transference, the instant in which Gooch's increasing physical management of his father becomes conventional dramatic gesture, Father's position in universal Manhood is endowed to Gooch.

In the "scene" that follows, Gooch becomes a "man of the family," with sufficient "energies and courage" to support his mother, to appreciate a lady who is "perfection itself," and to cope with confused arrangements and desultory attendance at the funeral services. He takes on his father's gentility in this moment, entering the gestured code of chivalry that makes death a discourse.

> Of course a *scene* followed. I knew that all my energies and courage were in demand and they were sufficient to bear me out. My poor mother was for some days cheerless, comfortless & almost given out. Barton Haxall put things (papers &c) right in the house. Miss Elizabeth Daniel was perfection itself & Miss Lucy Ball showed what she was made of. The next morning came and the funeral had been [?] for 4 o'clock—tho' there was some informality & it was not made known where he w'd be interred—badly managed. Mr. Woodbridge performed the service and I was the only blood relation who followed his body. Never having counted any body's favor or care—none of the Richmond hypocrites—nor rascal grandees who when in life were so courteous to him came to see the body interred. It was done in the Poor house burying ground on 22 day of April about 6 1/2 o'clock PM about 30 hours after like—silently and quietly, but those who stood around used no hypocracy but really. (157)

The next two pages of this volume are missing, so there is no evidence of Gooch's or his family's further response, except perhaps in their reluctance to address more of it to posterity. The diary next notes that Gooch wrote to his mother in July: "wrote to Ma—a foolish feeling letter" (164). But the set piece authoring such foolishness remains frozen in conventions, not in the feelings that in this case could have been equally conventional. The drama of this father's death portrays emotion as readily available and expected responses, supposed universals that inscribe a manhood that deserts Gooch in human form. But that manly position returns to him, as the ability to write this classically unified narrative. As in letters figuring "bravery" during the Civil War (chapter 5), this crisis portrays an abruptly static gendering of its protagonists, who assume fixed identities inherited from comforting commonplaces. This universal subject position is more like John Mortimer's note, "A moral being is one who gives up personal good for absolute good" than like its later, interiorized alternatives.

This is to suggest that Gooch, like Mortimer and his friends at the Philological Society, had not imbibed literary or psychologized "consciousness." He would note an evening reading *The Comedy of Errors* at the University of Virginia, but not mention sentimental fiction. Men in his account do portray codified emotion, but never intimate interactions; their scenes and cant phrases do not express emotion as a psychological state. Those states were perceived by many fathers precisely *as* fictions, as dangerous-to-morality holdovers from the irrational oratorical "eloquence" that Hume's many revisions of his "Art of Eloquence" between 1742 and 1770 had increasingly demeaned.[14] As in the works of Locke and others before him, Hume's treatise evolves not only a discourse of "science" but, more important, a new rhetoric of political calm that emphasized social and discursive politeness, increasingly separated reason from emotion, and relegated to literary and dramatic writing the gestures that the young Gooch requires in this crisis.

Gooch appropriates this supposedly excessive emotional narration that differs from rational persuasion by drawing on oratorical gestures that Enlightenment and nineteenth-century rhetoric openly ridiculed—the signals and physically realized expressions taken for granted since Quintilian noted "the gestures which accompany strong feeling, *and sometimes even serve to stimulate the mind*: the waving of the hand, the contraction of the brow, the occasional striking of forehead or side."[15] His account relies on ritualized emotions stimulated by physical and vocal gestures, not on identification or connected consciousness.

These melodramatic conventions consequently enable Gooch's writing to place him in a now recognizable identity, yet without entirely placing him in the modern space of psychological desires—what Nancy Armstrong analyzes as a normalized tendency toward "*self*-realization."[16] That discursive position, the internal autonomy that many mistakenly impose on Victorian women as their only possible source of agency against social forces is visible here only as Gooch's scribal labor, his bravery in crafting this narrative. But he does not abandon rhetorical precedents for this emotional agency, despite the vulnerability made obvious in these records. The privatized world of sensitive, unique females and males does not yet construct this commonplace grief, which here emphasizes the acceptance of adult male identity as the ritualized implication of his loss. He continues the Lockean labor that produces negotiable moral propriety at the temporal edge of a different discourse of "experience."

Nonetheless, Gooch's narrative, even in its theatrical conventions, inscribes a "sense of self" absent from Evelina Roane's differently addressed petition. Gooch's purpose, to organize his most important crisis, is fulfilled by activating manhood through elocutionary conventions whose resonance we too easily flatten in our inherited cooperation with Hume and his circle's rejection of eloquence. This rhetorical tradition persuades Gooch, at least, that he has survived a moment of disaster, taking from it an entitlement to universalize his grief and adolescent uncertainty over his father's dead body of wishes for him. He inscribes a self in terms of the education of the Fathers by occupying a "character" worthy of the endurance of educational conventions. But in the final analysis, Father moves inside the subject position of traditionally exteriorized heroism.

Stunned, Subdued Softness: Moving "My Father's Household"

Jennie Stephenson's simultaneously local and universal griefs complete this relocation, placing her father and others in a discourse of consciousness. That new discursive space offers her, with other later nineteenth-century writers, relief from an unacceptable postwar collective identity. Males acquire a new position made possible by a freshly invented Memory of a world only rumored to have existed.[17] In this relocation, as Philip Gooch's flirtation with a rhetoric of psychological realism suggests, the cultural productivity of the commonplace book tradition was finally absorbed into a largely silent, privatized, and individualized bourgeois discourse of privacy and isolation. Valuing originality above skillful management of a textuality that no longer produces viable postwar manhood, local authors like Stephenson resignify a tension between the literate productivity of their lost privileges and a critical understanding of cultural, economic, political, and social biases. They thereby produce a closing moment of difference within entitlements, a new common place to write disabled identity.

LeeAnn Whites argues that postwar patriarchs identified with their dependents, at least insofar as they were persuaded to become enclosed by domestic security and to acknowledge the superiority of men who had defeated them.[18] But this interpretation of martial defeat begs the question of how a shift in entitlement became an evident option for men who enacted it or for those who wrote their stories. The exemplary memoir examined here describes a "stunned, soft, subdued" patriarchy that helped construct the new position in memory that compensated for actual depletion of patriarchal power and responsibility. In place of *standing*, Stephenson's memoir suggests, patriarchs acquired feminized but unexpressed emotions. The exemplary defeat of this father becomes legible along the lines of a similar shift in many discourses of identity. This general substitution of subdued emotion for entitled action, visible in many later nineteenth-century personal writing assignments in schools, as it is in Stephenson's self-consciousness about authorship, privileges largely ineffectual privatized feeling over socialized personal authority.

Jennie M. Stephenson (1851–1916) wrote "My Father's Household Before,

During, and After the War" in 1897, to raise money for the United Daughters of the Confederacy's Shenendoah Chapter 32.[19] Members were asked "to write a reminiscence of the War Between the States." This request took other forms across the state. Beverly Dandridge Tucker, for instance, wrote poems for the unveiling of the monument to the Confederate dead in Gloucester County.[20]

Stephenson's forty-five typed pages were published serially in 1960 in the *Petersburg Progressive Index,* which commented, "We know of nothing of the kind to compare with [these memoirs] since the 'Moratock' papers of Thomas Pleasants Atkinson which *The Daily Index* published in 1866." But Jane Minge Friend Stephenson would have attributed this praise to her topic, not to her design. Nor would she have taken publication under her name to be an entitlement of the indisputable social status of her family. She was one of nine children of an extended family that included her mother's sixty-two first cousins and relations of her father, Charles Friend, who was descended from the Bolling family. His ancestors included the grandson of Pocahontas (see chapter 3) and Ann Friend, who faithfully listed her gentlemen escorts at the Union Theological Seminary in Richmond (discussed in chapter 5). The idea of authorship was, Stephenson says, appalling.

The memoir begins with this awkward, self-effacing explanation: "[Fulfilling the request to write] sounds appalling to some of us, who are more used to wielding the broom than the pen, but when one finds that the word reminiscence means a recalling to mind the things of the long ago, and yet so vivid, and so a part of us did the events of these stirring times become, that the effort once undertaken to rehearse them, will not prove so arduous" (1). This initial position as a broom-wielder is a temporary pose, not a consistently domestic persona or an absolute, lasting rejection of the inscribing phallus. Stephenson assumes many stances in this account of a cultural shift that foreclosed some identities and opened others to her, the people of the South, and especially her emblematic father. This cultural shift is accommodated here in a framed memory, a remnant of the "entire universe [that] is a social system," contained in one man, in one site in south-central Virginia.

The first section, "The Home," portrays White Hill, her father's plantation, to situate her recollection. It is in turn a locus of southern patriarchy, headquarters for Grant's troops during the siege of Petersburg, and finally an unrecognizable pile, to be rebuilt as a foundation under daily reminders of the humiliation and depletion that was the result, here and elsewhere, of this war. White Hill has been the scene of other local and universal changes of hegemony. On April 25, 1781, British and German troops had rested on its lawn; during World War I, it would be an army training camp. Stephenson's memoir projects any rearticulation of this order into the acts of one pair of its representatives, her father and General Grant. Her vision of the house after returning from ten months in North Carolina joins the two men in a physical space invested with two identical spirits at war:

> What of the old home that had been lost to us . . . as if it had dropped out of existence, as verily it had! . . . [N]o wonder *my Father was a changed man*, for this *the home of his birth and manhood*, had been a pride and a delight. . . . About mid-way in these works [federal earthworks on the front lawn] *is a tree, against which Grant is said to have leaned,* and looking over the thinly manned Confederate lines, wept, that they had baffled him so long. (40, emphasis added)

In these overlapping worlds, midway between the Revolution and modern international conflicts, one universe changed as the other wept in frustrated anticipation. The White Hill tree is a stable pole around which patriarchies take turns.

"The Home" and all the following sections make a trope of Stephenson's memory, deeply implicating it in revolving patriarchal structures that are realized as paternity. Initially focusing on a difference between youth and age, the memoir thematizes that difference as change throughout its incidents. It follows Stephenson's development from age eight to thirteen during the war years, always managing to make the double vision of youthful and mature "eyes" a lens viewing patriarchies in combat:

> Some of us were young in 1860, when the exciting discussions of secession were heard wherever men met, but "little pitchers have big ears," and my Father, the subject of this paper, was too much in earnest in upholding the Union for his little girl, then eight years old, to be impressed with the fact that some mighty question filled the air. And I confess here, hero though my Father then was, and still is, in my eyes, as you will see if you follow the reading of this sketch, I often felt the opponent had the best of the argument; though States Rights was a vaguer subject in my mind than it is now. (1)

The delicacy with which Stephenson attempts to superimpose her youthful views on her later opinion that her father's Union sympathies were misguided is achieved in this account's ever ready childishness. Here, that franchise is self-portrayal as a "little pitcher," only eight, watching "men" discuss mighty questions. "Some of us were young" reinforces her credibility as an aging veteran observer and permits this observer to resist judgments in the commonplace politics that swirls around each of this account's events.

This permission to dissent is necessary for many reasons. It upholds this text's attempt to persuade readers to support the United Daughters of the Confederacy, but it simultaneously allows Stephenson to be heard in a postwar "national" context, among "modern women." She claims membership in that newly established controlling space, a mobile position that has been vacated by a father's unfortunately lost patriarchal powers, in an anachronistic early note on travel to Mt. Vernon in 1896 and to Massachusetts just before this writing:

> When I was in Cambridge, Mass. last September, we took a room with a Mrs. N——. I learned she owned and greatly prized a pair of sisscors her brother had used in cutting the blood stain made by the first man shot on the Pawnee [a federal gunboat on the James River], from a piece of canvas. *I kept quiet.* She did not know that boat had caused the beginning of our family flight from the dear old home, that lasted five years. *I was in Boston to see the sights, not to convince them that Southerners were not traitors.* I think our gentle bearing rather confounded her, as *she thought provincial savagery was the only type outside of "the hub", for there she had been born, and never cared to know or see beyond it.* (18, emphasis added)

In contrast, Stephenson's flexible ethos is as varied as that of the postwar South that she writes to provide for, as one of its broom-wielding daughters who can also manage public discourse. That mobile character is the fulcrum on which she writes, to install a memory of the South in the new patriarchy of a nationalized dominant hegemony. It will paradoxically also gain credibility through its constructions of her and those like her, precisely as a memory of its Other.

This purpose, to shift from one to another credible "universal" order, takes as its best rhetorical strategy a persuasive emphasis on family unity and childhood associations. But it also, again with rhetorical acumen, resists precisely those blood relations. Like Lincoln's *Gettysburg Address* and *Second Inaugural*, its sources of tropological persuasion are organic, biological figures of unity. Stephenson's memoir seeks out their obvious force, heading sections after "The Home" with "The Social View of Life," "Kinships," "The Management of the Children," "The Cook," "My Father and the Children," "Plans for Education," "Father Joins the Army," "Left Home," "Scarcity," "Refugeeing," "Family Cares," "Again We Leave Home," and even "Hidden Treasures," a story similar to Lucy Butler's comedy of hiding family jewelry and plate (chapter 5). Each section differently narrates happiness, security, mutuality, and especially unity in blood ties, in images that represent the urgency of raising monuments, like this text, to what is lost:

> Ah friends, daughters, wives let us make sacrifices to raise monuments worthy of our loved and our dead. Let us be willing to tell the story of all they endured. Let us tenderly care for the Veteran as he sinks down in poverty, because of the loss during these four years that swept from him the prosperous beginning that others have . . . or possibly the exposure, privations and hardships of those four years. (25)

The fatherly propriety of a Ralph Wormeley or a Charles Mortimer is idealized here, but nonetheless articulated practically, as a lost material property that must now be maintained as the collective decorum among "friends, daughters, [and] wives." They will continue entitlements to maintain, if now not to "improve," their families, in material and discursive contributions. This universal system must be rewritten.

But to accomplish that preservative rearticulation of material resources *as* a new imaginary relationship to them, the economy of patriarchy must also now take into its accounts not only feminized domestic bliss, but the subject positions of a specific female writer and the defeated men whose entitlements her writing would preserve. Their familial language must be written for the now invisible patriarchs. But it will not preserve the South if it is inscribed only as the new course in general biology that Lincoln used to "reestablish" the actually novel organic Union. Before the Civil War, that national entity had few discursive privileges in any of its states.

Consequently, this reminiscence and Stephenson's authorship are also distinct from the "separate spheres" and "family values" that were at the time encoding her triumphant nationalist opposites. This text manages a different system of relationships and exchanges within them, in two specific ways. It first implies that its writer's literary sensibility owes much to direct observations of slavery, a vision that categorically excludes itself from the new national family. Additionally, it endows Stephenson's father, its "hero," with a burden that distinguishes him from his conquerors—a privatized psychology that changed discursive practices over his lifetime (1818–1871) might have forecast, but which this late-century document helps construct as a modern commonplace. Both of these moves allow this memoir to expose difference *within* entitled literate practice. Both make a space for the Other of elite literacy, the place where privilege is "authored" but cannot be fully authorized by either lost *or* emerging dominant hegemonies.

"Did We Not Love the Darkey?"

Considering the date of this writing, as well as the various sympathies of its readers in the United Daughters of the Confederacy, Stephenson's memoir's extensive attention to slavery raises evocative questions. Substantial segments of "The Home" and other vignettes of family life before and after the war are devoted to "servants," "negroes," and "darkies," or characters like Mammy and a driver, Peter. The memoir explicitly credits to the destruction of slave labor the demise of not only an economy and a "country," but also southern hospitality.

Friends and relations would come to stay days, weeks and months, as it suited them, without thought of being a strain on . . . the hostess. For hadn't she the trained cook, who stood in the kitchen with a half grown boy under her to do her biddy; and were there not house maids to dress, if need be, the visitor, or do any service for their comfort; and did not the butler know when to make distinctions?" (10)

Stephenson remembers southern women before the war as much less overwhelmed by drudgery than is claimed by historians attempting to rehabilitate them through identification with bourgeois domesticity. But more often, especially in its longest section, "Slavery," this memoir links Stephenson's adolescent observations of politics and war to the slaves' changing moods. Patriarchal doings alien to childhood happiness are written through local and personal events, portents from the slave quarters where Stephenson claims to have found daily attention and security that she remembers less often in interactions with her parents.

The section on slavery begins, "My Father was a firm, but a kind Master," and explains, "our family physician was sent for whenever there was a case of serious sickness," and "merchandise was not made of the negro in my home" (5–6). Instead, slaves had "sweet privileges" that suggest similar accounts in Toni Morrison's *Beloved*. Here, favors enacted both objectivity and sentimentality, making slaves into artificial life forms or life-sized dolls:

If a woman fell from the path of virtue, the first time she was forgiven, but with the second offence, she was told she would be sold. They were allowed the sweet privilege of making love for themselves. It was always known when Master was gong to be called out by a suitor, for the purpose of asking permission to enter into a life's union with the object of his choice. . . . A little moral disquisition was always accompanied the consent. The day was then fixed for the marriage, which was solemnized by Dr. Gibson, our pastor. . . . The bride received the finishing touches to her dress from the young sympathetic guests in the house. Supper was spread out in the kitchen, and when all was in readiness, Mother and the ladies of the family were called out to commend. . . . the fiddle went into the night beyond my knowledge. But the excitement of these marriages thrilled our young hearts, as if one of near kin was entering the bond of holy wedlock. For did we not love the darkey? Their joys were ours, as were their sorrows. (5–6)

Obviously, this language manages a paternal objectification of slaves, treating them as recipients of patriarchal care of the body in, and after, earthly life; they are granted medical care, sexuality and marriage, and teaching on Sundays in family Bible sessions: "Their favorite rendition of the Fourth Commandment was, 'Thou shalt do no manner of work'. The sentiment thus twisted, was pleasing to their natures, and very loathe were they to give up their version" (6). Even in death, in a burial ground in the middle of a field, the "negroe" lived under the father's (certainly qualified) sense of being "physically, morally, and spiritually" responsible (5). Father gives out Christmas gifts to servants dressed in lace, in ceremonies that identify them as "only grown children, and do you not remember the pleasure new shoes always gave you?" (8). This segment concludes with the well-regulated, "cheerful" context provided for slaves, addressing this memory to readers who are modern exponents of the region: "I have dwelt so fully upon the condition of the servants, and their relations to their master, because it is only by such means that the young South can form an idea of slavery as I saw it in my home, and in the homes of relatives we visited" (9).

"Rebellion in the Poor Darkey Heart"

This "young South" is to assimilate not only the elided servant/slave identity which Stephenson, like many others, confers upon African Americans. In addition, it must internalize her favorably prejudiced perspective as a survivor and amanuensis of the old. This pivotal place between youthful and aging memories, her account implies, can be figured in an analogy between her youthful encounters with manly political and military cataclysms and the slaves' encounters with freedom. Their changing reactions as the war becomes first rumor and then reality resemble her own progress out of Blakean innocence. They, like Stephenson, pass through cataclysmic change in the war, which is followed by their taking, like Stephenson, authorial positions of responsibility in the new organization of universals that the memoir intends to make real. Repeatedly, the language that describes this transit sets up two realms, those of Father and family, versus the slaves' whispers and openly hostile statements. One incident that entirely rewrites universal patriarchal politics within this home demonstrates the tension between two unevenly entitled yet concurrently shifting subjectivities.

This discursive operation of tensions and parallel developments fills a section entitled "A Rising Cloud." Here Stephenson asserts love for both her father and the slaves, as though her youthful gaze might bond these unalterably opposed forces that only together provided lost "hospitality" and security:

> Somewhere about this time, 1860, discord seemed rife. My confidence and love for my Father were unbounded, and my affection and sympathy for the servants were great. . . . All the servants were safe in our hands, and could say what they chose without fear of tale-bearing. On leaving the family and going to the nursery, where the seamstresses sat at their work, there again I heard whisperings of a change, and murmurings of discontentment, which grew as the days went on. I was filled with apprehensions. A comet appearing in the heavens about this

time added not little to my fear, for the superstition of the negro caused me to believe it was the forerunner of portentious events. (16)

Stephenson immediately admits that there is no official record of this comet,
crediting it to her "enlarged imagination." In that fantasy past, where slave
and servant were identical, the slave's movements toward freedom reposition
the place where patriarchy is authorized, moving it into domestic lines. In
more than economic ways, "something did happen in our midst" (16).

In a stunning record, Stephenson offers a memory that few narratives cor-
roborate but nothing in this text's copious internal evidence undermines.

> Some theft was committed on the farm that my Father had reason to believe the
> servants either did themselves or were parties to the transaction. He punished
> them by withholding the allowance of meat for a week. Many were the glum
> looks and disagreeable speeches we children heard about Master's withholding
> the allowance, and the hardships of their lot in general. But the week passed and
> no confession was made. The punishment was repeated. (16)

Readers expecting the rigid "slaverat" whom Samuel Simpson saw in such
situations (chapter 5) may assume the outcome of this standoff. But Stephenson's account neither denies the absolute power of her father's ownership nor
hides her memory of how slaves inaugurated shifting prerogatives within still
irremediably fixed conditions. They become the agents who resolve this dilemma:

> At the end of this week twelve men and one woman, all farm hands, came to the
> door to ask that they be sold. It was Saturday night. My Father told them to think
> over the matter the next day, and if they still wanted to change their Master, to
> meet him in town Monday morning; but there were influences abroad to stir all
> the rebellion in the poor darkey heart. They met him. He left for the South that
> evening, where he sold them for a good round sum. They were the first servants
> he had ever sold, save a handsome young woman, my Mother saw slap my oldest
> sister, when an infant. She did not tell my Father what the girl had done, but told
> him he must hire her out, she could never come in her presence again. But she
> gave trouble wherever she was hired, until he sold her. She had been the maid of
> the first Mrs. Friend [Charles Friend's deceased wife]. (16–17)

This intricate positioning and repositioning of subjectivities makes Friend an
absolute master over slaves who, in seeming contradiction, are "free," but
free only to change the face of patriarchal arrangements, and only free to do
so because of "rebellion" in the air. Yet Stephenson, here their author, views
their actions as results of terrible "influences," not only to justify their horrible "choice" to leave Father's beneficent paternalism. She additionally brings
into play the absolute freedom of her mother to exile a slave, but in one flat

sentence explains that slave's supposedly unaccountable violence to the family by suggesting her autonomous loyalty to another mistress, Mother's now dead predecessor. Stephenson tacitly excuses her mother's possible jealousy by projecting it onto that predecessor's maid, drawing attention instead to the slave's motives. Nonetheless, Charles Friend appears to have been stymied by these field hands. His "satisfaction" in this displaced affair of honor is "a good round sum," cash obtained in a distant, vaguely identified "South" where slaves are sold. That unspecified place is not the country that is unified by the defeat that situates this later writing. It is an earlier, fragmented collation of nether regions within and outside state boundaries, an internalized Other to Stephenson's just, memorialized home.

This anecdote of slaves successfully asking to be sold portrays subjectivity in disarray. Whether Stephenson's recall of this event is accurate or manufactured, she may have been told a family interpretation of it outside the event itself. But the slave's request and her father's compliance fit the tenor of rising rebellion that this section of her memoir wants to evoke. It plausibly represents actual negotiations immediately preceding the war. In any of these contexts, this story asserts that patriarchy was never fixed in the precise ways that later bourgeois commonplaces tell us it was. But it also assimilates this mobile patriarchy into emerging threats to it. Father is both actor and audience, a cause of and a witness to a change occurring in the mind's eye of this new authorship. From that new position, the memoir undertakes another vivid dismantling of Father and his home.

The account continues to build on its rhetorical connections between Stephenson's youth and shifting identities for a family's slaves. The slave community fragments into groups: loyal retainers who defend what they can of the family property, a few who accompany the family to its many places of refuge, and others who strike out for new lives:

> Our own servants were never in our employ after the surrender, save one, who rented a house of my Father's . . . and paid the rent in the family laundrying. . . . All the house servants did well where they settled, whether North or South. They always come to see us when we are near, and seem to take an affectionate interest in us, as we do in them. Most of the field hands are lost to our knowledge. (39)

After the war, family members hire servants as they can. Her father, she says, "could never farm with the hired negro to contend with" (41).

Despite Whites's account of renovated gender after the Civil War, Stephenson and her family do not actually "identify" with these slaves. Instead, their repositioning becomes a subtextual warrant for Stephenson's new local authorship. Their changed position allows her to write for money, if only as a donation, while negatively requiring that she do so in demeaning public labor. Stephenson wields *both* broom and pen, service and power, in a postcolonial position whose formation her narrative attributes to the slaves, not to the actions of either her father or the victorious Fathers. This new writerly subjectivity can preserve still dominant white universals, but it must muffle their force. It owns slaves now only in discourse, not legally, but still powerfully writing their identity. Stephenson, who is also an actor in this discursive shift, came to adulthood at sixteen, when she married a Confederate soldier, a human effect of the war. As family members take on the burdens these slaves put down, they activate the slaves' interpretation of the Fourth Commandment in their home. Its proscribed labor now passes from the father to the children, who must serve newly imposed local and national patriarchal orders that finally demand Stephenson's writing.

Rewriting the "Tiny Family Man in Our Heads"

Stephenson's account does fulfill its promise to be "about" the Father. But now inscribed under a different covenant with patriarchal universals, he is here *a* father, Charles Friend. He has a physical countenance, an "inner" life, and a memorial, his daughter's preservation of his decline. Stephenson introduces him as a patriarch among others in the family lineage, born at White Hill and endowed with a breathlessly enumerated catalogue of qualities that mix theatrical strategies and substance.

> A man of medium height, 5ft., 9 or 10 inches, rather slender, with the complexion of a planter, who look well to his business, eyes of light blue, that sparkled with fun, or looked sad or thoughtful, being reflectors of his soul, a nose like my own, mouth small and pretty, but hid by a full red beard, so often seen in Virginia. His hair was black. I am sure the world never called him handsome, but with a manner dignified and courteous, a mind filled with daily intercourse with the best authors, full of ready wit, but with a judicial cast of mind that made him weigh as in a balance every character that passed before him, a heart tender and generous, but shall I say it, too much swayed by prejudice, and a reserve that hid from sight his heart's deepest workings, which caused him to avoid partings, and at such times, possibly, to disappear, as if by magic, lest someone should see the trembling lip or the moistened eye, stern in some aspects, but indulgent to laxity, where no evil was apprehended; was it a wonder his home was always filled with guests, young and old? (1–2)

Constituted by "the best authors" and a judicial entitlement to "balance" one against another character, Charles Friend is also made of feeling. His "hidden" emotions cite separate military, literary, and religious discourses to fix a male gender that carries its defeats as psychological, not purely material, changes. Father's feelings shift the "character" written on the specimen patriarchal calendar begun with Tazewell's account of his grandfather forward (chapter 3). They are not exclusively Friend's ability to disappear, "as if by magic." This man, for instance, often visits White Hill's family cemetery for unaccountable reasons: he "felt a tie which drew him to this spot not infrequently" (4). Fear is possible as it was not before, as when Stephenson hears him say, "I have not made a cent from the farm in two years." She immediately declares, "My heart sank" (10). Father is only reporting usual zero balance from unindebted, wholly owned agriculture, but she, "childlike" and "suffering in silence," imagines that he is terrified of debtors' prison. Unlike earlier counterparts who remain indifferent to females, he also has firm tastes in women's clothing, wanting "Mother [to] wear black silk in winter and white in summer" (11). (Mother prefers, and wears, "fashion.") He keeps "goodies" in his desk for his children and refuses to follow a brother-in-law's advice to turn his grounds into a park for reasons emphasized as fondness and nostalgia, not simply traditional male practicality: "He ever thinking of his children, and loving the home of his nativity, was held back by the thought, that if so much money was invested in improvements, no one child could inherit the place" (13).

Friend's "goodness," which is necessary to accomplish the desires of this text, cannot be the manly responsibility of prewar commonplaces, a socially earned exterior that warrants the "esteem" and "love" of an emphatically social community. The memoir instead verifies Stephenson's assertion that heroism resides in interactions with individuals, not moments of valor in politics, education, or battle. This late nineteenth-century construction of patriarchal identity projects onto Friend inner voices that are rarely audible, imposing on a unified psychology diverse conventions circulated in socially regulatory oratory and this period's domestic fiction.

Friend's monument, this writing, thus provides alternative "character" for a privatized, often inarticulate male who is officially head of the renovated household that is no longer a primary unit of civic action. Readers consequently learn little of the citizenship that identifies republican forebears in other texts, but a great deal about the modern construction of specifically male gender, the position that Stuart Hall identifies as a liberal "tiny family man *inside our heads*" (see chapter 4).[21] There dwells the retained regulatory universal of the historical patriarchy that, Hall says, only appears to have attenuated over time. This identity, which Stephenson's memorial to her father's feelings empowers, may be politically either right *or* left of dominant hegemony, yet is still tied to the core patriarchal determination to preserve its property.

Having established Father as a sensitive subject, Stephenson's memoir also reports that he belonged to the Confederate Prince George Company and that "no man went more promptly or remained more faithfully at his post" (19). But Father's actual politics unfixes this syntactic parallelism, portraying his conflicted positions in staccato sentences:

> No glaymore of southern fire could blind him to the hopelessness of the success of the Confederacy. . . . He was called a croaker, but none met duty more fully. He only saw further than most into the future. When southern heroism is lauded, my heart swells with pride, knowing my Father was one of that host. My Father loved home peculiarly. The companionship of men as a body was distasteful to him. In a few months he would have been past the age for conscription. His health was always frail. No hope nerved and sustained his spirit for such action, but self and money were given to the cause. (19)

Here again, overlaid on political realism that other war fiction names as heroism, is Father's domestic psychology. His interjected politics are written as frailty, premature aging, and a distaste for the company of men, all of which certify that he "loved home peculiarly." He sends his wife his first army pay, significantly "the first money he had ever made" (21), and returns home for Christmas, "but gift making was a thing of the past" (24). On other visits he is "cheerless" at the neglect and betrayal of his overseer. In all these ways, Friend is represented not only as emergent interior Man, but a particular southern version of that psychological subject. His defeat establishes domesticity, if passive domesticity, as appropriately male.

The memoir historically situates the defeat of the Confederacy in the conquest of Petersburg, a protracted, agonizing battle that well warranted Grant's consternation. "In our family history," Stephenson begins, the beginning of this siege (June 9) became "Memorial day" (29). During the battle, federal troops mistake Charles Friend farming his corn for a troop of soldiers. This event, like other misrecognitions, repositions universal fatherhood in a heartbeat:

> The Yankees took the moving in the corn for military operations and kept up the firing all day. My Father gave orders to the men to cut loose the horses and escape as best they could. . . . We feared that he had been killed or captured. So suddenly had they taken possession of the old home not one feather's worth had been saved. (30)

Stephenson watches as a shell lands in the yard without exploding, "the last shell we ever looked to see." But "none ever exploded." Mammy crawls away to Petersburg, a young sisterly cousin is killed in North Carolina, and the family governess "had just lost a married sister." Grandmother secures an army wagon for escape "by the eloquence of her tears," and family women and children begin lives as domestic combatants, hereafter the memoir's positions of agency (30–31). They accomplish a series of household moves and they succeed in their attempts to procure food and to entertain guests, including Stephenson's husband-to-be. (The romance is only briefly noted.) By virtue of this shift of agency to the family women, the memoir becomes a story of how domesticity survives the fall of a universal order, but not the death of the father's support. During the siege, a shell lands next to him as he sits "at the side of the front steps of our home. *Very few families were left in place*" (33, emphasis added). Later, with only a brief furlough, Father must leave his wife alone "to face a double trouble," both the birth of a son and the infant's death six days later, "having no Father at birth or burial" (34).

These chronological textual moments do not verify literary subtleties in this local authorship, nor do they rescue this extraordinary text from extracanonical invisibility. What is at stake is a local authorship that substitutes one universal order for another, to rewrite a culture on the feminized and privatized bodies of both sexes, not only on the briefly noted community actions of a father. Men away at war cannot be remembered by a writer who does not recall them. But this memoir's construction of a domesticity that excludes mankind is emphasized even by the account's brief and isolated reference to Stephenson's first meeting with her husband and its condensed notice of his deeds. Against this brevity, the account devotes two pages to the fabric, style, and availability of clothing worn by herself and the other children, to which Father contributed only through "an interest in a boat that ran the blockade to Nassau" (36). Clothing, not enacted principles of character, is the material of inheritance. Women seek protected hiding places for family valuables, which are a precisely "personal" commonplace now moved to a different social order.

Consequently, this authorship portrays a return to the family home of the Father and finds there a story of shells that land, definitively erasing its structure, but do not explode. The patriarchal composition of the family must move, but the combat that forces this shift does not entirely destroy it. In this cultural parable, a "historical" aftermath of the war is anticlimactic. Charles Friend obtains what money he can get after the war by cashing in his life insurance policies. But this cash cannot prevent his greatest loss, a family's ability to educate its children: "Where now were all the hopes of college bred sons and daughters, of finished education. Where the start in life for these youths and maidens, just budding into men and women?" (42). This realignment mourns the duty of parents to "improve" family properties, especially their children. Father's primacy in the home is thereby destroyed: "My Father now took his place in the garden, and with the aid of Tom, kept us beautifully supplied with berries and vegetables, which he gathered with his own hands." He buys a half interest in a cow that already carries his brand, for "in those insulted times, there was no use in trying to prove ownership" (42–43). A brief note finally draws together the memoir's representations of the changes wrought by Stephenson's two master tropes: the dissolution of slavery and the constituting of Father's "feeling":

> An incident occurred, which took my Father's heart, and is worth of record. His foreman, Jim Johnson, came to him, bringing money he had laid by, and begging his Master to accept it. He said that he had been working for himself for more than a year, and did not need it, as he could easily make more. He was then a tenant at White Hill. (43)

As slaves who work for themselves as tenants support the master, the family children begin to play with the skulls of dead soldiers left on the property. These actions in the memoir's next section, "Traces of War," also include the purgation and deaths of family members of both sexes by an epidemic of dysentery. Finally, this realignment in memory registers a deadly cleansing that must take Father's heart in more than one sense. His demise as The Father, long before his physical death, is the poignantly recorded premature boundary on his life:

> It was not strange that some, like my Father always went about hereafter in a subdued, stunned softness, that made the hearts of those about him bleed to see. No murmuring only the quiet taking up of the things so new to him, and all with a spirit so chastened as to make him say for the first time in his life, he felt thankful for the necessities of life. My Mother's spirit was more elastic. She was not so crushed. . . . But she was not the head. . . . Her household duties, though much simpler, were left in somewhat the same shape, but to my Father, a whirlwind could not better have carried away his means of supporting and equipping this large household for life. (38–39)

Many historians have told this story and have drawn obvious inferences from it about the emergence of feminized bourgeois domesticity. But this text marks a particular and different discursive time and social space. This late-century example symbolically closes a specific discourse, a way of language whose geography, local traditions, and class assignments had always only unstably appropriated, reformed, or recalculated commonplace cultural properties. But Stephenson offers those processes—appropriation, reform, and recalculation—to a different but not yet entirely established consensus. In this specific yet common place, a nationally conceived internalized sensibility could not yet flourish, for experience stubbornly remains publicly intended persuasion. The memoir's rhetoric exposes the operations that shift class positioning, precisely as operations of skillful discourse. Insofar as it succeeds in endowing its readers with both a textual monument and an immediate sense of participating in privileged but absent entitlements, it exposes the "true biases" that enabled even later, standardized middle-class discourses of evaluative interpretation.

Commonplace traditions in ordinary writing exchange conventions and refix them as properties, in discursive practices that are easy to observe but impossible to stabilize. These locally authorized compositions highlight this location of "culture" in ordinary writing. Its visible, always situated political forces rearticulate universal principles that, it turns out, are never abstract. These examples move universal Mankind into the duty of a particular General Assembly, into elocutionary and theatrical conventions that allow a son to grieve over a father's death, and finally into the silently expressive psychology of "a man." Yet despite the authority of precedents that they endow to "experience," neither the privacy nor the publicity of their emerging subject positions are still only on loan. In the internal Lacanian subconscious cultural syntax that would, in its way, give these texts the status of artifacts, subject positions are less easily assumed and returned for general use. They less readily serve the socialized identity that assures the inheritance of flexible societies. These texts foreshadow a privatized individual identity who becomes yet another, differently productive commonplace. This subject, whose more limited results from writing absorb its propriety into material property, is often empty of its own commonplace histories—and therefore without their cultural power.

Notes

·

References

·

Index

Notes

Introduction

1. Jacques Derrida, "Signature Event Context," *Margins of Philosophy,* trans. Alan Bass (Chicago: University of Chicago Press, 1972), 330.

2. Stephen Justice, *Writing and Rebellion: England in 1321* (Berkeley: University of California Press, 1994).

3. Janice Radway, *Reading the Romance: Women, Patriarchy, and Popular Culture.* Chapel Hill: University of North Carolina Press, 1991.

4. Regenia Gagnier, *Subjectivities: A History of Self Representation in Britain, 1832–1920* (New York: Oxford University Press, 1991).

5. David Vincent, *Bread, Knowledge and Freedom: A Study of Nineteenth-Century Working Class Autobiography* (London: Europa, 1981).

6. Richard Hoggart, *The Uses of Literacy: Changing Patterns in English Mass Culture* (Fair Lawn, N.J.: Essential Books, 1957), 252–53.

7. Linda Brodkey, *Writing Permitted in Designated Areas Only* (Minneapolis: University of Minnesota Press, 1996).

8. Sharon Crowley, *The Methodical Memory: Invention in Current Traditional Rhetoric* (Carbondale: Southern Illinois University Press, 1990).

9. Cheryl Glenn, *Rhetoric Retold: Regendering the Tradition from Antiquity Through the Renaissance* (Carbondale: Southern Illinois Univerity Press, 1997).

10. Susan Jarratt, *Re-Reading the Sophists: Classical Rhetoric Refigured* (Carbondale: Southern Illinois Univerity Press, 1991).

11. Roland Barthes, *Mythologies,* trans. Annette Lavers (Paris: Editions du Seuil, 1957), 75.

12. Catherine Clement, *The Lives and Legends of Jacques Lacan, 1981,* trans. Arthur Goldhammer (New York: Columbia University Press, 1983), 6, 134.

13. See David Silverman and Brian Torode, *The Material Word: Some Theories of Language and Its Limits* (London: Routledge and Kegan Paul, 1980), 227–46.

14. Mary Beth Norton, *Founding Mothers and Fathers: Gendered Power and the Forming of American Society* (New York: Knopf, 1996), 24.

15. Ibid.

16. Ibid., 22.

17. Joel Pfister, "On Conceptualizing the Cultural History of Emotional and Psychological Life in America," in *Inventing the Psychological,* edited by Joel Pfister and Nancy Schnog (New Haven: Yale University Press, 1997), 17.

18. Richard Price, *Alabi's World* (Baltimore: Johns Hopkins University Press, 1990), xvi.

Chapter 1 · A World Lettered by Codes

1. George Kennedy, introduction to *Aristotle on Rhetoric: A Theory of Civic Discourse* (New York and Oxford: Oxford University Press, 1991), 27.

2. Roland Barthes, *The Semiotic Challenge,* trans. Richard Howard (Berkeley and Los Angeles: University of California Press, 1994), 92, emphasis added.

3. Robert Beverley, *History of Virginia,* in *Reading, Writing and Arithmetic in Virginia, 1607–1699,* Historical Booklet, Jamestown 350th Anniversary, no. 15, edited by E. G. Sivern (Williamsburg: Virginia 350th Anniversary Celebration Corporation: 1957), 3. These plans were jettisoned after the Indian massacre of George Thorpe, director of the college land, along with 346 settlers, and the termination of the charter of the Virginia Company in 1624.

4. See Homer Alton McKann, "History of Early Education in Middlesex County, 1669–1890," M.Ed. thesis, University of Richmond, 1942.

5. Aristotle, *Topica,* I.14.105b.

6. Quintilian, *Institutes,* trans. H. Caplin, edited by G. P. Goold (London: Loeb, 1981), X:5.11–14.

7. See Ben Jonson, *Discoveries: A Critical Edition with an Introduction and Notes on the True Purport and Genesis of the Book,* edited by Maurice Castelain (Paris: Librairie Hachette, 1906?).

8. Mary Carruthers, *The Book of Memory: A Study of Memory in Medieval Culture* (New York: Cambridge University Press, 1990), 178, emphasis added.

9. Ibid., 179.

10. Joan Marie Lechner, *Renaissance Concepts of the Commonplaces: An Historical Investigation of the General and Universal Ideas Used in All Argumentation and Persuasion with Special Emphasis on the Educational and Literary Tradition of the Sixteenth and Seventeenth Centuries* (New York: Pageant Press, 1963).

11. Ibid., 170–71.

12. Ibid., 166.

13. Mary Thomas Crane, *Framing Authority* (Princeton: Princeton University Press, 1933), 4. See also Susan Miller, "Secondary Renaissance Literacy: 'As an Author, I Take More Liberties,'" in *Rescuing the Subject* (Carbondale: Southern Illinois University Press, 1989), 80–100.

14. Max W. Thomas, "Reading and Writing the Renaissance Commonplace Book:

A Question of Authorship?" in *The Construction of Authorship: Textual Appropriation in Law and Literature,* edited by Martha Woodmansee and Peter Jaszi (Durham: Duke University Press, 1994).

15. Ibid., 411.

16. Roger Chartier, *The Order of Books,* trans. Lydia G. Cochrane (Stanford, Calif.: Stanford University Press, 1994).

17. Michel Foucault, *Language, Counter-Memory, Practice,* edited and trans. by Donald F. Bouchard, Sherry Simon (Ithaca: Cornell University Press, 1977), 113–38.

18. Chartier, *The Order of Books,* 56.

19. Lechner, *Renaissance Concepts,* 183.

20. Walter Ong, *Ramus: Method and the Decay of Dialogue* (Cambridge: Harvard University Press, 1958).

21. Ibid., 118.

22. Ibid., 119.

23. Ibid.

24. Chartier, *The Order of Books,* 88.

25. Ann Moss, *Printed Commonplace-Books and the Structuring of Renaissance Thought* (Oxford: Clarenden Press, 1996), 49.

26. David Simpson, *The Academic Postmodern and the Rule of Literature* (Chicago: University of Chicago Press, 1995), 35. Note that Simpson's "precise" point is so only in relation to the shift to republican monarchy in Addison's time. His comment does not indicate the mass literacy in England and America that waited on the late nineteenth century.

27. Cited in C. B. Macpherson, *The Political Theory of Possessive Individualism: Hobbes to Locke* (Oxford: Clarendon Press, 1962), 140; Simpson, *The Academic Postmodern,* 78, emphasis added.

28. Simpson, *The Academic Postmodern,* 17.

29. Marshall Alcorn, *Narcissism and the Literary Libido: Rhetoric, Text and Subjectivity* (New York: New York University Press, 1994), 19.

30. François Furet and Jacques Ozouf, *Reading and Writing: Literacy in France from Calvin to Jules Ferry* (Cambridge: Cambridge University Press, 1982), 316.

31. Ibid., 317, emphasis added.

32. Cited in Anne Ruggles Gere, "Kitchen Tables and Rented Rooms: The Extra Curriculum of Composition," *CCC* 45 (February 1994): 81–82.

33. Raymond Williams, "Marx on Culture," in *What I Came to Say* (London: Radius, 1989), 199–200.

34. Mikhail Bakhtin, *Rabelais and His World,* trans. Helene Iswolsky (Bloomington: Indiana University Press, 1984), 423.

35. Nancy Armstrong and Leonard Tennenhouse, eds., *The Violence of Representation* (New York: Routledge, 1989), 38.

36. See *Jefferson's Literary Commonplace Book,* edited by Douglas L. Wilson (Princeton: Princeton University Press, 1989); Kenneth A. Lockridge, *On the Sources of Patriarchal Rage: The Commonplace Books of William Byrd and Thomas Jefferson and the Gendering of Power in the Eighteenth Century* (New York: New York University Press, 1992).

37. See, for example, Pierre Bourdieu and J.-C. Passerone, *Reproduction in Education, Society and Culture* (London: Sage, 1977).

38. See Macpherson, *The Political Theory of Possessive Individualism,* 140; and Simpson, *The Academic Postmodern,* 78.

39. John Locke, *Second Treatise,* sec. 28, in *Two Treatises of Government,* edited by Peter Laslett (Cambridge: Cambridge University Press, 1967).

40. David Silverman and Brian Torode, *The Material Word: Some Theories of Language and Its Limits,* 238.

41. Quoted in Silverman and Torode, *The Material Word,* 243, emphasis added.

42. Richard Schwartz, "Patrimony and Figuration of Authorship in the Eighteenth-Century Literary Property Debates." in *Works and Days* 7, no. 2 (1989): 29, emphasis added.

43. Macpherson, *The Political Theory of Possessive Individualism,* 221.

44. John Locke, *A New Method of Making Common-Place Books* (London: Greenwood, 1706).

45. See Christopher Fox, *Locke and the Scriblerians: Identity and Consciousness in Early Eighteenth-Century Britian* (Berkeley: University of California Press, 1988), 14–23, for a review of the theological and philosophical controversy occasioned by Locke's proposal that identity is split into temporally sequential moments of shifting awareness, and therefore is not a spiritually accountable, perduring "character."

46. See, for example, Bruno Latour, "Literature," in *Science in Action* (Cambridge: Harvard University Press, 1987), 21–62.

47. The collection has been expanded by additional acquisitions since January 1990.

48. See note 3, above, and G. Chinard, *The Literary Bible of Thomas Jefferson* (Baltimore: Johns Hopkins University Press, 1928). Both editors focus on the dating of this book and its relationships to Jefferson's published documents.

49. Mss1D3545a, 1186–1238, sec. 39. This text was widely republished and variously attributed, e.g., to Bishop James Madison and to Patrick Henry.

50. Richard Beale Davis, *Literature and Society in Early Virginia* (Baton Rouge: Louisiana State University Press, 1973), 106.

51. Laurel Thatcher Ulrich, *A Midwife's Tale: The Life of Martha Ballard, Based on Her Diary, 1785–1812* (New York: Vintage Books, 1991).

52. Mary Forrest, preface to *Women of the South Distinguished in Literature* (New York: Derby and Jackson, 1861).

53. Mss1B6386, sec. 60–67, 32.

54. Mss1H7185b, 8500, sec. 46.

55. Elizabeth Virginia Lindsay Lomax, January 16, 1857, quoted in her *Leaves from an Old Washington Diary, 1854–1863* (New York: E. P. Dutton, 1943).

56. Mss1P4686a, sec. 36.

57. Mss1G8782b4723, 70–71, 73.

58. Ibid., 68–69.

59. MssUn3, 10. Inscription: "Abra[ham] Wilson, April 4, 1836."

60. Mss1W7275a9, kept in *A Theological Common-Place Book* (Cambridge: Hilliard and Brown, 1832), preface.

61. See also MssiM1395a100, sec. 28, Alexander Hugh Holmes Stuart's commonplace book, "Kept in *The Lawyer's Note Book* (Washington and Baltimore: Coale and Co. and E. J. Coale, 1831) by a Gentleman of the Bar." This book, another example of the printed commonplace book tradition, includes Stuart's law notes. Pp. 53–246 are blank, indicating how needful were the publishers' introductions urging the habit of using such books.

62. John Todd, *Index Rerum: or Index of Subjects; Intended as a Manual to Aid the Student and the Professional Man, In Preparing Himself for Usefulness*, 2nd ed. (Northampton, New York, and Philadelphia, 1835), 6. Further page references will be given in the text.

63. MssiB1938a216, sec. 14.

64. Georges Bataille, *The Accursed Share,* trans. Robert Hurley (New York: Zone Books, 1988), 21.

65. Ibid.

Chapter 2 · Writing Along New Lines

1. Lawrence Levine, *Highbrow/Lowbrow: The Emergence of Cultural Hierarchy in America* (Cambridge: Harvard University Press, 1988).

2. Ian Hunter, *Culture and Government* (London: Macmillan, 1988).

3. Ibid., 67.

4. Robert Owen, "First Essay," *A New View of Society,* 1813; in *Robert Owen on Education,* edited by Harold Silber (Cambridge: Cambridge University Press, 1969), 76, emphasis added.

5. Hunter, *Culture and Government,* 4.

6. Ian Hunter, "Aesthetics and Cultural Studies," in *Cultural Studies,* edited by Lawrence Grossberg, Cary Nelson, Paula Treichler (London: Routledge, 1991), 363.

7. Kristin Ross, introduction to Jacques Rancière, *The Ignorant Schoolmaster,* trans. Ross (Stanford: Stanford University Press, 1991), xix.

8. Hunter, *Culture and Government,* 5.

9. See, for example, Sivern, *Reading, Writing and Arithmetic in Virginia.*

10. See Edmund S. Morgan, *Virginians at Home: Family Life in the Eighteenth Century* (Charlottesville: University of Virginia Press, 1952), 9–13.

11. Cited in McKann, "History of Early Education in Middlesex County 1669–1890," 25.

12. Sivern, *Reading, Writing and Arithmetic,* 9.

13. The 1850 census counted 88,520 (or ca. 20 percent) illiterate free adults in a statewide population of 438,966. This figure was down from the reported 79 percent illiterate among adult whites in 1840. See Dale G. Robinson, *The Academies of Virginia: 1776–1861* (n.p., 1977), 57.

14. Cited in Bernard Bailyn, *Education in the Forming of American Society* (New York: Norton, 1972), 26. Here, as throughout, unusual spellings are retained without note to ensure the integrity of the texts and encourage their reading in historical context.

15. See Morgan, *Virginians at Home,* 5–29.

16. McKann, "History of Early Education in Middlesex County," 25.

17. Ibid., 17.

18. *Acts of Assembly,* 1810, chap. XIV, 15.

19. Literary Fund, Minute Books, 1811–1837, Record Group 27, Virginia State Library and Archives, Richmond, xxii.

20. McKann, "History of Early Education in Middlesex County," 39.

21. Robinson, *The Academies of Virginia,* 5.

22. McKann, "History of Early Education in Middlesex County," 81. See also Tom Fox, "From Freedom to Manners: African-American Literacy Instruction in the Nineteenth Century," *Composition Forum* 96 (1995): 1–12; and Ann Ruggles Gere and Sarah Robbins, "Gendered Literacy in Black and White: Turn-of-the-Century African-American and European-American Club Women's Printed Texts," *Signs: Journal of Women in Culture and Society* 1 (1996): 643–78.

23. Susanne Lebstock, *Virginia Women, 1600–1945: "A Share of Honor"* (Richmond: Virginia State Library, 1987).

24. Ibid., 62.

25. Quoted in Catherine Clinton, *The Plantation Mistress: Women's World in the Old South* (New York: Pantheon, 1982), 124.

26. Lebstock, *Virginia Women, 1600–1945,* 62.

27. Mss73LA380Is431, John R. Purdie, "History of Education in Isle of Wight County from Colonial Times," September 1, 1880.

28. Ibid., 15.

29. Linda Kerber, *Women of the Republic: Intellect and Ideology in Revolutionary America,* Institute of Early American History and Culture, Williamsburg, Virginia (Chapel Hill: University of North Carolina Press, 1980), 200.

30. Purdie, "History of Education," 6, emphasis added.

31. Morgan, *Virginians at Home,* 22–23.

32. Karl F. Kaestle, *Pillars of the Republic: Common Schools and American Society, 1780–1860* (New York: American Century Series, Hill and Wang, 1983). See also Nancy Armstrong and Leonard Tennenhouse, "Family History," in *The Imaginary Puritan* (Berkeley: University of California Press, 1992), 77–85.

33. Ibid., 9, emphasis added.

34. Thomas Jefferson, *The Writings of Thomas Jefferson,* edited by Andrew A. Lipscomb (Washington, D.C.: Thomas Jefferson Memorial Association, 1903–1904), 2:11, emphasis added.

35. Thomas Jefferson, quoted in James A. Bear, "An Address delivered during the celebration of the 25th anniversary of the Tracy W. McGregor Library, 1939–1964 (Charlottesville: n.p., 1967), flyleaf.

36. Harold Hellenbrand, *The Unfinished Revolution: Education and Politics in the Thought of Thomas Jefferson* (Newark, N.J.: University of Delaware Press, 1990), 97.

37. Kaestle, *Pillars of the Republic,* 51.

38. Ibid., 194.

39. Agnes Lee, letter of July 16, 1854, in *Growing Up in the 1830s: The Journal of Agnes Lee,* edited by Mary Custis Lee de Butts (Chapel Hill: University of North Carolina Press, 1984), 41. See also February 23, 1853, and May 13, 1855.

40. MssIL51e660, Agnes Lee, letter, December 9, 1866.

41. Lynne Templeton Brickley, "'Female Academies Are Every Where Establishing': The Beginnings of Secondary Education for Women in the United States, 1790–1830," unpublished manuscript, Harvard University Graduate School of Education, 1982, iii.

42. Ibid., 45, emphasis added.

43. Gerda Lerner, *The Majority Finds Its Past: Placing Women in History* (New York and Oxford: Oxford University Press, 1979), 51.

44. Bernard Bailyn, "Education as a Discipline: Some Historical Notes," in *The Discipline of Education,* edited by John Walton and James L. Keuthe (Madison: University of Wisconsin Press, 1963), 135. See also Clinton, *The Plantation Mistress,* 130.

45. Harvey Graff, *The Literacy Myth: Literacy and Social Structure in the Nineteenth-Century City* (New York: Academic Press, 1979); Michel Cole and Sylvia Scribner, *Culture and Thought* (New York: Wiley, 1974); Brian Street, *Literacy in Theory and Practice,* Cambridge Studies in Literate and Oral Culture (Cambridge: Cambridge University Press, 1984); Niko Besnier, *Reading and Writing on a Polynesian Atoll,* Studies in the Cultural Foundations of Language, no. 17 (Cambridge: Cambridge University Press, 1995).

46. MssiB2346b11330.

47. Lebstock, *Virginia Women, 1600–1945,* 62.

48. Both Richard Bennett, a governor of Virginia, and Richard Bennett Jr. made marks to "sign" the Remonstrance by the residents of Isle of Wight County supporting Governor Berkeley in the late seventeenth century. Richard Jr. had attended Harvard in 1655–1656 (Sivern, *Reading, Writing and Arithmetic,* 66).

49. See Susan Miller, *Rescuing the Subject,* 91–92.

50. Lebstock, *Virginia Women, 1600–1945,* 62.

51. Quoted in Thomas Woody, *A History of Women's Education in the United States* (New York: Science Press, 1929), 1:152.

52. Ibid., 1:146, emphasis added.

53. "Miscellaneous Notes," *Education* 2 (January 1881): 315, emphasis added.

54. Woody, *A History of Women's Education,* 1:271.

55. Ibid., 1:213.

56. Quoted in ibid., 1:407.

57. Mssi735c. See also Anne Lee Peyton, commonplace book, 1861–1888, in which newspaper versions of poems are pasted over carefully drawn math exercises (MssiP4686c1135). See also MssiD2278c280, sec. 5, which includes a printed report card form, August 1865, listing the following subjects (giving grades only for those in italics): Writing, Reading, *Spelling,* Grammar, History, Geography, Natural Philosophy, Chemistry, Arithmetic Mental, Arithmetic Written, *Algebra, Geometry,* Trig, Calculus, *Latin, Greek, French,* German, Composition or Declamation, and *Conduct.*

58. George E. Dabney, "Address 'On the Value of Writing,' Delivered before the Society of Alumni of the University of Virginia at their annual meeting" (Charlottesville: O. S. Allen and Co., 1849), Virginia State Library and Archives. I quote extensively from this pamphlet because of its general unavailability. Page references will be given in the text.

59. Walter Ong, *Orality and Literacy* (New York: Methuen, 1982); David Olson,

"From Utterance to Text: The Bias of Language in Speech and Writing," *Harvard Educational Review* 47 (1977): 257–81.

60. Edward Channing, "The Orator and His Times," in *Lectures Read to the Seniors in Harvard College* [1856], edited by Dorothy I. Anderson and Waldo Braden (Carbondale: Southern Illinois University Press, 1968), 16.

61. Dabney, "Address 'On the Value of Writing,'" 4.

62. See Winifred Bryan Horner, "Writing Instruction in Great Britain: Eighteenth and Nineteenth Centuries," in *A Short History of Writing Instruction: From Ancient Greece to Twentieth-Century America,* edited by James J. Murphy (Davis, Calif.: Hermagoras Press, 1990), 121–50.

63. Walt Whitman, *Complete Poetry and Selected Prose by Walt Whitman,* edited by James E. Miller Jr. (Boston: Houghton Mifflin, 1959), 455–502.

64. Steven M. Stowe, *Intimacy and Power in the Old South: Ritual in the Lives of Planters* (Baltimore: Johns Hopkins University Press, 1987), 5–49. See Mss1B6117a, 34–39, P[hilip] S[tanhope] Blanton, "Essay on Duelling," 1846.

65. See introduction.

66. See Susan Miller, *Textual Carnivals: The Politics of Composition* (Carbondale: Southern Illinois University Press, 1991), 48–61.

67. John Langbourne Williams, commonplace books, 1879, 1880, 1888, Mss55W6734, secs. 1, 3, 2.

68. Mss1P9318a, 160–61.

69. Mss55B6385, sec. 1.

70. Mss1H2485a, 112–13.

71. In "Specimens of the Compositions of the pupils of the Alexandria female seminary selected and written by themselves, 1853 and 1858," Mss54AL276, sec. 1, 31–32. Further references are given in the text.

72. Mss1D3545a, 962–67, sec. 21. This Julia is the aunt of the younger Julia Beverly Whiting (chapter 5). Also includes an undated essay on Christmas in which Whiting remembers family togetherness on Christmas Eve, the "bright coal fire," and the bringing forth of "nuts and golden Pippens": "Those were happy days, and regrets will sometimes rise that these last few years have made them too old for such childish joys."

73. Mss1P1855a, 319–22.

74. Mss1C7835a, 325–66, 451–605, 611–16.

75. Mss1C7835a, 325–66, sec. 18.

76. Frederick Douglass, *Narrative of the Life of Frederick Douglass, an American Slave, Written by Himself* (New York: Signet Books, 1968), 55.

77. Mss55R1564, sec. 1.

78. Mss1J3698b, 3–30.

79. Mss1W3286a, 478–537, sec. 24, 60 items.

80. Mss1H2485e, 125–26.

81. See Shirley Brice Heath, "Toward an Ethnohistory of Writing in American Education," in *Writing: The Nature, Development and Teaching of Written Communication,* vol. 1: *Variation in Writing: Functional and Linguistic-Cultural Differences,* edited by Marcia Farr Whiteman (Hillsdale, N.J.: Lawrence Erlbaum, 1981), 35.

82. Kenneth Burke, *A Rhetoric of Motives* (Berkeley: University of California Press, 1969), 38.

83. See Nancy Green, "Female Education and School Competition," in *Women's Being, Woman's Place: Female Identity and Vocation in American History*, edited by Mary Kelley (Boston: G. K. Hall, 1979), 127–41.

84. Mss2M6663a.

85. Mss2H24535a1.

86. I. A. Richards, *Philosophy of Rhetoric* (London: Oxford University Press, 1936), 40.

87. Pierre Bourdieu, *Distinction: A Social Critique of the Judgment of Taste,* trans. Richard Nice (Cambridge: Harvard University Press, 1984), 12 and *passim.*

Chapter 3 · Home Improvements

1. See Richard Beale Davis, *Literature and Society in Early Virginia: 1608–1840*, 152 ff., for a description of Fithian's diary account of the Carter household, into which he later married to become one of the "members" that family texts about education adopt.

2. Mss51M1326, sec. 1, 1–2. Further references are given in the text.

3. See Brickley, "'Female Academies Are Every Where Establishing'"; Catherine Clinton states the view that Brickley questions: "Female academies and seminaries fitted women strictly for their preordained role in plantation culture: that of a well-read elite serving as wives and mothers to the master class. Unlike their northern counterparts, these women could not use their education to explore new avenues of experience. . . . However equal women might be proclaimed to be in spiritual and intellectual terms, men were still the acknowledged authorities in social, political, and economic spheres" (*The Plantation Mistress,* 137).

4. See Clinton, *The Plantation Mistress,* 138: "Maria Campbell, the Virginia plantation mistress, advised her niece to value her education, for 'when the frosty part of life shall arrive, it will be a support for you under every vicissitude of life.' At the time she expressed this sentiment, Campbell was only twenty-six" (Maria Campbell to Elizabeth Russell, August 19, 1808, Duke University).

5. Elizabeth Fox-Genovese, *Within the Plantation Household: Black and White Women of the Old South* (Chapel Hill: University of North Carolina Press, 1988), 257.

6. See Suzanne Lebstock, *The Free Women of Petersburg: Status and Culture in a Southern Town, 1784–1860* (New York: W. W. Norton, 1984), the title of which captures this position.

7. See Carroll Smith-Rosenberg, *Disorderly Conduct: Visions of Gender in Victorian America* (New York: Oxford University Press, 1985), esp. chap. 2.

8. Michael Warner, *The Letters of the Republic: Publication and the Public Sphere in Eighteenth-Century America* (Cambridge: Harvard University Press, 1990), 27.

9. Stephanie Coontz, *The Social Origins of Private Life: A History of American Families, 1600–1900* (London and New York: Verso, 1988), 14.

10. Mss1EA765a181.

11. Warner, *The Letters of the Republic,* 27.

12. Mss54AL2761, sec. 26.

13. Mss55H6375, secs. 1, 2, 11–12, 17–21. Further references are given in the text.

14. Mss1P4686a, 96–118.

15. P. Peace, *An Address on the Improvement of the Conditions of the Labouring Poor* (Shaftesbury, 1852), cited in Asa Briggs, *The Collected Essays of Asa Briggs* (Urbana: University of Illinois Press, 1985), 1:32, n. 122.

16. See Ralph Wormeley's letters to his son Warner in London (chapter 6).

17. See Nancy Armstrong and Leonard Tennenhouse, eds., *The Ideology of Conduct: Essays on Literature and History of Sexuality* (New York: Methuen, 1987), 8–9.

18. Mss1B6386, secs. 60–67, 1. Further references are given in the text. See also chapter 5.

19. Steven Mintz, *A Prison of Expectations: Family in Victorian Culture* (New York: New York University Press, 1983), 33.

20. Jonathan Goldberg, "Bradford's 'Ancient Members,'" in *Nationalisms and Sexualities,* edited by Andrew Parker et al. (New York: Routledge, 1992), 62. Goldberg cites Edmund Morgan, *The Puritan Family* (New York: Harper, 1966, rev. of 1944 ed.), 75–78; and John Demos, *A Little Commonwealth* (London: Oxford University Press, 1970), 71–75. Both suggest that this practice served to maintain distance between parents and children, to prevent excessive attachment. That motive, to avoid affectionate expressions and attachments, does not apply here. See chapter 2.

21. Mss1P3496c515, 6. Further references are given in the text.

22. Mss1M9924a, sec. 12, 44–45. The family moved to Richmond after the school closed. Eliza married Samuel Hays Myers at Spring Farm, in Henrico County in 1827, and resided in North Carolina, Richmond, and Petersburg. She had two children, Edmund (b. 1829) and Caroline (b. 1844), evidently named for a half sister referred to often in this text. Her son wrote at her death: "The anxiety and trouble she underwent during the period of Sister Caroline's aberration of mind, previous to her being placed in the asylum at Raleigh, and the fatigue she would insist on undergoing, in her domestic duties and in nursing sick soldiers who were taken into our house, to save their lives from exposure in camps or ill-tended hospitals, were too much for her delicate frame, and she would not permit any one to relieve her from them."

23. Sheldon Hanft, "Mordecai's Female Academy," *American Jewish History* 79 (autumn 1989): 81–82.

24. Ibid., 75.

25. Pestalozzi's letters to J. P. Greaves emphasizing that he addressed only home techniques were published in London in the year of his death, 1827, as *Pestalozzi on Infant Education.* They were brought to the attention of Americans by an enthusiastic review in the *Ladies' Magazine* 3 (April 1830): 140, frequently reprinted. See Johann Heinrich Pestalozzi, *Letters on Early Education* (Syracuse: C. W. Bardeen, 1898).

26. Mintz, *A Prison of Expectations,* 31.

27. See note 22.

28. For example, Elizabeth Appleton, *Early Education* (London, 1820); Lydia Maria Child, *The Mother's Book* (Boston, 1831); Herman Humphrey, *Domestic Education* (Amherst, 1840); Isaac Taylor, *Home Education* (London, 1838). Rachel's attitudes toward Christian doctrines are not known.

29. On Rachel's correspondence with Edgeworth, see Hanft, "Mordecai's Female Academy."

30. In the family papers is also Eliza's "The Rose of Salency, Translated from the French, Corrected and revised by her sister, by Genlis, Stephanie Felicitie Ducrest de St. Aubin, comtesse de, afterwards marquise de Sillery, 1746–1830."

31. See Dean May and Maris A. Vinovskis, "A Ray of Millennial Light: Early Education and Social Reform in the Infant School Movement in Massachusetts, 1826–1840," Clark University Conference on Family and Social Structure, April 22, 1972, 1–3. May and Vinovskis explain the brief popularity of these schools as a result of public counter-sentiment that poor children should not be taken from their homes; the kindergarten movement in the 1860s was met as a new European contribution to American public education, not as a revival of the earlier experiment.

32. See notes 22 and 30.

33. MssiG8855d254, 1. Further references are given in the text.

34. MssiSch284a5, 19, emphasis added. Further references are given in the text.

35. MssiEd745a384, sec. 39.

36. Gregory S. Jay, *America the Scrivener: Deconstruction and the Subject of Literary History* (Ithaca: Cornell University Press, 1990), 313–38.

37. For instance, Carrie Lena Crawford Moffett (1854–1898), like many Victorian adolescents, frequently refers to the act of writing her diary record of her education. She omits names of schoolteachers and friends because "to name all would take almost a book," Mss10, no. 148, 2.

38. Compare, for instance, Sir Charles Adderley in *A Few Thoughts on National Education and Punishment* (1874): "The educating by the artificial stimulus of large public expenditure, a particular class, out of instead of in the condition of life in which they naturally fill an important part of the community, must upset the social equilibrium" (quoted in Briggs, *The Collected Essays of Asa Briggs,* 1:32–33, n. 122).

Part II · True Biases

1. T. J. Jackson Lears, "Sherwood Anderson: Looking for the White Spot," in *The Power of Culture: Critical Essays in American History,* edited by Richard Wightman Fox and T. J. Jackson Lears (Chicago: University of Chicago Press, 1993).

Chapter 4 · The Class on Gender

1. Thomas Cole, *The Origins of Rhetoric in Ancient Greece* (Baltimore: Johns Hopkins University Press, 1991), 48–49.

2. Mss55R1564, sec. 1.

3. See, for example, MssiW7153a, Mary Jane Townes Wimbish, commonplace book, n.d. Her school notes on logic, metaphysics, and philosophy include the following: "Synthesis, Or, Systematic review of the terms explained in this volume. The terms employed in the several departments of abstract and mental sciences, are readily separated into three Classes. The First Class containing those which belong to the Physiology of the human mind; and which designate its several faculties, and modes of feeling and acting, such for example, as seen sensation, emotions, imagina-

tion. B. The Second Class comprehends those terms which represent familiar abstract notions, such as expance, extension, substance, ode, etc. and which belong to metaphysics. The third Class are those that express the operations of the mind; its methods, and are typical processes in acquiring and communicating knowledge. These terms belong to Logic. We have therefore before us 1st. Mental Philosophy which treats of the nature of the mind. 2nd. metaphysics or the science of abstraction. 3rd. Logic or the method of gaining knowledge for ourselves, and conveying it to others" (1). Detailed notes on these categories then follow.

4. MssiB6386a, sec. 9, 60–61.

5. MssiW7153a1280.

6. See G. Stanley Hall, "Student Customs," *American Antiquarian Society* 14, n.s. (October 1900): 83–104. Hall describes "the conditions which actually do prevail in school and college, where picked youth and maidens . . . [are] within the largest practicable limits left free to follow their own will" (83). See also chapter 2.

7. Armstrong and Tennenhouse, *The Ideology of Conduct*, 1–2.

8. MssiH7842a1046, 7–8. The dates of his papers (1882–1936) suggests that Horner may have copied this essay at about age twenty-one. Further references are given in the text.

9. *The Ladies Book,* unattributed filler, April 1831, 2:216, emphasis added.

10. MssiD3545a, 1186–1238, sec. 39. This folder also includes an essay, "Narrow Escape of a Young Buffalo Hunter," signed only "W. D. R., 1885," and a poem about marrying for a second time. See also MssiM6663c4220, Caroline Pinkney, commonplace book, 1816–1834, for a description of the proper behavior of wives toward husbands along the lines of this essay: "When his daily toils are over, she should stand upon him as the morning kisses the flowers, which it loves to. . . ."

11. See Nancy Armstrong, "The Book of Class Sexuality," *Desire and Domestic Fiction: A Political History of the Novel* (New York: Oxford University Press, 1987), 61–69.

12. See Bertram Wyatt-Brown, *Southern Honor: Ethics and Behavior in the Old South* (New York: Oxford University Press, 1982), 272–91, for specifications of the "emotional chasm" generally separating husbands and wives on social, or homosocial, grounds.

13. Similar complaints by men about physically abusive wives were made to the Virginia legislature in various petitions for divorce. See Thomas Buckley, "Unfixing Race: Class, Power, and Identity in an Interracial Family," *Virginia Magazine of History and Biography* 102 (July 1994): 349–80. Buckley documents numerous examples in which men publicly described physical as well as mental abuse and begged for release from marriage. See chapter 7.

14. Peter Stallybrass and Allon White, *The Politics and Poetics of Transgression* (Ithaca: Cornell University Press, 1986), 5.

15. Ibid.

16. MssiW6717a2, sec. 2. Williams also kept a detailed account of his work in German, in another volume (1816–1859).

17. Mss2M3857c5.

18. Kenneth Lockridge, *On the Sources of Patriarchal Rage: The Commonplace*

Books of William Byrd and Thomas Jefferson and the Gendering of Power in the Eighteenth Century, 37.

19. Ibid., 75–77.

20. Ibid., 105.

21. Ibid., 108.

22. Ibid., 59–73.

23. Mss2M3857c5, 1. Further references are given in the text.

24. Donna Landry and Gerald MacLean, *Materialist Feminisms* (Oxford: Basil Blackwell, 1993), 131–32.

25. Mss1Ed745a384, 51.

26. This topic does not appear in these commonplace books, but for examples in other sources of references to sexuality by women, see Clinton, *The Plantation Mistress,* 207 ff.

27. Armstrong, "The Book of Class Sexuality," 20.

Chapter 5 · Gender as Discourse

1. For a critique of this assignment, see Gerda Lerner, *The Creation of Patriarchy* (New York: Oxford University Press, 1986); Armstrong and Tennenhouse, *The Ideology of Conduct.*

2. See, for example, Harriet Blodget, quoted in Cynthia Gannett, *Gender and the Journal: Diaries and Academic Discourse* (Albany: State University of New York Press, 1992), 128.

3. Support for this argument is wide, but it is particularly indebted to Mary Poovey, *Uneven Developments: The Ideological Work of Gender in Mid-Victorian England* (Chicago: University of Chicago Press, 1988); Thomas Laqueur, *Making Sex: Body and Gender from the Greeks to Freud* (Cambridge: Harvard University Press, 1990); Gayatri Chakravorty Spivak, *Other Worlds* (New York: Methuen, 1987); Joan Scott, *Gender and the Politics of History* (New York: Columbia University Press, 1988), 28–52.

4. See Kerber, *Women of the Republic: Intellect and Ideology in Revolutionary America,* 285.

5. Mss1V2345a311. The ca. 1901 date of this book places it later than the period analyzed in this study.

6. Charles W. H. Warner, "Education in Essex County, 1776–1976," *Essex County Historical Society Bulletin,* May 1980, 1.

7. Brickley, "'Female Academies Are Every Where Establishing,'" 56. Brickley also presents evidence that in the twelve Virginia female academies operating before 1830, the pattern of women going South to teach was well established by the early 1800s.

8. Cathy N. Davidson, *Revolution and the Word: The Rise of the Novel in America* (New York: Oxford University Press, 1986), 57.

9. Robinson, *The Academies of Virginia,* 57; see chapter 1.

10. Mss55M3812, 1.

11. Mss1R9337b17.

12. Mss55Un3, 10.

13. Blodget, quoted in Gannett, *Gender and the Journal,* 128.

14. R. S. Neale, *Writing Marxist History: British Society, Economy and Culture Since 1700* (Oxford: Basil Blackwell, 1985), 177.

15. Jay Fliegleman, *Declaring Independence: Jefferson, Natural Language, and the Culture of Performance* (Stanford, Calif.: Stanford University Press, 1993), 2, emphasis added.

16. Kathleen Woodward, "Anger . . . and Anger: From Freud to Feminism," in *Freud and the Passions,* edited by John O'Neill (Philadelphia: University of Pennsylvania Press, 1996), 73–95.

17. Joan Scott, "Experience," in *Feminists Theorize the Political,* edited by Judith Butler and Joan W. Scott (New York: Routledge, 1992), 37, emphasis added.

18. MssiM6663c3767. Account Book of Mary Washington Ball Minor Lightfoot. On the inside of the front cover is written: "Opened June 11, 1878, Account Book of Mollie W. B. Minor. No 607 A. 10th St., Richmond, Virginia. This book is the ending of the accounts received . . . in 1866." In another hand: "Account, Mrs. Ro. D. Minor, 'alias,' Mamma's Indebtedness."

19. Mss5H6375, 1. The volume also includes a list made in 1775 of revolutionary battles and events (12).

20. Mss55P1432, 1.

21. Fox-Genovese, *Within the Plantation Household,* 243.

22. MssiEd745a384, sec. 39. In a July 1864 letter to his father-in-law announcing that he would be moving his family west after the devastation of the war, "in search of a home for self, and family," Simpson closes with a note testifying to the habitual hiring-out of slaves and perhaps his impatience with his father-in-law's withdrawn support: "The Negro girl [Clary?] is hired in Lynchburg Va at Mr [?]. She is at your disposal at the end of 1864. With my best wishes" (MssiEd745a47, sec. 2).

23. MssiED745a384, sec. 116. Simpson's opinion of the treatment of the Indians is reiterated in Hugh Paul Taylor, "Notes concerning Shawnee Indian attacks in Tazewell co., Va, in 1786" (Mss2T2146a8). These notes, written ca. 1829 and signed "son of Cornstalk," were published in the *Mirror,* Fincastle, Virginia, in that year. (See *Virginia Historical Register* 5 [1852], 20–24.) Taylor's evidently fictionalized local history describes the Shawnee motive for the massacre: "As the Indians always viewed, with just indignation, our attempts to take from them their lands" . . . "the treaty of Hopewell, soon after produced a short sessation of hostilities—but as we still coveted their land, and precisted in taking possession of it, the war was soon renewed, and lasted several years" (1–2). Another sympathetic treatment of Native American culture is a school essay by J. M. Holladay, "The Lone Indian," MssiH7185b8500.

24. The "dosing" of slaves was, of course, a dangerous treatment also metcd out to whites, as noted on the typescript copy of the Henley family letters to their children at school concerning numerous illnesses and medications for them: "In spite of the heavy doses of medicine *[sic]* they survived! To Carrie, who from being the center of attention from her father and brother, the excitement of Bethany [her school] was curative, after their marriages" (MssiH3895a, sec. 1).

25. MssiW6717a2, 3.

26. MssiM6663a, 806–07, sec. 33; Payne also kept records of service in Cul-

pepper, Fauquier, Loudoun, and Rappahannock Counties before his imprisonment (Mss1P2936a5).

27. Mss1T3977b355.

28. Mss1B2924a, sec. 22.

29. Ibid., punctuation added. The list for 1855 is repeated under the names of Jinny and Lucinda; a note begins, "I owe old Lucinda," and lists other women's names in its columns. Sugar is listed for all, except in "Hrshoes, Lindsey, in 2," and gives amounts of "$1 or 50 cents." In later years, the almanacs in which Alexander wrote imitate ladies magazines, offering stories and "characters" of bachelors, widows, domestic tyrants, and "husbands." Clearly the "domestic" role imagined after the Civil War was oriented toward female householding, while in the earlier almanacs, the end pages are coded "male," offering the same sorts of conversion charts, planting information, and advice as in the archetypal beginnings of this genre. The publishers of these southern almanacs may have adjusted them to meet the needs of women who became heads of households after the Civil War.

30. Mss55B4567, 1.

31. Mss10, no. 148. This record of Moffett's marriage was written after she wrote her cousin about the choice to marry or not to marry: "Do either and you'll repent."

32. Mss1Ep734 b7, sec. 6.

33. Mss1G8785a325.

34. Mss55D4454, 1. The tenth list, omitted in this description, records Christmas cards received. It is the only such list in the collection and dates from the twentieth century, suggesting the relative novelty of this custom. Schoolchildren often wrote compositions about Christmas, but letters rather than cards appear to have been exchanged in the nineteenth century. See the essay, "Christmas," and report cards from James S. Hallowell of the Alexandria Female Seminary, Mss1D3545a962–967, sec. 21.

35. Mss1L51kg47, sec. 9, 53.

36. Mss55L9547, 1.

37. Mss1B6117a124, sec. 17.

38. Mss1W3286a, 478–537, sec. 24. See chapter 2.

39. Gift to author from Nathaniel Morrison, Welbourne, Loudon County.

40. See Jean E. Friedman, *The Enclosed Garden: Women and Community in the Evangelical South, 1830–1900* (Chapel Hill: University of North Carolina Press, 1985), esp. 27–31. Friedman's historical purpose is to verify that plantation women had as difficult a work load as that of rural laboring-class women. She cites especially the diary of Sally Nivison Lyons Taliaferro, 1861, VHS.

41. There are fifteen catalogued official documents; they do not include other uncatalogued playbills, tickets to performances, drawings, transcribed laws, and other miscellaneous artifacts. "Affidavit of Sally Johnson," Mss1W91127a60.

42. Mss2H8352a.

43. Mss1G8785a325, 35–42.

44. Ibid., 54–55.

45. Ibid., 24.

46. Mss1D3545a, 322–418, sec. 11, 1.

47. Ibid., 2–4.

48. Ibid., 4–5.

49. Mss1G8782b4727; and Mss1D9295c10. See also unidentified commonplace book, 1865–1871, Mss55Un3, 7, for a formula for sulfuric acid.

50. Mss51G7918, 1.

51. Mss55B4567, 1.

52. Mss1D9215c10; and Mss55H8375, 1.

53. Mss55B4567, 1, 2.

54. Mss55P1432, 1.

55. Mss1H9196aFA2. The first recipe is apparently dated June 1792 but may have been copied in the 1830s.

56. Stowe, *Intimacy and Power in the Old South*, 162.

57. Mss2Sp323a1. Further references are given in the text.

58. For a different explanation that assumes that gender difference constituted the prewar South and that the war heightened this subject position among whites while providing opportunities for black men to become "men," see LeeAnn Whites, "The Civil War as a Crisis in Gender," in *Divided Houses: Gender and the Civil War,* edited by Catherine Clinton and Nina Silber (New York: Oxford University Press, 1992), 2–21.

59. Mss55Un3, 7, 2, emphasis added.

60. Mss1Ed745a, 285–86, sec. 15. See also chapter 2.

61. Mss1P4686a360.

62. Mss1L8278a330.

63. Lawrence Levine, *Highbrow/Lowbrow: The Emergence of Cultural Hierarchy in America,* 16–81.

64. Mss1L8378a330, 102–04.

65. Ibid., 107.

66. Mss1Ed745a46, sec. 1.

67. Clinton, *The Plantation Mistress;* Fox-Genovese, *Within the Plantation Household,* chaps. 2–3.

68. See Stowe, *Intimacy and Power in the Old South,* 50–122, on correspondence to arrange planter marriages.

69. Mss1L8378a330, 132.

70. Ibid., 112, with additional emphasis.

71. See Bertram Wyatt-Brown, *Southern Honor: Ethics and Behavior in the Old South,* 172. Wyatt-Brown cites a Civil War veteran explaining that soldiers fought on bravely long after knowing their cause was lost: "'We were afraid to stop.' Afraid of what?" asked the Mississippi senator. 'Afraid of the women at home, John. They would have been ashamed of us.'" Drew Gilpin Faust quotes three other women writing, "Would God I were a man"; "how I wish I were a man!" and "I do sometimes long to be a man" ("Altars of Sacrifice: Confederate Women and Narratives of War," in *Divided Houses,* edited by Clinton and Silber, 176).

72. Mss1L8378a330, 137. Further references are given in the text.

73. Mss1D3545a, 962–67. Further references are given in the text.

74. Julia Whiting's copy of the letter does not indicate whether the blanks in her

transcription indicate illegibility or her grandmother's omission of references that might have been incriminating.

75. Mss2T2153a1; Lucy Penn Taylor was later Mrs. Basil Gordon.

76. Wyatt-Brown, *Southern Honor,* 231–32, documents the postponement of separating girls from boys at an early age, but he notes the separation of girls much younger than Lucy Taylor.

Chapter 6 · Learning to Spell Patriarchy

1. Quoted in Gerald Graff, *Professing Literature: An Institutional History* (Chicago: University of Chicago Press, 1987), 29.

2. Comment on "Public Celebrations," June 29, 1846, Mss1B6117a, 34–39. Philip Southall Blanton copied some of the teacher's penned comment directly under it in pencil, evidently bemused by it. His papers also include an essay "On Duelling" (1846) and a lengthy treatment of "Tetanus" (1851), written at the Jefferson Medical College, Philadelphia. I am grateful to Shirley Brice Heath for conversation that led to my noticing that student writing in this collection did not receive letter grades, but numbers one to five, sometimes but not regularly followed by comments. Very rarely were student essays corrected except for slight editing of their spelling. Teachers' rewriting never appears on these documents.

3. Henry Louis Gates, *The Signifying Monkey: A Theory of Afro-American Literary Criticism* (New York: Oxford University Press, 1988), *passim.*

4. Richard Beale Davis, *Literature and Society in Early Virginia: 1608–1840,* 55.

5. Exceptions include Regenia Gagnier, *Subjectivities: A History of Self Representation in Britain, 1832–1920.* See also David Vincent, *Bread, Knowledge and Freedom: A Study of Nineteenth-Century Working Class Autobiography.* In addition, Gauri Viswanathan describes how scholarly "Orientalism" was deployed to further the "reverse acculturation" that would suit colonials to rule while reintroducing natives to their own heritage as "buried under the debris of foreign conquests and depredations" (*Masks of Conquest: Literary Study and British Rule in India* [New York: Columbia University Press, 1989], 28). See also Richard Altick, *The English Common Reader: The Uses of Literacy: Changing Patterns in English Mass Culture* (Fair Lawn, N.J.: Essential Books, 1957), 252–53.

6. See Bertram Wyatt-Brown, *Southern Honor: Ethics and Behavior in the Old South,* 20.

7. Mary Ryan, *The Cradle of the Middle Class: The Family in Oneida County, New York, 1790–1865* (New York: Cambridge University Press, 1981), 231–32.

8. Mss1M6663c3757.

9. Ryan, *The Cradle of the Middle Class,* 232.

10. Davis, *Literature and Society in Early Virginia,* 45–46.

11. Ibid., 45.

12. Dexter A. Wright et al., *Gay's Standard Encyclopeaedia and Self-Educator: A Household Library of Scientific and Useful Information* (Richmond: B. F. Johnson, 1882).

13. John Tayloe, letter, *Etonian* 14 (January 15, 1913): 218.

14. Mss1EA765a, 179–87, sec. 17; see chapter 3 for Early's commencement address.

15. 1801–1805, Mss1W8945a. I have slightly regularized spelling and punctuation.

16. Ibid., emphasis added.

17. Ibid., Mss1W8945a3.

18. Ibid., Mss1W8945a5, additional emphasis added.

19. Ibid., Mss1W8945a9.

20. Ibid., Mss1W8945a10, emphasis added.

21. Ibid., Mss1W8945a11.

22. Ibid., Mss1W8945a17, sec. 3.

23. Mss52M6665, 1, 83–84, 86–87, 97.

24. Mss1M6663a, 810–11, sec. 35.

25. Charles Mortimer wrote to General Weedon on July 18, 1781, declining to offer further medical assistance to soldiers except as a consultant: "It was not in my power to give the sick assistance longer, for the following reasons. The want of medicines—my own indisposition often and sudden and never having any regular appointment from the State." From *Papers Relating Chiefly to the Maryland Line During the Revolution,* edited by Thomas Balch (Philadelphia: Printed for the Seventy-Six Society, T. K. and P. G. Collins, Printers, 1857); rpt. *William and Mary Quarterly* 27, 1st ser. (1918–1919): 80.

26. A footnote on a letter, April 6, 1786, identifies Billy Mercer as the "oldest son of General Hugh Mercer." Under this letter, in one of the many hands recorded in Mary Anne Randolph's commonplace book, is a practice imitation of its signature: "C Randolph." Other notes occur occasionally, added both as the letters were copied and, when in another hand, perhaps some time later.

27. Quoted in Victoria Bynum, *Unruly Women: The Politics of Social and Sexual Control in the Old South* (Chapel Hill: University of North Carolina Press, 1992), 49.

28. See Edward C. Carter II, ed., *The Virginia Journals of Benjamin Henry Latrobe, 1795–1798,* published for the Maryland Historical Society (New Haven: Yale University Press, 1977), 1:97, 175; 2:548–49.

29. Stowe, *Intimacy and Power in the Old South,* 161. Further references are given in the text.

30. Mss1H24895a, 1–43.

31. In May 1856, Robert Henley mentioned to his daughter, "Little Robert has been quite fretful. . . . I noticed today that he has one under tooth nearly through." Thomas's wife, Priscilla Henley, also wrote to Carrie in 1856.

32. David E. Wellbery, introduction to Frederick Kittler, *Discourse Networks: 1800/1900,* trans. Michael Metteer, with Chris Cullens (Stanford, Calif.: Stanford University Press, 1990), x.

33. Ibid., xvii–xviii.

Chapter 7 · Coda—Fundamentals of Authorship

1. Mss55H2318, 1. "The Southern Literary Messenger eagerly sought contributions from women writers and struggled to evaluate the torrents of unsolicited poetry [that] flooded their offices" during the Civil War (Faust, "Confederate Women and Narratives of War," 177).

2. Roger Chartier, *The Order of Books,* trans. Lydia G. Cochrane, 29–32.

3. Spivak, *Other Worlds,* 41.

4. Butler, "Contingent Foundations," 14.

5. Reproduced in Thomas Buckley, "'Placed in the Power of Violence': The Divorce Petition of Evelina Gregory Roane, 1824," *Virginia Magazine of History and Biography* 100 (January 1992): 29–78. I am indebted to students at the University of Utah for helping to shape this analysis. For both sexes, petitioning was an established mode of appeal. See Cynthia A. Kierner, "The Rhetoric of Equity and the Ritual of Dependence: Carolina Women Petition the Legislature, 1750–1800," Southern Historical Association conference, fall 1993.

6. Buckley, "'Placed in the Power of Violence," 63. Further references are given in the text. See Bertram Wyatt-Brown, *Southern Honor: Ethics and Behavior in the Old South,* 243–44, on other maternal custody assignments; his earliest example occurred in 1858.

7. Scott, "Experience," 22–40.

8. Letter to Fannie Edrington, MssiEd745a, 285–86, sec. 17.

9. MssiM6663c, sec. 32. For detailed minutes of the 1835 meetings of the Millbrook Academy (Albemarle County) Philological Society, see MssiH7185b852. See also Edward S. Jogres, LL.D., *The Uses of the Literary Society.* Address before the Literary Societies of Washington and Lee University (Richmond: Baughnian Stationery Co., 1892): "I know hardly anything more jejune, juiceless and insipid than the exercises in declamation required in school or college" (9).

10. MssiR9337b17, sec. 8.

11. MssiG5906a242.

12. Philip Gooch, *The Stethoscope, and Virginia Medical Gazetteer: A Monthly Journal of Medicine and the Collateral Sciences,* edited by P. Claiborne Gooch, A.M., M.D., vol. 1 (Richmond: Ritchies and Dunnavant, 1851). Editorial comments suggest that Gooch edited work by others; see "The Vapors," 199–203; "Trial for alleged Rape—curious question of fact—Judge, jury and counsel in a dilemma," 471–74.

13. MssiG5906a242, 139. Further page or date references are given in the text.

14. Douglas Hume, *Essays, Moral, Political, and Literary,* edited by Eugene F. Miller (Indianapolis: Liberty Classics, 1985).

15. Quintilian, *Institutes* X:3:21, emphasis added.

16. Nancy Armstrong, "Seduction and the Scene of Reading," *Desire and Domestic Fiction: A Political History of the Novel,* 203 ff.

17. Whites, "The Civil War as a Crisis in Gender," 19. For another perceptive explanation of this shift, see Nancy Schnog, "Changing Emotions: Moods and the Nineteenth-Century American Woman Writer," in *Inventing the Psychological,* edited by Joel Pfister and Nancy Schnog, 87–109.

18. Ibid.

19. MssiB6117a, TS, 16–18, 1. Further references are given in the text.

20. MssiE1595a, 1574–83, sec. 54.

21. Hall, *The Hard Road to Renewal,* 250.

References

Primary Materials Cited

Printed and Other Primary Sources

Dabney, George E. "Address 'On the Value of Writing,' Delivered before the Society of Alumni of the University of Virginia at their annual meeting." Charlottesville: O. S. Allen & Co., 1849.

Dulany, Rebecca Anne. Diary, 1855–1857; TS, 1991. Gift to the author from Nathaniel Morrison, Welbourne Plantation, Middleburg, Va.

Lomax, Elizabeth Virginia Lindsay. *Leaves from an Old Washington Diary, 1854–1863.* New York: E. P. Dutton, 1943.

Minute Books. Literary Fund (1811–1837). 2 vols. Record Gp. 27. Virginia State Library and Archives.

Virginia Historical Register 5 (1852): 20–24. Virginia State Library and Archives.

Manuscripts in the Virginia Historical Society, Richmond

Manuscripts are cited by manuscript number, author (where known),
type of document or title, and date of composition (where known).

Mss10, No. 148, Carrie Lena Crawford Moffett, commonplace book, 1872–1876, diary, 1871–1898.

Mss1735c. Peter Stubblefield, "Arithmetic Book."

Mss1B1938a216. Hugh White Sheffer, commonplace book, 1874–1877.

Mss1B2346b11330. Sextus Barbour, "Directions for Writing," ca. 1839–1841.

Mss1B2924a, William Rust Baskervill, commonplace book.

Mss1B6117a. P[hilip] S[tanhope] Blanton, essays, 1846; Anne Page Friend, commonplace book, 1879–1886; Jane Minge Friend Stephenson, "My Father's Household, Before, During, and After the War," 1897.

Mss1B6117a, 16–18, 1. Beverly Dandridge Tucker, poem, TS. See also Mss1E1595a, 1574–83.

Mss1B6386. Blair Bolling, continuation of memoirs of Robert Boilling, 1836.

Mss1C7835a, 325–66. Martha Elizabeth Coons, essays and school notes, 1858–1859.

Mss1C7835a, 451–605. George Dallas Coons, Latin exercises, 1859.

Mss1C7835a, 611–616. Henry Wilkins Coons, papers, 1859–1862.

Mss1D2278c280. (Daniel family papers.) Printed report card form, August, 1865.

Mss1D3545a, 322–418. John Peyton Dulany, "Affidavit."

Mss1D3545a, 962–967. Julia Beverly Whiting (?–1903), school records, 1859.

Mss1D3545a1151. Julia Beverly Whiting (1892–?), commonplace book, ca. 1935.

Mss1D3545a, 1186–1238. "Advice to a New Wife."

Mss1D925c10. Joseph Dupuy, commonplace book, 1845–1858.

Mss1D9295c9. Commonplace book, 1810–1865.

Mss1EA765a. Mary Virginia Early, essay; commencement address, 1842.

Mss1Ed745a, 285–286. John Edrington, letter, 1863; Samuel Simpson, letter, 1885.

Mss1Ed745a384. Samuel Simpson, commonplace book, 1879–1886.

Mss1Ed745a46. Ella Simpson, letter, 1861.

Mss1Ep734b7. Josephine Dulles Horner Eppes, commonplace book, 1850.

Mss1G5906a242. Philip Claiborne Gooch, commonplace book, 1839–1846.

Mss1G8782b4722, 4723, 4727, 4740. Hugh Blair Grigsby, commonplace books, 1824–1870.

Mss1G8785a325. Timothy Chandler, commonplace book, 1818–1823.

Mss1G8855d254. "Ann Eaght" essay.

Mss1H2485a, 112–13. John Robinson, commonplace book, 1735–1747.

Mss1H2485e, 125–26. William Ellzey Harrison, essay, "On Composition."

Mss1H3895a. Robert Henley, letters, 1836–1856.

Mss1H7185b8500, 8502. James Minor Holladay, commonplace books, n.d.; 1835–1842.

Mss1H7185b852. Minutes of the Millbrook Academy (Albemarle Co.) Philological Society, 1835.

Mss1H7842a1046. Alfred Byrne Horner, commonplace book.

Mss1H9196aFA2. Marianna Russell (Speace) Hunter and Jane Swann Hunter, commonplace book, 1791–1837.

Mss1J3698b, 3–30. Allen Talbot, commonplace book, 1860–1861.

Mss1J6496a. Lucy Newton Johnston, commonplace book, 1911–1918.

Mss1L51e660. Agnes Lee, letter, Dec. 9, 1866, TS.

Mss1L51kg47. Susan Elizabeth Roy Carter and Thomas Nelson Carter, commonplace book, 1875–1879.

Mss1L8378a330. Lucy Butler, commonplace book, 1859–1863, TS.

Mss1M1395a100. Alexander Hugh Holmes Stuart, commonplace book, 1831.

Mss1M6663a, 806–07. Robert Dabney Minor, commonplace book, 1840.

Mss1M6663a, 810–11. Mary Anne Fauntleroy Mortimer Randolph, commonplace book, 1851–1855.

Mss1M6663c32. John Fauntleroy Mortimer, Fredericksburgh Philological Society Minutes.

MssiM6663c3757. Landonia Randolph Minor, commonplace book, 1858–1869.

MssiM663c4220. Caroline Pickney, commonplace book, 1816–1834.

MssiM9924a. Rachel Mordecai, memoir, 1816–1820.

MssiP1855a, 319–22. Margaret J. Palmer, commonplace book, 1859–1860.

MssiP2936a5. Alexander Dixon Payne, memorandum book, 1863–1865.

MssiP3496c515. Littleton Waller Tazewell, memoir.

MssiP4686a, 96–118. Essay, "Education of Women and on Youth."

MssiP468a317. Eliza Gordon Scott, commonplace book, 1885.

MssiP4686a360. Frances Lee Jones, commonplace book, ca. 1865.

MssiP4686c1135. Anne Lee Peyton, commonplace book, 1861–1888.

MssiP9318a, 160–61. Virginia Eliza Price, school essay, commonplace books, 1849–1850, 1850–1851.

MssiR9337b. John Coles Rutherfoord, commonplace book, 1852–1856.

MssiR9337b17. John Coles Rutherfoord, speeches before House of Delegates, 1852–1856.

MssiSch284a5. John A. Scherer, diary, 1850–1908.

MssiT3977b355. William Harrison Shover, diary, 1845–1846.

MssiV2345a311. Lila Hardaway (Meade) Valentine, commonplace book, ca. 1901.

MssiW3286a, 478–537. Asa Dupuy Watkins, commonplace book.

MssiW6717a2. Frederick Williams, commonplace book, 1800–1859; autobiography, 1800–1834.

MssiW7153a81. Mary Jane Townes Wimbish (?–1865), commonplace book.

MssiW7153a1280. David Meade, commonplace book, 1869.

MssiW727sa9. John Henry Ducachet Wingfield, commonplace book, 1856.

MssiW8945a, 3, 5, 9–11, 17. Ralph Wormeley and Eleanor Wormeley, letters, 1801–1805.

MssiW91127a60. "Affidavit of Sally Johnson."

Mss2H24535a1. Burton Norvell Harrison, letter, 1890.

Mss2H8352a. Mary Howard, "Petition to Virginia Assembly," 1827.

Mss2M38567c5. Thomas Eugene Massie, commonplace book, 1855.

Mss2M6663a. Charles Minnigerode, letter, 1881.

Mss2Sp323a1. Conrad M. Speece, letter to Polly Hanna, 1791, TS.

Mss2T2146a8. Hugh Paul Taylor, "Notes concerning Shawnee Indian attacks in Tazewell Co., Va., in 1786."

Mss2T2153a1. Hugh Paul Taylor, letter, 1823.

Mss51G7918, 1. Edwin Gray, diary, 1778.

Mss51M1326, 1. "Copy of an account of Mrs. Anna Blanton McClure's early days in Virginia as given to her daughter, Mrs. Elizabeth McClure Calhoon in the 1930's," TS.

Mss52M6665, 1. John Minor, letterbook, 1809–1812.

Mss54AL276, 1. Mary McVeigh, "The Advantages of a Good Education," in "Specimens of the Compositions of the pupils of the Alexandria female seminary selected and written by themselves, 1853 and 1858."

Mss55B4567, 1. William R. Bernard and Jane Bernard, commonplace book, 1847–1850.

Mss55B6385, 1. Robert Bolling, "A Collection of diverting anecdotes, bonmots and other trifling pieces . . . 1764."

Mss55D4454, 1. Maria Martini DeRieux, commonplace book, 1806–1823.

Mss55H2318, 1. Eleanor Calhoun Harper, commonplace book, 1824–1885.

Mss55H6375, 1, 2; 3. Isaac Hite and his son Isaac Hite, commonplace books, 1776–1859; 1785, 1819–1899.

Mss55H8375, 1. Joseph and William Howard, commonplace book, 1765–1826.

Mss55L9547, 1. Ida Spooner Lownes, commonplace book, 1840.

Mss55M3812, 1. John Mason, speech, 1817; commonplace book, 1815–1818.

Mss55P1432, 1. Jane Frances Walker Page and Jane Byrd Nelson Walker, commonplace book, 1802–1845.

Mss55R1564, 1. Mary Jefferson Randolph, commonplace book, 1826.

Mss55Un3, 7. John Yates Beall, letter to unidentified keeper, commonplace book, 1865–1871.

Mss55Un3, 10. Commonplace book, inscription "Abra[ham] Wilson, April 4, 1836," sermon notes, 1722–1729.

Mss55W6734, 1–3. John Langbourne Williams, commonplace books, 1879, 1880, 1888.

Mss73LA380Is431. John R. Purdie, "History of Education in Isle Wight County from Colonial Times," 1880.

Books and Articles

Alcorn, Marshall. *Narcissism and the Literary Libido: Rhetoric, Text and Subjectivity.* New York: New York University Press, 1994.

Altick, Richard. *The English Common Reader: The Uses of Literacy: Changing Patterns in English Mass Culture.* Fair Lawn, N.J.: Essential Books, 1957.

Appleton, Elizabeth. *Early Education.* 2nd ed. London, 1820.

Armstrong, Nancy, and Leonard Tennenhouse, eds. *The Ideology of Conduct: Essays on Literature and History of Sexuality.* New York: Routledge, 1989.

———. *The Violence of Representation.* London: Routledge, 1989.

Armstrong, Nancy. *Desire and Domestic Fiction: A Political History of the Novel.* New York: Oxford University Press, 1987.

Bailyn, Bernard. "Education as a Discipline: Some Historical Notes." In *The Discipline of Education,* edited by John Walton and James L. Keuthe. Madison: University of Wisconsin Press, 1963, 125–38.

———. *Education in the Forming of American Society.* Chapel Hill: University of North Carolina Press, 1960.

Bakhtin, M. M. *Rabelais and His World.* Bloomington: Indiana University Press, 1984.

Balch, Thomas, ed. *Papers Relating Chiefly to the Maryland Line During the Revolution* (1857); rpt. *William and Mary Quarterly* 27, 1st ser. (1918–1919): 80.

Barthes, Roland. *Mythologies,* Trans. Annette Lavers. Paris: Editions du Seuil, 1957.

———. *The Semiotic Challenge.* Trans. Richard Howard. Berkeley and Los Angeles: University of California Press, 1994.

Bataille, Georges. *The Accursed Share.* Trans. Robert Hurley. New York: Zone Books, 1988.

Bear, Tracy. "An Address delivered during the celebration of the 25th anniversary of the Tracy W. McGregor Library, 1939–1964." Charlottesville, Va.: n.p., 1967.

Besnier, Niko. *Literacy, Emotion, and Authority: Reading and Writing on a Polynesian Atoll.* Studies in the Cultural Foundations of Language. Cambridge: Cambridge University Press, 1995.

Beverley, Robert. "History of Virginia." In *Reading, Writing and Arithmetic in Virginia, 1607–1699,* Edited by E. G. Sivern. Historical Booklet, no. 15. Williamsburg: Virginia 350th Anniversary Celebration Corp., 1957.

Bourdieu, Pierre. *Distinction: A Social Critique of the Judgment of Taste.* Trans. Richard Nice. Cambridge: Harvard University Press, 1984.

Bourdieu, Pierre, and J. C. Passerone. *Reproduction in Education, Society and Culture.* London: Sage, 1977.

Brickley, Lynne Templeton. "'Female Academies are Every Where Establishing': The Beginnings of Secondary Education for Women in the United States, 1790–1830, A Review of the Literature," unpublished manuscript, Harvard University Graduate School of Education, 1982.

Briggs, Asa. *The Collected Essays of Asa Briggs.* Vol. 1: *Words, Numbers, Places, People.* Urbana: University of Illinois Press, 1985.

Brodkey, Linda. *Writing Permitted in Designated Areas Only.* Minneapolis: University of Minnesota Press, 1996.

Buckley, Thomas. "'Placed in the Power of Violence': The Divorce Petition of Evelina Gregory Roane, 1824." *Virginia Magazine of History and Biography* 100 (January 1992): 29–78.

———. "Unfixing Race: Class, Power, and Identity in an Interracial Family." *Virginia Magazine of History and Biography* 102 (July 1994): 349–80.

Burke, Kenneth. *A Rhetoric of Motives.* Berkeley: University of California Press, 1969.

Bushnell, Horace. *Discourses on Christian Nurture.* Boston, 1847.

Butler, Judith M. "Contingent Foundations: Feminism and the Question of 'Postmodernism.'" In *Feminists Theorize the Political,* edited by Judith Butler and Joan W. Scott. New York: Routledge, 1992, 3–21.

Bynum, Victoria. *Unruly Women: The Politics of Social and Sexual Control in the Old South.* Chapel Hill: University of North Carolina Press, 1992.

Carruthers, Mary. *The Book of Memory: A Study of Memory in Medieval Culture.* New York: Cambridge University Press, 1990.

Carter, Edward C., ed. *The Virginia Journals Of Benjamin Henry Latrobe, 1795–1798.* Maryland Historical Society. New Haven: Yale University Press, 1977.

Channing, Edward. "The Orator and His Times." In *Lectures Read to the Seniors in Harvard College,* edited by Dorothy I. Anderson and Waldo Braden. Carbondale: Southern Illinois University Press, 1968.

Chartier, Roger. *The Order of Books.* Trans. Lydia G. Cochrane. Stanford: Stanford University Press, 1994.

Child, Lydia Maria. *The Mother's Book.* Boston, 1831.

Chinard, G. *The Literary Bible of Thomas Jefferson.* Baltimore: Johns Hopkins University Press, 1928.

Clement, Catherine. *The Lives and Legends of Jacques Lacan, 1981.* Trans. Arthur Goldhammer. New York: Columbia University Press, 1983.

Clinton, Catherine. *Plantation Mistresses: Women's World in the Old South.* New York: Pantheon, 1982.

Clinton, Catherine, and Nina Silber, eds. *Divided Houses: Gender and the Civil War.* New York: Oxford University Press, 1992.

Cole, Michel, and Sylvia Scribner. *Culture and Thought.* New York: Wiley, 1974.

Cole, Thomas. *The Origins of Rhetoric in Ancient Greece.* Baltimore: Johns Hopkins University Press, 1991.

Coontz, Stephanie. *The Social Origins of Private Life: A History of American Families, 1600–1900.* London: Verso, 1988.

Crane, Mary Thomas. *Framing Authority.* Princeton, NJ: Princeton University Press.

Crowley, Sharon. *The Methodical Memory: Invention in Current Traditional Rhetoric.* Carbondale: Southern Illinois University Press, 1990.

Davidson, Cathy N. *Revolution and the Word: The Rise of the Novel in America.* New York: Oxford University Press, 1986.

Davis, Richard Beale. *Literature and Society in Early Virginia: 1608–1840.* Baton Rouge: Louisiana State University Press, 1973.

DeButts, Mary Custis Lee, ed. *Growing Up in the 1830s: The Journal of Agnes Lee.* Robert E. Lee Memorial Association. Chapel Hill: University of North Carolina Press, 1984.

Demos, John. *A Little Commonwealth.* London: Oxford University Press, 1970.

Derrida, Jacques. "Signature Event Context." *Margins of Philosophy.* Trans. Alan Bass. Chicago: University of Chicago Press, 1972.

———. *The Post Card.* Trans. Alan Bass. Chicago: University of Chicago Press, 1987.

Douglass, Frederick. *Narrative of the Life of Frederick Douglass, an American Slave, Written by Himself.* New York: Signet Books, 1968.

Faust, Drew Gilpin. "Altars of Sacrifice: Confederate Women and Narratives of War." In *Divided Houses: Gender and the Civil War,* edited by Catherine Clinton and Nina Silber. New York: Oxford University Press, 1992, 171–99.

Ferguson, Kathy E. *The Man Question: Visions of Subjectivity in Feminist Theory.* Berkeley: University of California Press, 1993.

Fliegleman, Jay. *Declaring Independence: Jefferson, Natural Language, and the Culture of Performance.* Stanford: Stanford University Press, 1993.

Forrest, Mary. *Women of the South Distinguished in Literature.* New York: Derby and Jackson, 1861.

Foucault, Michel. *Language, Counter-Memory, Practice.* Edited and trans. by Donald F. Bouchard and Sherry Simon. Ithaca: Cornell University Press, 1977.

Fox, Christopher. *Locke and the Scriblerians: Identity and Consciousness in Early Eighteenth-Century Britain.* Berkeley: University of California Press, 1988.

Fox, Tom. "From Freedom to Manners: African-American Literacy Instruction in the Nineteenth Century." *Composition Forum* 96 (1995): 1–12.

Fox-Genovese, Elizabeth. *Within the Plantation Household: Black and White Women of the Old South.* Chapel Hill: University of North Carolina Press, 1988.

Friedman, Jean E. *The Enclosed Garden: Women and Community in the Evangelical South, 1830–1900*. Chapel Hill: University of North Carolina Press, 1985.

Furet, François and Jacques Ozouf. *Reading and Writing: Literacy in France from Calvin to Jules Ferry*. Cambridge: Cambridge University Press, 1982.

Gagnier, Regenia. *Subjectivities: A History of Self Representation in Britain, 1832–1920*. New York: Oxford University Press, 1991.

Gannett, Cynthia. *Gender and the Journal: Diaries and Academic Discourse*. Albany: SUNY Press, 1992.

Gates, Henry Louis. *The Signifying Monkey: A Theory of Afro-American Literary Criticism*. New York: Oxford University Press, 1988.

Gere, Anne Ruggles. "Kitchen Tables and Rented Rooms: The Extra Curriculum of Composition." *CCC* 45 (February 1994): 75–92.

Gere, Ann Ruggles, and Sarah Robbins. "Gendered Literacy in Black and White: Turn-of-the-Century African-American and European-American Club Women's Printed Texts." *Signs: Journal of Women in Culture and Society* 1 (1996): 643–78.

Glenn, Cheryl. *Rhetoric Retold: Regendering the Tradition from Antiquity Through the Renaissance*. Carbondale: Southern Illinois University Press, 1997.

Goldberg, Jonathan. "Bradford's 'Ancient Members.'" In *Nationalisms and Sexualities*, edited by Andrew Parker, Mary Russo, Doris Somer, and Patricia Yaeger. New York: Routledge, 1992, 60–77.

Gooch, Philip. *The Stethoscope, and Virginia Medical Gazetteer: A Monthly Journal of Medicine and the Collateral Sciences*. Vol. 1. Edited by P. Claiborne Gooch. Richmond: Ritchies and Dunnavant, 1851.

Graff, Gerald. *Professing Literature: An Institutional History*. Chicago: University of Chicago Press, 1987.

Graff, Harvey. *The Literacy Myth: Literacy and Social Structure in the Nineteenth-Century City*. New York: Academic Press, 1979.

Green, Nancy. "Female Education and School Competition." In *Women's Being, Woman's Place: Female Identity and Vocation in American History*, edited by Mary Kelley. Boston: G. K. Hall, 1979, 127–41.

Hall, David. "The World of Print and Collective Mentality in Seventeenth-Century New England." In *New Directions in American Intellectual History*, edited by John Hingham and Paul K. Conkin. Baltimore: Johns Hopkins University Press, 1979, 180–95.

Hall, G. Stanley. "Student Customs." *American Antiquarian Society* n.s. 14 (October 1900): 83–104.

Hall, Stuart. "Crisis and Renewal on the Left." *The Hard Road to Renewal: Thatcherism and the Crisis of the Left*. London and New York: Verso, 1988.

Hanft, Sheldon. "Mordecai's Female Academy." *American Jewish History* 79 (autumn 1989): 72–93.

Hareven, Tamara K. *Family and Kin in Urban Communities, 1700–1730*. New York: New Viewpoints, 1977.

Heath, Shirley Brice. "Toward an Ethnohistory of Writing in American Education." In *Writing: The Nature, Development and Teaching of Written Communication*.

Vol. 1: *Variation in Writing: Functional and Linguistic-Cultural Differences,* edited by Marcia Farr Whiteman. Hillsdale, N.J.: Lawrence Erlbaum, 1981, 25–46.

Hekman, Susan J. *Gender and Knowledge: Elements of a Postmodern Feminism.* Boston: Northeastern University Press, 1990.

Hellenbrand, Harold. *The Unfinished Revolution: Education and Politics in the Thought of Thomas Jefferson.* Newark, N.J.: University of Delaware Press, 1990.

Hoggart, Richard. *The Uses of Literacy: Changing Patterns in English Mass Culture.* Fair Lawn, N.J.: Essential Books, 1975.

Horner, Winifred Bryan. "Writing Instruction in Great Britain: Eighteenth and Nineteenth Centuries." In *A Short History of Writing Instruction: From Ancient Greece to Twentieth-Century America,* edited by James J. Murphy. Davis, Calif.: Hermagoras Press, 1990, 121–50.

Humphrey, Herman. *Domestic Education.* Amherst, 1840.

Hunter, Ian. "Aesthetics and Cultural Studies." In *Cultural Studies,* edited by Lawrence Grossberg, Cary Nelson, and Paula Treichler. London and New York: Routledge, 1991, 347–72.

——. *Culture and Government.* London: Macmillan, 1988.

Jaratt, Susan *Re-Reading the Sophists: Classical Rhetoric Refigured* (Carbondale: Southern Illinois University Press, 1991).

Jay, Gregory S. *America the Scrivener: Deconstruction and Subject of Literary History.* Ithaca: Cornell University Press, 1990.

Jefferson, Thomas. *The Writings of Thomas Jefferson.* Vol 2. Edited by Andrew A. Lipscomb. Washington, D.C: Thomas Jefferson Memorial Association, 1903–1904.

Jogres, Edward S. *The Uses of the Literary Society.* Literary Societies of Washington and Lee University. Richmond: Baughnian Stationery Co, Printers, 1892.

Jonson, Ben. *Discoveries: A Critical Edition with an Introduction and Notes on the True Purport and Genesis of the Book.* Edited by Maurice Castelain. Paris: Librarie Hachette, 1906?

Justice, Stephen. *Writing and Rebellion: England in 1321.* Berkeley: University of California Press, 1994.

Kaestle, Karl F. *Pillars of the Republic: Common Schools and American Society, 1780–1860.* New York: American Century Series, Hill and Wang, 1983.

Kennedy, George, ed. Introduction. *Aristotle On Rhetoric: A Theory of Civic Discourse.* New York: Oxford University Press, 1991.

Kerber, Linda K. *Women of the Republic: Intellect and Ideology in Revolutionary America.* Institute of Early American History and Culture, Williamsburg, Va. Chapel Hill: University of North Carolina Press, 1980.

Kierner, Cynthia A. "The Rhetoric of Equity and the Ritual of Dependence: Carolina Women Petition the Legislature, 1750–1800." Southern Historical Association Conference, Fall, 1993.

Kittler, Friedrich A. *Discourse Networks: 1800/1900.* Trans. Michael Metteer with Chris Cullens. Stanford, Calif.: Stanford University Press, 1990.

Lady's Book, Unattributed filler. Vol. 2. (April 1831): 216.

Landry, Donna, and Gerald MacLean. *Materialist Feminisms.* Oxford: Basil Blackwell, 1993.

Laqueur, Thomas. *Making Sex: Body and Gender from the Greeks to Freud.* Cambridge: Harvard University Press, 1990.

LaTour, Bruno. *Science in Action.* Cambridge: Harvard University Press, 1987.

Lears, T. J. Jackson. "Sherwood Anderson: Looking for the White Spot." In *The Power of Culture: Critical Essays in American History,* edited by Richard Wightman Fox and T. J. Jackson Lears. Chicago and London: University of Chicago Press, 1993, 13–38.

Lebstock, Susanne. *The Free Women of Petersburg: Status and Culture in a Southern Town, 1784–1860.* New York: Norton, 1984.

———. *Virginia Women, 1600–1945: "A Share of Honor."* Richmond: Va. State Library, 1987.

Lechner, Joan Marie. *Renaissance Concepts of the Commonplaces: An Historical Investigation of the General and Universal Ideas Used in All Argumentation and Persuasion with Special Emphasis on the Educational and Literary Tradition of the Sixteenth and Seventeenth Centuries.* New York: Pageant Press, 1963.

Lerner, Gerda. *The Creation of Patriarchy.* New York: Oxford University Press, 1986.

———. *The Majority Finds its Past: Placing Women in History.* New York: Oxford University Press, 1979.

Levine, Lawrence. *Highbrow/Lowbrow: The Emergence of Cultural Hierarchy in America.* Cambridge: Harvard University Press, 1988.

Locke, John. *Two Treatises of Government.* Edited by Peter Laslett. Cambridge: Cambridge University Press, 1967.

Lockridge, Kenneth A. *On the Sources of Patriarchal Rage: The Commonplace Books of William Byrd and Thomas Jefferson and the Gendering of Power in the Eighteenth Century.* New York: New York University Press, 1992.

Lomax, Elizabeth Virginia Lindsay. *Leaves from an Old Washington Diary, 1854–1863.* New York: E. P. Dutton, 1943.

Macpherson, C. B. *The Political Theory of Possessive Individualism: Hobbes to Locke.* Oxford: Clarendon Press, 1962.

Martin, Theodora Penny. *The Sound of Our Own Voices: Women's Study Clubs 1860–1910.* Boston: Beacon Press, 1987.

May, Dean and Maris A. Vinovskis, "A Ray of Millennial Light: Early Education and Social Reform in the Infant School Movement in Massachusetts, 1826–1840." Clark University Conference on Family and Social Structure, April 22, 1972.

McKann, Homer Alton. "History of Early Education in Middlesex County 1669–1890." MS Ed. thesis, University of Richmond, 1942.

Miller, Eugene F., ed. *Hume's Essays, Moral, Political, and Literary.* Indianapolis: Liberty Classics, 1985.

Miller, Susan. *Rescuing the Subject.* Carbondale: Southern Illinois University Press, 1989.

———. *Textual Carnivals: The Politics of Composition.* Carbondale: Southern Illinois University Press, 1991.

Mintz, Steven. *A Prison of Expectations: Family in Victorian Culture.* New York: New York University Press, 1983.

"Miscellaneous Notes." *Education* 2, no. 3 (January 1881): 315.

Morgan, Edmund. *The Puritan Family.* New York: Harper, 1966, rev. of 1944 ed.

Morgan, Edmund S. *Virginians at Home: Family Life in the Eighteenth Century.* Charlottesville: Dominion Books, of the University of Virginia Press, 1952.

Moss, Ann. *Printed Commonplace-Books and the Structuring of Renaissance Thought.* Oxford: Clarenden Press, 1996.

Mouffe, Chantal. "Hegemony and New Political Subjects: Towards a New Concept of Democracy." Trans. Stanley Gray. In *Marxism and the Interpretation of Culture,* edited by Cary Nelson and Lawrence Grossberg. Urbana: University of Illinois Press, 1988.

Neale, R. S. *Writing Marxist History: British Society, Economy and Culture Since 1700.* Oxford: Basil Blackwell, 1985.

Norton, Mary Beth. *Founding Mothers and Fathers: Gendered Power and the Forming of American Society.* New York: Knopf, 1996.

Olson, David. "From Utterance to Text: The Bias of Language in Speech and Writing." *Harvard Educational Review* 47 (1977): 257–81.

Ong, Walter. *Orality and Literacy.* New York: Methuen, 1982.

————. *Ramus: Method and the Decay of Dialogue.* Cambridge: Harvard University Press, 1958.

Owen, Robert. "First Essay." *A New View of Society.* 1813. In *Robert Owen on Education,* edited by Harold Silber. Cambridge: Cambridge University Press, 1969.

Pestalozzi, Johann Heinrich. *Letters on Early Education.* Syracuse, N.Y.: C. W. Bardeen, 1898.

Pfister, Joel. "On Conceptualizing the Cultural History of Emotional and Psychological Life in America." In *Inventing the Psychological,* edited by Joel Pfister and Nancy Schnog, 17–59.

Pfister, Joel, and Nancy Schnog, eds. *Inventing the Psychological: Toward a Cultural History of Emotional Life in America.* New Haven: Yale University Press, 1997.

Poovey, Mary. *Uneven Developments: The Ideological Work of Gender in Mid-Victorian England.* Chicago: University of Chicago Press, 1988.

Price, Richard. *Alabi's World.* Baltimore: Johns Hopkins University Press, 1990.

Quintilian. *Institutes.* Trans. H. Caplin. Edited by G. P. Goold. 2 vols. London: Loeb, 1981.

Radway, Janice. *Reading the Romance.* Chapel Hill: University of North Carolina Press, 1991.

Richards, I. A. *Philosophy of Rhetoric.* London: Oxford University Press, 1936.

Robinson, Dale G. *The Academies of Virginia: 1776–1861.* N.p: n.p., 1977.

Ross, Kristin, trans. Introduction to *The Ignorant Schoolmaster* by Jacques Rancière. Stanford: Stanford University Press, 1991.

Ryan, Mary. *The Cradle of the Middle Class: The Family in Oneida County, New York, 1790–1865.* New York: Cambridge University Press, 1981.

Schnog, Nancy. "Changing Emotions: Moods and the Nineteenth-Century American Woman Writer." In *Inventing the Psychological,* edited by Joel Pfister and Nancy Schnog, 3–16.

Schwartz, Richard. "Patrimony and Figuration of Authorship in the Eighteenth-Century Literary Property Debates." *Works and Days* 7, no. 2 (1989): 29–54.

Scott, Joan W. "Gender: A Useful Category of Historical Analysis." *Gender and the Politics of History*. New York: Columbia University Press, 1988, 25–52.

———. "Experience." In *Feminists Theorize the Political*, edited by Judith Butler and Joan W. Scott. New York: Routledge, 1992, 22–40.

Silverman, David, and Brian Torode. *The Material Word: Some Theories of Language and Its Limits*. London: Routledge and Kegan Paul, 1980.

Simpson, David. *The Academic Postmodern and the Rule of Literature: A Report on Half Knowledge*. Chicago: University of Chicago Press, 1995.

Sivern, E. G., ed. *Reading, Writing and Arithmetic in Virginia, 1607–1699*. Historical Booklet. Jamestown 350th Anniversary, no. 15. Williamsburg: Virginia Anniversary Corporation, 1964.

Smith-Rosenberg, Carroll. *Disorderly Conduct: Visions of Gender in Victorian America*. New York: Oxford University Press, 1985.

Spivak, Gayatri Chakravorty. *Other Worlds*. New York: Methuen, 1987.

Stallybrass, Peter, and Allon White. *The Politics and Poetics of Transgression*. Ithaca: Cornell University Press, 1986.

Stone, Lawrence. *Schooling and Society: Studies in the History of Education*. Baltimore: Johns Hopkins University Press, 1976.

Stowe, Steven M. *Intimacy and Power in the Old South: Ritual in the Lives of Planters*. Baltimore: Johns Hopkins University Press, 1987.

Street, Brian. *Literacy in Theory and Practice*. Cambridge Studies in Literate and Oral Culture. Cambridge: Cambridge University Press, 1984.

Tayloe, John. Letter. *Etonian*. Eton College: Stottiswood no. 14 (January 15, 1913): 218–19.

Taylor, Isaac. *Home Education*. London, 1838.

Thomas, Max W. "Reading and Writing the Renaissance Commonplace Book: A Question of Authorship?" In *The Construction of Authorship: Textual Appropriation in Law and Literature*, edited by Martha Woodmansee and Peter Jaszi. Durham: Duke University Press, 1994, 401–15.

Ulrich, Laurel Thatcher. *A Midwife's Tale: The Life of Martha Ballard, Based on Her Diary, 1785–1812*. New York: Vintage, 1991.

Vincent, David. *Bread Knowledge and Freedom: A Study of Nineteenth-Century Working Class Autobiography*. London: Europa Publications, 1981.

Viswanathan, Gauri. *Masks of Conquest: Literary Study and British Rule in India*. New York: Columbia University Press, 1989.

Warner, Charles W. H. "Education in Essex County, 1776–1976." *Essex County Historical Society Bulletin*, May 1980, 1.

Warner, Michael. *The Letters of the Republic: Publication and the Public Sphere in Eighteenth-Century America*. Cambridge: Harvard University Press, 1990.

Wellbery, David E. Introduction to Frederick Kittler, *Discourse Networks: 1800/1900*, ed. Wellbery. Trans. Michael Metteer, with Chris Cullens. Stanford: Stanford University Press, 1990.

Whites, LeeAnn. "The Civil War as a Crisis in Gender." In *Divided Houses: Gender and the Civil War*, edited by Catherine Clinton and Nina Silber. New York: Oxford University Press, 1992, 2–21.

Whitman, Walt. *Complete Poetry and Selected Prose by Walt Whitman*. Edited by James E. Miller Jr. Boston: Houghton Mifflin, 1959.

Williams, Raymond. "Marx on Culture." *What I Came to Say*. London: Radius, 1989.

Wilson, Douglas, ed. *Jefferson's Literary Commonplace Book*. Papers of Thomas Jefferson, 2nd ser. Princeton: Princeton University Press, 1989.

Woodward, Kathleen. "Anger . . . and Anger: From Freud to Feminism." In *Freud and the Passions,* edited by John O'Neill. Philadelphia: University of Pennsylvania Press, 1996, 73–95.

Woody, Thomas. *A History of Women's Education in the United States*. 2 vols. New York: Science Press, 1929.

Wright, Dexter A., et al. *Gay's Standard Encyclopeaedia and Self-Educator: A Household Library of Scientific and Useful Information*. Richmond: B. F. Johnson and Co., 1882.

Wyatt-Brown, Bertram. *Southern Honor: Ethics and Behavior in the Old South*. New York: Oxford University Press, 1982.

Young, Iris. "Gender as Seriality: Thinking about Women as a Social Collective." *Signs* 19 (spring 1994): 713–38.

Index